Finding the Lef
Arm of God

ALSO BY BRIAN M. ENDSLEY

Bums No More:
The 1959 Los Angeles Dodgers,
World Champions of Baseball
(McFarland, 2009)

Finding the Left Arm of God

*Sandy Koufax and the
Los Angeles Dodgers,
1960–1963*

BRIAN M. ENDSLEY

McFarland & Company, Inc., Publishers

Jefferson, North Carolina

LIBRARY OF CONGRESS CATALOGUING-IN-PUBLICATION DATA

Endsley, Brian M.
Finding the left arm of god : Sandy Koufax and
the Los Angeles Dodgers, 1960–1963 / Brian M. Endsley.
p.   cm.
Includes bibliographical references and index.

ISBN 978-0-7864-7415-8 (softcover : acid free paper) ∞
ISBN 978-1-4766-1894-4 (ebook)

1. Koufax, Sandy, 1935– 2. Baseball players—United States—Biography.
3. Pitchers (Baseball)—United States—Biography.   4. Los Angeles
Dodgers (Baseball team)—History—20th century.   I. Title.

GV865.K67E54 2015   796.357092—dc23   [B]   2015027056

BRITISH LIBRARY CATALOGUING DATA ARE AVAILABLE

On the cover: Sandy Koufax (National Baseball
Hall of Fame Library, Cooperstown, New York)

Printed in the United States of America

*McFarland & Company, Inc., Publishers
Box 611, Jefferson, North Carolina 28640
www.mcfarlandpub.com*

To my grandsons,
Cohen Brian Endsley
and
Aiden Daniel Endsley

Table of Contents

Part IV. 1963: Return to the Summit

Preface

This book is a continuation of the story begun in *Bums No More: The 1959 Los Angeles Dodgers, World Champions of Baseball*, which covered the Dodgers' first two years on the West Coast. We will now travel with the team through the next four years, from their precipitous decline in 1960 to their return to the summit in 1963. Where *Bums No More* chronicled the final triumph of the transplanted "Boys of Summer," this book is at its core the story of the Dodgers' volatile fortunes during the transformation of Sandy Koufax from a wild young left-hander with a career losing record to an artist with exquisite control of the baseball—a veritable Mozart on the mound.

My interest in the subject is personal. I grew up in Southern California transported by Vin Scully's broadcasts of the Dodgers' games. I personally experienced the heartbreak of their 1962 collapse and the exhilaration of their redemption in 1963. Where other books covering this period focus on the year 1962, I take a broader view. *Finding the Left Arm of God* explores in depth the changes that took place in the 2-year run-up to that pivotal year and its aftermath. It is structured as a narrative history of the Dodgers in the first four years of the 1960s set against the backdrop of the events that changed our world during John F. Kennedy's election year and fleeting New Frontier presidency.

The book is organized into four parts. Part I covers the team's plunge back into the baseball wilderness in 1960 after their 1959 World Championship season. It describes a transitional year which saw both the declining relevance of the aging "Boys of Summer" and the arrival of a new generation of exciting young players such as Frank Howard and the Davis boys, Tommy and Willie. We will see a 24-year-old Sandy Koufax struggle through his worst—and nearly his last—season.

Part II covers the intertwined fortunes of the Dodgers and Koufax in his breakthrough year of 1961. We will view the season through the prism of the metamorphosis of a *new* Sandy Koufax: from the turning point in spring training when he discovers the art of controlling the baseball; to his emergence as an All-Star; to his breaking of a

52-year-old league record for strikeouts in a season. At the same time we will see the team return to pennant contention in their last year in the Los Angeles Memorial Coliseum.

Part III is the triumph and tragedy of 1962, the Dodgers' first year in Dodger Stadium. We will relive the catastrophe that befell perhaps the finest Los Angeles Dodger team with Maury Wills as the new major league Stolen Base King, Don Drysdale as the Cy Young Award winner, and Tommy Davis as the batting champion and most prolific run producer in the National League since 1937. We will also see the crippling effect of losing Sandy Koufax to injury at mid-season.

Part IV completes the story with an exploration of the year 1963. Here we will see the dramatic one-year turnaround of the Los Angeles Dodgers from maligned "choke artists" to World Champions as Sandy Koufax blossoms fully into baseball's greatest pitcher. Enjoy the ride!

Prologue

It is minutes after winning the climactic Game 6 of the 1959 World Series 9–3 over the Chicago White Sox. Jubilant Larry Sherry and Duke Snider embrace in the visitors' locker room at Old Comiskey Park. The Los Angeles Dodgers have come back from an 11–0 Game 1 drubbing at the hands of the Go-Go Sox to win the Series, four games to two. Sherry has just saved the game for Johnny Podres, his second save in the Series to go along with two wins—all in relief. He will be named the Most Valuable Player of the Series. The old Brooklyn veteran Snider, after convincing manager Walter Alston that he was well enough to start in center field despite a bad knee, put the Dodgers ahead for good with a 2-run homer in the third inning off Early Wynn.

After their Game 1 humiliation, the Dodgers won the next three games, and were in position to end the Series in the fifth game in Los Angeles on October 6. They handed the baseball to their enigmatic 23-year-old left-hander Sandy Koufax before 92,706 at the Memorial Coliseum, still the largest crowd in World Series history. At this point in his career, the Dodgers were never sure which Koufax would show up. That year, on August 31 in Los Angeles, he struck out 18 San Francisco Giants to tie Bob Feller's record for most strikeouts in a game, thereby bringing the Dodgers to within one game of the first-place Giants. He then virtually disappeared during the September pennant stretch, losing his only two starts. But young Koufax pitched brilliantly in Game 5 of the Series, giving up only 5 singles over the first 7 innings. But since he had allowed the only run of the game to score in the fourth inning on a double play ground ball, the Sox escaped with a 1–0 do-or-die win to send the Series back to Chicago.

For the Dodgers, 1959 was a remarkable turnaround season. The year before, their first in Los Angeles, they finished in seventh place—next-to-last in the National League. No one gave them a chance on opening day, and by the end of May they were a mediocre .500 team. But beginning in June, General Manager Buzzie Bavasi started making some transformative moves. He recalled right-hander Roger Craig from St. Paul. Craig became the Dodgers' stopper, with a brilliant 11–5 performance for the remainder of the year.

From Spokane he brought up a 29-year-old rookie with five kids named Maury Wills to play shortstop. Wills became the glue that held the Dodger infield together, and led them to a crucial 3-game sweep of the Giants at Seals Stadium in late September. Bavasi recalled Larry Sherry from St. Paul. Sherry was 7–3 down the stretch as a reliever and spot starter before shining in the postseason.

After Roger Craig clinched a first-place tie with Milwaukee on the last day of the season with a complete-game victory over the Cubs in Chicago, the Dodgers and Braves began a best-of-three-game playoff series the next day in Milwaukee. The Dodgers had a history of bad luck in their two previous playoffs, losing a one-game playoff to the Cardinals in 1946, and a three-game playoff to the Giants in 1951 on Bobby Thomson's "shot heard around the world." The Milwaukee Braves were heavily favored to advance to their third straight World Series. But the Dodgers came from behind to win the opening game 3–2 in County Stadium as Larry Sherry pitched the last 7⅔ scoreless innings in relief. Twenty-four hours later at the Coliseum in Los Angeles, the Dodgers clinched the pennant with a dramatic come-from-behind victory in the bottom of the 12th inning. As Gil Hodges crossed home plate with the winning run, Vin Scully's voice reverberated across the airwaves: "We go to Chicago!"[1]

On this evening the Dodgers left Chicago as World Champions with high hopes for creating a new dynasty in Los Angeles.

Reflecting on the 1959 season, Dodger General Manager Buzzie Bavasi knew he had to shore up the team's offensive power. Despite the advantage of playing half their

games in the Los Angeles Memorial Coliseum with its 40-foot left field screen just 250 feet from home plate, the Dodgers were fifth out of eight National League teams in home runs with 148. Gil Hodges led the team with 25, but due to turn 36 the following April, he was well past his prime. In November of 1959, Bavasi disclosed to the press that he was seeking a right-handed power hitter to take advantage of the short left-field dimensions of the Coliseum. He announced his intention to talk to Bucky Harris of the Red Sox about Jackie Jensen, Parke Carroll of the Athletics about Bob Cerv, and Calvin Griffith of the Senators about Roy Sievers.[2] The Dodgers were especially interested in Sievers. The Senators' right-handed slugging first baseman led the American league with 42 home runs in 1957, and was third in 1958 with 39. After injuries caused him to fall off to 21 home runs in only 115 games in 1959,

Dodger General Manager Emil J. "Buzzie" Bavasi. Bavasi sought White Sox slugger Roy Sievers at the 1959 Winter Meetings (National Baseball Hall of Fame Library, Cooperstown, New York).

the rumor mill placed him on the trading block.[3] Bavasi saw Sievers as an attractive under-valued asset.

Major League Baseball's annual Winter Meetings began on December 7, 1959, in Miami Beach, Florida. Bavasi and the Dodgers offered infielder Don Zimmer and pitcher Danny McDevitt to the Senators for Sievers and Cuban pitcher Pedro Ramos. But Bavasi backed off when Senators owner Cal Griffith also wanted the Dodgers to throw in their power-hitting outfielder Don Demeter[4] or their top minor league prospect, Pacific Coast League batting champion Tommy Davis.[5] This proved to be a deal-breaker. The tone of the negotiations turned acrimonious, and ruptured the relations between the Dodgers and Calvin Griffith. When the Winter Meetings ended on December 9, Roy Sievers was still a Washington Senator and the Dodgers were still in need of a right-handed power hitter.[6] The negotiating positions of the two clubs—as well as their relationship—remained frozen when the inter-league trading deadline expired on December 15. The Dodgers had missed their chance.

Revenge of the Go-Go Sox

Six months after the Dodgers beat them in the World Series, the Chicago White Sox exacted their revenge by grabbing the player most coveted by the Dodgers. On April 4, a week before opening day, they took Roy Sievers from the Washington Senators in exchange for catcher Earl Battey, first baseman Don Mincher, and $150,000 cash.[7] The Dodgers would live to regret their failure to work out a deal for Sievers. Their home run production in 1960 would continue to decline to the lowest total since 1948. They would run up against Earl Battey in the 1965 World Series as the All-Star catcher of the Minnesota Twins.

Part I

1960:
Return to the Wilderness

One

Bright Beginnings

I hope to put pennants back-to-back on the Coliseum flag
pole.[1]—Walter O'Malley

Even though most of the baseball experts downplayed their chances of repeating
as World Champions, the Los Angeles Dodgers were hopeful as they completed their
spring exhibition season with an 8–4 win over the Giants in Sacramento on April 10,
1960. After all, the same experts had given them no chance the year before. The following day they optioned their highly touted power-hitting rookie, Frank Howard, to
Spokane.[2] That evening when they were feted by a star-studded capacity crowd of 1,200
at the Beverly Hilton Hotel at the Los Angeles Baseball Writers' Dinner emceed by Jerry
Lewis, there was no mention of the lackluster 12–10–1 spring exhibition record or the
aging of the team, only unbridled optimism.

All was calm in the country. President Eisenhower, in the last year of his second
term, was preparing to make his Easter pilgrimage to the Southern White House,
Augusta National Golf Club, with his new shortened back swing. Vice President Richard
Nixon, as expected, had already announced his candidacy for Ike's job. In the wake of
John F. Kennedy's win in the Wisconsin primary, a "Stop Kennedy" coalition was formed
by Senator Robert Byrd of West Virginia to prevent him from becoming Nixon's opponent.[3] Elvis Aaron Presley was safely back home in Memphis, having survived the U.S.
Army's 2-year project to tame him. His latest record, "Stuck on You," was #1 on the
charts.

Ed Roebuck, Comeback Kid

On April 11, the day the Dodgers announced their 28-man opening day roster,
number 37 Ed Roebuck was on it. It marked the culmination of a remarkable comeback
by the 28-year-old relief pitcher.

Escape from the Coal Mines

Edward Jack Roebuck was born in East Millsboro, Pennsylvania, on July 3, 1931. He was one of eight children from a Polish immigrant family that sent all of its male members to work in the coal mines. When Ed, the baby of the family, showed an early gift for baseball, the family was determined that he be given a chance to escape that fate. Unlike his four brothers, he was allowed to finish Brownsville High School, where his two no-hitters drew major league scouts like flies. The family pooled its resources to enable him to spend his summers playing baseball instead of toiling in the mines.[4]

In 1947, at age 16, he was invited five times by the Pittsburgh Pirates to work out at Forbes Field. He accepted the bus fare and meal money but declined their offer to sign a Class A contract. He subsequently declined Class AA contract offers from the Indians and the Red Sox. With his family behind him, he was determined to start at a higher level. By 1948, he had his sights firmly set on obtaining a Triple-A contract when Dodger scout Jim Murray took him to Ebbets Field to work out in front of Branch Rickey and George Sisler. The Dodgers were sufficiently impressed to sign him to a contract with their Class AAA Montreal team plus $2,500 in cash—the most money anyone in his family ever had at one time.[5]

Ed Roebuck resurrected his career in 1960 after arm problems nearly ended it (George Brace photograph).

Young Roebuck had his Triple-A contract. But because he entered into the transaction without the guidance of an agent, he was ignorant about the right of a team to "option" a player down to a lower level—a trap for the unwary. As a consequence, from 1949 to 1951 he was "optioned out" to Newport News (Class B) twice and to Elmira (Class A) once before he ever got to Montreal.[6] Beginning at Montreal in 1952, he put together three strong seasons as a starting pitcher, culminating in an 18-win season in 1954 made possible by his decision to limit his repertoire to just three pitches: a fastball, a curve, and a sinker—the pitch that would become his meal ticket.

A Dodger at Last

After 5½ years in the minor leagues, Roebuck made the Brooklyn Dodgers in the spring of 1955 as a relief pitcher. He responded to the call by saving 12 games for the World Champion Dodgers of 1955, and pitched 2 scoreless innings in the World Series. He continued to be a mainstay of the Dodger bullpen for the next two seasons. With an 8–2 record and a 2.71 earned run average, 1957 was his best year in Brooklyn. But it was also in 1957 that he first began to experience shooting pains in his right shoulder. He continued to pitch for the first three months of the 1958 season in Los Angeles as the pain got progressively worse. By July, it had become impossible for him to continue. July 19 was his final appearance of the year. On July 28 the Dodgers put him on the "voluntarily retired list."[7] It looked to everyone in the Dodger organization—except Ed Roebuck—that his career was over at 27.

The Journey Back

The following spring at Vero Beach he was reinstated by the Dodgers. But when they saw that he couldn't pitch, they put him on waivers. When no major league team agreed to pick him up for the $1 waiver price, the Dodgers released him "outright." Roebuck, who had always been a good hitter, set out to make it as a first baseman. He convinced Buzzie Bavasi to sign him to a contract with St. Paul, their Triple-A farm team in the American Association without a first baseman on its roster. He worked out at first base for two weeks in Vero Beach before leaving for St. Paul. The throws he made from first base made his arm begin to come around. But the Dodgers were not convinced, and he was shipped out to join the St. Paul Saints, who were playing their final exhibition games on the road in Texas. Saints Manager Max Macon asked Roebuck to pitch even though his arm was out of shape after concentrating his efforts at first base. The shoulder felt all right, but the switch to an unfamiliar position caused him to develop a sore elbow. A Fort Worth doctor diagnosed the problem as a broken bone. Roebuck balked when he was told the arm would have to be placed in a cast for six weeks.[8] When he told the Saints he was going back to Los Angeles to get another opinion, Max Macon told him he wasn't serious about baseball and suspended him. In the space of six weeks Roebuck's status had alternated from voluntarily retired, to reinstated, to released outright, to suspended.[9]

The first doctor he saw in Los Angeles took more X-rays and diagnosed the problem as bone chips instead of a break. He told Roebuck that he'd never pitch again—or even play golf. Roebuck refused to give up. He went to see the Dodgers' future team physician, Dr. Robert Kerlan, for a third opinion. Kerlan's diagnosis was a calcium deposit on the elbow, which he proceeded to dissolve in less than a week with one shot of cortisone. Roebuck bundled his wife and 5-year-old son into the car and drove them back to St. Paul to resume his career.[10]

When Roebuck got to St. Paul he was told that the roster was full, and that he would have to be placed on the disabled list. This was a mere pebble in the road compared to his previous setbacks, and in a few days he was given a chance to start. He pitched a 3-hit complete-game victory, his first complete game since 1954. He continued to surprise everyone with 12 more wins and 13 more complete games for the 1959 Saints. He followed that up with a perfect 9–0 record as a starter for Pete Reiser's winter league team at Escogido in the Dominican Republic. But when he received his 1960 contract from St. Paul with a 50 percent pay cut, he went to see Buzzie Bavasi in his Los

Angeles office before spring training. Bavasi told him, "I guess once you have a sore arm, no one will ever believe you can get rid of it."[11] Then he gave him a glimmer of hope by telling him he could work out with the Dodgers at Vero Beach "if he thought he could help the team."[12] Roebuck jumped at the chance. Under what he would later say was the most pressure he ever experienced in baseball, he fought for a job at Vero Beach wearing a Dodger uniform—though he was owned by a minor league team—with the burden of knowing that someone had to go before there would be room for him.

At the end of spring training, with the prospect of returning to the minors looming, the Dodgers sold outfielder Don Miles to Victoria in the Texas League. Buzzie Bavasi walked up to Roebuck in the Dodger Town lobby and told him, "Congratulations! We've purchased your contract from St. Paul."[13] Roebuck would always say it was the happiest moment of his career.

Worship Service in Blue at City Hall

On April 12 the Spring Street entrance to the City Hall was covered with "Welcome World Champion Dodgers!" posters, while thousands of rabid Dodger fans gathered at noon to celebrate the start of the 1960 season. In a reverential ceremony Los Angeles Mayor-celebrant Norris Paulson presented "Our Dodgers!" to the congregation; pro-

claimed Dodgers owner Walter O'Malley "King of the Day"; and received a gold lifetime pass to all Dodgers games in return. O'Malley then introduced Manager Walter Alston who, with the help of a dozen of his uniformed players, unfurled a huge 1959 World Champion pennant to be flown at the Los Angeles Memorial Coliseum.[14]

After the players had scribbled autographs on everything and everyone, they mounted convertibles for a trip down Broadway en route to the Coliseum. The Baseball Writers Association of America, discounting the Dodgers' 1959 Cinderella season as a mere temporary aberration, picked them to finish third in the National League.[15] All the experts, including Frank Finch, the principal Dodgers reporter at the *Los Angeles Times*, expected the Braves—with All-Stars Aaron, Mathews, Spahn, and Burdette—to resume building their dynasty in Milwaukee by winning their third pennant in four years in 1960.[16]

Twenty-three-year-old Don Drysdale made his third consecutive opening day start April 12, 1960 (George Brace photograph).

But today in downtown Los Angeles, the curbs were jammed with true believer Dodger fans undeterred in their optimism. Some fans, overcome with emotion, rushed the caravan to touch their heroes and personally deliver encouragement. A young girl, part of a troop of Brownies, admonished Gil Hodges, "Hey Gil, get a home run tonight!" An amused Hodges told his teammate sitting beside him, "That's 72 so far I'm supposed to get tonight." Thousands of faces and waving arms in skyscraper windows from the reinforcements working above pelted the procession with cascarones, hollow eggshells filled with confetti.[17]

Back to Reality—Opening Night at the Coliseum

That evening at the Coliseum, where only 50,000 were expected, a National League night game record crowd of 67,550 bundled-up Dodger fans turned out on a chilly opening night to see their World Champion Dodgers usher in the 1960 season.[18] Though still only 23 years old, Don Drysdale—the undisputed ace of the staff—was beginning his fifth big league season, and making his third consecutive opening day start for the Dodgers. The fearsome 6-foot 6-inch sidewinding, head-hunting Drysdale, from nearby Van Nuys, was 17–13 in 1959, leading the National League in both strikeouts with 242 and hit batters with 18.

Drysdale's pitching career had a serendipitous beginning. In 1953, between his junior and senior years at Van Nuys High School, he was the second baseman on the American Legion team coached by his father, Scott. When the team's pitcher failed to show up for a game, Drysdale was pressed into service. He pitched a complete-game victory in his first experience on the mound. After the game, his father introduced him to Brooklyn Dodger scout Goldie Holt, who just happened to be in the stands that day. "Have you ever thought about pitching?" Holt asked Drysdale.[19] A year later, after making the Los Angeles All-City team as a starting pitcher, he was besieged by scouts from the Yankees, Braves, White Sox, Pirates, in addition to Holt. In June 1954, a month before his 18th birthday, he turned down scholarship offers from Stanford and USC to sign a contract with the Brooklyn Dodgers. The day after graduation, he was sent to Bakersfield in the Class C California State League.[20] Two years later, after just a season and a half in the minors and a growth spurt of 4½ inches, he was a spot-starter for the Brooklyn Dodgers at the age of 19. The thirty-nine-year-old veteran, Sal "The Barber" Maglie, took young Drysdale under his wing to teach him the art of *shaving*—keeping batters from crowding the plate by pitching them high and tight.[21]

On this night at the Coliseum, California Governor Edmund G. "Pat" Brown headed the list of luminaries in the stands studded with Hollywood stars. National League President Warren Giles threw out the first ball.[22] With the exception of the pitcher's spot, the starting lineup for the Dodgers was virtually unchanged from the day they won the World Series six months before in Chicago:

	APRIL 12, 1960		OCTOBER 8, 1959	
1	Jim Gilliam	3B	Jim Gilliam	3B
2	Charlie Neal	2B	Charlie Neal	2B

APRIL 12, 1960			OCTOBER 8, 1959	
3	Wally Moon	LF	Wally Moon	LF
4	Duke Snider	RF	Duke Snider	CF
5	Gil Hodges	1B	Gil Hodges	1B
6	John Roseboro	C	Norm Larker	RF
7	Don Demeter	CF	John Roseboro	C
8	Maury Wills	SS	Maury Wills	SS
9	Don Drysdale	P	Johnny Podres	P

Though Norm Larker was supplanted by Don Demeter in the #7 spot in the opening night lineup, Larker would be a major factor in 1960.

Drysdale appeared to be in command until the Cubs' new third baseman, Don "Popeye" Zimmer, led off the top of the third inning with a home run. Drysdale and Zimmer had been Dodger teammates for the last four seasons, until fan-favorite Zimmer was unceremoniously dealt to the lowly Cubs four days earlier for three virtual unknowns,

Chuck Essegian accepting his 1959 World Series ring from Commissioner Ford Frick (National Baseball Hall of Fame Library, Cooperstown, New York).

plus $25,000 in cash. One of the unknowns coming over from the Cubs was a pitcher named Ron Perranoski, who would spend the entire 1960 season in the minors before establishing himself as one of the great Dodger relief pitchers beginning in 1961. When Zimmer, carrying a plate in his head as a result of two near-catastrophic beanings,[23] lofted Drysdale's 2–2 pitch over the left-field screen to put the Cubs ahead 1–0, Dodger fans rose to their feet to give their beloved Popeye a standing ovation. Drysdale was roughed up for another run on Tony Taylor's line-drive double, and was down 2–0 before he could get back to the dugout.[24]

After surviving his rocky 29-pitch third inning, Drysdale settled down to shut out the Cubs for the next eight innings, striking out another 11 batters, and even blasting a 410-foot triple off Cubs starter Bob Anderson in the seventh.[25] The Dodgers tied the game 2–2 in the fifth inning on a 2-run double off the left-field screen by Wally Moon. The game remained tied 2–2 as it moved into the bottom of the eleventh. After Cubs reliever Bob Elson retired the first two Dodger batters, Alston had a decision to make: whether to pull Drysdale for a pinch hitter. Drysdale was one of the best hitting pitchers in the league with 11 home runs at the Coliseum over the past two years. Tonight, he had dominated the Cubs since the third, but he had already thrown 165 pitches. For Alston, the elevated pitch count was dispositive. He looked down the bench and told Chuck Essegian to grab a bat. Essegian was a former Stanford football player and no ordinary pinch hitter. He had hit home runs in his last two major league at bats—both as a pinch hitter in the 1959 World Series.

Drysdale had lost his two previous opening-day starts in 1958 and 1959. He knew that the only way he could get credit for a win was for Essegian to keep the inning alive and for the Dodgers to pull it out with a run. Otherwise he would be charged with a "no decision." Elston's first pitch was wide of the strike zone, but his second pitch was a hanging curve that Essegian did not miss. He hit a towering walk-off home run over the 40-foot screen deep into the left-field seats. Drysdale was halfway up the runway to the showers when he heard the crack of the bat. He ran back onto the field to hug Essegian as he crossed home plate.[26] Chuck Essegian had now homered in his last three official at bats. Don Drysdale had his first opening-day victory, an 11-inning complete game with 14 strikeouts. As they walked off the field a few minutes before midnight, the Los Angeles Dodgers were off to a great start to the 1960 season with a 3–2 win.

Reflections on Rings, Flags and Ike's Last Pitch

The Dodgers spent their Monday off-day of April 18 preparing to travel to San Francisco for their first encounter with the Giants at Candlestick Park. The day before, Easter Sunday, as they celebrated with their fans the awarding of their World Series rings and the raising of the 1959 National League Pennant and World Championship flags at the Coliseum, everything seemed to be falling into place. Starting pitcher Larry Sherry, who had been promoted to the rotation as a reward for his MVP performance as a reliever in the Series, beat the St. Louis Cardinals 7–5. It was Sandy Koufax—his role still uncertain—who came out of the bullpen to save the game for Sherry. Old Boys of Summer Gil Hodges and Duke Snider each hit home runs. With their victory the

Dodgers completed a 3-game sweep of the Cardinals, and ended the first week of the season tied for first place with the Giants.

That Monday in Washington, D.C., President Eisenhower interrupted a golfing vacation in Augusta, Georgia, to open the American League season at Griffith's Stadium. It was the first time since 1903, the year the league was founded, that the A.L. opened a week later than the N.L. Commissioner Ford Frick had allowed the National League to stretch its schedule from April 12 to October 2 to accommodate the long travel distances between the eight N.L. cities, including two on the West Coast.[27]

Eisenhower had celebrated his Easter Sunday by attending services with his family at the Presbyterian church in Augusta before heading off to Augusta National Golf Club to play his seventh consecutive round in seven days on the same course where Arnold Palmer was crowned Masters Champion on April 10.

Today would be Eisenhower's seventh and final opening day ceremony. The year before, he passed up the honor in favor of total golf immersion in Augusta. Today, the Pitcher-in-Chief, in a suit and tie, removed his felt hat, put on his baseball glove, and tossed out two balls from his private box without benefit of a wind-up. The first was a high, hard one caught by Senators outfielder Bob Allison, last season's A.L. Rookie of the Year. It would have been a perfect last pitch for Ike. But to make up for his dereliction of duty the previous year, the good soldier made the mistake of releasing a second pitch, a feeble blooper fielded by a rookie Washington pitcher named Jack Kralick. After autographing both baseballs, Ike settled into his role as First Baseball Fan, armed with a scorebook, hot dog, peanuts, and large Coke.[28] Beside him, self-proclaimed baseball expert and presidential candidate Richard Nixon provided commentary.

Washington's Camilio Pascual, the Cuban right-hander with the legendary curve ball, struck out 15 Red Sox batters in an overpowering 10–1 complete game victory. Pascual broke Walter Johnson's Washington Senators' single game strikeout record of 14 that "The Big Train" set in 1910 and duplicated in 1924.[29] Only 41-year-old Ted Williams, beginning his nineteenth and final season, prevented a total Boston humiliation. As Williams came to the plate in the second inning, Nixon was heard telling Eisenhower, "This is probably his last season. Let's root for him." "That's a good idea," the president responded.[30] Williams complied with the executive order from the stands by hitting a Pascual fast ball over the 31-foot center field fence for a solo home run. The ball landed among some startled pedestrians on Fifth Street, more than 450 feet from home plate.[31]

Staying for the final out, Eisenhower completed his typically meticulous scoring of the game, and headed back to National Airport with a career "winning record"—having presided over four Senators opening day wins out of seven since 1953. "That's better than .500, and that's okay in baseball," Nixon assured him. Within an hour he was in the air aboard the Columbine III (aka Air Force One) preparing to attend to more important matters at Augusta National.[32]

Later that evening, aboard a United Airlines flight to San Francisco, as Walter Alston and the Dodger players reflected on the previous day's ceremonies at the Coliseum, they had to come to grips with some new realities: 1959 was past, the team was getting older, and the National League was greatly improved since last season. They would face challenges to their title not only in San Francisco and Milwaukee, but surprisingly, in Pittsburgh as well.

There's Something Going On in Pittsburgh

By the last day of April, the euphoria of opening night and the excitement of the World Championship ceremonies of Easter Sunday had faded. Before 85,065 on a Saturday night at the Coliseum, Willie McCovey and the arch-rival Giants beat Don Drysdale to win the rubber game of a 3-game series, 6–3, thereby throwing the Dodgers into fifth place with an 8–7 record. McCovey's ownership of Drysdale began on that day as he rocked him for the first 2 of the 12 career home runs he would hit off the big right-hander.[33] Drysdale lasted five innings. By then, he had allowed the Giants to take an insurmountable 5–0 lead. Sandy Koufax replaced Drysdale to start the sixth inning, but he was taken out before he could complete the inning after walking three batters. It was not a good day for what was to become one of the greatest righty-lefty 1–2 pitching combinations of all time.

Some 2,400 miles away in Pittsburgh, there was something unexpected going on. The Pittsburgh Pirates ended April in first place with an 11–3 record. The Pirates hadn't been to the World Series since 1927 when they were swept by Babe Ruth and the Yankees in four straight games. Most of the baseball experts picked them to finish out of contention again in 1960:

EXPERTS	PUBLICATION	PITTSBURGH— PREDICTED FINISH
Frank Finch	*Los Angeles Times*	4th
Baseball Writers Association of America	*The Sporting News*	4th
John Drebinger	*New York Times*	4th
J.G. Taylor Spink	*The Sporting News*	5th
N.Y. Writers Composite Poll	*The Sporting News*	5th

But as the Pirates entered May, Roberto "Bob" Clemente was hitting .377 with 4 home runs; Bill Mazeroski had 4 home runs; Dick Groat was hitting .349; Bob Friend was 3–0 with 2 shutouts; and Vernon Law, at 4–0 with a 1.25 ERA, was on his way to a Cy Young Award. These were not Joe Garagiola's Pirates of the early fifties with their laughable spaceman batting helmets. It was evident that there was something going on in Pittsburgh.[34]

	W	L	PCT.	*
Pittsburgh	11	3	.786	
San Francisco	10	5	.667	1½
Milwaukee	7	5	.583	3
St. Louis	7	6	.538	3½
Los Angeles	8	7	.533	3½

*Games behind leader

✳ ✳ ✳

On May 1 the Soviets shot down an American U-2 spy plane invading Soviet airspace on the eve of a crucial Big Four summit in Paris on a nuclear test ban treaty.[35] President Eisenhower and the State Department initially called the U-2 a weather plane. But with strong countervailing evidence—the plane, the pilot (Francis Gary Powers), and his film—in the hands of the Soviet Union, the U.S. soon had to admit that it was a spy plane, while maintaining that the mission was "justified." The incident caused the Paris summit to collapse when Eisenhower refused to knuckle under to Soviet Premier Nikita Khrushchev's demand for an apology. East-West relations further deteriorated when Soviet Foreign Minister Andrei Gromyko and American U.N. Ambassador, and eventual Nixon running mate, Henry Cabot Lodge locked horns at the Security Council.[36] Francis Gary Powers was later tried in Moscow, convicted of espionage, and sentenced to 3 years' imprisonment and 7 years of hard labor. The U-2 incident would set in motion a downward spiral of mistrust that would culminate in the Cuban Missile Crisis.

❈ ❈ ❈

Two

Changes, Losses, and a Glimpse at Greatness

There are no second acts in American lives.[1]—F. Scott Fitzgerald

Despite the Dodgers' disappointing fifth-place position heading into May, they possessed a weapon that could prevent most clubs from ever being counted out: pitching. Their starting rotation of Don Drysdale, Johnny Podres, Stan Williams, and Roger Craig was arguably the best in baseball. So far in 1960, Roger Craig was on pace to be even more of a force than he was in 1959. That would soon change.

Bad Luck for Roger the Dodger

At 30, Roger Lee Craig, from Durham, North Carolina, was the second oldest pitcher on the Dodgers' staff—next to 33-year-old Clem Labine. As a rookie in 1955, Walter Alston had enough confidence in him to let him start Game 5 of the World Series at Ebbets Field, where he beat the Yankees. By 1958 he was being shuttled between the minors and the big club due to "tendonitis" in his right shoulder. It was actually an undiagnosed torn rotator cuff—an injury that was not recognized in those days. When Carl Erskine retired suddenly in mid–June of 1959, Craig was brought up from Triple-A Spokane. When Dodger General Manager E.J. "Buzzie" Bavasi called to tell him to report immediately, he loaded his wife and three kids into the car and drove 1,300 miles nonstop to the Coliseum where he arrived in time to suit up for a night game with the Milwaukee Braves.[2] Craig did not waste his second chance with the Dodgers. He was a major factor in their winning the pennant with a dazzling 11–5 run in the last half of the season. He had become their stopper in September with wins in his last five decisions down the stretch. He maintained the momentum into 1960, with a complete-game win over the Cubs in Wrigley Field on April 27.

On May 2, Craig was attempting to keep his streak alive—with a seventh consecutive win—in a start against the Reds at the Coliseum. The Reds hadn't won a pennant since 1940. They came into the Coliseum in last place, but they had been a nemesis to the Dodgers. The Dodgers were just 9–13 against Cincinnati in 1959, their worst record against any opposing team.

Roger Craig, whom Walter Alston was counting on to be a key member of his rotation, was pitching well on this night without any support from his defense. He had shut out the Reds through the first four innings. He entered the fifth with a 1–0 lead, but errors by Maury Wills and Charlie Neal caused him to give up two unearned runs and the lead.[3]

He lost the lead again in the seventh when Billy Martin, the Reds' fiery problem-child second baseman, hit his first National League home run to tie the game at 3–3. Craig and Martin had a history: Martin had hit .429 against Craig in two World Series; he ruined Craig's shut-out with a line-single in Game 5 of the 1955 World Series, and hit a home run off him in Game 3 of the 1956 World Series. In those days, Martin was the All-Star second baseman on Casey Stengel's Yankees. But he was trouble. After the infamous Copacabana brawl incident of May 16, 1957, the clubbing, boozing debauchery of the Mantle-Ford-Martin triumvirate had become too much for the Yankees to tolerate. Martin—whom the Yankees deemed the catalyst—was traded to Kansas City a month later, essentially to "protect" Mickey Mantle. Martin lasted for just three months in Kansas City, and one season each for two other teams, before landing in Cincinnati in 1960. After bouncing between another two teams in two different leagues in 1961, his career would be over. But on this night in Los Angeles, he enjoyed resuming his torment of Roger Craig.

It was the eighth inning that proved disastrous for Roger Craig and the 1960 Los Angeles Dodgers. Clinging to a 3–3 tie, Craig got lead-off batter Vada Pinson to ground weakly to second base. But it turned into an infield single when Charlie Neal was unable to throw out the fleet Cincinnati center fielder. Reds left fielder Gus Bell followed with a ground ball through Neal's legs. Neal was charged with his second error of the game, and instead of the bases empty and two outs, Craig now had Bell on first and Pinson on third with none out. Next, he got future Hall-of-Famer Frank Robinson to hit another ball on the ground to shortstop Maury Wills. Pinson broke for the plate, but was trapped in a rundown when Wills threw home to prevent him from scoring the go-

The Dodgers were dealt a blow May 2, 1960, when Roger Craig suffered a broken collarbone in a collision at the plate with Vada Pinson (National Baseball Hall of Fame Library, Cooperstown, New York).

ahead run. Pinson lowered his shoulder into Craig, who was covering home plate, sending him reeling into a reverse somersault. Despite the violence of the collision, Craig tagged out Pinson and hung onto the ball. With Bell now on third and Robinson on second, Craig began to walk Lee Walls intentionally to load the bases. After lobbing three pitches, he knew there was something wrong with his shoulder, and had to come out of the game. He was replaced by his roommate, Larry Sherry. After Sherry struck out shortstop Roy McMillan for what should have been the third out, catcher Ed Bailey delivered the crushing blow: a base-clearing double to make the score 6–3, Cincinnati. All three of the runs were unearned and charged to Roger Craig.[4]

The Dodgers eventually lost the game 6–5. Roger Craig was charged with the loss, despite giving up only one earned run. Craig's six-game win streak was over, but that was the least of the Dodgers' worries. He was later diagnosed with a broken right collarbone.[5] The Dodgers had lost their 1959 meal ticket—he would not make another start for more than two months. The loss dropped the team back into fifth place with an 8–8 record. Now they were a .500 team with only two dependable starters.

The Tunnel

Already, the season had not been kind to Sandy Koufax. In his sixth year in the major leagues, he was still not a regular member of the starting rotation. When he did get a chance to pitch, he pressed and overthrew, trying to strike out every batter he faced. He tended to lose control of his emotions out of frustration when he gave up a hit or a walk. This led to a downward spiral of more overthrowing and increased wildness.[6] He had just come off a forgettable 3-walks-in-⅔-of-an-inning relief performance less than 48 hours before. In his only start on April 22, he had to be taken out of the game in the first inning before he could get anyone out, after giving up 5 runs, 5 hits, a walk, and a wild pitch.[7]

To get to the dugout at the Memorial Coliseum, the players had to walk through a tunnel from the dressing room that let them out behind home plate. Before the game of May 2, Koufax was making his way down the tunnel when he confronted General Manager Buzzie Bavasi approaching from the opposite direction. As they met, Koufax's frustrations boiled over:

> KOUFAX: "Buzzie, why don't you trade me? I want to pitch, and I'm not going to get a chance here."
> BAVASI: "How can we pitch you when you can't get anyone out?"
> KOUFAX: "How can I get anyone out when I'm sitting around in the dugout? If I can't do the job for you, why don't you send me somewhere where I can get a fresh start? Maybe you can even get a player you can use. I don't want to sit around and just watch."[8]

The Dodgers were getting their first hint that this might be their last year with Sandy Koufax.

The Changing of the Guard

On May 12, after losing two out of three games to the Pirates at the Coliseum, the Dodgers were still mired in fifth place, three games under .500. Buzzie Bavasi, knowing he had to do something to keep the season from slipping away, placed 38-year-old veteran Carl Furillo on the "inactive list," and recalled Frank Howard from Spokane.[9] Furillo

learned of his fate from the Dodgers' traveling secretary Lee Scott: He would not be making the trip with the team to San Francisco that night because Frank Howard was taking his place on the roster.[10] When Furillo called Commissioner Ford Frick the next day to inquire about his status on the inactive list, he was told that he must be on the disabled list because there was no such "inactive list." The Dodgers promptly recharacterized his status as the 30-day disabled list.

Just seven months before, Furillo was a hero in Los Angeles. As a pinch hitter in the 12th inning of the final game of the playoff series with the Milwaukee Braves, he drove in the winning run to send the Dodgers to the World Series. Five days later, he drove in the two deciding runs as a pinch hitter in Game 3 of the Series. But that was then. After he tore a calf muscle in the first week of the 1960 season, the latest of a series of leg injuries, he had contributed just two hits in ten at bats.[11] Up in Spokane, Washington, the Dodgers had a 6'7" outfielder named Frank Howard who was tearing up the Pacific Coast League with a .371 average, 4 home runs, and 24 runs batted in. The handwriting was on the wall for Furillo.

The shameful treatment of Carl Furillo remains a dark chapter in the history of the Los Angeles Dodgers (National Baseball Hall of Fame Library, Cooperstown, New York).

Skoonj

Carl Anthony Furillo, from Reading, Pennsylvania, had been with the Dodgers since 1946 after distinguishing himself with three battle stars and a Purple Heart as an infantryman in the Pacific Theater during World War II. *Skoonj*, as his teammates called him, soon established himself as one of the era's great right fielders. The players on other teams, wary of his powerful throwing arm, called him "The Reading Rifle." They didn't run on him. Don Drysdale recalled in his autobiography, "I saw him throw runners out at first base on balls that dropped in front of him and should have been singles. Amazing."[12]

Furillo reached his peak at 31 in 1953 with the Brooklyn Dodgers—the year they won 105 games under Charlie Dressen, but lost the World Series for the fifth consecutive time to the New York Yankees. That year he was the National League batting champion with a career best .344 average. When the Dodgers arrived in Los Angeles in 1958, Furillo's career was on the decline, but he led the team in runs batted in and was second to Duke Snider in batting average. It would be his last full season. Hobbled by leg injuries in 1959, he was relegated to a pinch hitting role, starting only 15 games in right field.

Going into the 1960 season, even Furillo's future as a pinch hitter was thrown into question when he pulled a muscle in his right leg at the end of spring training. General Manager Buzzie Bavasi observed at the time, "Furillo's condition complicated everything. If we were sure he could pinch hit, we know he'd be extremely valuable. If he can't, then the entire team must be switched around."[13]

Furillo managed to start two games in right field for the Dodgers on April 19 and 20 at the brand-new Candlestick Park in San Francisco, but was unable to complete either game. April 20 would be the last start of his career.

The Boy Giant

Frank Oliver Howard was born August 8, 1936, in Columbus, Ohio, weighing in at 13 pounds, six ounces. He was the third of six children born to John and Erma Howard. His father had to work long hours as a railroad machinist to support his family, and Frank did manual labor during the summers to help out. The summer of 1950, before entering high school, he gained 45 pounds and grew 5 inches in height while swinging a pick and shovel and running a jackhammer. At South High School in Columbus he was an outfielder-pitcher on the baseball team; but it was his prowess as a basketball player that brought him scholarship offers from several colleges.[14] Led by their 6'7" center Frank Howard, the 1954 South Bulldogs won the Ohio State High School Athletic Association Regional Championship.[15]

Howard chose Ohio State University, in his own hometown, and majored in physical education. In his junior year on the Buckeye basketball team, he was the runner-up high scorer in the Big Ten Conference and was selected on the second team of the Consensus All-America team along with Elgin Baylor. His 32 rebounds against BYU in 1956 is still the single-game Buckeye record. The Philadelphia Warriors drafted him in the third round of the 1958 National Basketball Association draft. But when the Los Angeles Dodgers offered him a whopping $108,000 bonus after he batted .336 as the Ohio State right fielder, he decided to forego the final two quarters of his senior year, and joined their Green Bay club in the Class B Three-I League. There, under manager Pete Reiser, he was an instant sensation, batting .333 with 37 home runs (including one that measured 550 feet) and 119 runs batted in. In a game at Rochester he hit three home runs over three different fences, the third one delivered with only one hand on the bat. Word traveled fast around the majors about the modest Boy Giant in Green Bay who responded to questions from the press about his Ruthian feats with a laconic "Yes sir" or "No sir."[16] It was in Green Bay that he met his future wife, Carol, a petite 5'1" beauty. He won the Three-I League Most Valuable Player Award by a landslide, and was called up at the end of the 1958 season by the Dodgers, struggling in their first year in Los Angeles.[17] In his second big league at bat, facing future Hall of Famer Robin

The Dodgers' 23-year-old 6'7" power-hitting sensation, Frank Howard (George Brace photograph).

Roberts, he hit a prodigious home run that hit a sign atop the left field roof at Connie Mack Stadium in Philadelphia.[18] His Dodger teammates called him Hondo, after the larger-than-life John Wayne character in the movie of the same name.

He moved quickly up the Dodger farm system in 1959. After just 63 games at Double-A Victoria in the Texas League, again under Pete Reiser, he was hitting .371 with 27 home runs and 79 runs batted in when he was promoted to Triple-A Spokane in the Pacific Coast League. There, under the tutelage of Bobby Bragan, he added another 16 home runs and 47 RBIs in 22 games. With a combined 43 home runs, 126 RBIs, and a .342 batting average, he was brought up at the end of the Dodgers' 1959 world championship season for another brief look. His second big league home run came in St. Louis on September 22, in the thick of an intense 3-team pennant race among the Dodgers, Giants, and Braves, when he hit a clutch 3-run pinch hit home run in the ninth inning off Cardinals' ace reliever Lindy McDaniel.

During Spring Training at Vero Beach in 1960, after 12 years as the Dodgers' first baseman, Gil Hodges was asked to groom Howard as his eventual replacement. But Howard was never comfortable there, preferring the outfield. To complicate matters, a sulking Howard had a run-in with Walter Alston after failing to show up for two consecutive Sunday exhibition games in protest over not getting enough playing time. Though he had been named the 1959 Minor League Player of the Year by *The Sporting News*, he still didn't make the big club when the Dodgers broke camp. Management's official line was, "We feel he needs experience at first base and [more] attention to his hitting."[19]

Back in Spokane, Frank Howard was clearly a misfit—a man among boys—again destroying Pacific Coast League pitching. On the day he was called up for the third time, the Dodgers were last in the National League in batting, but they had a Boy Giant with a wooden club on the way to join them when they started a 14-game road trip in San Francisco.

The Schism Is Complete

On May 17, the Dodgers gave Carl Furillo his unconditional release. He had been offered a demotion to Spokane at his same $32,000 salary, but he turned it down, knowing he had to remain on a major league roster to qualify for his 15-year pension. When the Dodgers paid him a severance amount of only $7,000, he threatened to sue them for the remaining $25,000 due on his contract.[20] Both sides dug in. Buzzie Bavasi maintained that since Commissioner Ford Frick informed him that he could not keep Furillo on the disabled list "as long as he could hit," he had placed him on waivers. When no team in either league wanted him at his $32,000 salary, his only alternative was to release him. Furillo took the position that he was wrongfully released under the Official Major League Players Contract, which prohibited trading or releasing a player when he is injured, and that he was therefore due payment from the Dodgers on his full contract, plus treatment for his injuries. The Dodgers' position was that he was released not because of a specific injury, but because of the fact that Furillo "is getting old."[21] As Buzzie Bavasi matter-of-factly put it, "We have to go for youth in a situation like this."[22]

In May of 1961, Furillo would receive $21,000 in a settlement with the Los Angeles Dodgers. But the rift would never heal. That spring he had written letters to all eighteen major league teams asking for a chance to pinch-hit and/or play the outfield, but nobody would hire him.[23] He would go to his grave believing that he had been released in contravention of the rules and that Major League Baseball blacklisted him after he stood up to the Dodgers.

With the release of Carl Furillo, the rapid dispersal of the Boys of Summer continued. By the end of the 1960 season, the Dodgers would have only seven players on the roster from their 1955 Brooklyn world championship team: Hodges, Snider, Gilliam, Craig, Podres, Koufax, and Drysdale.

A New Beginning in Milwaukee

On the day of Carl Furillo's unconditional release, a reeling Dodger team arrived in Milwaukee after losing two out of three to the Giants in San Francisco, still in fifth place, four games under .500. Frank Howard was in Furillo's old spot in right field. Despite having lost his last three starts in a row, Don Drysdale was given the ball and asked to right the ship. The Dodgers had to face right hander Bob Buhl, who had beaten them nine straight times at County Stadium since September 1955. Drysdale was gone after six innings, having given up home runs to Ed Mathews and Hank Aaron (one of seventeen that "Bad Henry" would hit off him).

Buhl was cruising with a 4–1 lead as he entered the eighth inning. Then the wheels began to fall off as the Dodgers loaded the bases with none out. Frank Howard, who had already hit the ball sharply off him with a line drive single and a fly out to the deepest part of the park, was next. On Buhl's 3–1 pitch, Howard hit a towering drive that landed in a clump of trees beyond the bullpen over 450 feet from home plate—an area of County Stadium rarely reached since its inception in 1953. The grand slam home run put the Dodgers ahead, 5–4. In the radio broadcast booth, an incredulous Vin Scully described what he had just seen: "Frank Howard just hit a ball into the trees in Milwaukee!" Before the inning was over, Dodger reliever Larry Sherry had finished off Buhl with another home run.[24]

It was a transitional day for the Dodgers as they escaped Milwaukee with a 6–4 win. Frank Howard put some new life—some punch—into their lineup. Their 5-year Bob Buhl jinx was over. Back in California, Carl Furillo was trout fishing as his attorney prepared his case against the Los Angeles Dodgers.

A Glimpse at Greatness

Sandy Koufax was a spot-starter when the Dodgers lost Roger Craig to a broken collarbone back on May 2. They responded by promoting him to the starting rotation now comprised of Don Drysdale, Johnny Podres, Stan Williams, and Koufax.[25] It was Koufax's turn when the Dodgers arrived in Pittsburgh on May 23, trapped in sixth place, five games under .500.

The Jewish Kid from Brooklyn

Sanford Braun was born in Brooklyn on December 30, 1935, to Evelyn and Jack Braun. Jack divorced Evelyn when Sandy was three and dropped out of his life. The boy spent most of his time with his grandparents as Evelyn worked as a certified public accountant. When he was nine his mother married Irving Koufax, a local lawyer. He acquired a new father and a new name: Sanford Braun Koufax.[26] The Koufaxes settled in a neighborhood of lower-middle-class Italians and Jews in the hamlet of Bensonhurst.[27] Sandy was known as a quiet kid, always with a basketball. By his senior year at Lafayette High School he was the captain of the basketball team who was attracting attention as a 6'2" guard with exceptional leaping ability.[28]

He entered the University of Cincinnati in the fall of 1953 without a scholarship. He walked onto the freshman basketball team and was awarded a partial scholarship after Coach Ed Jucker watched him practice. As the basketball season was winding down, Jucker, also the baseball coach, was having trouble finding players for the baseball team. Koufax approached him to deliver a typical Koufax understatement: "I can pitch." That winter he tried out inside the old Schmidlaff Gym, and made the 1954 varsity team as a pitcher. In his only season of intercollegiate baseball, he was 3 and 1 with a 2.81 ERA and 51 strikeouts in 32 innings.[29]

A 25-year-old Sandy Koufax is promoted to a full-time starter with the loss of Roger Craig to the disabled list (George Brace photograph).

Koufax returned home to Brooklyn after his freshman year, and took a job as a camp counselor in the Catskills. Scouts from several teams began to come around: the Yankees, Giants, Pirates, and Al Campanis from the Dodgers.

Al Campanis, a Greek-Italian from Cos in the Dodecanese Islands, graduated in 1940 from New York University, where he was the captain of his football and baseball teams. After serving in World War II, he played shortstop alongside Jackie Robinson at Montreal in 1946. He left the field after the 1947 season to manage in the Dodger farm system for two years until he found his calling in 1950: scouting.[30] Campanis knew talent, but he had never seen anything like this before. He was so impressed with Koufax the first time he saw him throw a baseball that he invited him to work out at Ebbets Field. On September 17, 1954, days before he was to return to the University of Cincinnati, manager Walter Alston and scouting director Fresco Thompson watched him throw from the Ebbets Field mound.[31] The Dodgers made a handshake deal with Koufax before he could leave the premises.

Irving Koufax negotiated the terms of a contract on behalf of his son: $20,000—$6,000 for the first year's salary and a signing bonus of $14,000. The deal, which qualified him as a "Bonus Baby," was reported in the *New York Times* on December 14, 1954.[32] Under the version of the bonus rule then in effect, a free agent who signed for more than $6,000 had to start out on the major league roster, and remain there for two years. The rule was originally adopted at the 1952 winter meetings, and was intended to discourage the richer teams (translated: the New York Yankees) from outbidding the poorer teams for the top talent. The Dodgers had to cut a little left-hander named Tommy Lasorda to make room for Koufax on the roster. As a consequence of the bonus rule, instead of developing in the minor leagues, Koufax languished for two years on the Brooklyn bench with an occasional start or a mop-up assignment in relief.

In 1955, at the age of 19, he started five games and even pitched two shutouts—though it would be four years before he pitched another. But in 1956, it was clear that he was still not ready, as he gave up 10 home runs in only 58⅔ innings. Don Drysdale, who joined him as a teammate that year, would recall 35 years later: "There's no question in my mind that those two years were pretty much wasted as far as Sandy developing his craft.... Instead of being spotted in the major leagues—he won 2 games in 1955 and 2 in 1956—he could have been developing better in the minors. He showed signs of brilliance but there was no way you could predict greatness for him, because of one factor—his control, or lack of it."[33]

In 1957, the Dodgers' last year in Brooklyn, Sandy Koufax was largely a .500 pitcher in the background without a defined role, and the team floundered toward a third-place finish as they prepared to leave town for the West Coast. His role began to change in 1958 when the Dodgers moved to Los Angeles. He was given 26 starts in a year when Don Newcombe was dealt to Cincinnati, Carl Erskine was in rapid decline, and Roger Craig was optioned out to Triple-A St. Paul.[34] With an 11–11 record he was third on the club in wins, but continued to struggle with his control, as evidenced by his 105 walks and league-leading 17 wild pitches. Though he was an unexceptional 8–6 in 1959, he displayed intermittent flashes of brilliance. He turned in a 16-strikeout performance against the Phillies in June—a new record for a night game.[35] On the last day of August, in a crucial game against the Giants before 82,794 at the Coliseum, he struck out 18 to break his own night game record and tie Bob Feller's major league record for most strikeouts in a single game. While he effectively disappeared during the Dodgers' September pennant drive, he reappeared on October 6 for Game 5 of the World Series against the Chicago White Sox. Again on a big stage—in front of a record crowd of 92,706 at the Los Angeles Memorial Coliseum—he pitched brilliantly for seven innings, giving up only one run in the fourth inning on a double play ground ball. Desperate to get on the scoreboard, the Dodgers had to remove him for a pinch hitter before he could complete the game. A win—likely a shutout performance—would have clinched the Series and thrust him into national prominence. But the one run he gave up turned out to be the only run of the game. He lost 1–0, and the Series moved on to a Game 6 in Chicago.

The Koufax No-hitter That Wasn't

When Sandy Koufax took the mound on the night of May 23 at Forbes Field in Pittsburgh, it looked like he was on his way to another undistinguished season. He had a 0–4 record with a whopping 5.16 earned run average. He had lost six straight games since his 18-strikeout performance at the Coliseum nearly nine months before.[36] On April 22 in St. Louis, he was chased in the first inning before he could get a single batter out, giving up three singles, a walk, a wild pitch, and a 3-run double to Stan Musial. Charged with 5 earned runs for zero innings completed, his ERA ballooned to a grotesque 15.00. On May 6 at the Coliseum in Los Angeles, he struck out 15 Phillies over nine innings, then lost his command and the ball game in the tenth when he allowed his seventh walk and a crushing home run to an aging Alvin Dark in his last year as a player. On May 19 at Crosley Field in Cincinnati, he took a 4–3 lead to the bottom of the ninth inning, only to lose on a walk-off triple by the ubiquitous Vada Pinson. It had already been a tough year.

Koufax's opponent would be a black pitcher named Bennie Daniels. Daniels, from Compton High School 10 miles south of the Los Angeles Memorial Coliseum, made his major league debut as the starting pitcher for the Pirates in the final game played at Ebbets Field on September 22, 1957.

Koufax got off to a typically erratic start in the first inning, walking two batters but striking out the side to escape unscathed. His shakiness continued into the second. After he retired the first two batters, he walked Bill Mazeroski to bring up the pitcher's spot. Bennie Daniels was a right-handed pitcher who batted left-handed. Daniels was unable to get around on Koufax's fast ball, but he managed to punch a 1–2 pitch into the opposite field for a single. After Koufax walked Bob Skinner—his fourth walk in the first two innings—he suddenly had the bases loaded with Dick Groat, the eventual 1960 batting champion, coming to the plate. But Koufax got Groat to ground out to shortstop Maury Wills to end the inning.[37]

The game was a scoreless tie going into the top of the seventh inning. Norm "Dumbo" Larker led off for the Dodgers. He came into the game hitting .360, but was hitless in his first two trips to the plate against Bennie Daniels. This time he hit Daniels' 0–1 pitch into the left-field gap for a double. With Larker standing on second base, Daniels retired right fielder Frank Howard and catcher Johnny Roseboro to come to within one out of escaping. But rookie Tommy Davis, hitting .138, ruined his shutout by lining a double into left field to score Larker. With first base open, Pirates manager Danny Murtaugh ordered Daniels to

An awkward off-field single by Pirates' pitcher Bennie Daniels at once spoiled Sandy Koufax's first no-hitter and the only no-hitter in the history of Forbes Field (National Baseball Hall of Fame Library, Cooperstown, New York).

walk Maury Wills intentionally to get to Koufax. Though Sandy Koufax was a notoriously bad hitter with a career .071 batting average, Walter Alston left him in the game only to see him watch a third strike go by with the bat on his shoulder.

The run scored by the Dodgers in the seventh inning would turn out be the only run of the game. The innocuous single by Bennie Daniels was Pittsburgh's last—and only—hit of the game off Sandy Koufax. He walked Don Hoak in the third, then Hal Smith in the sixth, and that was it as far as Pirate base runners were concerned. He mowed down the last ten batters in a row. There had never been a no-hitter thrown at Forbes Field since it opened in 1909.[38] But for an off-field hit by Bennie Daniels—a pitcher with a .170 lifetime average—Sandy Koufax would have become the first and last pitcher to accomplish the feat. Forbes Field would close on June 28, 1970, never having staged a no-hit game.

Buoyed by Sandy Koufax's performance at Forbes Field, the Dodgers won five more games in the last week of May. But at the end of play on May 31 the Dodgers were still in fifth place, one game under .500.

	W	L	Pct.	*
Pittsburgh	27	14	.659	
San Francisco	26	16	.619	1½
Cincinnati	22	20	.524	5½
Milwaukee	16	16	.500	6½
Los Angeles	20	21	.488	7

*Games behind leader

The good news was that big right-hander Stan Williams improved his record to 3–0 that day with an impressive win over the Cardinals at the Coliseum. The bad news was that the Dodgers still had not hit bottom.

Three

Out of the Woodshed
and into Contention

I don't want to take their money, and I've never done it as
long as I've managed the Dodgers, but this careless, sloppy
play must stop.[1]—Walter Alston

The Dodgers continued to struggle in June. In the first two weeks they lost eight
out of twelve games at home, with Sandy Koufax losing three consecutive starts. To
start the third week, Koufax won his first game since his 1-hitter in Pittsburgh, but the
Dodgers closed out their 19-game home stand on June 19 by losing two out of three to
the league-leading Pirates. The next night in Milwaukee, Henry Aaron spoiled Don
Drysdale's evening with two home runs for a 4–1 thumping. The one bright spot was a
brief one-inning relief appearance by Roger Craig after seven weeks on the disabled list.

The View from the Woodshed

On June 21, after arriving at 2:30 in morning from Milwaukee, the Dodgers hit a
new low in Cincinnati, falling 11½ games behind in sixth place after a 6–4 loss to the
Reds at Crosley Field.

	W	L	Pct.	*
Pittsburgh	38	21	.644	
Milwaukee	33	23	.589	3½
San Francisco	34	28	.548	5½
Cincinnati	30	31	.492	9
St. Louis	29	31	.483	9½
Los Angeles	27	33	.450	11½

*Games behind leader

Walter Alston's "Money Pitcher," Johnny Podres, was gone before he could complete the fifth inning. It wasn't the seven hits and two walks he allowed in 4⅓ innings that irked Alston. It was the poor judgment of grooving a 0–2 pitch to Wally Post that he hit over the center field fence in the fifth to put the Dodgers behind 5–0.

The Dodgers made a game out of it in the sixth inning when Norm Larker and John Roseboro hit a pair of 2-run homers off Reds starter Bob Purkey to pull within one run at 5–4. Larker's 4-for-4 performance catapulted him into the National League batting lead with a .344 average.[2]

Alston's frustrations intensified in the eighth inning when Maury Wills made an error to allow the Reds to score an unearned run, putting the Dodgers behind 6–4 and down to their last three outs. Alston went into overload when Frank Howard took a called third strike as the Dodgers went down meekly in the ninth inning.

Smokey

Walter "Smokey" Alston, from tiny Darrtown, Pennsylvania (population 179), played shortstop and third base for Miami University of Ohio, where he graduated with a B.S. in education in 1935. He was also a standout guard on the Miami basketball team.[3]

Dodger manager Walter Alston held a torrid woodshed session in the clubhouse at Crosley Field on June 21, 1960, after a dismal loss dropped the team into sixth place (George Brace photograph).

After graduation, he broke into professional baseball as a third baseman for Greenwood of the East Dixie League, where he showed promise with a .326 batting average. But by 1940 he was stuck in the low minors as a player-manager. To supplement his modest minor league salary, he taught high school biology and coached basketball. He worked his way up the Dodger farm system to become manager of the St. Paul Saints of the Triple-A American Association, where he won his first pennant in 1949. After winning another pennant at St. Paul, he took over the Dodgers' Triple-A farm team at Montreal in the International League, where he won another two pennants and the Little World Series in 1952 and 1953.[4] By then Alston had attracted the attention of the Dodger front office.

After winning 105 games for the 1953 Brooklyn Dodgers—the sixth most wins in National League history—and his second consecutive pennant, then Dodger manager Chuck Dressen dared to ask team President

Walter O'Malley for a two-year contract. But O'Malley offered him his customary one-year deal. When Dressen sent him an angry letter, O'Malley promptly announced that he had "accepted Dressen's resignation."

At a press conference on November 24, 1953, Walter O'Malley introduced Walter Alston as the new Dodger manager for the upcoming 1954 season. It was immediately obvious that the quiet, self-effacing Alston was a sea change from the previous flamboyant Dodger managers: the glib and sophisticated Leo Durocher and the peppery, wisecracking Chuck Dressen.

In 1954, Alston's first season as the Dodgers' manager, the team finished second to Durocher's World Champion Giants. But O'Malley didn't blame Alston. Roy Campanella had surgery on his hand, Johnny Podres had his appendix removed, and Don Newcombe struggled after returning from military service. O'Malley rehired him for 1955, and was rewarded with the first Dodgers' World Championship. Alston was voted National League Manager of the Year.

Then hard times returned to the Dodgers with Alston at the helm. He blew a 2-game lead to the Yankees in the 1956 World Series. In 1957, the Dodgers' last season in Brooklyn, he led the team to their worst finish in thirteen years. They finished seventh out of eight N.L. teams in 1958, the first year in Los Angeles. Critics called for his head, but O'Malley stuck with Alston for another year. Alston came through by leading a team of has-beens and underdogs to a world championship in 1959.

Lighting a Fire Inside the Woodshed

On June 21, before the players could return to their hotel, the usually mild-mannered Alston closed the clubhouse doors and read them the riot act at a rare late-night postgame meeting.[5] In a Jekyll and Hyde transformation, it was an irate Alston who tore into the players for their careless, sloppy play, threatening them with fines and extra workouts. No one was spared as he cited boneheaded base running, poor throwing by outfielders, and "too many fat two-strike pitches."[6] In the game the Dodgers had lost minutes before, Johnny Podres committed a mental lapse in the third inning when he dropped the ball while on the mound for a balk that allowed a gift run to score. Maury Wills was picked off first base. Don Demeter missed the cutoff man with a throw that sailed over catcher Joe Pignatano's head. Duke Snider missed the cutoff man while throwing to the wrong base.

A particularly sore spot for Alston was the carelessness displayed by the Dodger pitchers with 2-strike counts: "Look at the games we've lost on 2-strike hits this month alone. I don't expect our pitchers to bounce the ball up there when the count is 0 and 2. But they've just got to quit giving 'em good ones in these situations," he later told reporters camped outside the woodshed.[7] He got personal by singling out Duke Snider, Gil Hodges, and Charley Neal for their lack of offense, "They were our big gunners last season, and now they aren't hitting a lick."[8]

Alston's tirade jolted the Dodgers out of their malaise. They won six of the last eight games in June, and then made July their best month of the season.

The New Frontier Comes to L.A.

July 11–14 was the All-Star break. But it was an inopportune time for the Dodgers to take a break. They had just won six out of their last seven games. The year before, major league baseball began a 4-year experiment in playing two All-Star games. After playing both games in National League venues in 1959, this year's games would be played in American League parks: Municipal Stadium in Kansas City and Yankee Stadium in New York. Managers Walter Alston and Al Lopez, who squared off in the 1959 World Series, each led his league's All-Star team. Alston was gracious enough to showcase arch-rival Willie Mays by placing him in the leadoff position in the batting order. Mays led the N.L. to a 2-game sweep with a spectacular 6-for-8 performance including a double, triple, home run, 3 singles, and a stolen base.

Los Angeles

On Monday, July 11, with the Dodgers on All-Star break, the Democratic Party took over Los Angeles with their convention at the Sports Arena. Wednesday, July 13, they nominated a 43-year-old senator from Massachusetts named John F. Kennedy as their candidate for the presidency.[9] Twenty-four hours later, Kennedy named Texas Senator Lyndon Johnson as his running mate.[10] On Friday, July 15, while the Dodgers were in San Francisco, John F. Kennedy took over their home ballpark. He filled the Los Angeles Memorial Coliseum with eighty thousand people to deliver his formal acceptance of the nomination with his vision of a *new frontier*:

> For I stand tonight facing west on what was once the last frontier. From the lands that stretch 3000 miles behind me, the pioneers of old gave up their safety, their comfort and sometimes their lives to build a new world here in the West.... Their motto was not "Every man for himself," but "All for the common cause."
>
> Today some would say that those struggles were over, that all the horizons have been explored, and that all the battles have been won, that there is no longer an American frontier. But the problems are not all solved and the battles are not all won, and we stand on the edge of a *new frontier*—the frontier of the 1960s, a frontier of unknown opportunities and paths, a frontier of unfulfilled hopes and threats.
>
> The new frontier of which I speak is not a set of promises—it is a set of challenges. It sums up not what I intend to *offer* the American people, but what I intend to *ask* of them.... It holds out the promise of more sacrifice instead of more security.... Beyond that frontier are uncharted areas of science and space, unsolved problems of peace and war, unconquered pockets of ignorance and prejudice, unanswered questions of poverty and surplus.... I am asking each of you to be new pioneers on that new frontier.[11]

Thus Americans were called to join a cause that was to begin in six months' time.

San Francisco

After the All-Star break, the Dodgers began a weekend series with the Giants at Candlestick Park with a night game on July 15. Play had to be halted twice when heavy fog rolled in from the ocean, making it impossible to see the baseball. Both teams were the beneficiaries of some strange rulings. Charlie Neal was credited with a "double" when his pop fly dropped out of the fog in front of a surprised Don Blasingame near second base. The fog did not play favorites. Willie McCovey received a gift "triple" when his pop fly fell harmlessly to the ground among Moon, Snider, Neal, and Wills as they stared into the mist like the four blind mice. During the moments that baseball could be played, Ed Roebuck saved a 5–3 victory for Don Drysdale.[12] At this time last year, Roebuck was working his way back—against the odds—in the minor leagues. Today, he was the Dodgers' number one relief pitcher with 5 saves, an 8–1 record, and a 1.90 earned run average.

Making a Run in 3-D

On July 31, with Don Drysdale on the mound, the Dodgers had a chance to complete their best month of the season at the Coliseum against the Milwaukee Braves. For their rookie center fielder Tommy Davis, July of 1960 would be the month that he finally arrived.

Tommy D

Herman Thomas Davis was born in Brooklyn on March 21, 1939. Growing up on the Jefferson Avenue border between the Bushwick and Bedford-Stuyvesant sections of the borough, he idolized the Brooklyn Dodgers. Later as an established star with the Los Angeles Dodgers, he would recall his boyhood days at Ebbets Field: "When I wasn't playing ball, I used to go to Ebbets Field with my pals and figure out some way to get in. We used to sneak in with some of those big groups of kids that went to the games. I used to study the hitters—especially Gil Hodges and Pee Wee Reese. I didn't watch Jackie much for some reason. I was studying them, not trying to copy them. Nobody can copy another hitter's style. You've got to be yourself at the plate."[13]

Tommy Davis was all-around athlete at Boys High School in Brooklyn. He was

Rookie outfielder Tommy Davis came into his own in the summer of 1960 (George Brace photograph).

a New York City All-Star catcher on the baseball team. And at 6'2", he was an All-Public School basketball player. When he graduated from Boys High in 1956, he was offered a basketball scholarship to Providence University. But he had his sights set on baseball as both the Yankees and Dodgers descended on the Davis house.

Despite his love for the Dodgers, he was all set to sign a $4,000 bonus contract with the Yankees and report to their Birmingham Southern League affiliate. That was before super scout Al Campanis went to work on Tommy's mother. The future director of scouting for the Dodgers knew how to make a sales pitch—and at whom to pitch it. Davis would recall the biggest decision of his young life: "He was smart, that Campanis. He kinda saw that mother made the decisions around the house, so he began concentrating on her. He talked pretty good, and then she went to work on me. She said that after all, as long as the money [$4,000] was the same, I might as well sign with the Dodgers, since I was a Brooklyn boy."[14]

After he got a personal call from Jackie Robinson on the road in Cincinnati, his mind was made up. Tommy Davis signed with the Brooklyn Dodgers and set out for Hornell, New York, to join the Dodgers' Class D Pony League club, where he hit .325 in 43 late-season games. The next year, 1957, he led the Class D Midwest League with a .357 average for a Kokomo team managed by Pete Reiser. He jumped three levels in 1958, hitting a combined .304 as he split his time between Victoria in the Class AA Texas League and Montreal in the Class AAA International League. The 1959 season was the breakout year for Tommy Davis, and his last year in the minors. He batted .345 for the Triple-A Spokane Indians to win the Pacific Coast League batting title. Spokane manager Bobby Bragan changed his batting style from that of a straightaway hitter to a pull hitter: "He told me I'd have a better chance to make the majors if I'd pull the ball, so I changed my style right there."[15] He was called up by the Dodgers at the end of the season, and made his major league debut on September 22, 1959, in St. Louis when he struck out as a pinch hitter—his only major league at bat of the season.

At age 21, Tommy Davis was one of the hottest prospects in major league baseball when he made the big club coming out of Vero Beach in April 1960.[16] The Dodgers loved his bat, but they didn't know where to play him. For the first two months of the season he was shuffled in and out of all three outfield positions, and was even tried at third base. The uncertainty took its toll, as he ended May with a .155 batting average and was relegated to a mainly pinch-hitting role in June. The breakthrough came in July after the Dodgers settled on a place for him in center field.

He hit his first major league home run on July 10 against the Cardinals at the Coliseum. On July 20, he hit a walk-off 2-run home run off Elroy Face in the eleventh inning to give the Dodgers a 7–5 come-from-behind over the Pirates.[17] With the Dodgers surging on July 30, he hit two homers and drove in five runs against the Braves. His grand slam tied the game at 7–7 in the seventh. The Dodgers had only one problem as they prepared to extend their winning streak to four straight: Lew Burdette. Burdette came into the game from the bullpen in the ninth inning and shut out the Dodgers on one hit for the last three innings of the game. Lew was different. He was a pitcher who enjoyed hitting so much that he ran up to the plate with a bat in his hand. In the top of the eleventh inning, he jogged up to the plate and hit a home run off Larry Sherry to put the Braves ahead for good, 8–7. Then he spoiled the evening for Tommy Davis by retiring him for the last out of the game in the bottom of the eleventh with the tying run on base. But when number 12, Tommy Davis, took the field on the last day of July, he knew he had arrived.

Double D Turnaround

Don Drysdale was having a roller coaster of a season. He finished June with a 4–10 record after losing six games in a row and going nine straight starts without a complete game. He turned it completely around in the month of July by winning his next five straight decisions with two consecutive shutouts heading into his start on July 31.

Drysdale didn't have his best stuff this Sunday afternoon, but he had enough to contain the Braves' big bats. He took a 7–4 lead into the ninth before running out of gas. After Wes Covington doubled in a run to make the score 7–5, Alston brought in Ed Roebuck from the bullpen to get the final two outs. Drysdale got his sixth consecutive victory in July to even his record at 10–10 for the year. Tommy Davis contributed two more hits and drove in a run with a sacrifice fly. Now batting .252, he had raised his average nearly 100 points in two months.

The Dodgers finished the day with a 19–7 record for the month of July, in third place, only four games behind the league-leading Pirates.

	W	L	Pct.	*
Pittsburgh	57	39	.594	
Milwaukee	54	40	.574	2
Los Angeles	52	42	.553	4

*Games behind leader

July was also a good month for Roger Craig. After a two-month layoff needed to heal a broken collarbone, he returned to the starting rotation on the Fourth of July and won three straight decisions. The Dodgers had played the first three months below .500, but they were now in the pennant race.

Maury Wills, Leadoff Man

Maury Wills had been buried down in his usual eighth spot in the batting order since opening day. But beginning on June 12, he caught fire, putting together a 22-game, 34 for 75, .453 batting surge that raised his average from .222 to .313.[18] This prompted Walter Alston to try an experiment on the Fourth of July. For the second game of a twilight-night double-header in St. Louis he moved Maury Wills from the number eight hole into the leadoff spot. Jim Gilliam, their leadoff man since he joined the team as a rookie in 1953, was moved from the leadoff position to the second spot behind Wills. The experiment, which originally lasted three games, was repeated on August 2—and made permanent. The Wills-Gilliam 1–2 punch at the top of the lineup would transform the Dodger attack.

A 9-Year Struggle in the Minors

The year before, the Dodgers rolled the dice on a black 26-year-old rookie shortstop with 5 kids named Maury Wills. By the beginning of June 1959, it was evident to the Dodgers that their principal shortstop and heir apparent to Pee Wee Reese, Don Zimmer, was not working out. Not only was he batting only .202, but his range had mysteriously declined. Zimmer had been playing with a broken toe that he was able to conceal until someone noticed that the leather of his shoe had been cut away to provide freedom for his toe.[19] The Dodgers' backup, Bob Lillis, was batting .229 in 48 at bats and had committed four errors in his last two starts.[20] Buzzie Bavasi acted by calling up Wills from Spokane on June 5, 1959. His debut the following day in Milwaukee was inauspicious: 0-for-4 at the plate and 2 errors in the field. But it was also marked the end of a 9-year struggle to make it to the major leagues.[21] Years later, Buzzie Bavasi would recall, "Had Zimmer not broken his toe in 1959, the world might never have heard of Maury Wills."[22]

Maurice Morning Wills was a Baptist minister's son from Washington, D.C. He was a standout in baseball, football, and basketball at Cardozo High School. After graduation in 1950, the 5'10" 155-pound All-State T-formation quarterback turned down nine football scholarships, including offers from Ohio State, Syracuse and Rutgers, to pursue a professional baseball career—as a pitcher. He first went to a New York Giants tryout camp, where he was rejected for being too small despite striking out every batter he faced.[23] The Dodgers moved in to sign Wills to a contract with their Hornell club of the Class-D Pony League where he began in 1951 as a "mop-up" pitcher. But it was soon apparent that his future was not on the mound. Instead, he would struggle for the next eight years in the Dodger farm system as a "good field, no hit" shortstop.

After hitting a modest .253 at Triple-A Spokane in 1958, Wills was "conditionally purchased" by the Detroit Tigers. But when he reported to spring training in 1959, the Tigers had already acquired an established big-league shortstop from the Washington Senators named Rocky Bridges. The Tigers "returned" Wills to Spokane to avoid paying his purchase price of $35,000.[24]

It was a blow to find himself stuck again in the Pacific Coast League. But it was there that he made a career-changing breakthrough with the help of his manager, Bobby Bragan. Wills was a natural right-handed batter. Bragan converted him to a "switch hitter" to take advantage

Maury Wills took over the leadoff spot in the Dodger batting order for good on August 2, 1960 (George Brace photograph).

of his speed coming out of the left side of the batter's box. When the Dodgers needed a shortstop at the beginning of June 1959, Maury Wills was hitting .313 with 25 stolen bases in his first 48 games at Spokane.

For the first month, he and Don Zimmer went to war over the shortstop position. Maury Wills finally took over on July 4, 1959, in Chicago when Zimmer's batting average had disintegrated to .175.[25] Despite a hitting a merely satisfactory .260 in 83 games, his clutch play in key situations was a principal reason for the Dodgers' second-half surge to the National League pennant. He hit .345 for the month of September, and almost singlehandedly swept the Giants in a crucial 3-game series with a 7-for-13 performance at Seals Stadium in San Francisco on September 19 and 20. The Giants were knocked out of first place for good, while the Dodgers went on to beat the Milwaukee Braves in a playoff to advance to the World Series.

Though he played such a pivotal role in turning around the Dodgers' fortunes in 1959, Maury Wills had to fight for his job again the following spring at Vero Beach. All four of his competitors were white: Don Zimmer and Bob Lillis, whom he had already bested the prior year, and two promising rookies, Bob Aspromonte and Charlie Smith. The scrappy Wills won again despite a lukewarm endorsement by Walter Alston: "Wills is the shortstop until someone takes the job away."[26]

New Stolen Base Champ, New Offense

From the leadoff spot, Maury Wills could maximize his unique contribution: the stolen base. With Wills, Walter Alston abandoned giving the stolen base sign from the dugout, instead letting him use his own judgment as to the jump he needed and the pitch to run on. As a result, he was running practically unchecked from the day he took over the leadoff chores on August 2. He would steal 18 bases in August, including eight in a 3-day surge on the road in Philadelphia and Milwaukee.[27] He would add another 14 in his last 30 games for a total of 50 to unseat Willie Mays—who had led the league for the last four years—as the top National League base stealer. It was the most stolen bases in the NL since 1923.[28]

Since the 1950s, the Dodgers had depended on the home run with sluggers like Roy Campanella, Duke Snider, and Gil Hodges. Campanella was confined to a wheelchair after a tragic auto accident in January of 1958. Snider and Hodges, now seeing limited duty, would hit just 14 and 8 home runs, respectively, in 1960. After arriving late, with high expectations, enormous rookie Frank Howard would contribute only 23.

With fleet runners like Maury Wills, Jim Gilliam, and Tommy Davis occupying the first three spots in the batting order, August 2 marked the beginning of a new philosophy of offense—with the emphasis on speed. This transformation would be complete in September with the addition of Willie Davis, the fastest of them all.

❋ ❋ ❋

By the start of August, the battle lines were clearly drawn for the November presidential election. Richard Nixon had just defeated his only Republican opponent, Barry

Goldwater, at the GOP convention in Chicago, where he named U.S. Ambassador to the U.N. Henry Cabot Lodge, Jr., as his running mate. It would be Nixon/Lodge versus Kennedy/Johnson on November 8.

❀ ❀ ❀

Four

Facing Reality in
the Year of the Pirates

The Pirates are a team of Destiny.[1]—Dodgers third base
Coach Bobby Bragan June 18, 1960

I used four packs (of chewing tobacco) and don't remember
spitting.[2]—Pirates Manager Danny Murtaugh to reporters
after Game 7 of the 1960 World Series October 13, 1960

After their 19–7 surge in July, the Dodgers reverted to .500 baseball in August.
When they arrived in San Francisco on September 2 for a weekend series with the
Giants at Candlestick Park, they were 9½ games out, in fourth place. The Giants—led
by their left fielder, and future manager, Felipe Alou—ended any Dodger hopes of repeating as National League champs with a crushing 3-game sweep.

In the series opener, the Giants jumped on Johnny Podres early. By the third inning,
he was behind 4–0 thanks to a 2-run home run by Orlando Cepeda and two run-scoring
doubles by Alou. The Dodgers could never recover as they went down to defeat, 4–3.
In the second game, hard-luck Sandy Koufax completely shut down the Giants—but
for one mistake: a 2–2 pitch to Alou that he drove over the left field fence to lead off
the fourth inning. Alou's solo home run turned out to be the only run of the game as
Mike McCormick shut out the Dodgers 1–0 on six singles. The Giants completed the
sweep with an 8–3 win in the series finale on September 4.

Again, it was over early for the Dodgers as Alou put the Giants ahead 4–0 in
the first inning with a 3-run homer off Dodger starter Danny McDevitt. With 2
doubles, 2 home runs, and 6 RBIs for the series, Felipe Alou effectively ended the
Dodgers' season. Eleven games behind the high-flying Pittsburgh Pirates at the end of
play on September 4, Walter Alston and Buzzie Bavasi began planning for the next season.

* * *

41

On that day in Rome, an 18-year-old string bean from Louisville named Cassius Marcellus Clay won the Olympic gold medal for boxing in the light-heavyweight category with a stunning upset over an experienced Polish Olympian named Ziggy Pietrzkowski. The exuberant young Clay later told the *New York Times*, "I didn't take that medal off for 48 hours. I even wore it to bed. I didn't sleep too good because I had to sleep on my back so the medal wouldn't cut me."[3]

The Arrival of the 3-Dog

Of the 15 players Alston and Bavasi called up from their minor league system at the beginning of September, it was a 20-year-old outfielder with world-class speed named Willie Davis who attracted the most attention. In only his second year of professional baseball, he led the Pacific Coast League in six offensive categories:

Batting Average	.346
Runs	126
Hits	216
Doubles	43
Triples	26
Total Bases	347

His eye-popping 26 triples—irrefutable evidence of his blinding speed—broke a PCL record that had been established in 1903, the year the league was founded.[4] He would be named league Most Valuable Player.

The Kid Who Couldn't Hit and Couldn't Throw

William Henry Davis was a basketball and track star at Roosevelt High School in Los Angeles. Baseball was his third-best sport. In the spring he played baseball on Tuesdays and Thursdays, and participated in the sprints and the broad jump for the track team on Fridays. Davis was a natural athlete who showed up for track meets without any preparation. "I didn't know anything about broad jumping. All I did was run and jump," he would recall.[5] One Friday he jumped 25 feet, 5 inches, a new city record at the time. Although he could fly on the bases and in the outfield, there were two reasons why 15 major league scouts passed on him: 1. he couldn't hit; and 2. and he couldn't throw. Kenny Myers, from the Los Angeles Dodgers, was the one scout who saw something intangible in Willie Davis.[6]

When Kenny Myers signed Willie Davis in high school, he was a poor right-handed hitter with a weak throwing arm. Myers spent long hours molding him into a professional baseball player. He converted him to a left-handed batter to take advantage of his speed coming out of the batter's box. Davis spent a year stretched on his back, as Myers showed him how to get more "carry" on an outfielder's throw.[7] When Davis entered the Dodgers' farm system the year after he graduated from high school, Myers's work began to yield rapid results. His first stop was Reno in the Class C California League. At age 19, he led the league with a .365 batting average, and was named league Most Valuable Player. In the spring of 1960, he jumped four levels to the Spokane

Indians in the Pacific Coast League under manager Preston Gomez. For his sensational performance in that last season in the minor leagues, Willie Davis would be named Minor League Player of the Year by *The Sporting News*.

Quick Out of the Starting Blocks

On September 8, in his first major league at-bat at Crosley Field in Cincinnati, Willie Davis lined a single to right field off Reds left-hander Jay Hook. When right fielder Gus Bell looked up after momentarily bobbling the ball, he saw Davis streaking into second base. In the second inning, Davis was on second base with Maury Wills ahead of him on third. When Norm Larker blooped a single into left field, the speedy Wills was nearly run over by Willie Davis bearing down on him from behind with his long, loping strides.[8]

After a sensational MVP season in the Pacific Coast League, 20-year-old Willie Davis made his major league debut on September 8, 1960 (National Baseball Hall of Fame Library, Cooperstown, New York).

He continued to impress Dodger management for the remainder of the season with 2 home runs, a triple, 28 hits, and a .318 batting average. General manager Buzzie Bavasi would say, "He can go 50 feet farther for a ball than any other man alive."[9] The Dodgers had found their new center fielder, a converted track star in jersey no. 3 that his teammates would call "3-Dog."

Elimination Day

The reign of the World Champion Los Angeles Dodgers ended quietly on September 19 at Busch Stadium in St. Louis as Bob Miller and Lindy McDaniel combined to shut them out 1–0. When Wally Moon struck out for the last out of the game, they were mathematically eliminated with ten games left in the season.

Big Dodger right-hander Stan Williams pitched well, but got no support from an offense that could manage only 5 hits. Williams gave up a home run to Joe Cunningham in the sixth inning that turned out to be the only run of the game. But for a freak injury to Stan Musial, Cunningham probably would never have played. Musial injured his left elbow throwing the ball after fielding a single by Tommy Davis in the second inning. Cardinal Manager Solly Hemus had to bring in Cunningham off the bench to replace him.[10] The indignation of losing the elimination game was just another blow in the second-half slide of Williams. He had gotten off to the best start of his career with an 11–2 record through July. But when he hurt his shoulder on August 10, he lost four games in a row and was unable to complete any of seven consecutive starts.[11] After this night, his record was 14–9, and he would lose his only remaining start a week later.

On the night they were eliminated, there was one bright spot for the Dodgers. With one hit in four trips to the plate, Norm Larker was still in the lead—barely—for the National League batting title. At .325 he was ²⁶⁄₁₀₀ of a point ahead of Dick Groat of the Pittsburgh Pirates, who was still on the disabled list after Lew Burdette broke his wrist with a pitch on September 6. But Dick Groat wasn't Larker's only challenge. With 457 plate appearances, he was still 20 short of the 477 he needed to qualify for the batting title.

.00188 Points Apart, Worlds Apart

The Dodgers' season ended on a Sunday afternoon, October 2, at the Los Angeles Memorial Coliseum with a meaningless 4–3 win over the Chicago Cubs. With a crowd of 15,266, they set a new National League single-season record of 2,253,019. These Dodger fans came out on this day, not to set an attendance record, but to pull for their underdog first baseman, Norm "Dumbo" Larker, to win the batting title.

Larker had been in contention since batting .361 for the month of May after taking over the first base position from Gil Hodges. He came out of nowhere to lead the league with a .348 average on May 31, 4 points higher than the great Willie Mays. Mays surged at the end of June to take a .361-to-.354 lead over Larker on June 30. Larker moved back ahead of Mays by 2 points on the last day of July, .345 to .343. By August 31, Larker had blown past Mays .339 to .326, but Pittsburgh's Dick Groat, with a blistering .373 month of August, was now in the picture at .323. As Mays faded in September, it turned into a 2-man race between Larker and Groat. On September 6, when Lew Burdette broke Groat's left wrist with a pitch, sending him to the disabled list, Larker was ahead by 5 points:

Larker	.330579
Groat	.325044

Larker was unable to take advantage of Groat's absence, and when Groat returned from the disabled list on September 27 after missing 16 games, he found himself in a virtual tie with Larker:

Groat	.325044
Larker	.324706

Between September 28 and October 1, Larker had 3 hits in 12 at bats to lower his average to slightly below .323, but he became officially eligible for the title by crossing the threshold of 477 plate appearances. Groat missed two games and could only pinch hit in another, adding 2 hits in 6 at bats to maintain his average at .325:

Groat	.325132
Larker	.322654

Going into the final day of the season, the race for the N.L. batting title would be reduced to a one-game contest between two players who were only 2 points apart in batting average, yet worlds apart in every other way.

DUMBO

Norman Howard John Larker was the son of a coal miner from Beaver Meadows, Pennsylvania. He spent nine years in the minor leagues before getting his chance in the majors.[12]

He began his journey in 1949 at the age of 18 as a free agent with the Class D Mountaineers of Hazelton, Pennsylvania, a team unaffiliated with any major league club. During that first season he was struck in the side by a thrown ball, injuring his left kidney. The kidney became infected and had to be removed. He would play the rest of his career with one kidney.[13]

The Brooklyn Dodgers acquired him that winter and sent him to their Class C Greenwood, Mississippi, farm team for the 1950 season. He continued to shine as a first base prospect as he moved up the Dodger farm system until he became stuck for three years at Triple-A St. Paul, where he hit over .312 from 1955 to 1957. Granted, at 5'10", he was small for a first baseman. He had one kidney and a stomach ulcer. But he could hit. There was really only one thing that was blocking him: Gil Hodges.

He temporarily broke through the "Gil Hodges Blockade" when the White Sox drafted him at the close of the 1956 season. But the following spring in Sarasota, Florida, he found himself in a five-way battle for the first base job that he ended up losing to Jungle Jim Rivera. When the team got to Chicago in April of 1957, Sox manager Al Lopez handed him a train ticket back to St. Paul. As Larker would recall years later, "I thought this was going to be my big opportunity to crash the majors. Then the White Sox returned me to the Dodgers and I wound up back in St. Paul. It was pretty discouraging, pal."[14]

Norm Larker finally got his chance in 1958, the Dodgers' first year in Los Angeles. He made the team when the Dodgers broke camp in April, then saw limited duty as a pinch hitter and backup outfielder for the first two months. On July 1, with Hodges mired in a terrible slump, Walter Alston inserted him into the starting lineup in St. Louis. He responded with two home runs and a double. When Hodges returned to first base they transferred Larker to the outfield to keep his bat in the game. It was a Dodger tradition that everyone be given a nickname. Reese was called "Prune" because of the wrinkles on his face; Snider was "Snubby" for his short, little nose; and Hodges was "Moony" because of his big, round face.[15] The Dodgers gave Larker the name "Dumbo" for his oversized ears.[16]

After nine years in the minor leagues, underdog first baseman Norm "Dumbo" Larker came within a whisker of the National League batting championship in 1960 (National Baseball Hall of Fame Library, Cooperstown, New York).

In the Dodgers' world championship year of 1959, Larker got another chance when Hodges injured his neck running out a triple in San Francisco on May 7.[17] He took over at first base for the remainder of the series at Seals Stadium, contributing 5 hits. After Hodges returned to first at the end of May, Larker alternated between left field and right field while continuing to swing a hot bat. He played a key role in the Dodgers' sweep of a best-of-three-game playoff series with the Milwaukee Braves, by driving in three runs with five hits in eight at-bats. But it was a hard-nosed play on the bases by Norm Larker in the second and deciding game that had the biggest impact on the outcome of the series. With the Braves ahead 4–2 in the seventh inning behind Lew Burdette, Larker attempted to break up a double play by throwing a shoulder block into Milwaukee shortstop Johnny Logan at second base. He was unsuccessful in breaking up the double play, but Logan had to be carried off the field on a stretcher. Logan's replacement, Felix Mantilla, made the fatal throwing error in extra innings that cost the Braves the pennant and sent the Dodgers to the World Series.[18]

At Vero Beach in 1960, when Hodges began grooming Frank Howard as his heir apparent at first base, Norm Larker's future was in doubt. But when it became obvious that Howard was more comfortable in the outfield, he saw an opening. When Hodges's batting average dipped below .200 in May, the job was his.

Dick Groat, All-American

Richard Morrow Groat was the son of a successful realtor from Wilkinsburgh, Pennsylvania. In contrast to Norm Larker's hardscrabble background, his was privileged

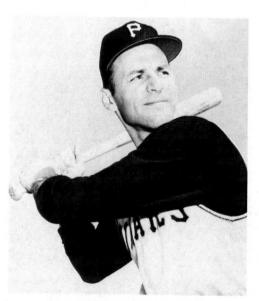

Pirate shortstop Dick Groat on his way to the World Series and the Most Valuable Player Award (National Baseball Hall of Fame Library, Cooperstown, New York).

and marked by early success. He was a natural basketball player who started shooting baskets at the age of five. At thirteen he could shoot hook shots with either hand, dribble the length of the court through an entire high school team, and sink set shots from 30 feet. At Swissvale High School (7 miles from Forbes Field) he had a 25-point scoring average, and made All-State his last two years.[19] He was also an outstanding shortstop in baseball, his second-best sport.

Groat went on to become a two-time All-American in both baseball and basketball at Duke University. His father encouraged him to seek a $100,000 baseball signing bonus during the Bonus Baby frenzy. On June 16, 1952, days after Groat graduated, Pirates General Manager Branch Rickey fended off seven other big league clubs to sign him for a reported $30,000 bonus. Groat turned down $65,000 from the Senators to accept Rickey's offer, on the condition that he play every day.[20] Three days later, as the Pirates' starting shortstop, he got his first major league hit off the Giants' Larry Jansen at the Polo Grounds.[21] As Rickey promised, Groat played every day and finished his rookie year of 1952 with a team-leading .284 batting average in 95 games.

At the end of the 1952 season, Branch Rickey gave him permission to play professional basketball. He had been drafted third overall by the Fort Wayne Pistons in the 1952 NBA draft. Groat played 33 games as a 5'11½" guard for the Pistons during the 1952–53 season. They had to fly him to the games in their company plane from the Duke campus, where he was finishing his bachelor of science degree. Though he never practiced with the team, he scored 12 points per game.[22]

Groat spent 1953 and 1954 in the U.S. Army, where he led the Fort Belvoir (Virginia) Engineers to the 1954 World Wide Army basketball title. The Pistons wanted him back after his discharge, but the Pirates would not allow it. Though some in the NBA maintained that he was certain to be second only to Bob Cousy as the league's second-best guard, his basketball playing days were over.[23]

When he returned from the Army in 1955, Dick Groat put together five solid years as the Pirate shortstop, highlighted by .315 and .300 batting marks in 1957 and 1958. Although he made the National League All-Star team in 1959, his .275 batting average and the Pirates' disappointing fourth-place finish made him expendable as Pittsburgh sought to add power to their lineup. Groat was a line-drive hitter whose top home run total was a mere seven in 1957.

At the baseball winter meetings in Miami in December 1959, Kansas City Athletics owner Arnold Johnson let it be known that his All-Star outfielder, Roger Maris, was available. Yankees General Manager George Weiss wanted Maris, a powerful left-handed pull hitter, perfect for the short right-field dimensions of Yankee Stadium. But Johnson wanted something that the Yankees couldn't provide: a top-flight shortstop. And after multiple trades throughout the 1950s with the Yankees, he was also wary of the A's being stigmatized as the "Yankees farm club." Pirates General Manager Joe Brown and Manager Danny Murtagh also wanted Maris. They were ready to deal when they met with Johnson in his suite at the Fontainebleau Hotel. Brown offered his package on paper:

TEAM	PLAYERS
Pirates	Dick Groat, shortstop; Ron Kline, pitcher; Bill Virdon, outfielder; Hank Foiles, catcher.
Athletics	Roger Maris, outfielder; Joe DeMaestri, shortstop; Hal Smith, catcher.[24]

The A's tentatively agreed, but asked Brown and Murtagh to step out momentarily to let Johnson and his aides have a few minutes of final deliberation. Out in the hallway, Murtagh started to have doubts. He told Brown, "Groat? He's the guy who has been holding us together." That was enough for Brown. He went straight down to the lobby, dialed Johnson's room, and told him, "Arnold, we can't possibly make that deal. We can't give up Groat."[25] The Groat-for-Maris deal, within minutes of being finalized, was never consummated. The Pirates kept Dick Groat. The Yankees swooped in to take Roger Maris as part of yet another multi-player New York-Kansas City deal.

Groat and Maris would meet in the World Series in three days. Both players would be named his league's Most Valuable Player for 1960.

Last Game, Last Chance

On October 2, when the day began, Larker's batting average that was .002477 points lower than Dick Groat's. The dreaded Dumbo stomach ulcer erupted with a vengeance during the last week of the season, but he refused to rest, needing to amass 477 plate appearances. He now had a chance to win the batting title on the final day of the season, and nothing was going keep him from playing. By the time the Dodgers took the field, Groat's game against the Braves in Forbes Field was over. Groat had gone 1 for 4 against his old friend Lew Burdette, thereby cutting his lead to .001953 points. Larker walked in the first inning, and grounded out in the third. In the fifth inning, he hit a high bouncing ball back to the mound that Cubs pitcher Moe Drabowsky prevented from going into center field, but hurriedly threw wide of first base, allowing Larker to reach base safely. It was a difficult play, but the Coliseum scorekeeper gave Drabowsky an error. When the scorekeeper later reversed his decision and ruled it a hit, there was a mixed reaction from the crowd: applause from fans hoping to keep Larker's chances alive, and boos from those sensing a "hometown call." He came to bat for the last time in the seventh inning to face Cubs right-hander Don Cardwell. With a hit he would win the batting title by four tenths of a point. But it was not to be for the coal miner's son they called Dumbo. Cardwell retired him on a routine fly ball caught by a young Billy Williams in left field. Norm Larker ended the season with a .323 average, .00188 points short of having his name recorded in the record book:

Groat	.324607
Larker	.322727

Instead, Dick Groat's name would go into the record book as the National League batting champion at .325.

The View from the Wilderness

The day after the season ended, Walter Alston and Buzzie Bavasi were on their way to Pittsburgh for the start of the World Series, not as participants like last year, but as seekers of home run hitting talent.[26] The Dodgers finished in fourth place with a record of 82 wins and 72 losses, 13 games behind the NL champion Pirates.

	W	**L**	**Pct.**	*
Pittsburgh	95	59	.617	
Milwaukee	88	66	.571	7
St. Louis	86	68	.558	9
Los Angeles	82	72	.532	13

*Games behind leader

As they looked back over the season from their vantage point in the National League wilderness, several themes became clear.

Imbalance

The Dodgers were blessed with arguably the best pitching staff in the league, but their hitting had declined from league best in their glory days in Brooklyn to mediocre. They knew they had to correct this imbalance to be contenders again.

Power Failure

At the end of the season, Alston identified lack of power as their biggest problem.[27] The Dodgers finished fifth out of eight National League teams in home runs with 126, a decline of 22 from the prior year, and their lowest annual number since 1948. Rookie Frank Howard led the team with 23, despite playing in only 117 games. No one else reached the 15 level. The decline from 1959 was mainly due to four players:

PLAYER	1959	1960
Hodges	25	8
Snider	23	14
Neal	19	8
Demeter	18	9

When Gil Hodges turned 36 in April, he had begun a precipitous decline. Hodges appeared in only 101 games in 1960—many as a pinch hitter. He hit only .198 for the year—his lowest batting average since 1947—in just 197 at bats. Duke Snider also appeared in only 101 games with a .243 batting average and 36 runs batted in after hitting .308 and driving in 88 the year before. Don Demeter was on pace for more than 20 home runs when he was lost to injury at mid-season. It was a disappointing season for second baseman Charlie Neal, who had 11 fewer home runs and dropped 31 points in batting average.

Dumbo Flying Solo

Norm Larker's near league-best .323 batting average has been discussed above. He was the Dodgers' only regular .300 hitter.

Strong Pitching

The Dodger pitchers led the league in strikeouts for the thirteenth straight season with a major league record 1,122 and in Earned Run Average for the second straight season at 3.40. Workhorse Don Drysdale continued to be their number one starter. He led the league with 246 strikeouts and had a 2.84 ERA. But with lack of offensive support, he barely won more games than he lost at 15–14. Stan Williams emerged as the number 2 starter with a 14–10 record. On the day the Dodgers were eliminated, despite a strong performance in defeat by Stan Williams, Walter Alston praised Williams by saying that he had "finally arrived." Alston's "money pitcher," Johnny Podres, turned in a solid 14–12 season. The Dodgers were counting on Roger Craig to be a bulwark of the rotation by building on his heroic performance of the second half of 1959. But he finished the season with a modest 8–3 record after spending most of May and June on the disabled list. Larry Sherry, the hero of the 1959 World Series, was given a chance to break into the rotation at the beginning of the season. But after three lackluster starts in April, it was obvious to Alston that Sherry was better suited for the bullpen. He finished with a 14–10 record, all but three of the decisions recorded as a relief pitcher. As good as he was, Sherry was upstaged by the surprising comeback performance of Ed Roebuck.

Triumph of the Comeback Kid

Relying on a devastating sinker ball for 90 percent of his pitches, Ed Roebuck became the Number 1 man in the Dodger bullpen. He had an 8–3 record, with a 2.78 earned run average and 8 saves in 58 appearances. There was only one reason he wasn't named Comeback Player of the Year: *The Sporting News* didn't initiate the award until 1965. Teaming with Larry Sherry, he gave the Dodgers an effective 1–2 punch in the bullpen to complement their outstanding starting rotation. But there was still one member of the Dodger pitching staff that remained an enigma: Sandy Koufax.

Koufax Adrift

In his sixth season, Sandy Koufax won just 8 games while losing 13. For him, 1960 was a year of inconsistency and frustration. He clashed with management over his lack of opportunities to start. When the Dodgers did use him, he lurched from dazzling performances such as a 1-hitter and two 15-strikeout games to games where he had to be removed early due to his inability to get the ball over the plate.

Injuries

The Dodgers had their share of injuries, both freak and nonfreak. Larry Sherry missed two weeks after he sprained his ankle by tripping over a bat. Don Drysdale injured his back when he slipped on a wet locker room floor while wearing his spikes, contributing to his 5-game losing streak in June. As we have seen, the Dodgers suffered a major blow on May 2 when Roger Craig broke his collarbone in a collision at home plate with Vada Pinson. Craig was unavailable for the next 55 games. Don Demeter was the Dodgers' principal center fielder until a collision with shortstop Maury Wills in the outfield on July 3 resulted in a season-ending wrist fracture. Before he hurt his shoulder in August, Stan Williams had a chance to win 20 games. Two years after his December 1957 surgery, Duke Snider was still plagued by a "trick knee."[28] By now he was keeping his career alive with the help of periodic cortisone injections.[29]

The Aging Boys of Summer

The Dodgers had to face reality: the Brooklyn Boys of Summer were getting old. Hodges was 36 and Snider was 34. Carl Furillo was released in May at 38, and Clem Labine was traded in June at 33. Pee Wee Reese, Roy Campanella, and Carl Erskine had already disappeared in the previous two years. Even "Junior" Gilliam was now 32.

New Faces—New Colors—New Sizes

As the Boys of Summer aged, the Dodgers continued to replace them with players who looked and played differently. By opening day, Maury Wills had won the shortstop wars with Don Zimmer. In Wills the Dodgers now had a permanent black shortstop who established himself as the league's premier base stealer. Tommy Davis and Willie Davis were young players of color who began distinguished careers in the Dodger outfield. Wills and the two Davis boys brought a striking new dimension to the offense: speed. The 6'7" Boy Giant, Frank Howard, rounded out the new outfield. His prodigious tape-measure home runs awed fans, opponents, and press alike. He would be named National League Rookie of the Year in November.

The Unanswered Question

Was 1959 a mere aberration? Both combatants in the 1959 World Series—the Dodgers and the White Sox—fell from pennant winners to also-rans. The Go-Go Sox dropped to third place as the Yankees rebounded from their "off year" to win their tenth American League pennant in the last twelve years. In the National League, the Dodgers made their run with a 19–7 month of July, and then played at an even .500 for the rest of the season. Clearly, this was not enough in the Year of the Pirates.

Game 7 of the 1960 World Series

Thursday, October 13, 1960. It was a beautiful fall afternoon in Pittsburgh. Walter Alston and Buzzie Bavasi had expected to be home by now. They arrived at Forbes Field eight days before prepared to make a quick deal for a power hitter over the four games this World Series was expected to last. After all, the Yankees were playing in their ninth World Series in the last eleven, and it was Pittsburgh's first trip to the fall classic since 1927, when Babe Ruth, who had hit an astronomical 60 home runs in the regular season, led the Yankees to a four-game sweep of the Pirates. What's more, the mighty 1960 Yankees had pulverized them 16–3, 10–0, and 12–0, and outscored them 42–11 through the first six games. But they had still not been able to put them away. By managing to eke out three close games, the scrappy Pirates surprised everyone by forcing a Game 7.

So here they were, Alston and Bavasi, back at Forbes Field, about to witness baseball's post–World War II era come to an end—with a bang. And this is what they saw.

Bottom of the Eighth—Fate Grabs the Yankees by the Throat

After falling behind 4–0 against the eventual Cy Young Award winner Vernon "The Deacon" Law, the Yankees surged to a 7–4 lead in the top of the eighth. Only six more outs and they could go home and wait for another World Series check. Little Bobby Shantz, a five-foot-six left-hander, was on the mound for the Yankees. He had been charged by New York's sixty-nine-year-old manager Casey Stengel to get the final six outs and bring the city of Pittsburgh back to reality. Their postwar Pirates had been a joke, finishing last (eighth) or next-to-last (seventh) in ten of the first twelve years beginning in 1946. By 1952 they were the laughingstock of baseball, losing 112 games and looking like children in bad space suits by wearing baseball's first mandatory batting helmets. Pittsburgh manager Danny Murtaugh finally began to turn things around when he took over for Bobby Bragan in mid-season 1957, leading the Pirates to two consecutive above-.500 seasons in 1958 and 1959, then winning their first National League pennant in thirty-three years in 1960.

Shantz had completely shut down the Pirates since coming in to begin the third inning, allowing only one hit and no runs over the last five innings. But now, with a 7–4 lead in the bottom of the eighth, he was beginning to tire. He immediately gave up a line single to right-center field off the bat of Gino Cimoli, the former Dodger journeyman outfielder from San Francisco pinch-hitting for Pittsburgh's ace reliever Elroy Face. Casey Stengel had two men warming up in the bullpen, as he had had from the beginning of the game. There was no tomorrow. Everyone must be ready to play, perhaps even Whitey Ford, who pitched nine innings to shut out the Pirates 24 hours before. The second batter, center fielder Bill Virdon, hit what looked like a perfect double-play ball: a sharp grounder toward Yankee shortstop Tony Kubek. It appeared that the Pirates would be down to their last four outs, down three runs, with no one on base. But fate intervened. The Forbes Field "alabaster plaster" infield had the reputation for being the hardest playing surface in baseball. The baseball took a lightning erratic hop, striking Kubek in the throat before he could get his hands up to protect himself, rendering him helpless in the dirt as both the batter and the base runner were safe: Cimoli at second, Virdon at first. Kubek had to be helped off the field and rushed to the hospital. Joe DeMaestri, who came over from Kansas City with Roger Maris eleven months before, replaced Kubek at shortstop. Instead of being down to their last four outs with the bases cleared, the Pirates had two runners on base, no outs, and the potential tying run coming to the plate in the person of Dick Groat, the National League batting champion. Groat promptly finished Shantz by lining his first pitch into left field to score Cimoli. The Yankee lead was down to two, at 7–5.

Stengel removed Shantz, and brought in right-hander Jim "Crazy" Coates. It would prove to be a controversial move. Pirate left-fielder Bob Skinner laid down a sacrifice bunt to move the tying runners, Virdon and Groat, into scoring position at third and second, respectively. The Pirates later revealed that they never would have attempted a bunt with Bobby Shantz—one of the game's best fielding pitchers—on the mound. Coates appeared to have things under control as he got Pittsburgh first baseman Glenn

"Rocky" Nelson on a harmless pop fly to right field, which Roger Maris calmly put away for the second out. All Coates had to do to get out of the inning was to deal with "Bobby," the Pirate fans' endearing name for their right fielder, Roberto Clemente. While Clemente finished the regular season with an impressive .314 batting average, in 1961 he would blossom into "The Great One" with the first of his four batting titles. Today, Clemente hit what should have been the last out of the inning, a high bouncing ground ball past the mound to first baseman Bill "Moose" Skowron, who merely had to toss the baseball to the pitcher covering first to end the inning and preserve the Yankees' 2-run lead. But where was the pitcher? Again, the Yankees paid a penalty for taking Bobby Shantz out of the game, as Coates exercised poor judgment by chasing after the slow roller himself instead of covering first base. Now Skowron had no one to throw the ball to because Crazy Coates was standing next to him with a confused look on his face. Clemente had an infield single, Virdon scored to bring the Pirates to within one run at 7–6, and Dick Groat moved up to third base as the potential tying run.

The Pittsburgh Pirates had one of baseball's best hitting catchers in Forest Harrill "Smokey" Burgess. But in a failed attempt to tie the game in the seventh, they removed the slothful Burgess for a pinch runner after he lined his second hit of the game in front of Mickey Mantle in center field. Thus the Pirates had to rely on their reserve catcher, Hal Smith, to tie the game. As we have seen, the Pirates obtained Smith—and very nearly Roger Maris—from the Kansas City Athletics in the inter-league trading sessions of December 1959. One of two fungible "Hal Smith" catchers in the National League–the other played for the Cardinals–the nondescript Smith had amassed only 32 home runs in five major league seasons before joining the Pirates. After four pitches from Coates, Smith had not taken the bat off his shoulder, passively allowing the count to move to 2–2. But on the fifth pitch he delivered a dagger: a two-out three-run home run over the left-field wall. The 36,683 people in Forbes Field, whose mood had swung from euphoria, to despair, and back to euphoria, were numb as they watched Jim Coates head for the clubhouse, Ralph Terry come in from the Yankee bullpen, and Don Hoak hit an inning-ending routine fly ball to Yogi Berra in left field. It would be the last time Berra would be able to get to a ball thrown by Ralph Terry in Forbes Field. But the damage was done. In a matter of minutes the Pirates had scored five runs to erase the Yankees' three-run lead, gone ahead 9–7, and begun their own countdown to a World Championship: only three more outs.

Top of the Ninth—The Mick Saves the Series

Danny Murtaugh brought in right-hander Bob Friend to get the final three outs in the top of the ninth inning. Friend was 18–12 during the regular season, but had already lost Games 2 and 6 of the Series. After giving up singles to the first two Yankee batters, second baseman Bobby Richardson and pinch hitter and former Pirate Dale Long, what little patience Danny Murtaugh had was gone with the tying runs on base, nobody out, and Roger Maris–already with two home runs in the Series–coming to the plate as the potential winning run. Murtaugh promptly pulled Friend and brought in his own little left-hander, Harvey "The Kitten" Haddix, to pitch to Maris. After winning twenty games with the Cardinals in 1953—his first full season in the major leagues—Haddix had bounced around with the Phillies, Redlegs, and now the Pirates, where he finished the regular season with an 11–10 record, teaming with former Cardinal teammate Wilmer "Vinegar Bend" Mizell (13–7) to form the southpaw half of the 1960 Pittsburgh starting staff.

Harvey Haddix would be best known for the tragedy that befell him on the night of May 26, 1959, in Milwaukee, when he pitched twelve perfect innings—the longest perfect game in baseball history—only to lose to the Braves in the thirteenth. Today he had a chance to rehabilitate his place in baseball history. Standing at the plate, Roger Maris was 0 for 4, but he had hit a home run off Haddix at Yankee Stadium in Game 5. Haddix induced Maris to foul out to catcher Hal Smith for the first out. Now he had to face the great Mickey Mantle, a switch hitter who would bat right-handed. So far, Mantle had destroyed Pirate pitching with three home runs, ten runs batted in, and a .375 batting average. Mantle could not be stopped as he lashed a single into right-center field. Clemente, with arguably the finest throwing arm in baseball, managed to cut the ball off, but had no play at the plate after bobbling the ball. Richardson scored from second base with Long taking third. The Pittsburgh lead had been reduced to one run, at 9–8.

Haddix now had to face the dangerous Lawrence Peter "Yogi" Berra, who has already driven in seven runs in the Series. Pitching carefully to the great clutch hitter, Haddix fell behind two balls and no strikes. Balls? Strikes? It mattered not a whit to Berra, a classic "bad-ball" hitter. Berra connected with Haddix's third pitch, sending a hot smash on the ground over the first base bag heading for the right field corner. Pirate first baseman Rocky Nelson made a great play to backhand the ball. All Nelson had to do was throw the ball to second base to force Mantle for the second out, and the return throw to first for the third out would beat Berra, by a mile since he had not even left the batter's box. The World Series would be over; the Pirates would win 9–8. So simple, but confusion reigned. Strangely, Nelson did not throw the ball to second, but stepped on first for the second out, thereby removing the force on Mantle. With the ball in his bare hand he attempted to tag Mickey Mantle who, in a split-second calculation, saw he had no chance to beat a throw to second, and was now desperately trying to get back to first. In an electrifying move of pure athleticism, lightning reflexes, and instinct, Mantle somehow avoided Nelson's frantic tag, stayed within the base line, and dived head first safely back into first base. Within two seconds after Berra put the ball in play, a Series-ending play had morphed into a freak play with a bizarre result: Nelson was holding the baseball face-down in the dirt, Mantle was sprawled in the same dirt with his hand safely on the bag, and McDougald, who had been brought in for Long, had scored to tie the game at 9–9. To those who saw it in real time–whether at Forbes Field or on national television–it was a thrilling, unforgettable moment: Mickey Mantle had just saved the World Series, not with one of his 500-foot home runs, but with a brilliant base-running maneuver. Hard-luck Harvey Haddix had blown the save, but managed to get Moose Skowron to ground out to shortstop. The Yankees and Pirates went to the bottom of the ninth tied, 9–9.

Bottom of the Ninth—Maz Ends It

Ralph Terry, the 24-year-old right-hander from Big Cabin, Oklahoma, tried to hold Pittsburgh in the bottom of the ninth and force the game into extra innings. Bill Mazeroski, number 9, with the familiar plug of chewing tobacco bulging from his left cheek, was the first batter. "Maz," also 24 years old, was from Wheeling, West Virginia. In his fifth year with the Pirates, he was recognized as one of the National League's premier second basemen. He already had seven hits in the Series, including a 2-run home run in Game 1 that turned out to be the game-winning blow. The Yankees knew that Mazeroski was a high fastball hitter. Ominously, Terry's first pitch was a fastball that sailed high and out of the strike zone. Mazeroski would later say that he nearly chased it, but managed to check his swing. Yankee catcher John Blanchard made a quick trip to the mound to remind Terry to keep the ball down to Mazeroski. But it was no use. Terry's second pitch was another high fastball, this time up in Mazeroski's eyes—shoulder high at the top of the strike zone. He did not miss it, sending a long arching drive to left field. Every baseball fan has seen the slow-motion film of Yogi Berra going back to the left field wall before looking up in resignation as the baseball disappears over the red

Pirate second baseman Bill Mazeroski wins the 1960 World Series with an iconic home run off Ralph Terry in the bottom of the ninth inning of Game 7 (National Baseball Hall of Fame Library, Cooperstown, New York).

bricks and ivy to the left of the 406 sign. To Berra's left, the Longines clock at the top of the scoreboard reads 3:35 p.m. Mazeroski, knowing he had hit the ball over Berra's head, but thinking it was going to carom off the wall, ran full speed until he nearly reached second base. It was at that point that he saw one of the umpires give the home run signal: a circling motion with his right arm. As Mazeroski rounded second base he was joined by an army of Pirate fans swarming onto the field. To the author, watching this scene in real time, it was a crushing blow. Just minutes before he had seen his hero, Mickey Mantle, save the World Series with a thrilling feat of athleticism. Now all was lost. This emotional rollercoaster of a game, now in free-fall, concluded as Mazeroski, leaping, holding his batting helmet, his crew cut exposed, waving his arms, escorted by his flock, touched third base, which he would later never remember doing. Now, all he had to do was to navigate through the multitude guarding home plate and step on it to make it official. But not to worry, he was guided in by a bald guy in a jacket from the box seats. The voice of the Pittsburgh Pirates, Bob Prince, described the chaos on the field: "They're ripping this field apart. They're going after home plate. They're going after everything." His broadcast partner, Jim Woods, observed, "I don't see how Maz reached home plate. This is the wildest scene since I was on Hollywood Boulevard the night World War II ended." After two hours and thirty-six minutes, it was over. Harvey Haddix was the winning pitcher. The Pittsburgh Pirates were World Champions of baseball for the first time since 1925.

※　※　※

In four hours Americans would see Soviet Premier Nikita Khrushchev, who had camped on New York's Park Avenue for the past 25 days, give his shocking farewell to America as he pounded his shoe in anger on a table at the United Nations. An hour later, John Kennedy in New York and Richard Nixon, by split screen in Los Angeles, collided in their third televised debate before beginning the last round of the 1960 presidential campaign.[30] In another 25 days, John F. Kennedy was elected the 35th president of the United States by a plurality of only 120,000 votes, the smallest margin since 1888.[31]

※　※　※

The Winter of His Discontent—Sandy Koufax at a Crossroads

On December 30, Sandy Koufax stood at a crossroads on his twenty-fifth birthday. The 1960 season was the low point in his career. He never recovered from a horrendous 1–8 start. Though he was still plagued by the inconsistency and wildness evident since 1955, he had shown occasional flourishes of brilliance. He struck out 15 Phillies on May 6, but lost the game after walking 7 and giving up 2 home runs. There was the near no-hitter of May 23, a one-hit shutout of the Pirates at Forbes Field. On May 28, after striking out 15 Cubs and walking 9 in 13 innings, he lost the game in the 14th. He put together two consecutive complete-game victories away from the Coliseum at the beginning of August: an 11-strikeout performance on August 7 in Philadelphia, followed by a shutout of the Reds with 13 strikeouts on August 11 in Cincinnati. But he relapsed into the familiar pattern of drifting in and out of command until he stabilized for another two consecutive complete-game victories on the road in September: a 10-strikeout win on September 8 in Cincinnati, and an 11-strikeout performance on September 13 in Philadelphia, his eighth—and last—win of the season.

The strikeouts had always come easy for Koufax, and 1960 was no exception. He struck out an amazing 197 batters in only 175 innings, but he walked 100. His record for the season was 8–13 with a 3.91 earned run average. But more importantly, after six seasons in the major leagues, he had a career losing record of 36–40.

The Wooden Box and the Garbage Pile

In the Coliseum clubhouse after the last game of the season on Sunday, October 2, Sandy Koufax had pondered what to do with his wooden box. The wooden box was where each player put his equipment at the end of the season. The boxes then became shelves in large steamer trunks to be transported to Vero Beach the next spring. Disgusted with his performance for the season and uncertain about his future, Koufax put nothing into his wooden box. He grabbed a new pair of baseball spikes and his best glove—just in case he wanted to play softball on Sunday afternoons in the park—and threw everything else into the garbage pile.[32] This strange behavior was observed by an incredulous custodian named Nobe Kawano, and provoked the following confrontation:

> KOUFAX: "There it is. Do whatever you want with it."
> KAWANO: "What are you shipping down?"
> KOUFAX: "Nothing, including myself."
> KAWANO: "If you want to quit, go ahead. But I wish you'd leave your arm."[33]

Koufax left with his softball gear, and Kawano contemplated what to do with the rest.

Choices

Sandy Koufax had no wife, and no family to support. He was in position to take a chance. He and a partner had already gone into business together representing the manufacturer of several electrical lines.[34] He had recently confided in Carl Erskine that he also had an opportunity to buy into a radio station, and that he was seriously contemplating leaving the game.[35] He looked back, wondering whether he should have finished college instead of leaving after one year to sign the bonus contract.

In his autobiography, Koufax described how he struggled after the 1960 season to come to grips with the idea that he had failed at 25: "To leave at the end of a successful career is one thing; the time that it's tough is when you haven't made it, when you've done nothing, when it's an admission—no matter how graciously you choose to explain it to yourself—that you've been licked."[36] But the thing that troubled him the most was the idea of walking away from baseball, not only before he had achieved success, but knowing that he had not worked as hard as he could have and given himself every possible chance to make it.[37] It was by engaging in this self-assessment process that Sandy Koufax talked himself out of quitting. He decided to give it one more year—"one last all-out effort."[38] As soon as the decision was made, he sold his interest in the rep business to his partner, and began preparing for the 1961 season.

Part II

1961:
The Great Awakening
of Sandy Koufax

Five

Leo

The first time there is any second-guessing, that's it.[1]—
Buzzie Bavasi

At the beginning of 1961, the Dodgers didn't yet know how lucky they were to have Sandy Koufax—or how close they were to losing him. Instead of an enormous Koufax retirement crisis, they had a mere coaching crisis: two vacancies needed to be filled. Third base coach Bobby Bragan left to become director of player personnel and farm director for the new Houston club, which would make its debut in the National League in 1962 as the Colt .45s. First base coach Greg Mulleavy was suddenly "reassigned" to a scouting position due to his health. Clay Bryant, manager of the Triple-A Montreal Royals, was promoted to take Bragan's spot. The Dodgers then made a controversial choice from outside their system to replace Mulleavy.

The Return of Leo the Lip

After nine years and 99 days of trying to erase the memory of October 3, 1951, from their minds, the Dodgers did the unthinkable: they put Leo Durocher back in a Dodger uniform. It was on that date in 1951 that Durocher, as manager of the New York Giants, presided over the dismantling of the Brooklyn Dodgers at the Polo Grounds in New York. Just two months before, on August 11, Dodgers' right-hander Ralph Branca had beaten Warren Spahn and the Boston Braves to give Brooklyn a seemingly insurmountable 13½ game lead over the Giants. By the end of play on September 30—the last day of the season—the lead had vanished, sending the Dodgers and Giants into a best-of–3-game playoff series. In the bottom of the ninth inning of the deciding third game of October 3, it was Branca—in relief of Don Newcombe—who was called on to face Bobby Thomson with two runners on base and the Dodgers clinging to a 4–2 lead. Branca had been an important part of the Dodgers' starting rotation since 1947, when he won 21 games. But it would be one pitch—one mistake—that he would be remembered

61

for: an errant fast ball up in the strike zone that the "Flying Scot" hit into the lower deck of left field stands. The "Shot Heard Around the World" sent the Giants to the World Series, the Dodgers home, and Giants' announcer Russ Hodges into his immortal "The Giants Win The Pennant!! The Giants Win The Pennant!!" hysterics. The pitch effectively ended Branca's career. He would never start another game for the Brooklyn Dodgers. Leo Durocher would continue to manage the Giants for four more years, including their 1954 world championship season.

A Lip's Journey

Leo Ernest Durocher was born July 27, 1905, in West Springfield, Massachusetts, the youngest of Clara and George Durocher's four sons. The Durochers struggled to make it in a poor French Catholic neighborhood where their name was pronounced *Doo-roe*-shay. Their living standard further eroded when George, an engineer for the Boston and Albany Railroad, suffered a heart attack that limited his role and earning capacity with the railroad. Clara was forced to take a job as a maid in a Springfield hotel.[2] Young Leo worked a number of odd jobs to help the family, including delivering papers, shoveling snow, mowing lawns, picking tobacco, and hustling pool.[3]

In high school Leo participated in football, basketball, and track. But it was in

On January 9, 1961, the Dodgers announced the hiring of Leo Durocher as their new third base coach (George Brace photograph).

baseball that he was extraordinary, having been tutored as a shortstop by fellow Springfield resident, and future Hall of Fame shortstop, Walter "Rabbit" Maranville. Leo was headed for Holy Cross, the eastern baseball powerhouse of the day that had offered him a scholarship, when it all fell apart after the hotheaded Durocher struck a teacher. He was suspended for thirty days, and never went back to finish high school. After dropping out at age 16, he went to work for the Boston and Albany Railroad, where he began playing for their baseball team. He soon jumped to the Wyco Electric Company, and its baseball team, for more money.[4]

At 17, he added a year to his age and asked for a tryout with the local Springfield professional baseball club. He was summarily rejected for being too small. A year later, he was two inches taller and ten pounds heavier, and a family friend named Jack O'Hara arranged for him to attend a two-week tryout camp held by the Class A Hartford Senators in the Eastern League. His confidence was so fragile that he asked Wyco Electric for a two-week leave of absence. At the end of the tryout camp, he was sent home by Paddy O'Connor, the gruff Irish manager of the Senators, and returned to his job at Wyco Electric. A few days later, after O'Hara lobbied O'Connor on his behalf, he was recalled by Hartford and given a contract for $150 per month for the 1925 season. Five months later, he was purchased by the New York Yankees. By September, the 20-year-old kid from Springfield was in the same dugout in Yankee Stadium with Babe Ruth and Lou Gehrig, and even appeared in the last two games of the season as a pinch hitter and a pinch runner.[5]

It was obvious to the Yankees that Durocher needed more seasoning, and he spent the next two seasons in their minor league system, at Class A Atlanta in 1926 and Class AA St. Paul in 1927. By 1928 he was back in a Yankee uniform. Legendary Yankee manager Miller Huggins—a jockey-sized fellow little man—took Durocher under his wing and worked on building his confidence. Huggins gave him a chance to break into the lineup as a second baseman when Tony Lazzeri broke two ribs. He encouraged the weak-hitting, but slick-fielding, Durocher, assuring him that if he used his head on the baseball field, there would always be a place for him in the game. With Lazzeri back at second base in 1929, Huggins moved the regular shortstop Mark Koenig to third base and made Durocher the new Yankee shortstop. Things came to an end for Durocher in New York when his mentor, advocate, and father figure Huggins died of a stroke 11 days before the end of the season at the age of 51. After an ugly run-in with Yankees owner Ed Barrow over salary the following February, Durocher was punitively sold to the Cincinnati Reds—a last-place team—on February 5, 1930.[6]

In 1933, in the middle of his fourth season with the lowly Reds, Durocher was given a reprieve when he was traded to the ascendant St. Louis Cardinals. The next year he was a key part of the immortal Gas House Gang, with Dizzy Dean, Pepper Martin, and Joe Medwick, that won the 1934 World Series. Durocher, who lost his hair over the course of that pressure-packed season, was shortstop and team captain for manager Frankie Frisch. By the end of the 1937 season the rivalry between Frisch and aspiring manager Durocher had become so disruptive that Frisch gave Cardinals General Manager Branch Rickey an ultimatum: "It's me or Durocher."[7] On October 4, 1937, Leo Durocher was traded to the Brooklyn Dodgers.

Durocher was the shortstop of the hapless seventh-place 1938 Brooklyn. He realized his dream the next year when Dodgers General Manager Leland Stanford (Larry) MacPhail named him player-manager. Under Durocher the 1939 Dodgers improved to third place. By 1941, he had brought the first National League pennant to Brooklyn in 21 years with a 100–54 season as the manager in the dugout—with the young Louisville sensation, Harold "Pee Wee" Reese, entrenched at shortstop. Durocher's Dodgers won 104 games the next year, but finished second to the Branch Rickey's St. Louis Cardinals. When MacPhail resigned as Brooklyn general manager at the end of 1942 to join the U.S. Army, the 61-year-old Rickey left the Cardinals to replace him. Durocher managed the Dodgers under Branch Rickey for the next six years, with a break in 1947 when he was suspended for the season by baseball Commissioner Albert B. "Happy" Chandler for his "association with known gamblers."[8] Midway through the 1948 season, friction between Rickey and the abrasive Durocher caused by the suspension, his outspoken nature, a clash over the decision to sell second baseman Eddie Stanky to the Boston Braves, and the Dodgers' poor performance on the field, reached a breaking point. By now, having been already ejected from 63 games for his notorious confrontations with umpires, he was known as "Leo the Lip." On July 16, 1948, Branch Rickey and New York Giants owner Horace Stoneham—an unholy alliance for the ages—worked out a deal whereby Leo Durocher would be released from his Brooklyn contract to allow him to become manager of the bitter rival Giants. The next day, Leo was sitting in the dugout at Forbes Field in Pittsburgh wearing a Giants uniform.

For Durocher's first 2½ years as manager of the Giants, they played modest .517 baseball, never finishing higher than third place. Then 1951 happened. In the last six weeks of the season the Dodgers collapsed, and the Giants went on a 39–8 run (including the 3-game playoff). Aided by "The Miracle of Coogan's Bluff" on October 3, Durocher brought the World Series back to the Polo Grounds for the first time since 1937. But his finest hour with the Giants was October 2, 1954, when Leo's boys completed a 4-game sweep of the Cleveland Indians in the 1954 World Series, "The Little Miracle of Coogan's Bluff."[9] After completing his contract with the Giants with a third-place finish in 1955, Durocher left to embark on a new career as color commentator on *Major League Baseball on NBC with Lindsey Nelson*. But after thirty years on the field and in the dugout, Durocher was never comfortable in the broadcast booth.

I'm Just a Coach

On January 9, 1961, at the press conference at the Statler Hilton Hotel, the ground beneath Los Angeles shook as Leo Durocher appeared in a Los Angeles Dodgers cap and jersey number 2 as their new third-base coach (to accommodate Leo, Clay Bryant, third base coach for all of a month, would be bumped to first base). It was the same number he wore in 1948, his last year as the manager of the Brooklyn Dodgers before committing his mortal sin of turning coat and taking over as field manager of the New York Giants. But today, all was forgiven as current Dodger manager Walter Alston told reporters, "We've got Leo on our side again, and I'm glad to have him with us."[10]

A reporter asked Durocher the question that was on everyone's mind: whether he considered his new job as a stepping stone to another managerial role. "I'm not looking for anything. I'm happy to be with the Dodgers—and that's it,"[11] he replied. Durocher actually had to ask Dodger General Manager Buzzie Bavasi for a job after leaving NBC and drifting as "an unemployed amateur golfer" for fifteen months. As a celebrated manager in his own right, he attempted to dispose of the sensitive issue of the second-guessing of Walter Alston before anyone else could raise it: "I'm just a coach. Alston's the manager."[12] A wary Bavasi, positioned between Alston and Durocher, reinforced the nature of the arrangement by way of a not-so-subtle warning, "The first time there is any second-guessing, that's it."[13]

The New Frontier Opens in Washington

The "New Frontier" officially began on January 20, 1961, at 12:51 p.m. on a bright 22-degree day in Washington, D.C., as 43-year-old John F. Kennedy was inaugurated as the 35th president of the United States. In front a crowd of 50,000 people, and with the 70-year-old retiring President Dwight D. Eisenhower looking on, the new president proclaimed, "Let the word go forth from this time and place, to friend and foe alike, that the torch has been passed to a new generation of Americans...."[14]

After Kennedy took the oath of office from U.S. Chief Justice Earl Warren, Richard Nixon was the first one—after Justice Warren—to shake his hand. The grounds were blanketed with an early morning 8-inch snowfall, the first to afflict an inauguration since 1909. It was quickly characterized by the pundits as "Nixon's revenge."

Six

Turning Point in Florida

con•trol *n*   the ability of a baseball pitcher to control the
location of a pitch within the strike zone[1]

It took me six years to get it through my thick skull.[2]—Sandy
Koufax

After making the decision to give it one more season on the day before New Year's
Eve—his twenty-fifth birthday—Koufax immediately began working out with a renewed
sense of purpose. Then in January, Koufax underwent a tonsillectomy that led to a
serendipitous breakthrough in his conditioning philosophy. For two weeks he couldn't
eat because he couldn't even swallow. Before he could eat again, he had lost 30 pounds,
dropping from 200 to 170. He usually prepared to report to camp a little overweight,
at around 205 pounds, then worked himself into shape. This year, due to the tonsillectomy, he would report in at 184. For the first time, he brought his weight up to the opti-
mum level by building muscle with exercise, proper diet, and adequate rest. As a result,
he reported to camp in the best shape of his life. For the rest of his career he would
come into camp underweight.[3]

Koufax Reports to Spring Training

On February 20, 1961, the day the Dodger pitchers and catchers reported to Vero
Beach, Sandy Koufax had not planned to be there. When he showed up with only a
glove and a pair of spikes, he was surprised to find the rest of his gear waiting for him
in his locker. Fortunately, on the last day of the 1960 season, when he had thrown everything else into the trash can in the clubhouse at the Coliseum, clubhouse custodian
Nobe Kawano recovered it from the trash and kept it for him.

66

The Gospel According to Alan Roth

In camp, Koufax began to pay closer attention to Alan Roth, the club statistician. Up in the radio booth with Vin Scully, Roth had charted every pitch of every game the Dodgers played since 1947. He meticulously registered the hits: who made them, where they went, who was pitching, what the count was, and how many men were on base. For Walter Alston and the coaching staff he produced two sets of index cards, one blue and one yellow. The blue cards had the name of every opposing pitcher and how each Dodger hitter had performed against them. There was a yellow card for every opposing batter. On these cards were the names of the Dodger pitchers with their yearly and lifetime records against that batter.[4]

By analyzing his yellow cards, Roth discovered two important things about Koufax. First, contrary to convention, the left-handed-throwing Koufax was less effective against left-handed batters than against right-handed batters. Consequently, he was not taking advantage of his "natural advantage" against lefties. According to Roth, this was caused by the break on his curve ball. The curve ball of most left-hand pitchers broke away from left-handed batters. But Koufax's curve ball broke straight down.

The second thing Roth disclosed to Koufax was that his control was what was preventing him from reaching his potential. In 1960, he was still averaging 5.14 walks per 9 innings compared with the league average of 3.19. And when he was behind in the count, batters hit .286 against him. But when he was ahead they hit only .146.[5]

Joe Becker

Dodger pitching coach Joe Becker played in only 40 major league games as a catcher for the Cleveland Indians in 1936–1937. He then managed in the minors for several years before taking over the Brooklyn pitching staff in 1955. In the spring of 1961 he was the only professional pitching coach Sandy Koufax ever had. Koufax now worked with him to address the two issues raised by Allan Roth. First, Becker got him to alter his grip on the baseball. By moving his fingers slightly on the ball when pitching to lefties, he was able to throw a curve that broke slightly away, as well as down.[6] He could now exploit his natural advan-

Dodger pitching coach Joe Becker changed Sandy Koufax's grip on the curve ball and tightened his windup (George Brace photograph).

tage against left-handed batters. With two curve balls, the devastating 12-to–6 curve for right-handed batters and a "modified" curve for left-handed batters, he would be a force to be reckoned with.

Next, with a slight mechanical adjustment, Becker tightened up his windup. The shorter windup helped Koufax with his control. It also helped him to better hide his pitches. When Wally Moon came over from St. Louis in 1959, he told Koufax that the Cardinals noticed that when pitching from a stretch, he brought his hands up higher for a fastball than for a curve, thus tipping his pitches.[7] Thanks to Joe Becker, batters would no longer know which of Koufax's pitches was coming.

Epiphany at Lennie's

Lennie's, a bar within walking distance of the batting cage at Vero Beach, was a favorite hangout for Dodger regulars, including the scout who discovered Willie Davis, Kenny Myers. On the night of March 22, 1961, Myers, smoking his usual cigar, was holding court over a contingent of players including Norm Sherry, Ed Roebuck, and Sandy Koufax. Myers, who had been working with Koufax, wanted to prove a point: Sandy had a flaw in his motion. Myers took the cigar out of his mouth, marked a spot on the wall, and said to Koufax, "Sandy, take an imaginary baseball and try to hit that spot."[8] Koufax got up and went into his windup. At the point where he had reared back so far that he lost sight of the target, Myers stopped him: "Wait, Sandy, how can you hit that spot if you can't even see it?"[9] He then offered a suggestion: "Why not try taking your hands back and keeping your head level?"[10]

When Koufax implemented this simple change, it produced two results. First, he was able keep his eyes on the catcher's mitt—The Target. Second, it lowered his release point, thereby helping to correct a tendency to throw pitches up above the strike zone whenever he began to press.

Turning Point in Orlando

In Vero Beach on March 23, 19 days before the opening day of the 1961 season— the season Sandy Koufax promised himself would be his last if he could not turn his career around—the Dodgers split the team into two squads to look at as many prospects as possible. Squad A, made up of the veterans, traveled with Walter Alston and the coaching staff to Lakehurst to play the Detroit Tigers. Squad B, made up primarily of young players from minor league rosters, traveled to Orlando to play the new American League expansion Minnesota Twins. Sandy Koufax and catcher Norm "Catcher Face" Sherry (older brother of Larry) went with Squad B to work on Sandy's curve ball and changeup. Only three pitchers were scheduled to make the trip to Orlando: Koufax (who was assigned to pitch the first five innings), Ed "Wally Weird" Palmquist, and a 27-year-old rookie named Willard Hunter. Koufax had struggled to this point in the exhibition season. In three appearances, he had completed 6 innings with 5 earned runs and 8 walks.

Complications arose before Squad B could get out of Vero Beach. A disoriented Wally Weird, nursing a hangover, missed the plane. Now they were down to two pitchers. On the plane, designated manager Gil Hodges told Koufax he would have to go at least seven innings. In Orlando, the complications only escalated. When Hodges was beaned in batting practice, he was rushed to the hospital for X-rays. Dodger trainer Bill Buhler went with him, thus leaving no one to give Koufax his usual pre-game rubdown. Pressed into emergency service, the versatile Nobe Kawano improvised an Oriental massage with Joy Oil.[11]

Koufax's roommate, catcher Norm Sherry, encouraged him to try a new approach today: "You haven't got a thing to lose, because none of the brass are here. If you get into trouble, let up, throw the curve, and try to pitch the fastball to spots." But by the time Koufax took the mound, he was in

Dodgers backup catcher Norm Sherry convinced Koufax to "take the *grunt* out of the fastball" in the B game in Orlando of March 23, 1961 (George Brace photograph).

a distracted state. The plan went out the window from the start. Behind the plate, Sherry called for Koufax to start off with curve balls and changeups. But when Sandy couldn't get these over the plate, he became frustrated and began to shake off Sherry and resort to the fast ball. Koufax fell into a familiar pattern: the more he pressed, the harder he threw his fastball, and the higher the ball sailed—up and out of the strike zone—until he had walked the first three batters on 12 pitches.

Taking the "Grunt" Out of the Fastball

With the bases loaded and Koufax yet to throw a strike, Norm Sherry went to the mound with some calming words to try to settle him down: "Sandy, you know we're shorthanded. Take the *grunt* out of the fastball. You know you've got to throw the ball over the plate or we'll be here all day. Why don't you take something off the ball and just let them hit it?"[12]

With Sherry back behind the plate, Koufax wound up and began to throw his fastball without pressing. It was as if he was saying to the batters, "Here, hit the ball." He struck out the side. When Koufax walked off the mound, Sherry told him with Berra-esque clarity, "I'll tell you something, you just now threw harder trying not to than when you tried to."[13]

Koufax relapsed in the fifth inning. He began overthrowing and walked the bases loaded again with no one out, bringing Norm Sherry to the mound for a second time. "Think about what you're doing," Sherry said. "Be a pitcher. Make them swing the bat, and maybe you'll get out of the inning."[14] Koufax regained his focus and his control. He was able to get ahead in the count, throw his fastball to *spots*, and strike out the side— this time, blowing away the sluggers Harmon Killebrew, Jim Lemon, and Bob Allison in succession.

Norm Sherry had offered similar advice to Koufax before, but Koufax had always tuned him out. Koufax would recall, "I had heard it all before. Only, for once, it wasn't blahblahblah. There comes a time and place where you are ready to listen."[15] The result was dramatic. Koufax pitched a 7-inning no-hitter with eight strikeouts. "I was still throwing hard," he would recall. "I was just taking the *grunt* out of the ball. When I got ahead of the batter, I went for spots. I found that I was hitting the spots with amazing regularity."[16]

March 23, 1961, would be a turning point in the career of Sandy Koufax, the transformation from a thrower to a pitcher. Five years later, he would recall, "That day in Orlando was the beginning of a whole new era for me. I came home a different pitcher from the one who had left [Vero Beach]."[17] He went on to finish his spring exhibition season with a shutout, the first pre-season complete game of his career, and a run of 22 scoreless innings.

The Dodgers would finish their spring exhibition season with an undistinguished 13–15 record, narrowly ahead of the Milwaukee Braves. But they had a new, more confident Sandy Koufax with a new windup that allowed him to keep his eye on the target and put the ball over the plate, and a new curve ball that made him more effective against left-handed batters. And he had a new attitude with better control over his emotions. He would no longer fall into the destructive pattern of pressing, and throwing the ball harder and harder when he was frustrated. As he prepared to leave Florida, Koufax remarked to reporters of his transformation, "It took me six years to get it through my thick skull."[18] If the National League batters were expecting the old Koufax in 1961, they were in for a surprise.

	W	**L**	**Pct.**
Pittsburgh	18	11	.621
St. Louis	16	10	.615
San Francisco	15	11	.577
Philadelphia	14	11	.560
Chicago	14	13	.519
Los Angeles	13	15	.464
Milwaukee	12	15	.444
Cincinnati	12	17	.414

At the bottom of the heap, the Cincinnati Reds appeared to be headed for yet another year out of the running. After all, they had not won a pennant since 1940.

Seven

April—A Full Moon
and a New Koufax

In 1961 a whole new world opened up to me.[1]—Sandy
Koufax

As the Dodgers prepared to open their last season in the Coliseum, they were the heavy favorites to win the National League pennant:

EXPERTS	PUBLICATION	DODGERS—PREDICTED FINISH
L.A. Writers Composite Poll	*Los Angeles Times*	1st
Baseball Writers Association of America	*The Sporting News*	1st
Associated Press	*Washington Post*	1st
Arthur Daley	*New York Times*	1st
J.G. Taylor Spink	*The Sporting News*	1st

To take the pressure off, the ever cautious Walter Alston attempted to downplay the media expectations: "I'm enthusiastic about our chances, but I'm not sure. This could be the most unpredictable team I've ever managed. The veterans and rookies are both big ifs."[2]

Losing Roebuck

On April 6, five days before opening day, the Dodgers received a blow from Phoenix. Their team doctor, Dr. Robert Kerlan, announced the results of his examination of relief pitcher Ed Roebuck, who had been unable to pitch a single inning in spring training because of an old shoulder injury: "acute and chronic adhesive capsulitis." Roebuck, whom the Dodgers were counting on to continue his outstanding bullpen work of the prior year, was sent home and immediately placed on the disabled list.[3] The one positive note was Kerlan's guarded prognosis. He said that ordinarily he would take a dim view of a pitcher's future in such a case. But the fact that Roebuck had overcome such an injury before caused him to be cautiously optimistic.[4]

Opening Day on the New Frontier

At 1:27 p.m. on April 10 at Griffith Stadium in Washington, D.C., 80 days after he was inaugurated at the East Portico of the Capital building—2¼ miles away as the crow flies—President Kennedy threw out the first ball to open the new baseball season before the game between the Washington Senators and the Chicago White Sox. Whereas Eisenhower had delivered a "feeble blooper" as his last opening day pitch a year ago in the same stadium, the youngest president in history released his pitch with characteristic Kennedy "vigga"—a whizzing fast ball that sailed over the heads of all the awaiting Senators and White Sox players, except Jim Rivera, the Sox outfielder, who was playing him deep.[5] Though it was a cold and overcast day, the young president remained hatless and coatless for most of the game. The torch had indeed been passed to a new generation.

Kennedy, an avid Red Sox fan from Boston, was now the ceremonial First Senators Fan. But this was the New Frontier, and these were not the same Washington Senators that every president since William Howard Taft in 1910 had adopted. Those Senators were now in Minneapolis, where they had changed their name to the Minnesota Twins. These Senators were one of the two new expansion teams cobbled together from the expansion draft of the previous October. As the new Senators ran onto the field, the public address announcer introduced them in the spirit of the occasion: "Ladies and gentlemen, meet the New Frontier Senators."[6]

Unfortunately for the new president and the other 26,724 fans in attendance, the new Senators were not much better than the old Senators. After handing the White Sox a gift of 4 errors, they went down to an ignominious 4–3 defeat. With his pitching duties over, Kennedy, accompanied by Vice President Lyndon Johnson, returned to the White House to finish his first 100 days.

❋ ❋ ❋

At that hour, 3,500 miles away in Nicaragua, 1,400 CIA-trained Cuban exiles were making final preparations for an invasion of Cuba at the Bay of Pigs.

❋ ❋ ❋

Opening Night in L.A.

The next night in Los Angeles, manager Walter Alston picked Don Drysdale to make his fourth consecutive opening game start. He would face veteran Philadelphia right-hander Robin Roberts, who had started every opening game for the Phillies since 1950. Tonight, with his twelfth in a row, he would tie the Phillies' record set by the immortal Grover Cleveland Alexander. There were some dramatic changes to the Dodger starting lineup from the previous year's opener.

	APRIL 11, 1961		APRIL 12, 1960	
1	Maury Wills	SS	Jim Gilliam	3B
2	Willie Davis	CF	Charlie Neal	2B
3	Tommy Davis	3B	Wally Moon	LF
4	Duke Snider	RF	Duke Snider	RF
5	Wally Moon	LF	Gil Hodges	1B
6	Norm Larker	1B	John Roseboro	C
7	Charlie Neal	2B	Don Demeter	CF
8	John Roseboro	C	Maury Wills	SS
9	Drysdale	P	Drysdale	P

The lineup opened with speed at the top. Maury Wills was now firmly entrenched as the Dodger leadoff man. He would be followed by rookie centerfielder Willie Davis, widely regarded as the fastest man in the major leagues, and Tommy Davis, seeking to find a new home on third base. Jim Gilliam was absent from the opening lineup for the first time since his rookie year of 1953. Gil Hodges had been the Dodgers' starting first baseman since 1949. Today he was relegated to the bench to begin what was to be his last year in Dodger blue. The former great Dodger center fielder, Duke Snider, was now confined to right field by a "trick knee." The only member of the old Boys of Summer in the starting lineup, Snider was coming off a fine .389 spring exhibition season, but he would turn 35 in September.

The crowd of 50,665 was studded with Hollywood celebrities, led by Gary Cooper and Danny Kaye. The Glendale banker, Charles "Casey" Stengel, watched from the stands after being "retired" as manager of the New York Yankees the previous October.[7]

Drysdale was on his game, striking out eight Phillies in seven innings. His only mistake was a hanging curve ball that Johnny Callison hit over the right-center-field fence for a 2-run homer in the third inning. Otherwise, Philadelphia could manage only four singles against him. Larry Sherry came in to pitch the final two innings, adding another five strikeouts—for a combined total of 13—to save the 6–2 win for Drysdale. An enthusiastic Alston praised Sherry's performance: "I thought Larry Sherry looked the best since 1959. He was really good out there."[8]

Wally Moon began what would be a tor-

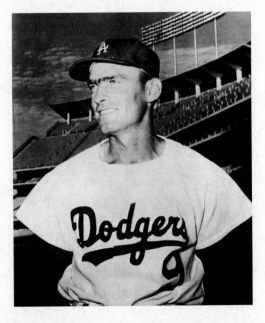

Wally Moon tore up National League pitching in the month of April with his patented "Moon Shots" (National Baseball Hall of Fame Library, Cooperstown, New York).

rid April for him in the Year of the Home Run when he launched the first of his "Moon Shots" off Robin Roberts in the second inning, a sliced fly ball over the left field screen. Thanks to Drysdale, Sherry, and Moon, the Dodgers started the 1961 season with a bang.

❋ ❋ ❋

Three hours after the last pitch at the Coliseum, the Soviet Union announced it had put the first man into space: Major Yuri Gagarin, a 27-year-old air force test pilot. Gagarin orbited the earth for 108 minutes in a 10,395-pound sputnik called Vostok 1.[9] By orbiting the first astronaut and returning him safely to earth, the Soviets got a temporary leg up in the space race with the United States.

❋ ❋ ❋

The Great Shin-Kicking Match

Any time the combustible elements of Leo Durocher and Hall of Fame umpire Jocko Conlon came together on the same baseball field, as they did on April 16, there was a high probability of an explosion.

Jocko Conlon, NL umpire with a notorious hair-trigger temper, engaged with Leo Durocher in The Great Shin-Kicking Match of April 16, 1961 (George Brace photograph).

The Accidental Umpire

John Bertrand Conlon was born December 6, 1899, in Chicago, Illinois. After 12 years as a 5'7" minor league center fielder, he was brought up by the Chicago White Sox in July of 1934. He became an umpire quite by accident the next season when regular umpire Red Ormsby was overcome by the heat in a game between the White Sox and the Browns in St. Louis. In those days, only two umpires were assigned to each regular season game. If one was incapacitated, a player with a "reputation for honesty" could be pressed into service. Conlon, sitting on the bench with no known criminal record—the perfect candidate—was asked to fill in. And he took to the role. After the White Sox gave him his unconditional release as a player on November 6, 1935, he made the transition from player to umpire complete by beginning in the minor leagues the next year. In 1941, he began his major league career in the National League where his polka-dot tie, balloon chest protector, and mercurial quick smile–quick snarl became his trademarks.[10]

The Spark

On this Sunday afternoon, Conlon, the hair-trigger-tempered banty rooster of a man was the plate umpire in a game between the Dodgers and the Pirates before over 27,000 at the Coliseum. Conlon had already ejected Durocher numerous times, the first being in 1943 when Leo was manager of the Brooklyn Dodgers.

The inevitable spark was set off in the fourth inning. Leo was prowling somewhere in vicinity of the third base coach's box, which had been rendered invisible since before the game's first pitch. Not one to be boxed in, Leo had made it a ritual to obliterate the white chalk lines immediately upon taking the field. After Wally Moon led off the inning with one of his signature inside-out-swing home runs over the left field screen, Pirate pitcher (and 1960 Cy Young Award winner) Vern Law got Norm Larker to hit a towering pop fly between home plate and first base—a sure out. But catcher Hal Smith—yes, the same "Hal Smith" who saved the Pirates from elimination in Game 7 of the 1960 World Series with a 3-run home run in the bottom of the eighth inning—lunged for the ball, which appeared to everyone in the park to tick off his glove into fair territory before spinning into foul territory. Everyone except Jocko Conlon, that is. Larker was on second base when Conlon called the ball foul, ruling that Smith's glove had never come in contact with the ball. An angry mob of Dodgers, including Alston and Durocher, charged Conlon, arguing that Smith had touched the ball before it went foul. Conlon was not persuaded, and ordered Larker back to home plate, his "gift double" erased from the record book. The Dodgers never scored, Durocher returned to the dugout, case closed.

Only it wasn't closed. Durocher threw a towel in derision onto the field. Right on cue, the testy Conlon immediately ejected Leo. Instead of heading for the showers, Durocher decided to deliver an appeal of Conlon's decision in person—nose to nose, shin to shin. In the kicking frenzy that ensued in the dust in front of home plate, as in the fog of war, there were conflicting interpretations of what actually happened. Durocher asserted that he merely kicked a "little dirt" on Conlon's shoes, and that Conlon's attempt to kick some dirt back at him misfired when Jocko's spike-less shoe skidded off the ground and landed squarely on Leo's shin.[11] Jocko, a former boxing referee, asserted that it was Leo who scored the "first kick," and that the match had ended in a draw, at two kicks apiece. Perhaps, but Leo always maintained there was a gross imbalance in the damages. Since Jocko was wearing shin guards underneath his pants and iron plates on the toes of his shoes to protect him from foul balls, every time Jocko kicked Leo it raised a lump on his shins. But every time Leo kicked Jocko it bruised his toes.[12] Ironically, it was the hot-tempered Don Drysdale who was the peacemaker, separating the two combatants before any blood could be spilled. The Dodgers eventually won the game, 13–6, in a 3-hour, 35-minute marathon to bring their record to 3–3 and into a fourth-place tie with the Pirates.[13] Wally Moon hit his third home run of the season and raised his batting average to .471.

The next day, National League President Warren Giles suspended Durocher for three games. In a bizarre rationale, Giles informed Dodger General Manager Buzzie Bavasi: "Jocko was wrong. He shouldn't have done it, but I'm suspending Durocher."[14] Since he was coming into the game with 97 career ejections, Leo's reputation did not help him. The league's message to the Dodgers was clear: Leo the Lip—now aka Leo the Toe—would be kept under control. That evening the Dodgers were dealt another blow when Bob Gibson broke Duke Snider's elbow with a fastball. Snider, with his weight lighter than any time in ten years and playing without a knee brace for the first time since his operation in the winter of 1957, had gotten off to one of his best starts. Now he would be lost to the Dodgers for five weeks.[15]

❋ ❋ ❋

On the same day, April 17, 1961, 1,400 armed Cuban exiles landed at the Bay of Pigs on the southern coast of Cuba.[16] Two days before, six repainted American B-26 bombers bombed and strafed Cuban airfields. This had destroyed half of Castro's air force, but it had also alerted him that an attack was imminent.

Young President Kennedy, in office for less than 90 days, had inherited "Operation Zapata" from the Eisenhower administration, an operation already in an advanced stage of preparation. The landing force was actually a group of fiercely anti–Castro exiles that the CIA had recruited, equipped, and trained for an invasion of their homeland. The CIA confidently expected the invasion to ignite a popular uprising that would result in the demise of the Castro regime. Though Kennedy had the option of canceling the plan, on April 15 he decided to go forward based on the unanimous recommendations of his intelligence and military advisors, and by his own desire to project an image of toughness.

Fiasco

Kennedy had at his disposal a U.S. aircraft carrier several miles offshore. But he rejected a plan to use navy planes to support the invasion for fear of exposing U.S. involvement. The invasion force encountered unexpected reefs that prevented their supplies from coming ashore until high tide. Meanwhile, Castro's planes promptly destroyed the invaders' tiny air force and sank two of the loaded merchant ships as they approached the island. At the end of the first day, the invaders were pinned down on the beachhead by the Cuban militia. By the end of the third day, 114 of the invaders were killed and nearly 1,200 were taken prisoner. There was no popular uprising.

The consequences of the Bay of Pigs would be devastating for President Kennedy and U.S. foreign policy. The fiasco profoundly shook the confidence of the young president and his administration, and encouraged Nikita Khrushchev and the Soviet Union.[17]

❋ ❋ ❋

Roger Craig started his second game of the season on the night of April 18 at the Coliseum against the St. Louis Cardinals. As was the case four days before when the Phillies pounded him for two home runs in six innings, Craig was bitten by the gopher ball—this time compliments of Dodger-killer Ken Boyer. Boyer tied the game 2–2 with a home run off Craig in the third, then tied the game again at 3–3 with another home run off him in the fifth.

Fortunately for Craig, Wally Moon put him in position to win his first game of the season by knocking in two runs with a single and a "Moon Shot" home run over the left-field screen to raise his batting average to an eye-popping .480. With the Dodgers back in front 5–4, Alston brought in rookie reliever Ron Perranoski in the eighth inning to hold off Boyer and the Cardinals.

The "Throw-In"

Ron Perranoski came to the Dodgers as an afterthought from the Chicago Cubs. On April 8, 1960, he was part of the trade that sent Don Zimmer to the Cubs for infielder Johnny Goryl, outfielder Lee Handley, and $25,000 cash. To sweeten the deal the Cubs added a left-handed minor league pitcher named Ron Perranoski—in baseball terms, a "throw-in."[18]

Ronald Peter Perranoski grew up in Fair Lawn, New Jersey, 35 minutes away from Yankee Stadium. He played baseball and basketball at Fair Lawn High School, where he attracted the attention of scouts—college and professional—by pitching 56 consecutive scoreless innings. He accepted a scholarship offer from Notre Dame, then changed his mind and went to Michigan State. Though he had always dreamed of playing for the Yankees, in 1958 he signed a $21,000 bonus contract with the Chicago Cubs at the "advanced" baseball age of 22. At the time he thought he would have a better chance to make it to the majors in the Chicago system: "I never would have signed with them [Yankees] or the Dodgers. I knew I had to come up fast because of the years I spent in college."[19] Perranoski spent all of 1958 and 1959 trying to make it as a starting pitcher in the Cubs' farm system.

On April 8, 1960, Perranoski was a private in the Army at Fort Leonard Wood, Missouri, when he received a wire informing him that his contract had been "assigned to Montreal." He didn't know whether or not he still belonged to the Cubs until, during a card game, his sergeant showed him a sports page clipping saying that he had been traded

In 1961 left-handed relief pitcher Ron Perranoski became a fixture in the Dodger bullpen. He spent the previous year in the minor leagues after coming to the Dodger organization as a "throw-in" in the April 8, 1960, trade with the Chicago Cubs (George Brace photograph).

to the Dodgers.[20] His manager at Triple-A Montreal, Clay Bryant, took one look at his sinking fastball—the ideal pitch for inducing batters to ground into rally-killing double plays—and converted him to a relief pitcher. For the 1960 season he split his time between Montreal and St. Paul for a combined record of 12–11, giving up only 5 home runs in 57 games. After his 1-year apprenticeship, he made the Dodgers' 1961 roster and was assigned Larry Sherry as his roommate.

On this night in Los Angeles, Perranoski did what he would become famous for: he pitched 1⅓ hitless, scoreless innings to save his first game for the Dodgers. When Ken Boyer, already with two home runs, came to the plate in the ninth as the potential tying run, the "throw-in" struck him out. Alston had a new weapon in the bullpen, and particularly satisfying for Bavasi and O'Malley, he had been acquired on the cheap.

A New April Koufax

Sandy Koufax was a notorious slow starter. April had never been kind to him. In fact, he had never won a game in the traditional starting month of the baseball season since he joined the Brooklyn Dodgers as a bonus baby in 1955. That would change in 1961.

It was a *new* Sandy Koufax who took the mound on Friday night, April 21, at the Coliseum to face the Cincinnati Reds. Ever since his catcher-confidant-roommate, Norm Sherry, helped him to make a breakthrough a month ago in Orlando, he approached the game with a new philosophy: he did not need to press; he did not need to throw the baseball as hard as he could; he could pitch to spots; he would be a pitcher.

The Dodgers' left fielder, Wally Moon, was beginning to attract attention across the baseball world with a cluster of "Moon Shots." His solo home run in the second inning was his seventh in only the ninth game of the season. That combined with Johnny Roseboro's 2-run homer in the same inning off Reds starter Jay Hook gave Koufax a 3–0 lead to work with. Sandy's only test came in the third inning when he gave up a game-tying 3-run home run to Frank Robinson, who would go on to be the Most Valuable Player of the league.[21] It was a blow that would have rattled the old Koufax. But this was a new Sandy Koufax. He did not resort to overthrowing out of frustration, but steadied himself to get out of the inning without any further damage.

Over the next six innings he gave up only two hits while striking out nine batters. He pitched a complete game with eleven strikeouts. It was his first career win, as well as his first career complete game, in the month of April. It evened his record to 1–1 for the season. The ascendancy of Sandy Koufax had begun.

April Ends on a Full Moon

On April 30 the Dodgers closed out the first month of the season with a Sunday double-header split at Wrigley Field in Chicago. In the first game, Don Drysdale struck out nine Cubs and allowed only one unearned run in the first seven innings before coming out for a pinch hitter in the eighth trailing, 1–0. Larry Sherry came in from the bullpen to shut out Chicago over the final two innings. Tommy Davis finally got the Dodgers on the scoreboard in the top of the ninth with a 2-run home run to win the game, 2–1, for Sherry. The Cubs knocked out Roger Craig in the second inning of the second game with a 7-run outburst en route to a 10–5 Chicago win.[22] Sandy Koufax made a meaningless 1-inning relief appearance just to get in some work between starts. While he made no impact on a game that was essentially out of reach, by now it was evident that he was finally on the right path to a breakout year.

Meanwhile, 93 miles away up in Milwaukee, an ailing Willie Mays was debating whether to sit out the game between the Giants and Braves at County Stadium. At the last minute he told Giants manager Alvin Dark to pencil him into the lineup card. Mays rallied to put together one of the greatest games of his career: 4 home runs and 8 runs batted in. The Giants' 14–4 rout of the Braves left them in first place by a half game over Pittsburgh and a full game over the Dodgers at the end of April.

	W	L	Pct.	*
San Francisco	10	6	.625	
Pittsburgh	9	6	.600	½
Los Angeles	10	8	.556	1
Chicago	8	8	.500	2
Milwaukee	6	6	.500	2
St. Louis	7	9	.438	3
Philadelphia	6	9	.400	3½
Cincinnati	6	10	.375	4

*Games behind leader

At this point in the season, the last-place Cincinnati Reds were not on anyone's radar.

In a month's time, Roger Maris and Mickey Mantle would hold the nation spellbound with their dual assault on Babe Ruth's single-season record of 60 home runs. But today, the Dodgers' Wally Moon, after an explosive start, was leading Major League Baseball with 8 home runs, and the National League with a .417 batting average.

Eight

Koufax Takes Off!

I can throw the ball where I want to now.[1]—Sandy Koufax,
Los Angeles June 10, 1961

With his first career April win under his belt, and after winning his second game
of the season on May 7 in Pittsburgh, the next start for Sandy Koufax was May 12
against the Cubs at the Coliseum. As was to become an increasingly common occur-
rence, he had a no-hitter going. This time it was the seventh inning before leadoff batter
Billy Williams broke it up by slicing a fly ball off the left field screen for a double. Koufax
answered by striking out the side to strand Williams on second and escape with his
4–0 lead in tact. He then began to founder. In the eighth, he narrowly escaped a bases-
loaded situation to preserve the shut-out. By the ninth he had reverted to his old pattern
of pressing—walking three batters, serving up a triple, struggling just to hang on. The
last walk, coming with the bases loaded and two outs, forced in a run to ruin his shutout,
and force him out of the game after 8⅔ innings and 11 strikeouts. The Dodger bullpen
hung on to save his third win, 4–2.

❊ ❊ ❊

On May 14, an angry mob of white segregationists attacked and burned a bus of
Freedom Riders outside Anniston, Alabama. The Freedom Riders were trained volun-
teers sent by CORE (Congress of Racial Equality) to test the U.S. Supreme Court's guarantee of the right to integrated travel in interstate buses established in December 1960
in the *Boyton v. Virginia* case. Minutes later, a Ku Klux Klan posse severely beat a second
busload when it arrived at the Trailways station 65 miles away in Birmingham. Attorney
General Robert Kennedy immediately sent federal marshals to evacuate the battered
CORE riders.[2]

❊ ❊ ❊

Losing the no-hitter, the shut-out, and nearly the game against the Cubs, had an
adverse effect on Koufax's confidence and set the tone for his next start on May 16

against the Braves at the Coliseum. It was a shaky outing, in which he lasted only 4 innings, walked 3 batters, gave up 5 earned runs, and lost his second game of the season, 3–2. The loss dropped the Dodgers into a 3-way tie for fourth place. The "new" Koufax had hit a wall. His record was 3–2. Another loss, and he was back to being a .500 pitcher still drifting through a mediocre career. As usual, the Giants would have a say in the matter.

The Dodgers traveled to San Francisco on May 19 for a 3-game series with the Giants. They won the first two, then called on Koufax to complete a sweep on Sunday, May 21. The inconsistency of his last two outings continued. In the fourth inning the Giants got to him for 2 runs on a home run by Tom Haller, a single by Felipe Alou, a sacrifice fly by Harvey Kuenn, and a double by Jose Pagan. After four innings of work, he was behind, 2–0, when he began to find his rhythm. He proceeded to no-hit the Giants for the remaining 5 innings. The Dodgers scored 3 runs in the fifth on home runs by John Roseboro and Junior Gilliam. That was enough to give Koufax an important come-from-behind 3–2 win. It was a complete game 4-hitter that raised his record to 4–2, and another turning point in his season and his career. With three days to prepare for his first confrontation with Bob Gibson in St. Louis, he was on the way up.

* * *

That same Sunday in Montgomery, Alabama, civil rights leaders Martin Luther King and Ralph Abernathy flew in from Atlanta to help a group of bandaged Freedom Riders holed up in a church next to the Alabama state capitol, where they were recovering from the previous day's violent attack at the Montgomery bus station. King, Abernathy, and fifteen hundred local Negroes held a community meeting inside the church while a mob of three thousand angry white people outside overturned and burned cars, threw rocks through the church windows, and repeatedly battered the doors in an attempt to get at the Freedom Riders.[3]

* * *

An Early Koufax-Gibson Classic

On May 25, 1961, Sandy Koufax and Bob Gibson collided for the first time in their careers on a Thursday evening in St. Louis. In his third year with the Cardinals, the 25-year-old Bob Gibson came into the game with 2–0 record. He had just shut out the Cubs with 11 strikeouts in his last start at Wrigley Field on the 21st.

Pack Robert Gibson, Jr., was born in Omaha, Nebraska, on November 9, 1935, as the youngest of Pack and Victoria Gibson's seven children. His father died of tuberculosis three months before Pack Jr. was born. Fortunately, his older brother Josh—15 years his senior—filled the void as a father and mentor.

Gibson's first home was a wooden shack without heat or electricity on Omaha's North Side. His childhood was plagued by health problems, including rickets and asthma. The family later moved up to a government housing project, albeit still in the ghetto. It was there that Josh began working with Bob to teach him the fundamentals of baseball and basketball.[4]

He entered Omaha Technical High School in the fall of 1949 as a 4'10", 90-pound freshman. Because of a heart murmur, he had to obtain a doctor's permission to compete in sports. In two years, at 6' and 175 pounds, he was a standout on the track, basketball, and baseball teams. While he was an outstanding baseball player, his best sport was basketball. He made All-State, and had his heart set on playing for Indiana University. When Indiana informed him, "[W]e already have filled our quota of Negroes,"[5] he had to settle for a basketball scholarship to Creighton University. As the only black basketball player at Creighton, he averaged over 20 points per game while continuing to develop

Bob Gibson became a full-time starter for the Cardinals in 1961 under new manager Johnny Keane. Gibson collided with Sandy Koufax for the first time at Busch Stadium on May 25, 1961 (George Brace photograph).

as a top baseball prospect. By the time he graduated in 1957, he was being pursued by both the Harlem Globetrotters and the St. Louis Cardinals. Gibson signed a $3,000 bonus contract as a pitcher-outfielder with the Cardinals, with both parties in agreement that he could delay his start for a year to allow him to play basketball with the Globetrotters.

Through 1957 Gibson continued with both sports, as "Bullet Bob" with the Globetrotters, and as a pitcher at Triple-A Omaha in the Cardinal organization. In 1958 he accepted a $4,000 offer from Cardinals General Manager Bing Devine to quit basketball and devote his full energies to baseball. In 1959 and 1960, "Hoot" Gibson was being shuttled between the Cardinals' bullpen/starting rotation and their Triple-A teams, mainly due to the racial prejudice of Cardinals manager Solly Hemus. Hemus had warned Gibson and his black teammate Curt Flood that they would never make it in the major leagues, and that they should "try something else."

On this night, the two future Hall of Fame pitchers put on a show at Busch Stadium. Bob Gibson was heading for his second consecutive shutout until he gave up a solo home run to Tommy Davis in the top of the seventh. Davis was leading the club at the time with a .307 average. His home run into the left-centerfield stands not only snapped Gibson's streak of 20 consecutive scoreless innings, it turned out to be the only run of the game. Koufax began the ninth with a one-hitter and a 1–0 lead when he began to run out of steam as Curt Flood and Bill White singled. With one out, good fortune intervened. Dodger nemesis Ken Boyer hit what appeared to be the game-tying hit, a line drive into right field. But Duke Snider, recently returned from the disabled list after Gibson broke his elbow with a fastball on April 17, charged in to make a one-handed catch, then threw to Jim Gilliam at second base for a game-ending double play. Koufax and Gibson both struck out 8 batters in a game that saw only 1 run and 8 hits between the two teams. With the 1–0 shutout, Sandy Koufax improved his record to 5–2 and brought the Dodgers to within a half game of the first-place Giants.[6]

❊ ❊ ❊

Earlier that day, despite President Kennedy's call for a "cooling off period," a busload of Freedom Riders arrived in Jackson, Mississippi, where they were arrested for breach of the peace for trying to use "white only" restrooms and lunch counters. At the same time in Washington, D.C., Kennedy delivered an extraordinary second 1961 State of the Union address to a joint session of Congress. He announced to the nation that he would ask Congress to approve a program to send men to the moon. He also declared, "The great battleground for the defense and expansion of freedom today is the whole southern half of the globe," but he never mentioned racial injustice at home or the Freedom Rides.[7]

❊ ❊ ❊

Sandy Koufax and the Dodgers opened a new home stand at the Coliseum on May 29 with a Monday night game against Larry Jackson and the Cardinals. Just like the Koufax-Gibson collision four days before in St. Louis, this was another classic pitcher's duel—only this one would be decided by balks. With just two pitches—a rising fastball and an unhittable curve—Koufax turned in a dominating performance. He shut out the Cardinals over the first seven innings. This was matched by Jackson, and the game was a scoreless tie into the bottom of the eighth inning before the Dodgers finally got to him. Jackson issued his only walk of the game to John Roseboro. After the St. Louis infield misplayed two bunts, the Dodgers had the bases loaded, and Jackson was forced out of the game. The Cardinals' ace reliever and Dodger killer, Lindy McDaniel, then balked home Roseboro from third. Willie Davis blooped a single into left field to score Koufax to make it 2–0, Dodgers. Since both runs were charged to Jackson, McDaniel was able to run his scoreless streak against Los Angeles to 28⅔ innings.

Koufax took a potential second consecutive shutout into the ninth inning with Ken Boyer again standing in the way. Boyer opened the inning with a triple. Just like the Dodgers, the Cardinals were the beneficiaries of a rare run-scoring balk as Koufax balked home Boyer to make it 2–1, Los Angeles. When Koufax recovered to strike out the side, it was over. He struck out a total of 13 Cardinals to improve his record to 6–2. This night in Los Angeles was a milestone for Sandy Koufax. His career record was now an even .500, at 42–42. It would never approach that level again. The win kept the Dodgers a nominal .001 points ahead of the Reds and within a game and a half of the league-leading Giants.[8]

The Acquisition of Daryl Spencer

The Dodgers, in the market all spring for a right-handed power hitter, had their eye on veteran Cardinal shortstop Daryl Spencer. Spencer was a strong right-handed pull hitter, perfect for the Los Angeles Coliseum. And he could also play second and third base. The next day, May 30, Buzzie Bavasi acquired Spencer in exchange for the Dodgers' backup shortstop Bob Lillis and rookie outfielder Carl Warwick. That same night Spencer was in the Dodger lineup at third base. Tommy Davis, considered a defensive liability at that position, returned to the outfield.

The Dodgers ended May with a tough 8–7 loss to the surging Reds at the Coliseum. It was the sixth consecutive win for the Reds, who went into a tie for first place with the Giants. The loss snapped the Dodgers' 3-game winning streak, dropping them alone into third.

	W	L	Pct.	*
San Francisco	26	16	.619	
Cincinnati	26	16	.619	
Los Angeles	27	19	.587	1

*Games behind leader

❅ ❅ ❅

It was at this time that President Kennedy sent 400 Green Berets to Vietnam as "special advisors" to train the South Vietnamese Army in counterinsurgency techniques in the fight against Viet Cong guerrillas. It was the beginning of a U.S. presence that would grow to over half a million.

❅ ❅ ❅

On June 3, the newly-acquired Daryl Spencer hit a ninth inning sudden-death home run off Juan Marichal to beat the Giants 4–3 in front of 66,059 fans at the Coliseum. The home run gave Sandy Koufax (7–2) his fourth consecutive complete-game victory and moved the Dodgers into first place by a game over Cincinnati.[9]

❅ ❅ ❅

On the same day in Vienna, Austria, an ashen President Kennedy emerged from a

The Dodgers acquired veteran infielder Daryl Spencer in a May 30, 1961, trade with the Cardinals (George Brace photograph).

one-on-one meeting with a belligerent Soviet Premier Nikita Khrushchev. The two-day summit was proposed to discuss a range of topics including Laos, the broader Indochina, and nuclear disarmament. But the incendiary topic of Berlin dominated the meeting. Khrushchev threatened Kennedy with war over Berlin: "Force will be met with force. If the U.S. wants war, that's its problem."[10] Kennedy later told the _New York Times_ that the summit had been "the roughest thing in my life. He just beat the hell out of me." Kennedy had been advised not to rush into a high-level meeting. Khrushchev left Vienna with the impression that Kennedy was weak and inexperienced. It would set a dangerous precedent for future Cold War relations between the two leaders.

❋ ❋ ❋

The National League's Winningest Pitcher

On Sunday afternoon, June 11 at the Coliseum, Sandy Koufax beat the Phillies 6–3. It was his sixth consecutive complete-game victory, and improved his record to 9–2, the most wins in the National League. He fell behind 3–1 in the third inning when the Phillies' Lee Walls touched him for a 3-run home run. But he calmed down to shut out the Phillies over the remaining 6⅔ innings, allowing only 2 more hits and striking out 10. With 14 hits, including 3 home runs, the Dodgers completed a 3-game sweep of Philadelphia to end the day in a virtual tie for first place with the Cincinnati Reds.[11]

The Dodgers flew to San Francisco the next day for a brief 2-game series with the Giants, who pleasingly knocked them out of first place by beating Roger Craig and Stan Williams on successive days at Candlestick. Back in Los Angeles on June 14, Drysdale lifted them back into first by a half game over Cincinnati with a home run and a brilliant 5-hit, 7–0 shutout of the Cubs. At the end of play on June 15, they remained in that position as they waited for the Milwaukee Braves to come to town.

Stopped by the Lew Burdette Show

On June 16, 32,860 fans came to the Coliseum on a Friday night to see Sandy Koufax extend his 6-game winning streak in the opening game of a 3-game series with the Braves. What they saw instead was the Lew Burdette Show.

Lew Burdette snapped Sandy Koufax's 6-game winning streak with a home run and a 5-hitter at the Coliseum on June 16, 1961 (George Brace photograph).

Selva Lewis Burdette was a perpetual thorn in the side of the Dodgers. He had already beaten them eight straight times at the Coliseum. With two outs in the fifth inning of a scoreless tie, in typical Burdette style, he ran up to the plate with a bat in his hand and hit a surprised Koufax's first pitch over the left-field screen for a solo homer. It was his sixth career home run in the Coliseum. Koufax thought he had made a good pitch. Alston called it a "perfect pitch, a curve ball low and inside—just where it was supposed to go."[12] Regardless of the esthetics, Koufax and the Dodgers were behind, 1–0, after five.

On the mound, Burdette made the Dodger hitters look inept for the first six innings with an assortment of pitches coming out of a mass of gyrations—including a widely reputed spitball. *New York Times* sportswriter Red Smith once said of Burdette, "There should be 3 pitching statistics for Burdette: Wins, Losses, and Relative Humidity."

In the seventh inning the "old" Koufax reappeared. "I hurt myself by forgetting everything I had learned," he would recall.[13] After he walked Gino Cimoli and Frank Bolling, and sent Cimoli to third base with a wild pitch, he began to stamp around the mound in frustration. He then reverted to brute strength to Ed Mathews, walking him on five pitches to load the bases. With Henry Aaron strolling to the plate with a .452 career batting average against Koufax, Alston took the ball out of Koufax's hand and gave it to Larry Sherry. Sherry got Aaron to fly out, but walked home Cimoli on a close 3–2 pitch to Joe Adcock to make it 2–0, Milwaukee. Charlie Neal spoiled Burdette's shutout with a solo home run in the bottom of the inning. It was the last hit for the Dodgers, who quietly went down in order the rest of the way to a 2–1 loss. With his 5-hit one-man show, Burdette ended Koufax's 6-game winning streak and set the Dodgers back to a half-game behind the Reds.

The Dodgers split the remaining two games of the weekend series with the Braves to fall a full two games behind Cincinnati. As they prepared to embark on a 15-game road trip, they needed to call on Sandy Koufax to keep them in the pennant race.

Masterpiece at Wrigley Field

The road trip started on June 20 in Chicago. Last year, at this point in the season, Sandy Koufax was adrift with a record of 2–8. Today, he pitched a dazzling 2-hit, 3–0 shutout over the Cubs in Wrigley Field to bring his record to league-leading 10–3. He struck out 14 batters to bring his season total to 111—also the best in the National League.

The Dodgers scored all three of their runs in the top of the seventh off Cubs starter Glen Hobbie. Roseboro led off with a single. Daryl Spencer hit a double play ground ball to shortstop that Andre Rodgers threw away, advancing Roseboro to third and Spencer to second. After Koufax struck out, Maury Wills singled home Roseboro, and Charlie Neal knocked in Spencer and Wills to make it 3–0. With Koufax in complete command—utilizing only a fastball and a curve—the game was virtually over.

Koufax still had a no-hitter with two out in the seventh inning when Ernie Banks hit a clean single to left field. He had his second career 1-hitter until his old Brooklyn teammate Don Zimmer hit a single to center with one out in the ninth. It took Koufax only two more pitches to erase him with a double play to end the game.[14] It was another truly dominating performance. He issued only two walks—both to Billy Williams. Williams was the only Chicago runner to reach second base. The Cubs hit only three balls to the outfield—all for outs.

With the gem by Sandy Koufax, the Dodgers leaped over the Giants and back into second place, a game and a half behind Cincinnati. They went on take three out of four games from the Cubs heading into a big 3-game weekend series with the Reds at Crosley Field in Cincinnati.

The Perils of Pitching to Frank Robinson

Coming into Cincinnati on June 23, the Dodgers found a Reds team that was on fire. They had just won eight of their last nine games thanks Frank Robinson's 4 home runs, 15 RBIs. and .463 batting average. They again led the National League by two games over the second-place Dodgers. Don Drysdale (5–4), who had never won a game at Crosley Field, faced Jim O'Toole (6–6) in the opener. Drysdale walked the torrid Frank Robinson the first two times he faced him, once intentionally. He made the mistake of pitching to him the third time in the sixth inning while leading 4–2 with a runner on third base. Robinson tied the game 4–4 with a line drive home run over the center field wall, and Drysdale was gone with no chance to win his sixth game. The Dodgers would go back to walking Robinson, but the damage was done. Robinson had put them in position to be beaten, 5–4, on a bases loaded single by shortstop Eddie Kasko in the bottom of the ninth. It was a bitter 1-run defeat for the Dodgers, who were now three games behind.[15]

The next day, June 24, Sandy Koufax (10–3) did not have any better luck with Frank Robinson. Koufax had a 2–0 lead with two outs in the third inning when a defensive lapse by Charlie Neal prolonged the inning and opened the floodgates. An annoyed Koufax walked Vada Pinson on four pitches to load the bases for Robinson, who cleared them with his second consecutive double off Koufax. Gene Freese followed with a 2-run home run. Sandy Koufax managed to survive the inning, but it would be his last. Instead of moving on to the fourth with a 2–0 lead on the way to his eleventh win, he was out of the game after three, trailing 5–2.

In what turned into a wild game, the Dodgers were down to their last out, trailing 7–6 in the top of the ninth inning—and about to fall to four games behind Cincinnati— when pinch-hitter Frank Howard tied the game with a home run off Reds reliever Bill Henry. Two batters later, Junior Gilliam hit a 2-run homer off Henry to give the Dodgers a 9–7 come-from-behind win. It was the fifth home run of the game for the Dodgers, who now led the National League with 93 in 69 games.[16] Sandy Koufax escaped with a no decision as rookie reliever Ron Perranoski picked up his fourth win.

On Sunday, June 25, Stan Williams (6–6) and Joey Jay (8–4) squared off before a standing-room-only crowd of 28,763 at Crosley Field for the series finale. Williams got off to a rocky start in the first inning, giving up three runs on two hits and a balk. The only thing the Dodgers did right was to walk Frank Robinson intentionally. When Alston came out to question the balk, he was ejected. They were behind 3–0 after one with

Leo Durocher in control. Joey Jay shut them down until the seventh inning, when they scored two runs on two walks, an error, a single by Daryl Spencer and a double by Maury Wills. When Jim Gilliam tried to score the tying run on Wills's double, Frank Robinson threw him out at home plate.

Durocher understood the importance of the game and used Sandy Koufax, Roger Craig, Ron Perranoski, and Don Drysdale to try to keep it from slipping away. But the Dodgers never recovered from the first inning, going down to a 3–2 defeat to lose the series two games to one. They had no answer for Frank Robinson. Even though they held him hitless, he still made a play to beat them. The Dodgers left Cincinnati in the same position they were in when they arrived: three games behind the Reds.

On June 29 in Pittsburgh, Sandy Koufax (10–3) pitched the rubber game of a 3-game series with the Pirates on a muggy night at Forbes Field. The Reds had already lost their day game at Wrigley Field, and the Dodgers could cut Cincinnati's lead to a game and a half. Koufax tore through the Pirate lineup for the first seven innings, striking out 9 batters while allowing just 4 hits and no runs. He took a 2–0 lead into the eighth and struck out the first two batters. The humidity began to take its toll on Koufax as Bill Virdon and Johnny Logan singled, bringing Walter Alston out to the mound. Alston made the risky decision to let Koufax pitch to Roberto Clemente. Clemente was having his breakout year, hitting .335 at this point in the season. Clemente lined Koufax's first pitch into left field for a game-tying 2-run double. It was his last pitch of the game. Larry Sherry was brought in to get Dick Stuart. Stuart hit a high bouncing ball that Jim Gilliam got his glove on before it trickled into left field to score Clemente for the go-ahead run.[17] Don Hoak followed with a triple to score Stuart to make it 4–2, Pirates. The Dodgers entered the ninth inning in a state of shock, having blown a 2–0 lead with 4 outs to go and Koufax on the mound. El Roy Face set them down in order on seven pitches. It was a galling loss for Koufax and the Dodgers. He lost a shutout and a golden chance for his eleventh win, and the team lost a chance to gain on the Reds, remaining two and a half games behind.

Thanks to a dazzling performance by their 21-year-old rookie center fielder Willie Davis, the Dodgers ended the month of June with a 10–6 win in Philadelphia on June 30. Davis ran out from under his cap as he stretched two doubles into triples to drive in three runs. He saved two more runs with an impossible one-handed, twisting stab of Pancho Herrera's 425-foot drive hit over his head into the deepest part of Connie Mack Stadium. It was a ball that no one except Willie Davis—the fastest man in major league baseball—could have reached.[18] With the win, the Dodgers stayed two and a half games behind Cincinnati in second place as they headed into July.

	W	L	PCT.	*
Cincinnati	45	28	.616	
Los Angeles	43	31	.581	2½
San Francisco	41	31	.569	3½

*Games behind leader

The Dodgers completed a 3-game sweep of the Phillies on July 2 and moved on to Milwaukee for a 2-game series with the Braves.

A Koufax Gem Saved by Wills

On July 3, four days after his debacle in Pittsburgh, Sandy Koufax took on the Braves on a cold and rainy night in County Stadium. He pitched brilliantly for eight innings, allowing only three hits and striking out seven batters. With the game tied 2–2 in the top of the ninth and the Dodgers down to their last three outs, he was pulled for a pinch hitter. He was headed for another no decision unless the Dodgers pulled it out now. Two batters later, Maury Wills singled home John Roseboro for the go-ahead run. Wills had tripled in the Dodgers' first run in the first inning and was now hitting .323 to move into a tie with Wally Moon as the club's top batter.[19] Larry Sherry came in from the bullpen to hold the Braves scoreless in the ninth and save the game for Koufax.

Sandy Koufax now led the league in wins with an 11–4 record and in strikeouts with 135. Through 77 games—at the halfway point in the season—he had already equaled his 1958 mark for most wins in season. On July 6 he would be named to his first All-Star team.

Schooled by Robby

In Los Angeles on July 9, the Sunday before the first All-Star break, the Dodgers were hopeful of gaining a split in their 4-game series with the Cincinnati Reds to stay within 3 games of first-place Cincinnati. Joey Jay (11–4), tied with Sandy Koufax for most wins in the National League, was on the mound for the Reds, against Roger Craig (3–4) for the Dodgers. Craig hadn't won a game since May 20, in what would be his last year in Los Angeles. But there was a bigger problem for the Dodgers: Frank Robinson. Robinson, on his way to the league Most Valuable Player award, came into the game hitting .318, and was already 4 for 9 in the series with a double and a home run. Out of respect—and fear—the Dodger pitchers simply referred to him as Robby.

Frank Robinson was born August 31, 1935, in Beaumont, Texas, and raised—mostly by his mother—in a rough section of West Oakland, California. The youngest of 11 children, he learned early to be aggressive—just to survive at the dinner table. He was a tall, skinny kid who was drawn to the baseball diamond near his mother's house, where he played every afternoon until dark.

Frank Robinson led the Cincinnati Reds to the World Series for the first time in 21 years in his MVP year of 1961 (George Brace photograph).

Frank's absentee father told his brothers, "Frank will never make a big-league baseball player."[20] This stinging rebuke gave him a fierce determination to prove his father wrong.

McClymonds High School in Oakland, where he entered as a freshman in the fall of 1950, was the scene of a life-changing experience for young Frank. It was there that he met George Powles, a white coach who molded many impoverished black children into professional athletes.[21] Under Powles, he played baseball, as well as basketball alongside future NBA Hall of Famer Bill Russell. From Powles, Robinson learned to think positively and play aggressively. The result: in June 1953, one week after graduating from McClymonds, 17-year-old Frank Robinson signed a contract with the Cincinnati Reds for a bonus of $3,500.[22] Off he went to Ogden, Utah, to play the second half of the season in the Class C Pioneer League, where he hit .348 with 17 home runs in 72 games.

Robinson was in the minor leagues for only two more years, mostly in Columbia, South Carolina, in the Class A South Atlantic League. It was there that he was shocked by the racism of Jim Crow America. He was turned away at movie theaters and restaurants. Traveling with the Columbia Reds, he was unable to leave the team bus to get food or use the bathroom. He could not lodge with the team. He had to be shunted across town to either a rented room without air conditioning, the YMCA, or a private home. Once on the field, fans attacked him with stigmatizing taunts and jeers such as "Hey, nigger" or "Coon boy!"[23]

In 1954, his first year in Columbia, he had an eye-opening season worthy of promotion: 25 home runs and a .336 batting average. But when he hurt his shoulder the following March in spring training with the Reds, he was sent back to Columbia for 1955. His situation quickly became a crisis. He couldn't throw and he couldn't swing, and his batting average plummeted to .190. When the team left for Charlotte, North Carolina, a depressed Frank Robinson decided he was going home. His teammate, Marv Williams, decided he wasn't going to be the only black on the team, and told Robinson he wasn't going on to Charlotte, either. After considerable thought, Robinson realized he would be throwing his life away by deserting the team. It was a turning point for the 19-year-old Frank Robinson. He and Williams decided to join the team in Charlotte, where they were the beneficiaries some unexpected good fortune. Since the game they missed had been rained out, they hadn't officially "missed" anything.[24]

On Opening Day 1956, a hardened 20-year-old Frank Robinson was in the starting lineup as the left fielder for the Cincinnati Reds. His minor league experiences in the South had sharpened his cutthroat style. In the batter's box, he dared pitchers to hit him by literally hanging over the plate. They were only too willing to oblige, drilling him a league-leading 20 times that first season. When they hit him, he would take his base, then take it out on their infielders. He soon established a reputation as the league's most aggressive base runner, barreling into second basemen, knocking shortstops into the outfield, ripping tendons and ligaments, and breaking limbs.[25] National League pitchers had good reason to back him off the plate. That first season he set a new Major League record for rookies with 38 home runs.

In his first five years, Robinson established himself as one of the National League's premier power-hitting outfielders, averaging 33 home runs and 90 runs batted in. But he would have a transcendent, breakout season in 1961.

Today at the Coliseum, Robinson got to Roger Craig early with a 2-run home run in the first inning. By the time Craig allowed the Reds to load the bases in the top of the third, he was removed. Sandy Koufax came in from the bullpen, but he couldn't stop the Reds from scoring their third and fourth runs as they put the game out of reach at 4–2, Cincinnati. Koufax held the Reds until the fifth, when he was unable to stop Frank Robinson from hitting yet another line drive—although this one was a mere single. Desperate to stay within reach of the Reds, the Dodgers brought in their other premier starter, Don Drysdale, from the bullpen. But it was no use. The Reds pounded Drysdale for another 3 runs to make it 7–2, Cincinnati after five.

Drysdale Boils Over

The 90-degree heat at the Coliseum did not help the mood of the hot-tempered Drysdale. In the sixth, he buzzed leadoff batter Don Blasingame's head before getting Blasingame to pop up. Then he sent a message to Vada Pinson with two inside fast balls. When Pinson doubled, Drysdale boiled over. When his first pitch to Frank Robinson sent him sprawling in the dirt, umpire Dusty Boggess issued a warning to Drysdale along with an automatic $50 fine. After Drysdale's next pitch knocked Robinson down again, Reds manager Fred Hutchinson charged out of the dugout to complain to Boggess. Drysdale was undeterred. His next pitch struck Robinson in the arm. That was enough for Boggess. Drysdale was summarily ejected.

Tour de Force

In the eighth inning, with the Reds enjoying a commanding 8–3 lead, it was Dodger reliever Turk Farrell's turn to face Frank Robinson. And it was not pretty. Robinson hit Farrell's first pitch on a line over the left-field screen for his second 2-run homer of the game. But Robinson was not done with Farrell. In the ninth inning with the bases loaded, he punished him again with base-clearing 3-run double to make the final score 14–3, Cincinnati. Frank Robinson was finally on his way out of Los Angeles, but not before going 4 for 4, with a double, 2 home runs, and 7 runs batted in to raise his batting average 10 points in one day to .328.[26]

Instead of splitting the series with the Reds, the Dodgers ended up losing three out of four to fall five games behind Cincinnati going into the first All-Star break.

	W	L	Pct.	*
Cincinnati	54	30	.643	
Los Angeles	49	35	.583	5
Pittsburgh	42	35	.545	8½

*Games behind leader

Sandy Koufax, All-Star

Two days later on July 11, Sandy Koufax made his first All-Star appearance in San Francisco. With the NL leading, 3–2, in the ninth inning, he was brought in to face just one batter, the AL right fielder who was having a pretty good year. Roger Maris, already with 33 home runs in the first 83 games, hit Koufax's first pitch for a ringing single into right field. After only one pitch, he gave way to Giants' ace reliever Stu Miller. Miller would achieve immortality one batter later when a gust of wind at Candlestick Park blew him off the mound like a tumbleweed. The umpires charged Miller with a balk, allowing the American League to tie the game at 3–3. Willie Mays scored the fourth and winning run for the NL before his hometown fans in the tenth on Roberto Clemente's game-winning single. Clemente would go on to win his first of four batting titles with the Pirates.

The Low Point

On July 15, a Saturday afternoon at the Coliseum, the Dodgers lost their second straight game to the last-place Philadelphia Phillies, 7–2. As a result, the Dodgers lost a 3-game series to a Phillies team that came into Los Angeles playing .291 baseball. Sandy Koufax, seeking his twelfth win, was bombed by the worst hitting team in the league for five earned runs on eight hits—including two doubles, a triple, and a home run—in 7⅓ innings. The loss dropped his record to 11–6, and the Dodgers were now six full games behind the Cincinnati Reds

July 15 was the low point of the 1961 season for the Los Angeles Dodgers. Things would begin to turn around the next day as the Dodgers began a 19–3 run and the Reds began a 6-game losing streak.

A Koufax Save and the Asterisk Bomb

On July 17, Sandy Koufax got a rare save when he came in from the bullpen in the eighth inning against the Pirates at Forbes Field to rescue a staggering Stan Williams. Williams, who had started the inning with a 6–2 lead, gave up solo home runs to the first two Pirate batters. Koufax was given a chance to recover from his demoralizing performance at the hands of the Phillies before the team headed for Cincinnati. He retired the next six batters in a row, including the red-hot Roberto Clemente, who was batting .359. In the process he saved Stan Williams's tenth win and completed a 2-game sweep for the Dodgers.

That day in New York, Commissioner Ford Frick called a press conference at his office in Rockefeller Plaza to address an escalating controversy. In the first year of the new 162-game American League schedule, Roger Maris and Mickey Mantle were threatening the most sacred record in sports: Babe Ruth's 60 home runs. With 35 home runs through the first 88 games, Maris was 14 games ahead of Ruth's 1927 pace. Mantle was close behind with 33. Frick, a personal friend of Ruth, made the following announcement:

> Any player who may hit more than 60 home runs during his club's first 154 games would be recognized as having established a new record. However, if the player does not hit more than 60 until after his club has played 154 games, there would have to be some distinctive mark in the record books to show that Babe Ruth's record was set under a 154-game schedule and the total of more than 60 was compiled while a 162-game schedule was in effect.[27]

Thus the infamous asterisk controversy was born without any mention of the word "asterisk."

Momentum Shift at Crosey Field

Major League Baseball Commissioner Ford Frick (George Brace photograph).

The Dodgers returned to Cincinnati on July 19 for a 2-game series at Crosley Field. The Reds had just lost three games in a row to cut their lead to 3½. Johnny Podres, having his finest season, beat the Reds with a complete game 8–3 victory in the opener to improve his record to 11–2.

The next night, Sandy Koufax (11–6) faced Cincinnati's ace, Joey Jay (13–4) in the concluding game. The Dodgers pounded Joey Jay for nine runs and ten hits, including home runs by Norm Larker, Duke Snider, Wally Moon, and Willie Davis, before he was driven from the game after five innings. Koufax got off to a shaky start, falling behind 1–0 when Vada Pinson doubled and the ubiquitous Frank Robinson—now hitting .341—drove him in with a line-drive single. Then Koufax found his rhythm, shutting out the Reds the rest of the way for a 10–1 complete-game victory. It was another milestone for Sandy Koufax. His twelfth win was a new personal best.

The Dodgers left Cincinnati sensing that the momentum had shifted. Just five days before, they were six games behind the Reds. Now they trailed by only a game and a half. And Koufax, who hadn't won a game since July 3, was back on track.

Soaring Over Pittsburgh

After the trough of July 15, the Dodgers looked like a different team as they concluded the month of July with an 8-game winning streak. They concluded their 11-game road trip with a weekend series in Pittsburg. Podres won his thirteenth game in the opener on July 28. He was pitching a shutout until Dick Stuart unloaded on him with a 2-run homer with two out in the seventh. When he waivered again in the ninth, Dick Farrell came in from the bullpen to get the final out for a 6–4 Dodger win—their sixth in a row.

Koufax (13–6) and fellow left-hander Harvey Haddix (6–5) met in the second game on July 29. After winning his thirteenth game with a complete-game 10-strikeout effort four days before in Philadelphia, Koufax turned in what was a largely a lackluster performance. In six innings of work, he gave up two runs on eight hits, while striking out seven. With the Dodgers trailing 2–1 in the seventh inning, Walter Alston took him out for a pinch hitter, thus leaving him on the hook for a loss. The Dodgers came from behind to win it 5–4 in the ninth on a game-tying pinch home run by Duke Snider and a tie-breaking pinch single by Ron Fairly.[28] Ron Perranoski won his sixth game in relief, and Sandy Koufax had his fifth no decision of the year to stay at 13–6. With their seventh consecutive win, the Dodgers went into a virtual tie (ahead by .002) for first with the Reds.

Don Drysdale completed the 3-game sweep of the Pirates on Sunday, July 30, the last day before the second All-Star break. Drysdale and rookie relief sensation Ron Perranoski combined for a 7–3 win. Despite giving up three hits to Roberto Clemente—whose average had now reached .360—Drysdale (9–6) ended his 3-game losing streak with a strong 6-hit, 8-strikeout performance over the first eight innings. After the first two batters reached base in the ninth, Perranoski came in to retire the next three in order to end the game.

The Dodgers went into the second All-Star break running on all cylinders. They had just won their eighth game in a row to take over first place by themselves, a half-game ahead of Cincinnati.

	W	L	PCT.	*
Los Angeles	62	38	.620	
Cincinnati	63	40	.612	½
San Francisco	54	46	.540	8

*Games behind leader

They were hitting: Wills was at .301, Tommy Davis .314, and Wally Moon .327. They were first in the league in pitching. Sandy Koufax, now in control of his temper—and the baseball—was tied with teammate Johnny Podres for second in the league in wins, was first in strikeouts, and was on his way to his second All-Star game.

Koufax at Fenway

The second 1961 All-Star game was played at Fenway Park in Boston on July 31. Maury Wills was the starting shortstop and leadoff man for the National League, with John Roseboro, Don Drysdale, and Sandy Koufax also representing the Dodgers.

NL manager Danny Murtaugh put Koufax into the game in the fifth inning with the AL ahead, 1–0. He gave up a lead-off single to Brooks Robinson, then converted a bunt back to him into a double play to erase Robinson, and got Norm Cash—leading the majors with a .365 average—to ground out. Koufax was left in to pitch the sixth with the score tied, 1–1. After Al Kaline reached base on an infield single, the capacity crowd of 31,851 rose in anticipation as Mickey Mantle came to the plate hitting .329

with 39 home runs (1 behind Roger Maris's 40). Koufax, who had not given up a home run in his last 35⅓ innings, blew him away on three pitches. He then got Mantle's teammate, Elston Howard (batting .351), to ground out to third. Koufax faced one batter over the minimum in his two shutout innings. The national television audience got a glimpse of Sandy Koufax in his transitional year before he ascended to the otherworldly level of his last five.

Nine

Showdown in August

You scared hell out of me. I thought I'd just gotten my pink slip.[1]—Walter Alston to club statistician Alan Roth after Roth left a pink stat sheet for him the night of the Dodgers' tenth straight loss

On August 2 at the Coliseum, in their first game after the second All-Star break, Juan Marichal ended the Dodgers' 8-game winning streak with a 1-hit, 6–0 blanking. Tommy Davis prevented a no-hitter with a line-drive single in the fifth inning. Felipe Alou sent Podres to his third defeat with two home runs and four runs batted in. Despite two sub-par performances by Sandy Koufax, the club bounced back to go on another 7–1 run over the next ten days.

The Pinnacle

On August 13, Stan Williams (10–8) faced off against Bob Gibson (8–8) on a Sunday afternoon at the Coliseum. Back on July 6, Gibson finally escaped racist Cardinal manager Solly Hemus, who had been shuttling him between the bullpen and the starting rotation for nearly two years. Johnny Keane, Gibson's former manager at Omaha, replaced Hemus as manager. From that day to the end of his career, Bob Gibson would be a starting pitcher.

Stan Williams had one of his best games of the season. He shut out the Cardinals 8–0 on eight hits with eight strikeouts. The Dodgers beat Bob Gibson for the fourth time in the season. Gibson was gone after two innings with the Dodgers in front, 4–0. It was the high water mark for the 1961 Dodger pitching staff: their third consecutive complete-game victory—even without a contribution from Koufax. Drysdale, Podres, and Williams gave up just one earned run in 27 innings.[2] The game would prove to be both the pinnacle and the hinge of the Dodgers' season, as they completed a 19–3 run to take a 2½-game lead over Cincinnati.

	W	L	Pᴄᴛ.	*
Los Angeles	69	40	.633	
Cincinnati	70	46	.603	2½
San Francisco	60	50	.545	9½

*Games behind leader

Noticeably, the Dodgers scored their eight runs without the benefit of a home run. To date, their leading home run hitter, Johnny Roseboro, had only 16 and ranked 16th in the league.[3] Frank Howard was a major disappointment with just 11. Daryl Spencer, who had hit six home runs after coming over from St. Louis at the end of May, broke a bone in his knee sliding into Ed Mathews in Milwaukee on the Fourth of July. By now it was evident that there was a power imbalance at the top of the NL standings. The Reds had Frank Robinson, already with 33 home runs. The Giants had Cepeda with 31 and Mays with 30.

* * *

That day East German soldiers armed with machine guns threw barbed wire across the line that divided East and West Berlin. It would be the first step in sealing the border for the next 28 years.[4] Emboldened by Kennedy's showing of weakness two months before at the Vienna summit meeting, Soviet Premier Khrushchev gave the go-ahead to begin erecting what would become the Berlin Wall.

* * *

The Beginning of the End

On the eve of a 3-game series with Cincinnati, the momentum was broken on August 14 as the Cardinals pounded Don Drysdale 5–0 at the Coliseum. It would be the start of a disastrous 10-game losing streak.

The Reds came into Los Angeles on August 15 trailing the Dodgers by two games in the standings to begin a critical 3-game series at the Coliseum. The opener, a Tuesday night game before 47,515, was a head-to-head matchup between both team's premier pitchers: Joey Jay (16–7) for the Reds and Sandy Koufax (13–7) for the Dodgers. After surging through June and July, Koufax was coming off two disappointing outings at home to begin August. On the 4th he was beaten by the Cubs after serving up 2 home runs to their 6'4" right

Right-hander Joey Jay, the first little leaguer to make it to the major leagues, would win 21 games for the 1961 Reds and finish 5th in the MVP voting (George Brace photograph).

fielder, George Altman. This was followed by a lackluster no decision performance against the Braves on the 8th.

Tonight the Dodgers needed Koufax to be on his game to preserve their lead. But he was unable to deliver. The Dodgers got to Jay for two runs in the first inning. But the truculent Frank Robinson hammered Koufax for a 2-run double to tie the score in the fifth. It was his 20th RBI of the season against the Dodgers. In fact, Koufax never could hold the Reds that night. In the sixth, Wally Post got to him with a towering home run into the left-center-field seats. After six innings he was out of the game, trailing 4–2. After his rocky first inning, Joey Jay settled down to shut out the Dodgers on four singles over the final eight innings to give the Reds a 5–2 win.

Koufax's inability to beat the Reds proved consequential. It allowed them to move to within one game of the Dodgers in the standings, with a double-header between the two clubs scheduled for the next evening. After their first sixteen head-to-head meetings, the Dodgers and Reds were now deadlocked at eight wins apiece.[5]

As the Dodgers and Reds worked out prior to their August 16 twi-night double-header, it was evident that they would be playing in front of an enormous crowd. That crowd would ultimately reach 75,364, a new league record for a night game.[6] The thrifty Walter O'Malley did not like to schedule double-headers at the Coliseum. Two games for the price of one was not his style. While the Reds had already played fifteen double-headers, the Dodgers had played only three.

Since the Dodgers had only four starters, double-headers put big pressure on Walter Alston's rotation. Consequently, Alston was forced to give reliever Larry Sherry (4–2) a rare start in the first game against Cincinnati's Bob Purkey (13–7). Sherry, who was making his first start since April of 1960, was clearly no longer comfortable in that role, and he would not last long. The Reds got to him for four runs in the first inning. In the third, after Vada Pinson lined a double off him, a frustrated Sherry promptly sent Frank Robinson into the dirt on his back with a high fast ball. But as always with Robinson, there was a cost. He dusted himself off and sent Sherry's next—and final—pitch over the left-field screen for his 34th home run of the season. With the Dodgers behind 6–0, Walter Alston immediately removed Sherry. The carnage inflicted on the 1961 Dodgers by Frank Robinson was reaching epic proportions: 6 home runs, 23 runs batted in, and a .432 batting average.

At the same time, the Dodger hitters could do nothing against right-hander Purkey. They could manage only four singles, as Purkey shut them out 6–0. The two teams were now tied for first place going into the second game of the double-header.

The second game was a contest of left-handers: Johnny Podres (15–3) made his regularly scheduled start for the Dodgers against the Reds' Jim O'Toole (11–9). The Dodger hitters were even more pathetic against O'Toole, managing only two singles. Meanwhile, Gene Freeze and the Reds pulverized Podres. After the Cincinnati third baseman got to him with a solo home run in the fourth and a 3-run home run in the eighth, the game was out of reach at 5–0 in favor of Cincinnati. Frank Robinson was trouble enough. But Freeze had just surpassed him as Cincinnati's top home run producer against the Dodgers with eight. When it was over, O'Toole had shut out the Dodgers again—this time 8–0. It was the first time the Dodgers had been shut out in both games of a double-header since 1935.[7]

Just 48 hours before, the Dodgers had led the Reds by two games. Now they trailed Cincinnati by a full game.

	W	L	Pct.	*
Cincinnati	73	46	.613	
Los Angeles	69	44	.611	1
San Francisco	62	50	.554	7½

*Games behind leader

On the eve of beginning a new road trip in San Francisco, the Dodger offense was in hibernation, having scored only 2 runs in their last 37 innings.

On Losing Ten in a Row

The Giants were only too happy to extend the Dodgers' losing streak in a 3-game week-end series beginning August 18 at Candlestick. In the opener, Don Drysdale had the Giants shut out until his worst nightmare, Willie McCovey, hit a home run in the seventh to make it 1–0, Giants. In the ninth, the Dodgers were one out away from being shut out again on three hits when Jim Gilliam tied the game 1–1 with an RBI single off Stu Miller to send the game into extra innings. But Orlando Cepeda ended it in the tenth with a solo home run off Larry Sherry.

The drought persisted as Juan Marichal and Stu Miller shut them out 5–0 the next day. In the finale on Sunday, August 20, Sandy Koufax lasted only three innings. The Giants pounded him for six earned runs on eight hits, including home runs by Willie Mays and Felipe Alou. The 11–8 loss was the fifth consecutive start without a win for Koufax and the seventh consecutive loss for the Dodgers.

Reds left-hander Jim O'Toole. On August 16, 1961, O'Toole teamed with Bob Purkey to knock the Dodgers out of first place with a double-header sweep in front of 75,364 at the Coliseum.

Things continued to deteriorate for the Dodgers in St. Louis. Johnny Podres lasted just 3⅓ innings in a 5–4 loss to the Cardinals on August 22. Don Drysdale could not stop the slide the next night. He took a 7–4 lead into the bottom of the eighth when the Cardinals tied the game on home runs by Bill White and Ken Boyer. Before the inning was over, Curt Flood had put the Cardinals in front 8–7 with an RBI single off a struggling Larry Sherry. The Dodgers went quietly in the ninth for their ninth straight loss. After the Cardinals destroyed Stan Williams and five other Dodger pitchers 10–1 the next day, the losing streak had reached ten straight with a date with the Reds to begin in 24 hours in Cincinnati.

Fatal Weekend in Cincinnati

The Dodgers came staggering into Cincinnati with their longest losing streak since 1944. It had been a disastrous 10-day slide that caused them to fall from first place, 2½ games ahead of the Reds, to second place, 3½ games behind them. It coincided with a major batting slump, with the Dodgers hitting only .143 with no home runs and only 3 runs scored in the first six games of the losing streak. The gravity of the situation caused General Manager Buzzie Bavasi to cut short his La Jolla vacation to fly in and join the team at Crosley Field. At a press conference before the game, Bavasi gave Walter Alston a much needed vote of confidence: "[W]e have as high a regard for Alston's managerial ability now as before the team went into the slump."[8] But Bavasi did not disclose what was really on his mind: this 4-game weekend series was critical to preventing the season from slipping away.

Koufax Stops the Free Fall

In the Friday night opener, Alston was counting on Sandy Koufax (13–9) to step up and be the stopper. Only he didn't know which Koufax would show up. His All-Star left-hander had been ineffective in his last five starts, with three losses and two no decisions since July 29. The stoic Koufax did not reveal until after the season that he had been fighting a month-long losing battle with the flu.[9]

From the start it was clear that Koufax was not his overpowering self. But like all great pitchers, he made the best of the stuff that he had. After allowing a solo home run to the Reds' little second baseman, Elio Chacon, in the third, and yet another Frank Robinson double coupled with an RBI single to Gene Freese in the fourth, Koufax held the Reds scoreless on 2 singles over the final five innings. He was finally able to get some offensive support. Frank Howard drove in three runs with two home runs, and Duke Snider drove in two more with a home run and a triple—all off Reds starter Bob Purkey. The 7–2 complete-game win by Sandy Koufax stopped the Dodgers' 10-game losing streak, and moved them to within 2½ games of the Reds.[10]

Saved by Perranoski

On August 26 the Dodgers and Reds resumed the series with a Saturday day game in another battle of the left-handers. Alston went with Johnny Podres (15–4); the Reds went with the seldom used Jay Hook (1–2). Hook had made only one start since April, and his rustiness showed. He never survived the Dodgers' 4-run second inning outburst, leaving after 1⅔ with the Reds down, 4–0. The Dodgers—sparked by another mammoth shot over the center-field wall by Frank Howard—continued to destroy a parade of

Cincinnati pitchers, building up a 10–1 lead going into the bottom of the seventh. Perhaps it was the huge lead—a shutout except for a solo home run in the sixth by the irrepressible Frank Robinson—that caused Podres to lose focus at that point in the game. He never got another batter out. After allowing three straight singles and a grand slam home run to Vada Pinson to cut the Dodger lead to 10–5, he had to be relieved by the unpredictable Larry Sherry.

The outcome of the game began to look in doubt in the bottom of the eighth inning. After getting the first two batters out, Sherry gave up a home run to Gordy Coleman, walked Elio Chacon, and surrendered a ground-rule double to Reds shortstop Leo Cardenas. With the dangerous left-handed-batting Pinson coming to the plate, Alston pulled Sherry and brought in left-handed reliever Ron Perranoski. Fortunately for Podres and the Dodgers, Perranoski disposed of Pinson with one pitch.[11]

Perranoski went on to retire the Reds in order in the ninth to preserve the Dodgers' 10–6 win. Podres was credited with his sixteenth victory, and the Dodgers moved up to within 1½ games of Cincinnati. They were in position to regain first place with a sweep of the Sunday double-header scheduled to conclude the series the following day.

A Sunday Debacle at Crosley Field

The Dodgers and Reds concluded their 4-game series on August 27 with a Sunday double-header at Crosley Field. In the first game, Stan Williams (11–0) faced off against the league's winningest pitcher, Joey Jay (18–8). Since Williams's brilliant shutout of the Cardinals on August 13, he had failed to last more than five innings in his next two starts, losing both.

Game 1—Dodgers Blow a Lead and the Season

In the first game, things began well for Stan Williams and the Dodgers. They built up a 5–1 lead against Joey Jay, knocking him out of the game before he could finish the seventh inning. But Williams began to fall apart in the bottom of the seventh. After he gave up a 3-run home run to Gene Freese, and walked the next batter, Alston removed him and brought in Ron Perranoski. Perranoski was able to get the Dodgers out of the seventh with a 5–4 lead. If he could hold it for two more innings, the Dodgers would actually go ahead of the Reds by .001 points in the standings.

The Dodgers gave Cincinnati a gift to open the eighth inning when second baseman Charlie Neal booted Jerry Lynch's leadoff ground ball. It would prove to be a costly error, as Leo Cardenas ended Perranoski's outing by tripling home Lynch to tie the score at 5–5. At that point a reluctant Walter Alston was forced to bring in Larry Sherry. It proved to be a disastrous move. Sherry walked Eddie Kasko intentionally, then allowed Wally Post to slam a pinch double down the third base line that scored Cardenas with the run that put the Reds ahead for good, 6–5. After the Reds brought in Jim O'Toole from the bullpen to retire the Dodgers in order in the ninth, it was over.

The loss proved to be a missed opportunity of catastrophic proportions for the

Dodgers. Instead of moving ahead of Cincinnati by a percentage point, they were now 2½ games back going into the second game of the double-header.

Game 2—Drysdale's Crosley Field Nightmare Continues

The shock of blowing a 5–1 lead in the first game was difficult to shake off. The Dodgers asked Don Drysdale (10–7) to salvage the second game and give them a 3–1 series win. It was a tall order for Drysdale, who had never won a game or completed a game in eight career starts at Crosley Field. The Reds called on a journeyman spot-starter named Ken Johnson (4–6), recently acquired from the American League, whom the Dodgers had never seen before.

It was not to be for Drysdale and the Dodgers. Before the sixth inning was over, they were behind 6–1, and Drysdale was out of the game. Once again, Perranoski was brought in to hold the Reds in the seventh. But it proved to be futile. Cincinnati lit up Perranoski for two more runs with two doubles and a triple to put the game out of reach. The Dodgers went down to a crushing 8–3 defeat in a game they were never in, at the hands of the unheard-of, but surprisingly difficult, Ken Johnson.[12]

It was the third double-header loss to the Reds for the season and a bitter turn-around for the Dodgers. After coming into Cincinnati with the potential to knock the Reds out of the lead, they left town in the same position as when they arrived: 3½ games behind. There were still 31 games to go, but none remaining with the Reds, who had just won the season series, 12 games to 10. The Dodgers' pennant ambitions had been dealt a devastating blow. *The Sporting News* would later look back on August 27 as the turning point in the 1961 season.[13]

	W	L	Pct.	*
Cincinnati	78	52	.600	
Los Angeles	71	52	.577	3½
San Francisco	68	55	.553	6½

*Games behind leader

Koufax Stops the Bleeding in Chicago

On August 29, in their first game after the double-header debacle in Cincinnati, the Dodgers once again called on their new stopper, Sandy Koufax (14–9), to right the ship—this time against the Cubs and their big right-hander Don Cardwell (11–11) at Wrigley Field.

With the wind blowing in from Lake Michigan, it was likely to be a pitcher's duel. And Koufax had a no-hitter—now becoming a regular possibility—until two batters were out in the bottom of the seventh inning. The no-hitter vanished when he gave up a RBI single to Chicago catcher Dick Bertell on a harmless fly ball that Wally Moon lost in the sun. The Dodgers could manage only three hits against Don Cardwell through the first eight innings, but two of them were sufficiently placed to produce a 2–1 lead going to the bottom of the ninth.

Koufax began to tire in the ninth. He walked the leadoff batter, Andre Rodgers. After he retired the next two batters, the Cubs got their second—and last—hit as Ron Santo singled Rodgers to third, representing the tying run. Alston had Sherry and Perranoski ready in the bullpen, but he decided to stay with Koufax. It took him only one more pitch to retire Bertell on a pop foul to wrap up a 2–1 victory.[14]

The 2-hit, 12-strikeout performance improved Koufax's record to 15–9. With six or seven potential starts remaining, it looked like 1961 was sure to be his first 20-win season. And he was starting to attract attention across the baseball world. With 212 strikeouts, he was closing in on the National League record of 267 set by Christy Mathewson in 1903. After this game, *Los Angeles Times* columnist Jim Murray called Koufax a "rare specimen," who was finally rewarding the Dodgers for their five years of patience.[15] Despite the effort by Koufax, the Dodgers could gain no ground on the Reds, who shut out the Pirates 3–0 at Forbes Field.

The next day, August 30, the Dodgers completed a sweep of the 2-game series at Wrigley Field as Johnny Podres beat the Cubs 5–2 for his seventeenth win of the season. Podres and Koufax were on track to be the Dodgers' first twin 20-game winners since Don Newcombe (20–9) and Preacher Roe (22–3) in 1951.

Ending August the Hard Way

On August 31, the Dodgers ended the month of August with a tough 2–1 loss to the Braves in Milwaukee despite a complete-game 6-hitter by Don Drysdale. After a scorching 19–7 month of July, they slipped to 11–15 in August. They were now three games behind Cincinnati with 28 games left to play.

	W	**L**	**Pct.**	*
Cincinnati	79	53	.598	
Los Angeles	73	53	.579	3
Milwaukee	70	57	.551	6½
San Francisco	69	57	.548	7

*Games behind leader

The Eyes of the Nation on M&M

The Dodgers-Reds pennant race took second stage to what was going on over in the American League. The eyes of the nation were on Roger Maris and Mickey Mantle as they chased Babe Ruth's single-season record of 60 home runs set in 1927. Through August, Maris had 51 home runs and Mantle had 48 with 29 games to go in the new 162-game expansion year season.

* * *

The Berlin Wall, hastily constructed in 18 days from prefabricated blocks of concrete, was completed on this day to finish sealing the border and stop the mass emigration to the West that had reached 2,000 per day on August 12. East Berliners would now need a special permit to cross the border.

❀   ❀   ❀

Roger Maris and Mickey Mantle (M&M) on their way to a record 115 home runs between them (National Baseball Hall of Fame Library, Cooperstown, New York).

Ten

The Coliseum Era
Comes to an End

Our team has been built on speed. But how could the Davis boys, Wills, or Gilliam go from first to third at the Coliseum on a ball hit to a left field fence which is just behind short-stop?[1]—Walter Alston

It took Warren Spahn only an hour and 59 minutes to shut out the Dodgers 4–0 on September 2 at County Stadium in Milwaukee. Spahn came into the game with an abysmal 16–31 record against the Dodgers, and had not shut them out since 1949.[2] Sandy Koufax went down to his tenth defeat as the Dodgers ended a disastrous 5-win/10-loss road trip 3½ games behind Cincinnati, with seven straight games with the Giants to begin the next day. Koufax, now 15–10, never recovered from a shaky 3-run first inning set up by a Maury Wills error. It was not Koufax's night. He had only two strikeouts in seven innings, and even gave up a home run to Sammy White, a backup catcher who came into the game batting .176.

Living by the Giants, Dying by the Giants

The Dodgers returned to Los Angeles on September 3 to begin a 4-game series with the Giants at the Coliseum. In the opener Podres beat the Giants 5–4 for his eighteenth win. This was followed by a 4–0 shutout by Don Drysdale on September 4, and a 4–2 complete game victory by Stan Williams on September 5.

On September 6 Sandy Koufax (15–10) and Jack Sanford (10–8) met in the series finale. Neither pitcher survived for long. Sanford lasted only ⅔ of an inning. In between striking out Giants in bunches, Koufax was bitten by the home run ball. He allowed three in the first three innings. He came out of the game before he could complete the fifth inning with ten strikeouts, but down 5–3. The Dodgers scored five runs in the eighth for a come-from-behind 9–5 win. Koufax was fortunate to escape with a no decision. The 4-game sweep of the Giants brought them to within one game of the Reds as they prepared to fly to San Francisco.

The war with the Giants took a different turn when it resumed in San Francisco on September 8. Johnny Podres gave up home runs to Mays and Cepeda in the first inning, and left the game behind 4–0 before he could get the second out. Giants left-hander Mike McCormick pitched a complete-game 7–3 win. With home runs by Mays and McCovey, the Giants bombed Drysdale and the Dodgers 9–6 the next day. The Dodgers were desperate to prevent a sweep on Sunday, September 10. After starter Stan Williams fell behind 3–0 after four innings, they brought in Sandy Koufax from the bullpen. But Orlando Cepeda greeted Koufax with a 3-run home run in the fifth— his 40th of the year. It was another no decision for Koufax, who struck out five batters in two innings of relief. The Dodgers could cobble together only three hits against Billy Loes and Stu Miller as they went down, 7–1, for their eighth consecutive loss at Candlestick Park.

It was a devastating weekend for the Dodgers. They came into San Francisco only one game out of first place, and left four games behind Cincinnati. The Giants spoiled their last chance to make a serious run at the Reds.

	W	L	PCT.	*
Cincinnati	85	56	.603	
Los Angeles	78	57	.578	4
Milwaukee	76	61	.555	7

*Games behind leader

Last Night in the Cement Prison

On Wednesday night, September 20, in Los Angeles, the Dodgers prepared to play their last game at the Memorial Coliseum. Back on April 18, 1958, when they played their inaugural game there, it was a celebration played in front of a crowd of 78,672, including the governor of California and a large contingent of Hollywood stars. Tonight, with 10 games left in the season and the pennant race all but over, a modest crowd of 12,068 diehard fans showed up to say goodbye.

The Coliseum, an oval football stadium jerry-rigged for baseball with a left field screen a mere 251 feet from home plate, was supposed to be a temporary 2-year arrangement until Dodger Stadium could be completed. Lawsuits and Chavez Ravine construction delays turned it into a 4-year sentence in a cement prison. The Dodger pitchers, who had to pitch with the left field screen looming over their shoulder, were the happiest to be leaving. Sandy Koufax, who had the honor of closing out their time on Figueroa Street, was probably the happiest of the lot. He came into the game with a 16–23 record and a 4.50 ERA at the Coliseum. Tonight, it took Koufax 205 pitches—over 13 innings— to get out of there. The 3–2 win over the Cubs brought his season record to 18–11. His 15 strikeouts gave him 259 for the season to tie Christy Mathewson for the third highest total in National League history that the New York Giants' left-hander accomplished in 1908.[3]

While the Dodgers ended the Coliseum era with a victory and a 4-year record of 172–137, they remained five games behind the Reds with nine games left to play. But the real story of their last game in the Coliseum was the transformation of Sandy Koufax. A year before, he was on the verge of quitting with a career losing record. He was now an All-Star, second only to Warren Spahn as the premier left-hander in the National League. And with two more regularly scheduled starts, he had a legitimate chance for his first 20-win season.

In January of 1958, three months before the first major league baseball game was played in Los Angeles, Ford Frick ignored the pleas of the baseball experts not to allow cheap home runs in this "cow pasture" on South Figueroa Street to jeopardize Babe Ruth's record.[4] Shortly before midnight on September 20, 1961, the lights went out on major league baseball at the Los Angeles Memorial Coliseum after 308 regular season games, 3 World Series games, and 1 All-Star game were played without a single rain-out—and without the wholesale destruction of baseball's home run records. Frick was off the hook as far as the Coliseum issue was concerned. But this day in Baltimore was also the final day of the 154-game "time limit" he had imposed on Roger Maris and Mickey Mantle to break Ruth's record. Maris hit number 59 in the third inning, but went hitless for the rest of the game, thus elevating the asterisk controversy to national prominence.

Another Elimination Day

On September 26 in Pittsburgh, the Dodgers came into Forbes Field to play a twilight-night double-header with the Pirates. The Reds had already won a day game in Chicago to increase their lead to 4½ games over the second-place Dodgers. With 6 games left in their season, the Dodgers' challenge was stark: sweep the double-header, or be eliminated.

Stan Williams came through in the first game. The Dodgers gave him five runs to work with in the second inning, and he carried a 5–1 lead into the eighth before giving up a 2-run home run to Dick Stuart. Williams continued to fade in the ninth, and had to be relieved by Ron Perranoski after two Pirates reached base. But the Dodgers were able to hang on and win 5–3. They were still alive.

In the second game Alston had to call on Don Drysdale to prolong the season, knowing that Pittsburgh was his toughest opponent. The Pirates had beaten Drysdale in his last seven tries, and it was evident by the third inning that he was not going to break the cycle. They buried him in a 5-run avalanche before he could complete the inning. The Dodger hitters could do nothing against Pittsburgh's starting left-hander, Joe Gibbon. But for a sixth inning pinch single by the Dodgers' 23-year-old rookie, and former classmate of Sandy Koufax at Lafayette High School in Brooklyn, Bobby Aspromonte, Gibbon would have pitched a no-hitter. Gibbon lost the no-hitter, but his 1-hit 8–0 shutout returned the Dodgers to 4½ games behind Cincinnati. And with only four games remaining, they were mathematically eliminated from the pennant race.[5]

* * *

That same night in New York, Roger Maris hit his 60th home run at Yankee Stadium. The third inning homer off the Orioles' Jack Fisher tied Babe Ruth's single season home run record set in 1927. Across town in Greenwich Village, a 20-year-old folk singer named Bob Dylan played Gerdes Folk City. In the audience was *New York Times* music critic Robert Shelton. In his column the next day, Shelton called Dylan "a cross between a choir boy and a beatnik."[6] His review captured the elusiveness of the University of Minnesota dropout who changed his name from Robert Allen Zimmerman and hitchhiked to New York City that January: "Mr. Dylan is vague about his antecedents and birthplace, but it matters less where he has been than where he is going, and that would be straight up."[7] In a month's time, record producer John Hammond would sign Dylan to a then unheard-of 5-year contract with Columbia Records, a deal that was derisively called Hammond's Folly.

❋ ❋ ❋

Hunting Christy Mathewson on the Road to Twenty

In the last four games of the season, with the pennant race over, Walter Alston wanted to give Sandy Koufax every chance to win twenty games. On the night of September 27 in Philadelphia, he started him on only two days' rest. Koufax was 18–12 and just five strikeouts short of Christy Mathewson's National League record of 267 set in 1903.

Koufax started strong, facing the minimum of six batters in the first two innings. He took a 1–0 lead into the third when the Dodger defense gave way behind him. With the Phillies' leadoff batter on first base, Maury Wills booted a sure double play ball, putting runners on first and second with none out. After Philadelphia's pitcher Jim Owens sacrificed the runners to second and third, Koufax bore down and struck out second baseman Bobby Malkmus, which should have been the end of the inning. But the extra out allowed third baseman Tony Taylor to come to the plate and double home both runners. It would be the last hit in the game for the Phillies. But instead of surviving the inning with a 1–0 lead, Koufax was now behind, 2–1.

In the sixth, Koufax struck out two batters to break Mathewson's 58-year-old record. But he was getting no support. The run the Dodgers scored back in the first inning turned out to be their only run in a game that ended as a heartbreaking 2–1 loss for Koufax, who turned in a masterful 3-hit complete-game performance with seven strikeouts. Had he won his nineteenth on this night, Walter Alston was prepared to let him start the last game of the season in Chicago, again, on two days' rest. But it was not to be. Sandy Koufax ended his breakout 1961 season with an 18–13 record and a new NL single season record 269 strikeouts.[8]

Drysdale Lays Down a Marker

On September 28 the Dodgers concluded their 2-game series in Philadelphia with Don Drysdale on the mound for his last start of the season. In this, his sixth year in the major leagues, the Dodgers had expected him to break through to the 20-game level. Though he began the game with a disappointing 12–10 record. Drysdale threw a dazzling 6-hit shutout with eight strikeouts. For good measure, he hit a single and his fifth home run of the season in the Dodgers' 10–0 cakewalk at Connie Mack Stadium. It was a performance that would portend the greatness of his next season.

Off the Radar in Chicago

With two games left in the season, the Dodgers gave rookie right-hander Phil Ortega a chance to start on September 30 in Chicago. Ortega was signed in 1959 as a free agent out of Mesa High School in Mesa, Arizona. They brought him up at the beginning of September despite a disappointing 8–14 stint at Triple-A Spokane.

On this day, he turned in a sparkling performance at Wrigley Field. In a rain-shortened game, Ortega pitched five innings with nine strikeouts and no walks. He allowed just three hits, including his only mistake of the day: a solo home run to Cubs' catcher Sammy Taylor in the second inning. The Dodgers could produce only one run against Chicago's starting pitcher, left-hander Dick Ellsworth, a sacrifice fly by Gil Hodges in the first inning. The Cubs scratched together an unearned run in the fourth caused by a Maury Wills error to take a 2–1 lead. When the rains opened up a few minutes later, the game was called, and Ortega was charged with the loss.

On the last day of the 1961 season, Sunday, October 1, the Dodgers beat the Cubs 8–2, and only the 4,325 at Wrigley Field noticed. The attention of the baseball world was riveted on Yankee Stadium, where Roger Maris had his last chance to break Babe Ruth's home run record. And it was there at 2:42 p.m. in the fourth inning that Maris hit his 61st home run off the instantly immortalized Tracy Stallard to break the record. Since this was the era before curtain calls, a reluctant Maris had to be pushed out of the dugout by his teammates to doff his cap and accept the accolades of the crowd.

Meanwhile in Chicago, Stan Williams turned in a strong 7-inning performance, allowing only one run while striking out nine for his fifteenth win of the season. His 15–12 record of 1961 would be his career best. The Dodgers finished the season in second place, four games behind Cincinnati.

	W	L	Pct.	*
Cincinnati	93	61	.604	
Los Angeles	89	65	.578	4
San Francisco	85	69	.552	8

*Games behind leader

※ ※ ※

In Saigon, South Vietnam's president, Ngo Dinh Diem, pronounced that his struggle with Communist insurgents was now a "real war." In a speech before the National Assembly, Diem Diem said, "It is no longer a guerrilla war that we have to face, but a real war waged by an enemy who attacks us with regular units fully and heavily equipped and who seeks a strategic decision in Southeast Asia in conformity with the Communist

International."[9] On this day the number of U.S. "special advisors" in Vietnam was approximately 3,000.

❋ ❋ ❋

Led Out of the Wilderness on the Arm of Sandy Koufax

The Dodgers' emergence from the N.L. wilderness in 1961 was largely attributable to the transformation of Sandy Koufax. In ten months he had gone from an adrift enigma, to an 18-game-winning All-Star and league record holder for most strikeouts in a season. The contrast with 1960 was stunning. He entered the season with a career 36–40 losing record (.474). He reached the .500 mark on May 29 and would never approach that level again. And 1961 was only the start of an amazing upward trajectory. He would eventually end his career at 165–87 (.655).

	WINS	LOSSES	W–L %
1960	8	13	.381
1961	18	13	.581
Change	+10	—	+.200

The 1961 season marked the end of his role as a spot-starter. Koufax was elevated to co–Ace of the Staff with Don Drysdale. Walter Alston now had greater confidence in Koufax, allowing him to complete more than double the number of games as the previous year.

	INNINGS PITCHED	GAMES STARTED	COMPLETE GAMES
1960	175	26	7
1961	255⅔	35	15
Change	+80⅔	+9	+8

As we have seen, Sandy Koufax set a new National League record with 269 strikeouts. But the transformation to the "new" Koufax can be seen most vividly in his numbers relating to bases on balls. The changes he made in Florida—correcting the flaw in his windup that had prevented him from keeping his eye on the target, breaking the habit of throwing the ball too hard under pressure, and keeping his emotions in check—paid off in the prize that had always eluded him: control (of the baseball). In 1961 he walked 34 percent fewer batters per every 9 innings than the previous year.

	BB	BB/9
1960	100	5.14
1961	96	3.38
Change	−4	−1.76
% Change	—	−34.2%

In his first six years the "old" Koufax had an average strikeouts-to-walks ratio of 1.69. In 1961 it jumped by 42 percent over the previous year to a league leading 2.80. And it was only the beginning. He was about to enter a period in which his annual strikeouts-to-walks ratio would reach as high as 5.38.

	STRIKEOUTS	BB	SO/BB
1960	197	100	1.97
1961	269	96	2.80
Change	+72	−4	+0.83
% Change			+42.1%

As Alan Roth's statistical analysis made clear to him in the off-season, staying ahead in the pitch count would be a key to his improvement. 1961 saw a 10 percent improvement in his ability to stay ahead of the batters.

AHEAD IN THE COUNT	
1960	29%
1961	32%
Change	+3%
% Change	+10%

For Sandy Koufax, 1961 was a hinge year between his first six years—the *lost* period—and his final five years—the *otherworldly* period.

A One-Moon Offense

Wally Moon had the finest season of his career, leading the team with a .328 batting average and 88 runs batted in. After his blistering .417 month of April he leveled off until September, when he hit .361 with 22 runs batted in down the stretch. Norm Larker, after losing the 1960 batting title on the last day of the season, returned to being a utility player as his batting average plunged from .323 to .270. The Dodgers were hurt by a lack of power. While they were second in the league in runs scored, they finished fifth out of eight NL teams in home runs with 157. For the first time since 1948, no Dodger had 20 home runs. John Roseboro led the team with 18 and Moon had 17. After hitting 23 home runs in his Rookie-of the–Year season, Frank Howard could produce only 16. The Dodgers looked for a big year from Duke Snider after he walked into camp 10 pounds lighter and tore up spring exhibition pitching with a .389 average. They even shortened the distance of the right-center-field power alley in the Coliseum for him: from 413 feet to 390 feet. Their challenge was keeping him in the lineup. He hit his second home run of the season on April 17 off Bob Gibson. But after Gibson broke his arm the next time up, he didn't hit another home run until June 22. Snider finished with 16 home runs in only 233 at bats. Daryl Spencer, who was brought over from the Cardinals at the end of May to supply some much-needed right-handed power, had six game-winning hits in June with a combination of six home runs and five doubles. The Dodgers received a damaging blow on the 4th of July when he broke a bone in his knee barreling into Ed Mathews. Spencer hit only one more home run for the year. These meager production numbers stood in sharp contrast to those of their NL rivals: the Reds with Frank Robinson's 37 and the Giants with Cepeda's 46 and Mays's 40.

The Collapse of the Pitching Staff

Considered the best in baseball, the Dodger pitching staff collapsed at the end of the season, despite leading the league in strikeouts for the fourteenth straight year with 1,105. As we have seen, Sandy Koufax had a breakout season. He seemed assured of his first 20-win season before tailing off at the end. He won only two games in August and three in September—one in relief. Though at 18–5 Johnny Podres had his best season as a Dodger, he did not win a game after September 3 and did not complete any of his last eight starts. He missed nearly two weeks in the middle of September to be with his seriously ill father in Burlington, Vermont. The other two members of the starting rotation performed near the .500 level: Don Drysdale (13–10) and Stan Williams (15–12). The fearsome Drysdale led the league in hit batters for the fourth straight year with 20. Roger Craig began the season as the fourth starter, but had to be taken out of the rotation in June after home run balls caused his ERA to explode. He finished with a 5–6 record and a 6.15 ERA, and gave up 22 home runs in only 112 innings.

With Ed Roebuck on the disabled list for the first 138 games, Alston was counting on Larry Sherry in the bullpen. Sherry saved twelve games before he was lost for three weeks in July due to a sprained ankle. He could save only one game in the last two months of the season. Rookie Ron Perranoski was a pleasant surprise with seven wins, six saves, and a 2.65 ERA. But he was the only member of the Dodger bullpen to pitch consistently well.

The Davis Boys—A Year Away

Willie Davis and Tommy Davis tailed off after whirlwind starts. In his second year in the majors, Tommy Davis began with a flourish before hitting a wall. After 9 errors in his first 30 games, the Tommy-Davis-as-third-baseman experiment was essentially over with the acquisition of Daryl Spencer at the end of May. Now Alston did not have to hold his breath every time a ball was hit to the left side of his infield, and Tommy could concentrate on his hitting. At the second All-Star break on July 31, he was hitting a robust .314 with 15 home runs and 55 RBIs in the first 100 games. But when regular season play resumed he went into a horrendous 1-for-34 slump and had to be benched for a week. He never hit another home run for the rest of the season, drove in only three more runs, and finished with a batting average of .278—essentially flat with the previous year. The Dodgers' 21-year-old rookie center fielder, Willie Davis looked like a sure-fire Rookie of the Year with his spectacular performance of May 27 in Milwaukee, when he pounded the Braves' pitching for two home runs, a triple, and five runs batted in. After 38 games he had 8 home runs and a .297 batting average. But he hit only .111 in the critical month of August and finished the season at .254, well out of the running for top rookie honors.

Mr. Consistency

Maury Wills at shortstop was a lone example of consistency for the Dodgers. He was the starting shortstop and leadoff batter for the National League in both All-Star games. He led the league in stolen bases for the second straight year with 35. He batted .282—.380 at Crosley Field—and finished ninth in the voting for Most Valuable Player. At the age of 28, he was one year away from superstar status.

The 1961 World Series

It was pandemonium at the Greater Cincinnati Airport on the night of September 26 when the Reds returned from Chicago after clinching their first pennant since 1940.[10] Their only problem was that they had to play the powerhouse 1961 Yankees in the World Series. The Yankees played .673 baseball to win the AL pennant by eight games. The team set a new major league record with 240 home runs, including 115 by two players: Maris (61) and Mantle (54). Their ace, left-hander Whitey Ford, won 25 games and lost only 4. Their top reliever, Luis Arroyo, was 15–5. Their catcher, Elston Howard, hit .348 with 21 home runs. Their backup catcher, John Blanchard, also hit 21 home runs—in only 243 at bats. They were overwhelming favorites to win the Series. And if that wasn't enough for the Reds to contend with, the Yankees were highly motivated to avenge their shocking defeat at the hands of Bill Mazeroski and the Cinderella Pittsburgh Pirates of the year before.

The nation expected Maris and Mantle to put on a home run show as the Series opened in New York on October 4. But it was Whitey Ford who stole the show. He shut out the Reds 2–0 on two hits. Mantle, who was hobbled by an abscessed hip that caused him to miss the last four games of the regular season, did not play. An exhausted Roger Maris took Mantle's place in center field and went 0-for-4.

The Reds' 21-game winner, Joey Jay, beat the Yankees 6–2 in Game 2 on October 5 at Yankee Stadium. The Series moved to Crosley Field on October 7. Mickey Mantle gamely put himself in the lineup but went 0-for-4. Roger Maris, 0-for-10 in the Series, came to the plate in the ninth inning of a 2–2 tie and hit a game-winning home run off Bob Purkey. That was essentially it for Cincinnati as they had to face Whitey Ford again in 24 hours.

On October 8, Ford shut them out for the second straight time, 7–0, to go up three games to one. He extended his World Series scoreless streak to 32 consecutive innings, thereby breaking Babe Ruth's record of 29⅔ scoreless innings set in 1918. Ford would later say about 1961, "It was a bad year for the Babe." In the fourth inning Mantle limped to the plate and hit a vicious line drive into left-center field that ordinarily would have been a stand-up double for him. But he stopped at first base, blood from his abscessed hip visibly soaking through his pants. He left the game to a standing ovation from the Crosley Field fans, and was not seen again in the Series.

Game 5, played in Cincinnati on October 9, was a mere formality. The Reds showed up, but were crushed 13–5. Despite Mantle and Maris's hitting only a collective .120 (3 for 25), the Yankees easily defeated an overmatched Reds team in five games, thanks to the tour de force performance by Series MVP Whitey Ford.

Alston to Return

On October 9 in Cincinnati, the closing day of the World Series, Buzzie Bavasi announced to the press that Walter Alston would return for his ninth season as Dodger manager in 1962. It had been the Dodgers' custom to name their manager during the winter meetings in December. Bavasi made the announcement early to end the speculation—rampant since the Dodgers' 10-game losing streak in August—that Alston was in danger of losing his job to Leo Durocher.[11]

The Dispersion of the Boys of Summer

The National League leadership stayed over in Cincinnati to conduct their special Expansion Draft the next day, October 10, at the Netherland Hilton Hotel. The league planned to expand to ten teams in 1962 with the addition of the New York Mets and the Houston Colt .45s. Each of the eight existing teams was required to submit a list of 15 eligible players to league president Warren Giles. Each would lose a minimum of five and a maximum of seven players in the pool selections.[12] Of the Dodgers' list of 15 eligible players, 6 were taken:

TO THE METS	TO THE COLT.45S
Roger Craig, P	Bob Aspromonte, 3B
Gil Hodges, 1B	Norm Larker, 1B
Turk Farrell, P	
Jim Golden, P	

The loss of Craig and Hodges furthered depleted the Boys of Summer cohort in Los Angeles. And after Charlie Neal was traded to the Mets for Lee Walls on December 15, only five former Brooklyn Dodgers remained on the roster: Snider, Podres, Koufax, Drysdale, and Roebuck. The loss of two first basemen would put the Dodgers in the position of having to rapidly develop Frank Howard and Ron Fairly. The 37-year-old Hodges would play for one more year with the Mets before becoming field manager of the Washington Senators in 1963.

Part III

1962:
The Best of Times,
the Worst of Times

Eleven

The Dodger Stadium Era Begins

Finally we'll be able to play *baseball*.[1]—Walter Alston on the
new Dodger Stadium

I'm just fine, really wonderful. I haven't slept in a week.[2]
—Walter O'Malley the morning of the dedication ceremonies

The Dodgers emerged confident from spring training with an 18–12 exhibition
season record. The biggest surprise of the spring was the resurrection of Ed Roebuck.
After spending 138 games of the 154-game 1961 season on the disabled list, Alston had
given up on him. He would rejoin Larry Sherry and Ron Perranoski as a key member
of the Big 3 in the Dodger bullpen. For the second straight year, *The Sporting News* poll
of Baseball Writers Association of America members picked the Dodgers to finish first
in the National League. The Giants were picked to finish second, the Braves third, and
the defending league champion Cincinnati Reds fourth.

Opening Day in Dodger Stadium

Four years, six months, and two days after Walter O'Malley sent a telegram from
Brooklyn instructing then Los Angeles mayor Norris Paulson to "Get your wheelbarrow
and shovel. I'll meet you in Chavez Ravine,"[3] Dodger Stadium opened on April 10, 1962,
with a Tuesday day game against the Reds. The 56,000-seat stadium was built at a cost
of $23 million—minuscule by modern standards. In contrast to the jagged dimensions
of the improvised playing field in the Coliseum, Dodger Stadium was perfectly sym-
metrical: 330 feet down the foul lines, 390 feet to the power alleys, and 410 feet to
center field. This was a pitcher's park. Not only was the area between the power alleys
a graveyard for fly balls, there was an unusually expansive foul territory, and a layer of
"dead air" that would settle over Chavez Ravine after sunset. The Reds immediately

Walter O'Malley and Walter Alston taking in the festivities on opening day at Dodger Stadium (National Baseball Hall of Fame Library, Cooperstown, New York).

claimed that the red crushed brick infield was even harder than the "alabaster plaster" in Forbes Field. And there was an elegance to Dodger Stadium. The left and right field bleachers were not bleachers; they were "pavilions." There was an unobstructed view from every seat in the park. Walter O'Malley's armchaired private box in the center of the Exclusive Stadium Club was equipped with a stock market ticker.

Walter Alston's first decision was a sensitive one: Who would get the honor of starting the first game at Dodger Stadium? Don Drysdale had started the last three openers. What about Sandy Koufax, who blossomed into one of the League's premier left-handers last season? In his autobiography, Koufax revealed that it was the one honor that he really did go after, but that he had read in the paper a day or two before that Alston said he wasn't going to open with him because he was "too nervous."[4] In the end Alston chose Johnny Podres, winner of the deciding game of the 1955 World Series, Alston's first championship. The Reds had planned to go with their own ace left-hander, Jim O'Toole, until he cut the middle finger of his pitching hand by forcing a suitcase into the trunk of his car. Instead, they would go with right-hander Bob Purkey, coming off a 16–12 season.

The starting lineup reflected the dislocations of an expansion year. Larker and Neal were gone, to Houston and New York respectively. But 35-year-old Duke Snider, beginning his final season with the Dodgers, was still the cleanup batter. And shortstop Maury Wills was again the leadoff batter as he began what was to be his historic fourth season.

	APRIL 10, 1962		**APRIL 11, 1961**	
1	Maury Wills	SS	Maury Wills	SS
2	Jim Gilliam	2B	Willie Davis	CF
3	Wally Moon	LF	Tommy Davis	3B
4	Duke Snider	RF	Duke Snider	RF
5	John Roseboro	C	Wally Moon	LF
6	Ron Fairly	1B	Norm Larker	1B
7	Daryl Spencer	3B	Charlie Neal	2B
8	Willie Davis	CF	John Roseboro	C
9	Johnny Podres	P	Don Drysdale	P

Five minutes after Mrs. Kay O'Malley threw out the first ball to Dodgers catcher John Roseboro, Podres delivered the first pitch of the Dodger Stadium era—a ball to the Reds' bald-headed shortstop, Eddie Kasko. The 52,564 fans in attendance got their first hint that the day might not end well for the Dodgers when his next pitch was lined into left field for a double. The game had been sold out for days, but a ticket foul-up caused the crowd to fall nearly 3,500 short of capacity. Two batters later, Vada Pinson hit another line drive into left field—this one a single to drive home Kasko. Podres got the reigning NL Most Valuable Player, Frank Robinson—who destroyed Dodger pitching the previous year with 7 home runs, 26 runs batted in, and a .388 batting average—to ground into a double play and escape the inning without further damage, behind 1–0.

Alston had named Duke Snider the Dodgers' first team captain since Pee Wee Reese. Snider delivered their first hit in Dodger Stadium with a sharp single to center field in the bottom of the second. Purkey would later say that he only "heard" the ball go by his head after it disappeared in a sea of white shirts behind home plate. Podres and Purkey were locked in a 2–2 tie as the game moved into the top of the seventh inning. Podres retired the first two batters before Pinson hit his second double of the game. The question became: what to do with the fearsome Frank Robinson? After a trip to the mound, Alston gave the order to walk Robinson intentionally and pitch to left fielder Wally Post. The strategy backfired. Post hit Podres's first pitch over the 410-foot sign in dead center field to give the Reds a 5–2 lead. The first home run in Dodger Stadium would turn out to be the deciding blow of the game.

The Meaning of Tommy Davis

Conspicuously absent from the starting lineup, Tommy Davis was beginning his third year in the major leagues at the age of 23. After winning a Pacific Coast League batting title in 1959, he put together two solid but somewhat disappointing offensive seasons— .276 in 1960 and .278 in 1961. At Vero Beach a frustrated Buzzie Bavasi said of him, "He doesn't know how good he can be ... he never wakes up until he gets two strikes on him."[5] The Dodger brass even criticized Davis for smiling in his spring program photo. Determined to make him more aggressive at the plate, Walter Alston decided to put him in the hands of Dodger coach Pete Reiser, who had managed him in the lower minors. As Reiser described his mission, "I want him mad at everyone in the world when he goes up there, including me."[6]

In the bottom of the eighth with two runners on base and the Dodgers still behind 5–2, the Reds pulled Bob Purkey and brought in left-hander Bill Henry to pitch to Duke Snider, representing the tying run at the plate. Alston coun-

A new intimidating Tommy Davis, the result of Pete Reiser's meanification project (National Baseball Hall of Fame Library, Cooperstown, New York).

tered by bringing Tommy Davis in off the bench to pinch hit for Snider. Davis and Henry engaged in a 7-pitch struggle that ended with Davis's grounding into a rally-killing double play. It was an inauspicious start to what would be one of the greatest offensive years in league history.

The Dodgers went on to lose their first game in Dodger Stadium by a score of 6–3.[7] On the bright side, those who made it into the Taj O'Malley were able to avail themselves of a new delicacy, the Dodger Dog, at only 25 cents apiece. What's more, they were able to exit the modern multi-tiered parking levels within 30 minutes of the last pitch. But they also noticed that O'Malley had not seen fit to install a single drinking fountain.

Sandy Koufax, Second Choice

Sandy Koufax was passed over for the inaugural game in Chavez Ravine, but he started the second game on the night of April 11 against the Cincinnati Reds. It was Chinatown Night at Dodger Stadium and Koufax was wheeled in from the bullpen in a rickshaw in front of 35,296 people. Just as he did in the inaugural game, pesky Reds leadoff man Eddie Kasko opened the game with a double. Only this one was a harmless pop fly that left fielder Wally Moon lost in the new lights and that Maury Wills almost made a spectacular over-the-shoulder catch on. Koufax took a 1-hitter—that could have been a no-hitter—into the ninth inning with a 6–0 lead when the big boys in red finally woke up. Pinson led off with a single and Robinson followed with the first of his league-leading 51 doubles. Wally Post, hero of the inaugural game, ruined the shutout with a hot smash to third base that Daryl Spencer couldn't handle to score Pinson. To build his confidence, Alston left Koufax in to face Reds first baseman Gordy Coleman. It took Koufax one pitch to induce Coleman to ground into a double play, with Robinson scoring from third with the second Cincinnati run. He then struck out rookie third baseman Tommy Harper to end the game and give the Dodgers a 6–2 win. Although it was not pretty at the end, Sandy Koufax's first victory of 1962—and the Los Angeles Dodgers' first win in Dodger Stadium—was a 4-hit complete game with seven strikeouts.[8]

Back in the fourth inning, Duke Snider pulled a muscle in his left leg sprinting to home plate to score the Dodgers' fourth run. After trying to play through it, he had to be taken out of the game in the seventh. He would not be able to start another game for eight days. Snider's misfortune was a fortuitous break for Tommy Davis. Davis took Snider's place in right field the next night and never came out of the starting lineup the rest of the season.

In his next start after the Chinatown Night win, Koufax suffered a setback when Hank Aaron and the Milwaukee Braves closed out their first visit to Dodger Stadium on April 15. The first two times he faced Aaron, Koufax struck him out on six pitches, carrying a no-hitter into the fifth inning. But before he could finish the seventh inning, Aaron had knocked him out of the game with a home run. Aaron finished with 3 hits and 2 runs batted in. Koufax was charged with his first loss as the Dodgers went down to a 6–3 defeat. Maury Wills, batting an anemic .118, quietly stole his second base of the season in the first inning off young Braves catcher Joe Torre.

After beating the Reds on the road in Crosley Field on April 19, Koufax turned in another historic performance on the afternoon of April 24 in Wrigley Field. With 144 pitches—96 for strikes—he struck out 18 Cubs to tie the major league record he shared with Bob Feller and improve his record to 3–1. He struck out the side in the first, third, and ninth innings.[9] The modest Koufax was the most surprised person in the park by his performance. Just before the first pitch he yelled to his third baseman, Andy Carey, "Be alive down there, I don't think I have it today!"[10] Tommy Davis was beginning to draw attention. He had a home run and a single to raise his batting average to .367, and drove in 4 runs to bring his season total to 20 in only his twelfth game. The Dodgers closed out their road trip on April 26 by pounding the Cubs 12–5 to win the series two games to one. By now Tommy Davis was on fire. He had a single, a double, and a triple to raise his average to .397. The Dodgers left Chicago in fourth place with a 10–6 record.

Jammed

Back home in Los Angeles, the Dodgers began a 4-game weekend series with the Pirates on April 27 at Dodger Stadium. In the Friday night opener, Don Drysdale pitched a complete-game 10–2 victory to bring his season record even with Koufax's at 3–1.

On Saturday afternoon, April 28, Koufax became locked in a pitcher's duel with Pirates right-hander Earl Francis. The Pirates scratched together a run in the fourth inning to take a 1–0 lead. After Koufax retired the first two batters, he gave up a single to Donn Clendenon, issued his only walk of the game to ex–Milwaukee Brave Johnny Logan, filling in at third base for Don Hoak (back at the hotel—sans wisdom teeth—recovering from oral surgery), and served up a seeing-eye ground ball single to reserve catcher Don Leppert that scored Clendenon.

The Dodgers scored an unearned run off Francis in the bottom of the sixth to tie the game at 1–1. Johnny Roseboro hit a 2-out single. Daryl Spencer hit a ground ball to third base that Logan threw away. By the time Roberto Clemente recovered the baseball in the right-field corner, Roseboro had crossed the plate with the tying run.

Both pitchers went all the way to the bottom of the ninth inning with the game tied 1–1. As he had the entire game, Francis continued to get the Dodgers to hit the ball on the ground. He got Jim Gilliam to ground out to second baseman Bill Mazeroski. He got Wally Moon to hit another ground ball to Mazeroski that glanced off his glove for an infield single. Moon moved into scoring position when Francis got Duke Snider to ground out to first base. Tommy Davis, who was hitless in his 9 previous at bats, hit the fourth ground ball of the inning into left field to score Moon with the winning run.

Pirates right-hander Earl Francis, a spot starter with a 16–23 career record, would play a key role in the Dodgers' 1962 fortunes (National Baseball Hall of Fame Library, Cooperstown, New York).

This game, won 2–1 by the Dodgers, had many ramifications. The loss knocked the Pirates out of first place. It was a heartbreaking loss for Earl Francis, who had allowed 6 hits and only 1 earned run. Sandy Koufax, also with a 6-hitter, became the first 4-game winner in the National League. But for his game-winning hit in the ninth, Tommy Davis's hitless streak would have grown to a potentially season-threatening 0-for-21. But it was a seemingly innocuous infield single by Sandy Koufax in the third inning that would have a lasting impact on the Dodgers' season.

No one expected anything from Koufax when he came to the plate in the bottom of the third with a perfect .000 batting average, 0-for-14 for the season. Walter Alston was usually content to see him take a seat on the bench after 3 pitches. This at bat was an exception. After taking the first three pitches with the bat on his shoulder, he was ahead in the count, two balls and one strike. Earl Francis decided to come back with an inside fast ball. With the ball boring in on him, Koufax, batting right-handed, just tried to fight it off to protect himself. Simply put, he was *jammed*. The ball slammed against the handle of the bat just above his hands. These were the days before batting gloves. Koufax's hands were ringing as the ball ricocheted off his bat handle and rolled through the pitcher's mound and up the middle. Dick Groat made a good play behind second base, but Koufax beat his throw to first. Koufax had his first hit of the season, but something was not right. In his autobiography, Koufax would recall that as he made contact with the ball the heel of the bat "had sort of pinched into the palm of the hand"[11]—his left, pitching hand. It caused a bruise so painful that he kept checking his palm for the rest of the game expecting it to turn black and blue. He finished the game and tried to put it out of his mind.

The Pirates rebounded the next day to sweep a Sunday double-header by beating Johnny Podres 6–1 in the opener and the Dodgers' 19-year-old rookie phenom, Joe Moeller, 1–0 in the second game. Moeller, a strapping 6'5" right-hander less than a year out of Mira Costa High School in nearby Manhattan Beach, had the Pirates shut out on two hits through the first six innings of a scoreless tie. Dick Stuart hit his first pitch in the seventh over the left-field fence for the eventual game-winning solo home run.

The Dodgers finished April in fourth place. The Giants were riding high in first place, playing .750 baseball. The defending league champion Reds were already three games under .500 in seventh.

	W	L	Pct.	*
San Francisco	15	5	.750	
Pittsburgh	13	5	.722	1
St. Louis	11	4	.733	1½
Los Angeles	13	8	.619	2½
Houston	7	8	.467	5½
Philadelphia	8	9	.471	5½
Cincinnati	8	11	.421	6½
Milwaukee	8	11	.421	6½
New York	3	13	.188	10
Chicago	4	16	.200	11

*Games behind leader

Twelve

A Season Goes Numb

Sandy, your finger looks like a grape. How can you pitch with that? Are you crazy?[1]—Sam Lichtenstein, uncle of Sandy Koufax

With four wins, Sandy Koufax put together the best April start of his career. It began to unravel in May. On May 2, in his first start after the jamming, he had a rough outing against the Cubs at Dodger Stadium. The Los Angeles press played up his 1,000th career strikeout—a 3-pitch disposal of Ron Santo in the second inning—but he was largely ineffective.[2] Though he struck out 8 batters in 6⅓ innings, he gave up 8 hits and 3 runs. The result was a 3–1 loss. On May 8 in Houston against the expansion Colt .45s he lasted only 5⅔ innings. He took a 6–1 lead into the sixth inning, struck out his seventh and eighth batters, but couldn't finish the inning.[3]

With Koufax in the clubhouse, Larry Sherry blew the save by allowing Houston to tie the game at 6–6 before the Dodgers came back to win it in the tenth, 9–6. On May 12 in St. Louis, Koufax was gone after six innings, behind 4–3 after allowing 9 hits and 4 runs. He escaped with another no decision when the Dodgers tied the game in the ninth inning before losing it 6–5 after midnight in the fifteenth on a wrong field bloop single by Julian Javier off the Dodgers' seventh pitcher, Don Drysdale. It was a costly loss that would come back to haunt the Dodgers at the end of the year. Had Drysdale retired Javier, the game would have gone into the record book as a 5–5 tie since the 12:50 curfew had passed eight minutes before the winning run crossed the plate.[4]

A Numbness at Chavez Ravine

Koufax failed in his fourth try for win number five on May 17 at Dodger Stadium against Houston. He fell behind 2–0 in the first inning by giving up three hits and a walk. After he gave up two more runs on another five hits—including a home run—

and hit two batters, Alston took him out at the end of the sixth inning, behind 4–0. When the Dodgers came back again to win the game in the tenth, Koufax was off the hook with another no decision. But it was beginning to cause concern in the front office that he appeared to have hit a wall. In his mind, he wasn't doing anything differently from what he had done in April. Reflecting back on it two months later, Koufax would pinpoint the middle of May as the time he first noticed a numbness begin to develop in the index finger of his pitching hand.[5]

The strong-willed Koufax ignored the numbness and pressed on, rationalizing that he had spent too much of his life *not* pitching to consider giving up any of his turns in the rotation.[6] He was determined to turn things around, and took the first step on May 21 when the Giants visited Dodger Stadium for the first time. The Dodgers, having just lost three straight to the Cardinals over the weekend, started Koufax against the Giants' Billy O'Dell (5–2). Koufax came through with an overpowering 5-hit, 10-strikeout, complete-game performance in front of crowd of over 45,000. His only mistake was a 2–2 pitch to Orlando Cepeda that the Baby Bull hit into the left field pavilion to lead off the seventh inning.[7] Tommy Davis, who had dipped below .300 the day before against the Cardinals, lit up O'Dell with 2 doubles, a home run, and 3 RBIs in an 8–1 thumping of the Giants. Koufax's first win since April 28 stopped the Dodgers' slide and ignited a 13-game winning streak.

On May 26 Koufax struck out 16 Phillies at Dodger Stadium with another 5-hit complete game to record his sixth win. Tommy Davis again provided the main support with a 3-for-4, 2 RBI performance to raise his average to .326. The Phillies put their first two batters on base in the ninth, but Koufax blew away the last three on strikes.[8] The 6–3 win was the sixth straight for the Dodgers.

Return to New York

On May 30 the Dodgers made their first appearance in New York in five years with a Memorial Day double-header against Casey Stengel's Amazin' Mets expansion team at the Polo Grounds. Sandy Koufax, who was passed over in favor of Johnny Podres for the honor of opening Dodger Stadium, made his regularly scheduled start in the first game, with Podres scheduled for the second game. It was Koufax who had made the last pitch for the Brooklyn Dodgers on September 29, 1957.

The Dodgers, who had always been despised in the Polo Grounds and who betrayed the Brooklyn faithful by abandoning them for the West Coast, were stunned by how well they were treated by the overflow crowd of 55,704. Number 4, Duke Snider, caused a sensation before the game when he emerged from the clubhouse in center field and nonchalantly strolled in to the batting cage. An incredulous Snider would comment after the game, "It was the best crowd I ever saw, anywhere."[9] The outspoken Leo Durocher, who hadn't been in the Polo Grounds since the last day of the 1955 season, was swarmed by an army of New York writers as he held court around the batting cage. While Snider got most of the attention, the crowd gave thunderous ovations to all the other former Brooklyn Dodgers: Drysdale, Koufax, Gilliam, Roebuck, and Podres. The crowd saved the longest ovation for Gil Hodges, now wearing a Mets uniform. Hodges, long admired and respected on both sides of the East River, was the only member of the old Boys of Summer who was never booed in the Polo Grounds.

In the first game, the Dodgers had spotted Koufax to an overwhelming 10–0 lead after batting in their half of the fourth inning. But it was evident that he was not at his best. In the bottom of the fourth the Mets got to him for three runs and five hits, including a leadoff home run that Gil Hodges hit to the delight of the crowd.

Maury Wills came into the game batting .239 with one career home run—that being a routine fly ball that cleared the left-field screen the year before in the Coliseum. Batting left-handed in the fifth inning, and already with two hits, he hit a line drive over right-fielder Joe Christopher's head that rolled to the fence 449 feet from home plate. He circled the bases for an inside-the-park home run. Batting right-handed in the top of the ninth against left-hander Wilmer "Vinegar Bend" Mizell, Wills hit a fly ball that dropped into the overhanging left field deck—a mere 256 feet from home plate—for his second home run of the game to put the Dodgers ahead, 13–4. He became the sixth player in major league history to hit a home run from both sides of the plate in the same game.

Duke Snider caused a sensation before the Dodgers' first game at the Polo Grounds in 5 years on May 30, 1962 (National Baseball Hall of Fame Library, Cooperstown, New York).

Koufax was noticeably laboring as he entered the bottom of the ninth. He had already thrown 137 pitches. After the Mets pounded him for another four hits and two runs to make the score 13–6, Alston came out to the mound to ask him if he wanted to let someone else come in to get the last out. In his autobiography Koufax revealed why it was so important for him to finish the game himself: "I had left as a hanger-on; I was returning, presumably, as a pitcher."[10] He was left in to face ex–Milwaukee Brave Felix Mantilla with runners on first and second. It was Mantilla's throwing error in the bottom of the twelfth inning at the Coliseum on September 29, 1959, that had sent the Dodgers on to the World Series in Chicago. Koufax's first offering to Mantilla was a wild pitch, allowing both runners to move into scoring position. But on the next pitch he got Mantilla to fly out to Tommy Davis in left field. Koufax had his seventh win, albeit a ragged 13–6, 13-hit, 160-pitch effort in which he struck out 10 hapless Mets.

In the clubhouse after the game, Koufax noticed that his index finger had grown more numb and cold with what he described as a "dead look about it."[11] When he pressed his thumbnail into it, the flesh didn't immediately recover like healthy tissue does. Instead, the nail created a lasting impression as if his finger were made of wax. Although the condition of the finger was alarming to Walt Alston and the trainers, they assumed that it would go away and heal on its own.[12]

In the second game Gil Hodges electrified the crowd with two more home runs—both off Johnny Podres in the first six innings to give the Mets a 4–3 lead. Willie Davis broke a 5–5 tie in the top of the ninth with a line drive into the upper deck in right field to give the Dodgers a double-header sweep and their tenth win in a row. After his heroic 3-home run effort, 38-year-old Gil Hodges was now hitting .316.[13]

The Dodgers closed out the month of May by beating the Mets 6–3 the next day to complete a 3-game sweep. Maury Wills had three more hits and stole three bases to bring his season total to a league-leading 27. Tommy Davis had three hits and drove in two runs to move into a tie with Orlando Cepeda for most RBIs in the league with 49. Willie Davis was now seventh in the league in batting with a .329 average and Tommy was eighth at .328. At the end of play on May 31 the Dodgers' winning streak stood at eleven games and they were only a half game out of first.

	W	L	Pct.	*
San Francisco	35	15	.700	
Los Angeles	34	15	.694	½
Cincinnati	27	17	.614	5
Pittsburgh	26	18	.591	6

The Dodgers moved on to Philadelphia to play a rare 5-game series with the Phillies. They swept a double-header on June 1 to increase their winning streak to thirteen games and move into a tie for first place with the Giants, but lost the next two. It was Sandy Koufax's turn to start on June 4 for the deciding game of the series. He beat the Phillies 6–3 by pitching his fourth consecutive complete game, allowing only three hits and striking out thirteen. In the bottom of the ninth he was actually one strike away from a 2-hit shutout when an obscure 26-year-old rookie pinch hitter named Jacke Davis hit a 2–2 pitch over the center field fence for a 3-run home run.[14] Davis could now say that the only home run of his 48-game major league career came off Sandy Koufax.

Ever since his 160-pitch game on May 30 in New York, Koufax's index finger had continued to grow number. But he continued to come up with justifications for ignoring it: he was the only left-handed starter left on the team since Podres was having problems with his elbow; he threw both his fast ball and his curve ball off his *middle* finger; the index finger was not essential to his grip—it only held the ball in place.

Moving into First Place on the Back of Maury Wills

On June 8, a humid Friday night in Houston, the Dodgers opened a 4-game series with the Colt .45s at Colts Stadium, a temporary 33,000-seat park thrown together in five months for two million dollars. The field dimensions were Texas-sized: 360 feet down the foul lines, 395 feet to the power alleys, and 420 feet to center field. The members of the grounds crew wore ten-gallon hats and cowboy boots. The fans were shown to their seats by lady ushers called Trigger-Ettes.[15] But the distinguishing feature of the park was the oppressive heat and humidity. Since there was virtually no shade, more than 100 people had to be treated for heat-related illnesses on opening day. Eventually the club had to convert its schedule to all night games until the Astrodome was built in 1965. The first major league Sunday night game would be played on June 9, 1963.

Koufax started the game for the Dodgers. In Pittsburgh three days before, he had to come in from the bullpen in the ninth inning to save a game for Drysdale. Tonight he had to come out of the game leading 2–1 in the sixth inning, exhausted from the humidity. Ed Roebuck blew his first save of the season, and the game went into extra innings. Past midnight, in the thirteenth inning with the teams hopelessly dead-locked at 3–3, Maury Wills drew a lead-off walk from Don McMahon. He stole second base with a head-first slide on McMahon's first pitch to Jim Gilliam. After Gilliam flied out, Wills stole third base on McMahon's first pitch to Willie Davis. Two pitches later Wills scored the go-ahead run on Willie Davis's sacrifice fly to deep center field. Larry Sherry held off the Colts in the bottom of the thirteenth to win the game, 4–3. Maury Wills had literally *stolen* the game from Houston. Koufax had another no decision, but the Dodgers leapfrogged over the Giants into first place by a half game. It was the first time since August 15, 1961, that they held sole possession of first place.[16]

Sandy Koufax, Home Run Hitter

The Dodgers concluded a 19-game road trip with three games in Milwaukee. On June 12 the Braves chased Johnny Podres in the second inning on their way to a 15–2 thrashing. The Dodgers had no answer for Hank Aaron. He was perfect 3-for-3 with two singles, a walk, a home run, and three runs batted in. However, the Braves showed mercy when they took him out of the game after the sixth inning. Old friend Lew Burdette pitched a complete game 6-hitter.

The next night Warren Spahn and Sandy Koufax squared off in front of a sparse County Stadium crowd of 14,913—although the second largest Milwaukee crowd to date. When Koufax came up to bat with one out in the fifth inning leading 1–0, Warren Spahn—15 years his senior—didn't take him seriously. Not only was he was batting .093 for the season, he had never hit a home run in seven years in the major leagues. But that was about to change. On the first pitch Spahn threw him one of his stock screwballs—albeit with nothing on it. Koufax took a wild swing at the ball and was surprised to feel solid contact. He was even more surprised when the ball came screaming off his bat, went into a towering orbit, and disappeared into the left-field stands. Now he had no choice but to go into some sort of a home run trot. By the time he reached first base he could hear someone screaming at him. It was Spahn. He was so furious at Koufax that he called him every profane name he had learned in Europe with the U.S. Army during World War II as he circled the bases. Ed Mathews added even more abuse as he rounded third.[17] Koufax could not get into the dugout fast enough.

Koufax continued to shut out the Braves until the sixth inning, when shortstop Roy McMillan led off with a home run to cut the Dodgers' lead to 2–1. It was the third and last hit for the Braves as Koufax retired the last twelve batters in order. His home run turned out to be the deciding run. His record was now 9–2, and the first-place Dodgers increased their lead to two full games over the Giants, who were in the middle of a 4–12 "June Swoon."[18]

Another Gibson-Koufax Masterpiece

On June 18 at Dodger Stadium, Sandy Koufax (9–2) and Bob Gibson (8–4) went head to head for the third time. The last time they met—September 24, 1961, at Busch Stadium in St. Louis—Gibson prevailed to deny Koufax his nineteenth victory and foreclose any possibility of his first 20-game season.

On this Monday night a crowd of 33,477 was treated to a joint masterpiece. For the first eight innings Gibson and Koufax matched each other with simultaneous shutouts. Gibson had given up just two singles—both to Wally Moon. He had walked four batters, the first being Maury Wills back in the first inning, when Wills promptly stole second base for his 36th steal of the season. In the 69th game of the season he now had more steals than he had the entire previous year. Koufax had walked no one and allowed only four singles: two to Stan Musial, and two to Julian Javier.

The game went to the ninth inning as a scoreless tie. In the top half with two outs, Ken Boyer hit the Cardinals' fifth single off Koufax, who then had to face 41-year-old Musial. Stan was having his last great year with a .331 batting average. Boyer took the bat out of Musial's hands when he was thrown out attempting to steal second to end the inning. In the bottom of the ninth Gibson retired leadoff man Ron Fairly on one pitch. He next had to confront the red-hot Tommy Davis. In the first Gibson-Koufax confrontation of May 25, 1961, it was Davis who hit a Gibson fast ball into the Busch Stadium left-field seats in the seventh inning to give Koufax a 1–0 victory. Tonight Gibson struck him out the first two times he faced him—on curve balls. Behind in the count 1–0, Gibson made the mistake of trying to sneak a fastball by Tommy Davis. Davis was looking for it and ended the game with a tremendous home run to the back of the left-field bullpen.

The 1–0 shutout was the sixth straight win for Sandy Koufax, and it was an unmitigated masterpiece. It was the first complete game of his career in which he didn't walk a batter. He had a 3-ball count on just two batters. Only one Cardinal reached second base. Wally Moon made the only outfield putout of a Cardinal hitter in the ninth inning.[19] Koufax struck out nine and Gibson matched it with eight. The Dodgers extended their lead to a game and a half over the Giants. Koufax was now 10–2.

The First Koufax No-hitter

It was Sandy Koufax's turn to pitch on the last day of June at Dodger Stadium against the New York Mets. The Dodgers were in a rough patch of their 20-game home stand. Not only had they already lost 3-game sets to the Astros, Reds, and Braves to slide back into second place, they had been bombed 10–4 the night before by a 19–52 Mets team.

On this Saturday night the crowd of 29,797 became aware that they were witnessing something special as the lights began to take effect in the first inning. Not one of the Mets' first three batters could make contact with the baseball. Koufax struck out the side on nine pitches. He would later call it the best inning he ever pitched.[20] In the bottom of the first, the Dodgers scored four runs off ex–Cardinal right-hander Bob Miller, the first player taken in the expansion draft. A triple by Willie Davis, RBI singles by Tommy Davis and Frank Howard, a 2-run double by John Roseboro, and Miller was gone. Obscure relief pitcher Ray Daviault, in his first and only year in the majors, was brought in to retire the .091-hitting Koufax. After one inning Sandy Koufax had a 4–0 lead—and he had no-hit stuff.

In the top of the second the Mets' cleanup batter, Frank Thomas, hit Koufax's first pitch sharply into the hole between shortstop and third base heading for left field. Maury Wills made a dazzling backhanded stab of the ball deep in the hole and threw him out at first base. It was the last ball put into play by the Mets that had any chance of being a hit. Koufax struck out the next two hitters—looking—and the second inning was in the books.

Koufax rolled through the next five innings striking out six and allowing no hits. He walked three batters, but was the beneficiary of an error-free defense and two double plays. Solly Hemus, former Cardinal manager and oppressor of Bob Gibson, was picked up by the Mets in the off-season and installed as third base coach by Casey Stengel. After every inning as Koufax walked off the mound, Hemus would work on him by reminding him, "You know something? You've *still* got a no-hitter."[21]

In the eighth Koufax's control became an issue as he had to make 27 pitches. He walked ex–Reds second baseman Elio Chacon—now playing shortstop with the Mets— and fell behind with a 3–2 count on two other hitters. But he managed to escape unscathed by getting Jim Hickman to fly out and by striking out Cliff Cook and Chris Cannizzaro.

The crowd at Dodger Stadium was on its feet as Koufax took the mound for the ninth inning. He walked the leadoff batter, Gene Woodling, for his fifth walk of the game. Joe Christopher came in to run for Woodling. He got Richie Ashburn to ground out to Maury Wills for the first out. The next two batters, Rod Kanehl and Felix Mantilla, were always tough outs for Koufax. He got Kanehl to ground out to Gilliam on an 0–2 pitch. Mantilla now stood between Sandy Koufax and a no-hitter. With the count at 2–1, Koufax got him to hit the ball on the ground toward Maury Wills at shortstop. Wills fielded it cleanly and flipped to second baseman Larry Burright to force Christopher for the final out. Sandy Koufax had his first no-hitter. The people in the field level box seats swarmed onto the field to join the Dodger players mobbing Koufax as a shower of cushions rained down from the stands.

It was a truly dominating performance by Koufax. He struck out 13 batters. Not one runner reached second base. Quietly in the background, Tommy Davis had two singles to displace Stan Musial as the National League's leading batter at .339. When he drove in the first run of the game in the first inning, he increased his league lead in runs batted in to in 81 in the first 80 games. The Dodgers ended June in the same position they were in when they started the month: a half game behind the Giants. Koufax was now 11–4.

	W	L	Pct.	*
San Francisco	51	28	.646	
Los Angeles	51	29	.638	½
Pittsburgh	44	32	.579	5½
St. Louis	43	33	.566	6½

Streaking into July

After the euphoria of the no-hitter dissipated, Koufax and the Dodgers had to come to grips with the fact that his finger was not getting any better six weeks after the numbness first appeared. But he was winning and the team was now playing at its best level of the season. The next day Don Drysdale opened July by beating Roger Craig and the Mets, 5–1, on a Sunday afternoon at Dodger Stadium. Like Koufax the night before, he struck out 13 batters. Drysdale-Koufax was fast becoming the most outstanding right-left combination in baseball. While Koufax had eleven wins, a no-hitter, and a league-leading 183 strikeouts in 150 innings, Drysdale was leading the league with a 14–4 record.

The Dodgers concluded their 20-game home stand on the Fourth of July with a double header with the Phillies. They overwhelmed them 16–1 in the first game with Koufax throwing a 150-pitch 5-hitter with ten strikeouts. In the second game young Joe Moeller and Ed Roebuck combined to beat them 7–3 to sweep the double-header and complete a 4-game sweep of the series. Tommy Davis was 5 for 6 with 5 runs batted for the day to raise his batting average to .344 and his RBI total to 87. Big Frank Howard drove in seven runs. After taking their seventh straight double-header, the Dodgers had a 6-game winning streak and were back in first place by a half game over the Giants. When the upstart second-year Angels also swept their Fourth of July double-header in Washington, D.C., displacing the Yankees to take over sole possession of first place by a half game, there was talk of a Freeway World Series in Los Angeles.

The next day the Dodgers flew to San Francisco to begin a 4-game series with the Giants. The Giants had shaken off their "June Swoon" and were playing well, having just feasted on Mets pitching in their own Fourth of July double-header at Candlestick Park, pounding them 11–4 and 10–3. Willie McCovey was 3 for 3 with 7 RBIs in the first game, and Willie Mays had 2 home runs and 5 RBIs in the second game. The Giants had a frightening lineup. Mays was batting .313 with 24 home runs. But Felipe Alou was hitting in the cleanup spot with a .332 average. There seemed to be no holes in the lineup. Harvey Kuenn was batting .315, Jim Davenport .320, Orlando Cepeda .313, and Willie McCovey .323.

The 4-Day War at Candlestick

The war at Candlestick began with a Thursday day game on July 5 in front of a disappointing crowd of only 24,915. Don Drysdale (14–5) started for the Dodgers, Mike McCormick (4–2) for the Giants. The Dodgers continued their torrid hitting of the day before in Los Angeles. By the middle of the fifth inning they had torched McCormick for three home runs to take a 6–1 lead. They scored five more runs against Giants relievers Bobby Bolin and Don Larsen. After his tormentor Willie McCovey homered off him in the sixth, Drysdale breezed through the rest of the game to an 11–3 win. He hung 0-for-4 collars on Willie Mays and Orlando Cepeda, striking out Mays twice and Cepeda three times. With their seventh straight win, the Dodgers increased their lead to a game and a half.

Friday night, July 6, 41,569 jammed into Candlestick to see right-handers Juan Marichal (11–5) and Stan Williams (7–4). After the Giants pounded Williams for four runs in the third inning and Ed Roebuck for five runs in the fifth and another three runs in the sixth, they were ahead by nine. Marichal went all the way to 5-hit the Dodgers, 12–3, with 13 strikeouts. The Dodgers' lead was whittled back to a half game.

Willie Mays was 0 for 9 in the series when he came to the plate the next day against Johnny Podres with two outs in the first inning. He hit Podres's first pitch over the left-field fence to put the Giants ahead, 1–0. That set the tone for day. In the first five innings against Podres, the Giants built a 4–0 lead. They increased it to 9–0 in the sixth by routing Larry Sherry and Ron Perranoski. Meanwhile the Dodger hitters could manage only 3 hits against Giants starter Jack Sanford and 2 hits against Stu Miller out of the bullpen on their way to a lopsided 10–3 defeat. At the end of this Saturday afternoon the teams had switched places: the Giants into first and the Dodgers back to second. A half game separated them with the series to conclude in less than 24 hours.

Pitching with a Knife Stuck in Your Finger

Sunday afternoon, July 8, was the last day before the first All-Star break. The largest crowd of the season, 41,717, packed Candlestick Park. Walter Alston gave the ball to Sandy Koufax (12–4). Alvin Dark also went with a left-hander, Billy O'Dell (10–6). As Koufax warmed before the game, he knew that there was something seriously wrong with his index finger. Not only had it turned a reddish color, but pain was now an issue. It was so tender that when he merely rested it against the ball to grip his curve, it felt like it was being cut by a knife. But if he couldn't use the finger even in this limited way, his curve ball would be rendered useless.[22] This was a crucial game with first place on the line. If he couldn't throw a curve, he would have to go forward with only one pitch: the fast ball.

By the time Koufax blew away the Giants in order in the first and second innings, it was obvious to them that he was throwing nothing but fast balls. The Giants knew what was coming, but they still couldn't hit it as Koufax took a no-hitter into the seventh inning. Jim Davenport reached first base safely when his ground ball took a bad hop off Dodger second baseman Larry Burright's arm. Orlando Cepeda moved Davenport to third base with a clean single up the middle. But the Giants left the runners stranded on first and third when Koufax struck out Felipe Alou to end the inning. The game remained a scoreless tie after seven innings.

The Dodgers already had eight hits off Billy O'Dell, but he had managed to pitch out of trouble until the eighth. Willie Davis hit his first pitch for a line drive double to right field. After he gave up his third single to Tommy Davis and another double to Frank Howard, he was down 2–0. With a 2-run cushion, Koufax continued to blow his fast ball past the Giants, retiring them in order in the bottom of the eighth.

By the ninth inning the problem with Koufax's finger had reached a critical mass. Part of his hand—the tissue between the finger and his thumb—had gone numb. Pinch hitter Bob Nieman led off with a line single to left field. Though it was only the third hit off Koufax, Don Drysdale got up in the Dodger bullpen. Koufax proceeded to strike out Harvey Kuenn, but it took ten fast balls to do it. He walked Jim Davenport on six pitches to put the tying run on first base with Willie Mays coming to the plate. After Koufax fell behind 2–0 to Mays, and his pitch count had reached 141, he was not allowed to continue. Alston brought in Drysdale to finish walking Mays to load the bases. Drysdale got Cepeda on a pop foul to Roseboro behind the plate for the second out. Felipe Alou, batting .330, would be the Giants' last chance with the bases loaded. Alou drove Drysdale's first pitch hard up the middle heading for center field. It looked like a sure game-tying base hit. But Maury Wills speared the ball behind second base and flipped it to Larry Burright to get a force out on Mays to end the game.[23]

Koufax had his thirteenth win, and Drysdale was credited with his only save of the season. The 2–0 win gave the Dodgers a split of the 4-game series and put them back in first place by a half game over the Giants. The two teams would stay locked in the same 1–2 position for the remainder of the regular season.

	W	L	PCT.	*
Los Angeles	58	31	.652	
San Francisco	57	31	.648	½
Pittsburgh	52	34	.605	4½

The Orange, Black and Blue Truce at the All-Star Game

Five Dodgers were picked for the National League All-Star team scheduled to play in Washington, D.C., in two days: Tommy Davis, Maury Wills, John Roseboro, Sandy Koufax, and Don Drysdale. After the first 89 games, Tommy Davis was leading the league with a .353 batting average and with 90 runs batted in. Koufax was 13–4 with a league-leading 202 strikeouts in 167⅔ innings. Drysdale was the league leader in wins with a 15–4 record. Maury Wills already had 46 stolen bases. The Giants matched them with five All-Stars of their own: Juan Marichal, Felipe Alou, Jim Davenport, Willie Mays, and Orlando Cepeda.

The Dodgers wanted Koufax to skip the All-Star game and see a vascular specialist. They called National League President Warren Giles to try to get him excused, but were turned down. The league was suspicious about contending teams inventing last-minute injuries to protect their starting rotations. The best the Dodgers could do was to ask National League manager Fred Hutchinson to not use Koufax in the game.[24]

Don Drysdale started for the National League at the 3-month-old D.C. Stadium on July 10. He shut out the American League for the first three innings, striking out three batters—including Roger Maris and Mickey Mantle. The Giants and Dodgers buried the hatchet for the day and worked together to achieve a 3–1 win. Juan Marichal took over for Drysdale and continued the shutout for two more innings. Maury Wills came in in the sixth inning as a pinch runner for Stan Musial. Wills promptly stole second base off Camilio Pascual and scored the first run of the game. After taking over at shortstop for Dick Groat, Wills singled to lead off the eighth inning, then proceeded to take over the game. When the Giants' Jim Davenport singled into left field, Wills caught Rocky Colavito by surprise by not stopping at second base. By the time the ball was relayed from left field to second, it was too late—Wills was already on his way to third. AL right-fielder Leon Wagner was next to be caught off guard by Wills. When he nonchalantly caught Felipe Alou's shallow pop fly in foul territory behind first base, Wills broke for the plate to make the final score 3–1, Nationals. Marichal was the winning pitcher, Maury Wills was the Most Valuable Player, but the truce was over.

Roger Craig was the number 1 starter for Casey Stengel on the 1962 Amazin' Mets expansion team (George Brace photograph).

Fred Hutchinson had graciously allowed Koufax to be a spectator on the bench. Koufax's finger was turning steadily redder, but the Dodgers were trying to keep his condition a secret. At this point not even Walter O'Malley knew about it.[25] After the All-Star game, Koufax flew to New York to get ready for his next start.

On July 12 the Dodgers opened a 3-game series with the Mets in New York with two rookies from their 1955 world championship team—Roger Craig and Sandy Koufax—facing off against each other at the Polo Grounds. The atmosphere was markedly different from the celebration on May 30 in front of 55,000. Rain had been falling most of the day to hold the crowd down to a mere 15,000. As Koufax warmed up before the game he noticed that the finger had begun to turn blue. After attempting a couple of balloon curves that came nowhere near the plate, he again had to throw nothing but fast balls. With his one pitch he rolled through the first five innings with a 2-hit shutout when a new complication arose. A blood bister had formed on the tip of the index finger, causing dead blood to seep down and collect in the tissue below. In the sixth, Frank Thomas, looking for the fast ball, lined one into left field for a double. Koufax was able to prevent him from scoring, and took a 2–0 lead into the seventh. He retired leadoff man Elio Chacon on one pitch, then walked Chris Cannizzaro. He struck out Roger Craig on three pitches, and got Richie Ashburn to ground out to end the inning. But the numbness was now so pronounced that he had lost all feeling for the baseball. When he revealed that to Walter Alston in the dugout, Alston removed him. Larry Sherry came in to save the win for Koufax by shutting out the Mets over the last two innings. The Dodgers won the game 3–0, but the "Koufax problem" was now a full-blown crisis. For the first time it made it impossible for him to finish a game.[26]

In New York, Koufax's uncle, Sam Lichtenstein, came to see him at the Dodgers' hotel. Lichtenstein was horrified by the condition of his finger, which looked like a bright reddish-blue swollen piece of overripe fruit. At Lichtenstein's insistence, Koufax went to see another uncle in New York—this one an osteopath. Uncle number 2 quickly recognized a loss of circulation from a likely blood clot, and warned him to get immediate treatment. Koufax brushed it aside.

A Monster Season Derailed

To this point in the season Sandy Koufax had a 14–4 record with a 2.06 ERA and 208 strikeouts in 174⅔ innings. He was on pace for a monster season: 25–7 and 374 strikeouts. But that was about to change in Cincinnati.

The Dodgers swept their three games in New York, split a 2-game series in Philadelphia, and arrived in Cincinnati on July 17. It was Koufax's turn to start against fellow All-Star Bob Purkey, also with 14 wins. While warming up before the game, Koufax knew from the extreme pain in his finger that he was a long shot for completing the game. A teammate even advised him to inform Alston that he would have to withdraw since he could barely hold the baseball.[27] But he insisted on going forward.

Leo Cardenas was the first batter Koufax faced in the bottom of the first inning. Cardenas lined his seventh pitch into center field for a single. Koufax struck out Eddie Kasko and got Vada Pinson to fly out to Willie Davis in center field for the second out, but he had already thrown 17 pitches. Next he had to face the dreaded Frank Robinson, batting .336. On the first pitch—a fast ball that everyone in the park knew was coming—Robinson nearly tore the glove off third baseman Jim Gilliam with another line-drive single. Wally Post, who ruined the Dodgers' inaugural game in Dodger Stadium, proceeded to ruin the heroic effort by Sandy Koufax. Post ripped a 2–2 pitch off the left field wall for a base-clearing double. Koufax hung on to get the third out, but he knew he was finished. The finger had literally split open. In the dugout, Walter Alston and Dodger trainer Bill Buhler were alarmed by the look of the injury—a raw open wound with no blood flowing out of it. Alston immediately removed Koufax. The Reds went on to win the game 7–5 by pounding Ed Roebuck for three home runs before going through three more Dodger pitchers. It went into the record book as the fifth loss of the year for Sandy Koufax. The loss to the Dodgers would be fatal.

The Dodgers were still trying to conceal the seriousness of the injury. In the *Los*

Angeles Times the next day it was reported that Koufax "had to surrender after falling behind after one inning when a blood blister developed on the tip of his finger and something went wrong with his shoulder."[28] But minutes after Koufax was removed from the game, Bill Buhler was on the phone to Buzzie Bavasi and team doctor Robert Kerlan in New York.

At the end of play on July 17—the day they lost Sandy Koufax—the Dodgers clung to a one-game lead over the Giants.

	W	L	Pct.	*
Los Angeles	62	33	.653	
San Francisco	61	34	.642	1
Pittsburgh	57	35	.620	3½

Thirteen

Life Without Koufax

You don't know how close you were to losing that finger.[1]—
Dr. Robert Kerlan to Sandy Koufax

After losing the series and Sandy Koufax in Cincinnati, the Dodgers moved on to Chicago while Koufax returned to Los Angeles to be examined by a second team doctor, Dr. Robert Woods. Woods personally accompanied Koufax to the offices of vascular specialist Dr. Travis Winsor. Together Winsor and Woods performed an arteriogram— an elaborate test to measure the blood flow in his left arm. It showed that the blood was flowing normally through the elbow, the forearm, the wrist, and into the palm of his hand. But below the palm—in the index finger—the circulation was reduced by about 85 percent by a closing off of the artery.[2]

They saw two possible diagnoses: (1) a blood clot; or (2) a rare disease known as Raynaud's Phenomenon. A blood clot could be dissolved; Raynaud's Phenomenon was incurable. They addressed the blood clot possibility first. An arterial blood clot would likely have been caused by a trauma. But the palm showed no evidence of a bruise. Had he tried to stop a ball with his bare hand, or had he been hit a pitch? Nothing came to mind. They were at an impasse. After repeated prodding, Koufax finally remembered being jammed by the Pirates' Earl Francis in Chavez Ravine back on April 28. Now all the pieces fell into place: it was a blood clot. Dr. Winsor began treatments to widen the artery, thin the blood, and dissolve the clot.[3]

Still on a Roll Without Number 32

Alston hesitated to put Koufax on the disabled list and risk losing him for a mandatory 30 days when he might recover sooner. Already with the smallest pitching staff in the majors—nine men—Alston would try to get by with eight, including three rookies.[4] Fortunately for the Dodgers, the loss of Koufax coincided with two positive developments: (1) the start of one of the hottest stretches of the season for the team; and

(2) the peaking of Don Drysdale in his greatest season. On July 22 they completed a 3-game sweep of the Cubs in Wrigley Field. In Game 2 Don Drysdale won his seventeenth game. Tommy Davis drove in six runs in the series to give him 102 for the season. They concluded a 19-game road trip on July 25 in St. Louis with Drysdale winning his eighteenth game to give the Dodgers a two-games-to-one series win over the Cardinals. The Dodgers had a one-game lead and two days to prepare for another showdown with the Giants in Los Angeles.

The war between the Giants and Dodgers resumed in the form of a weekend series beginning Friday night, July 27, at Dodger Stadium. Johnny Podres (7–7) beat the Giants 3–1 with a 5-hit complete game. All-Star game winner Juan Marichal (13–7) lasted only six innings. The big blow was a 3-run home run by Frank Howard off Marichal in the third.

On Saturday afternoon, July 28, Stan Williams (9–6) squared off against Jack Sanford (13–6). Sanford was chased in the fourth inning after the Dodgers tied the game at 3–3. After Frank Howard and Tommy Davis hit home runs off Bobby Bolin, the Dodgers had a 7–4 lead after five. The Dodgers went on to win the game, 8–6, as Ed Roebuck—now 7–0—got the win in relief.

It was Don Drysdale (18–4) against Billy O'Dell (12–8) in the series finale on Sunday afternoon, July 29. The Dodgers pounded O'Dell and the Giants 11–1 to sweep the series. Frank Howard had a home run, 3 singles, and 5 runs batted in to raise his batting average to .321. Drysdale threw a stellar 6-hit complete game for his nineteenth win of the season. Only a solo home run by Willie Mays in the seventh inning prevented a shutout. Maury Wills stole his 51st base to eclipse his personal best of 50 he set in 1960. Frank Howard destroyed the Giants with 3 home runs and 12 runs batted in for the series. It was the last game to be played in the month of July. With 12 home runs and a .381 batting average, Howard would be named NL Player of the Month, edging out Drysdale, who was 6–0 in July.[5] At the second All-Star break the Dodgers had increased their lead to four games over the Giants:

	W	L	Pct.	*
Los Angeles	71	35	.670	
San Francisco	67	39	.632	4
Cincinnati	61	42	.592	8½

Johnny Podres started the second All-Star game the next day at Wrigley Field in Chicago. Podres pitched two shutout innings, giving up two singles and striking out two. Unlike the first game, there was no heroic Giant-Dodger collaboration. The American League won the game, 9–4. The 1962 season would be the last year of the experiment of having two All-Star games.

Number Twenty Comes Early for Big D

Back at Dodger Stadium after the second All-Star break, the Dodgers began August by splitting two games with the Pirates. On August 3 they began a 4-game weekend series with the Cubs with Don Drysdale (19–4) going for his twentieth win. Drysdale almost didn't survive the first inning. He was shelled for two singles, a double, and a triple—all line drives—and three runs. Ignited by two singles, a triple, and two stolen bases by Maury Wills, the Dodgers came back to score eight runs, Drysdale was able to settle down and shut out the Cubs over the final eight innings on his way to a complete-game 8–3 victory. With 63 games left in the season, he became the Dodgers' first twenty-game winner since Don Newcombe in 1956. It was the earliest an NL pitcher had reached win number 20 since Jim "Hippo" Vaughn on August 1, 1918.[6] The Dodgers went on to win three out of four from the Cubs.

On August 7 the Dodgers completed a 2-game sweep of the Mets as Drysdale got win number 21 with a gritty 7–5 complete-game victory without his best stuff. Two days later they concluded an 11–2 home stand by taking two straight from the Phillies. Over the 13 games at Dodger Stadium, Maury Wills stole 11 bases to reach the 60 mark. Tommy Davis drove in 12 runs to give him 115 for the season. Frank Howard drove in 20. As the Dodgers prepared to leave town for San Francisco after winning 17 out of their last 21 games, their lead over the Giants had grown to 5½.

One of the noticeable characteristics of the Dodgers during their 17–4 run was how loose and relaxed they were. The players gave much of the credit to Leo Durocher. As the third base coach, it was his job to take Alston's signs from the bench and relay them to the batter and to the base runners. After Koufax went down, Durocher took it upon himself to shake up the team. He began to switch the signs to change the Dodgers' style of play from Alston's conservatism to a more wide-open style. In his autobiography he recalled, "Alston would give me the take sign, and I'd flash the hit sign. Alston would signal the bunt, and I'd call for the hit-and-run."[7] He was clearly overstepping his bounds, but the players loved it. They told him, "Just keep going, Leo. We never played like this before."[8] The downside was an increase in the tension between Durocher and Alston.

The status of Sandy Koufax remained uncertain. He stayed behind in Los Angeles to continue a series of treatments—some problematic—under the care of Dr. Winsor. One involved a daily 2-hour intra-arterial injection of a highly experimental "wonder" drug for dissolving blood clots. The drug later had to be taken off the market. When the blood began to flow back into his index finger, it caused an infection to take over the area surrounding the cuticle.[9] Hand specialist Dr. John Boyes had to be brought in to find the cause. After Dr. Boyes removed the nail of the index finger and drained the infected area, Koufax was finally out of the woods.[10]

Joyless in Mudville

Still haunted by the collapse of 1959, the *San Francisco Chronicle* headline, "Will Giants Choke Once Again?" expressed the pessimism of Giants fans as the weekend series with the front-running Dodgers began on Friday night, August 10. Johnny Podres (9–7), with a 5-game winning streak, took on fellow left-hander Billy O'Dell (13–10) to open the series before a sellout crowd of 40,304 at Candlestick Park. With a win the Dodgers could open up a commanding six-and-a-half-game lead. In an obvious attempt to neutralize Maury Wills, the Giants ordered the grounds crew to flood the infield areas where he could do the most damage: first base, second base, and the shortstop area. Seventy-four years after Ernest L. Thayer's poem, "Casey at the Bat," appeared in the *San Francisco Examiner*, the Giants seemed intent on making a reality of the mythical Mudville on windswept Hunter's Point. What's more, they refused to cut the infield grass in a not-so-opaque conspiracy to prevent Dodger ground balls from making it through to the outfield.

Giants' manager Alvin Dark stopped the Dodgers' momentum by turning his infield into a quagmire in a weekend series at the Candlestick Park August 10–12, 1962 (National Baseball Hall of Fame Library, Cooperstown, New York).

The Dodgers jumped on O'Dell for two runs on four singles in the top of the first. The Giants scored a run in the bottom of the first on a solo home run by Mays. They tied the game on a sacrifice fly by Pagan in the second. So far, Alvin Dark's guerrilla tactics were working. Wills reached base safely in his first two at bats, but did not attempt to steal.

The game remained a 2–2 tie as it moved to the bottom of the sixth. Podres got Chuck Hiller to ground out. He next got Mays to swing and miss on a 2–2 pitch. Roseboro, who had dropped the ball, tagged Mays for what everyone in the park believed to be the second out—everyone except plate umpire Ed Sudol. After Mays dropped his bat in resignation and took a step toward the dugout, Sudol belatedly signaled that the bat had made contact with the ball for a "foul tip." The call set off a raucous rhubarb. In a flash, Podres and Roseboro were in Sudol's face hurling vehement objections. Leo Durocher stormed out of the Dodger dugout and had to be restrained after he was ejected. But it proved to be an exercise in futility as Mays returned to the batter's box, and the floodgates opened. Mays lined Podres' next pitch into left field for a double. Instead of pitching to Orlando Cepeda as the potential third out, Podres walked him intentionally to load the bases for Felipe Alou. Alou lined a 0–2 pitch off the glove of Maury Wills to put the Giants ahead, 3–2. Jim Davenport beat out a dribbler up the third base line for an infield single to reload the bases. Tom Haller finished Podres with a ringing 2-run single into right field. Ed Roebuck came in from the bullpen with nothing. He walked Jose Pagan to load the bases for the third time. The pitcher, O'Dell, singled in two more runs. After leadoff batter Harvey Kuenn followed by doubling home the sixth run of the inning, the game was out of reach, at 8–2.[11]

After surviving his rocky first inning, Billy O'Dell retired 24 of the next 25 batters he faced for a complete-game 11–2 win. The phantom foul tip in the sixth inning killed any chance of the Dodgers' expanding their lead. Instead, it had been reduced to 4½.

Don Drysdale (21–4) and Billy Pierce (10–3) met on Saturday afternoon, August 11, in front of another turn-away crowd of 41,268 at Candlestick. Minutes before the first pitch, Head Groundskeeper Matty Schwab and his henchmen went to work with their four hoses. When they were done, the conditions were worse than the previous night. There were huge mud puddles around first and second base, and the over entire short-stop area. Predictably, the Dodgers howled in protest. Under the rules, it was up to the chief umpire—Al Forman—to decide whether the field was in playable condition. If he considered it unfit, he could suspend play until the condition was remedied by the grounds crew. Forman allowed play to go forward and set off a ticking time bomb in the process.

Again, the Dodgers got off to an early lead in the first inning. After Jim Gilliam reached safely on an error and Pierce hit Willie Davis in the hip with a pitch, Tommy Davis hit an 0–1 pitch over the right-field fence for a 3-run home run. Pierce and the Giants were down 3–0 after half an inning.

Play was interrupted in the second inning when Wills, armed with a mud cocktail, and Walter Alston carried on a heated protest with the umpire crew in the quagmire at the shortstop area—the main bone of contention. Wills would later say that it was like trying to play shortstop in a rice paddy. By the time the irate Wills came up to the plate to lead off the third inning, he was determined to continue the argument with umpire Al Forman from the batter's box. When Pierce was slow in delivering the first pitch, Wills stepped out of the box. Forman ordered him back in. Wills complied, but continued arguing. The crafty Pierce, recognizing a chance to push things over the edge by allowing Wills to continue his tirade, ignored Forman's signal to begin throwing. At this point Forman snapped, and ejected Wills. To the Giants, the only thing better than slowing down Maury Wills was not having to deal with him.

Drysdale took a 3–2 lead to the bottom of the sixth inning. He struck out Haller and Pagan, but gave up a double to Felipe Alou and hit Davenport on the left wrist, causing him to suffer a hairline fracture. Pierce was scheduled to bat next. Although he had limited the Dodgers to two singles after the first inning, Alvin Dark brought in Drysdale's nemesis, Willie McCovey, to hit for him. Drysdale and McCovey became embroiled in a 7-pitch struggle. The odds of McCovey's hitting a ball hard improved with each pitch until he hit the last one 440 feet over the right field fence. It was a 3-run jolt from which Drysdale and the Dodgers would not recover. The Giants went on to win the game, 5–4; Drysdale was charged with his fifth loss; and the lead was reduced to 3½ games.

Barring a playoff, Sunday, August 12, was to be the Dodgers' last appearance of the year in San Francisco. Already down two games to none, they had to face Juan Marichal in front of 41,812—the largest crowd to date at Candlestick. With their stopper, Sandy Koufax, back in L.A., they had to call on Stan Williams to salvage the series finale.

Before the game the audacious Matty Schwab held a water hose on the "takeoff strip" at first base for several minutes, to the delight of the crowd. This time the Giants had gone too far. The umpires held up the start of the game and ordered two wheel-barrows of sand to be dumped on the offending area.[12] In addition to the sand, the game would be played on what had by now become high, waving grass in the infield, which had not been mowed in four days.

The biggest game of the year to this point for the Dodgers turned into a clown show in blue. In the second inning they fell behind 1–0 when a passed ball by Roseboro allowed the Giants to score an unearned run off Williams. The Dodgers' only run came in the fourth when Ron Fairly hit an errant Marichal pitch halfway up the right-field bleachers to tie the game at 1–1. They could manage only two singles after that, but handed the Giants another unearned run in the fifth on a wild pitch and an error. Marichal coasted to 4-hit, 5–1 win.

The Giants succeeded in shutting down Maury Wills. He stole no bases and scored only one run in the series. The Dodgers hit an anemic .153 over the three games. To add a final insult to their injury, after the last pitch the grounds crew came out to ceremoniously mow the infield. As the Dodgers prepared to leave San Francisco for what they expected to be the last time, their lead had been cut to 2½ games. It was a pennant race again.

	W	L	Pct.	*
Los Angeles	79	40	.664	
San Francisco	76	42	.644	2½
Cincinnati	71	46	.607	7

Sandy Koufax, Question Mark

The Dodgers were reeling when they arrived in Pittsburgh on August 14 for a 3-game series with the Pirates. The Pirates beat Johnny Podres 2–1 the first night to trim their lead to a precarious game and a half. Their only run was a solo home run by Podres—the first of his career. Don Drysdale was beaten the next night, 6–3. It was the fifth consecutive loss for the Dodgers, and the first time since May that Drysdale had lost two games in a row. The only good news came from Los Angeles, where Sandy Koufax had begun a limited remedial throwing program. On the night of August 16, Stan Williams and Ron Perranoski salvaged the series finale with a 7–3 win to halt the losing streak. But the first signs of panic were already beginning to appear as Walter Alston and Leo Durocher bumped heads in the Forbes Field dugout. The volatile Durocher was set off when Ron Fairly missed a sign: "Someone should take those guys' money, someone better wake 'em up!"[13] Alston blew up in front of the players: "What do you mean? I'm the only one who has the right to take their money. I've had enough of this. You take care of the coaching, and I'll take care of the managing!"[14] After the Mudville series in San Francisco. Walter Alston made his first major personnel change in two months: Wally Moon, who had been waiting patiently on the bench, was inserted in left field and Tommy Davis was returned to the uncomfortable position of third base. Davis responded by going 1 for 15 in the Pittsburgh series.

After a month of treatments, Koufax rejoined the team on August 17 in Cincinnati—the site of his last appearance—as the Dodgers began a 4-game series with the Reds. He was relieved to hear from Dr. Robert Kerlan that everything had cleared up nicely. But what Dr. Kerlan told him next was very sobering: he had come very close to losing his finger. The bluish color that first appeared on July 12 in New York was the sign of a "pre-gangrenous condition." What's more, the subsequent infection could have spread to the bone and caused osteomyelitis. In either case—gangrene or a bone infection—the doctors would have had to amputate.[15] At this point Koufax was a question mark. The goal was for him to stay in shape while the finger continued to heal, with an eye toward possibly using him in September.

The Dodgers won two out of the first three games with the Reds to increase their lead to 3½ games over San Francisco at the end of play on August 19. Don Drysdale pitched a 3-hit complete game victory on that Sunday afternoon at Crosley Field to snap his personal 2-game losing streak and improve his record to 22–6. The series finale was played in sweltering 102-degree heat the evening of August 20. Stan Williams pitched a solid seven innings before turning the game over to Ron Perranoski with a 3–2 lead. Warren Spahn had already beaten the Giants in Milwaukee, and the Dodgers had an opportunity to open up a 4½ game lead. In the bottom of the ninth, Perranoski was one out away from making it happen. He just had to get Gene Freese with Frank Robinson on second base. But Freese dunked Perranoski's first pitch into center field to score Robinson with the tying run. The game moved to the bottom of the tenth as a 3–3 tie. Larry Sherry, who had replaced Perranoski, soon found himself in a thankless position: Frank Robinson, batting .344, back up at the plate with the bases loaded. Robinson ended it with a grand slam home run over the left-field wall. The Giants had dodged a bullet. Maury Wills batted .389 and stole five bases in the four games at Crosley Field, but the Dodgers could only come out with a split. Their lead remained stuck at 3½ games.

Minutes from Losing Leo

On August 24, eight days after Leo Durocher had his run-in with Alston in the dugout at Forbes Field, the Dodgers came close to losing him at the site of his greatest triumph as a manager—the Polo Grounds in New York. On this Friday night the Dodgers opened a 3-game series with Casey Stengel's farcical Mets with Don Drysdale on the mound seeking his twenty-third win. After losing eight out of their last twelve games on the road, they were counting on getting well at the Polo Grounds, where they were unbeaten in six games.

The Dodgers were on the field taking infield practice when the public address announcer asked that a physician report to the visitor's clubhouse. A rumor that Durocher had suffered a heart attack spread like wildfire through a crowd of nearly 40,000 that showed up to celebrate "Gil Hodges Night." Dr. Wade A. Hastings, a baseball fan from Malone, New York, responded to the call. By the time he reached the clubhouse, after being twice misdirected to the wrong end of the field, he found the 57-year-old Durocher in anaphylactic shock resulting from a massive allergic reaction to a penicillin shot. A non-physician, Dodger trainer Bill Buhler, had been giving him periodic penicillin injections for a groin injury Durocher suffered when Warren Spahn accidentally kicked him in the groin during a pre-game clowning match in Milwaukee. This was the first time there was a reaction. Walter Alston ran all the way to the clubhouse to be told by the ashen Durocher with a wan smile, "I'm going, Walt, go get 'em for me."[16] For half an hour Alston and Dodger trainers Bill Buhler and Wayne Anderson fought to keep Leo from losing consciousness. Alston massaged his limbs, Anderson administered oxygen, and Buhler gave him artificial respiration, giving Dr. Hastings time to arrive with a saving intravenous injection of adrenalin. While the revived Durocher was later joking and kidding as he awaited the arrival of an ambulance to take him to New York's Roosevelt Hospital, Dr. Hastings was giving reporters a chilling assessment, "Without help, he would have been dead in a few minutes."[17]

The night that had gotten off to a bad start for the Dodgers in the Polo Grounds clubhouse did not get any better on the field. Drysdale had pitched four complete-game wins in a row against the Mets. But by the fourth inning he had already given up home runs to "Marvelous" Marv Throneberry, "Choo Choo" Coleman, and Rod Kanehl and was behind, 3–2. He made it to the bottom of the eighth with the score tied 3–3 before Kanehl knocked him out of the game with a bases-loaded single that kept alive a fatal 3-run rally. The final result was a shocking 6–3 loss to the 32–96 Mets that trimmed the Dodgers' lead to 2½ games. Maury Wills singled and stole his sixty-ninth base in the first inning, then went silent at the plate while committing two errors at shortstop in the last two innings.[18] Leo Durocher recovered in time to watch the proceedings on television from his hospital room.

After their Friday night disaster, the Dodgers swept the final two games in New York. Stan Williams and Ron Perranoski beat Roger Craig 8–2 on August 25. Before the game Sandy Koufax disclosed his uncertain future to the press: "It's sort of useless right now. The finger is raw and I can hardly put any pressure on the ball. I have no idea when I'll be able to pitch."[19] On Sunday, August 26, they celebrated their last game of the year at the Polo Grounds with a merciless 16–5 thrashing of the Amazin' Mets, who did their best to help out with five errors. Pete Richert, a 22-year-old left-hander who was brought up from the minors at the beginning of the month to help fill the large hole left by Koufax, pitched seven innings for his third win. Maury Wills scored three runs with a walk, a single, and a double. As was now the case in every National League park—except Candlestick—each time Wills reached base, the crowd began a chant of "Go! Go! Go!" Wills responded by stealing three bases to give him seventy-two, eight shy of the post–1900 NL record. The Dodgers closed out a disappointing 15-game road trip in which they dropped 9 games, and prepared to return to Los Angeles—with Leo in tow—clinging to a 2½ game lead.

Closing Out August in First Place

The Dodgers opened a new home stand on August 28 in Dodger Stadium against the Reds. Minutes before the first pitch in the opener, the resurrected Leo Durocher had already kicked all the white chalk from his third base coaching box. Johnny Podres went on beat Bob Purkey and the Reds, 8–1, with a complete-game 8-hitter. Purkey, who entered the game with a 20–4 record, was finished after four innings thanks to home runs by Duke Snider and Tommy Davis. The next night, August 29, Don Drysdale made his second attempt at win number 23 in a pitcher's duel against fellow 20-game winner Joey Jay (20–10) in front of a huge crowd of 49,603. Drysdale pitched well for seven innings, but he was removed in the seventh for a pinch hitter with the Dodgers behind, 1–0. In the bottom of the ninth Jay was one out away from a 2-hit, 1–0 shutout when Duke Snider tied the game with a run-scoring triple. The game went to the bottom of the thirteenth inning tied 1–1 with Jay still on the mound for the Reds. After Tommy Davis singled and Lee Walls doubled, Jay walked Snider intentionally to load the bases for Roseboro. Roseboro hit Jay's next pitch—his 180th of the game—into center field to score the winning run. Ed Roebuck, who came in from the bullpen to pitch the last four scoreless innings, was the winning pitcher. Roebuck's record was now a perfect 9–0.

The next night, August 30, the Dodgers continued to have trouble against Reds pitching. This time it was Jim O'Toole who took a 2-hit, 5–0 shutout into the bottom of the ninth inning before they could finally get to him. The Dodgers put together five singles for four runs against O'Toole, Bill Henry, and Jim Brosnan. Brosnan hung on at the end to retire Jim Gilliam with the bases loaded to preserve a shaky 5–4 win for O'Toole.

The month of August concluded as the Dodgers began a weekend series with the Braves at Dodger Stadium on Friday, August 31. Young Pete Richert was again asked to fill in for Koufax. Richert turned in a satisfactory five innings before turning the game over to Ed Roebuck. Roebuck shut out the Braves over the last four innings to secure an 8–3 win for the Dodgers. The Dodgers prepared to enter September with a 2½-game lead over the Giants.

	W	L	Pct.	*
Los Angeles	88	47	.652	
San Francisco	85	49	.634	2½
Cincinnati	82	54	.603	6½

Tommy Davis finished August with a .342 batting average and 128 runs batted in, both tops in the National League. Drysdale led the league in wins with 22, and Maury Wills led the league in stolen bases with 73.

❊ ❊ ❊

On August 31, Senator Kenneth Keating (R–NY) reported to the Senate that there was evidence of Soviet missile installations in Cuba. Keating urged President Kennedy to take action.

❊ ❊ ❊

Fourteen

Black September

It's a record. Whether we say it's a record in 162 games or not, there's no question it's a record: The most bases ever stolen in a season.[1]—Ford Frick on Wills's breaking Cobb's record

The Dodgers were four games ahead with only seven games left to go. Nobody on the club had a thought that we could possibly lose.[2]—Sandy Koufax

The Dodgers got off to a flying start in September by completing a 3-game sweep of the Milwaukee Braves at Dodger Stadium. Podres beat them, 5–3, on September 1, and Drysdale shut them out, 8–0, on September 2 for his twenty-third win. They had now won 7 of their last 8 games to take a 3½-game lead over the Giants. But there were signs of trouble in two of the most important areas: pitching and defense.

A Pitching Staff at the Brink

The thinness of the pitching was beginning to be a concern. Alston had nine pitchers listed on his roster, including Koufax, who was still unavailable. Larry Sherry didn't see any work for two weeks due to a sore shoulder. On September 2, the day he was going to return, he suffered a freak mishap when he stumbled on the clubhouse steps and twisted his right ankle. That made it effectively a seven-man pitching staff, and put even more pressure on the overworked bullpen pair of Ed Roebuck and Ron Perranoski.

On September 4 a desperate Buzzie Bavasi was granted special permission to bring up a promising right-handed relief pitcher named Jack Smith from Omaha in the American Association. The 26-year-old Smith was 17–7 with 19 saves at Omaha, but had ten days left to go in his AA season. While the general rule prohibited major league teams

146

from promoting such a player before the end of his season, an "emergency clause" allowed them to replace a player who was inactive for 15 or more days. Since Sandy Koufax met that test, Smith was on his way to Los Angeles. The other 15 players the Dodgers called up that day to bring the roster up to the maximum of 40—including pitcher Joe Moeller, shortstop Dick Tracewski, and third baseman Ken McMullen—had to wait until the conclusion of their respective seasons.[3]

Dodger Defense—a Liability

On September 2 the Dodgers were ninth in the National League in defense. Only the Amazin' Mets were lower. They had 30 more errors than they had at this point in the 1961 season.[4] Maury Wills, now focusing on setting base-stealing records, had been particularly erratic. Through September 2 he already had 27 errors at shortstop. They had the fewest double plays in the league. And these numbers didn't reflect the inordinate number of misjudged fly balls that had dropped in for singles, doubles, and triples. In center field the speed of Willie Davis often covered up his bad judgment. A frustrated Walter Alston summed up his defense problem: "This is our weakest link. The trouble is we can't get some of our young players to think ahead."[5] The 1962 Dodgers were weak up the middle. In addition to center field and shortstop, second base was yet another problem area. Here they found themselves increasingly dependent on veteran Jim Gilliam to take over for the error-prone rookie, Larry "Possum" Burright.

The Final Showdown That Wasn't Final

The Dodgers held a 3½ game lead over the Giants as the two teams began a crucial 4-game series on September 3 at Dodger Stadium. The Giants came into the series having lost their last ten games in Los Angeles including all five this season at Dodger Stadium. Now they needed to take at least three out of four to pick up any ground on the Dodgers.

It was an angry Labor Day crowd of 54,418 that showed up for the opener with images of the quagmire and wild grass conditions at Candlestick Park of August still fresh in their minds. Many brought duck whistles. A local barber's union sent a telegram to the front office offering to cut the Dodger Stadium infield grass for free. Alvin Dark went with right-hander Jack Sanford (19–6), winner of his last thirteen decisions. Alston went with Stan Williams (12–9).

Willie Mays came into the game hitting only .196 for the year against the Dodgers. But in the third inning he broke a 1–1 tie with a 3-run home run off Williams that turned out to be the deciding blow. By the time the Giants knocked Williams out of the game in the fourth, they had built up an insurmountable 6–1 lead. Phil Ortega and Ron Perranoski held the Giants scoreless over the last four innings, but by then it was too late. Sanford, who had not completed a game against the Dodgers since May of 1959, pitched a complete-game 8-hitter for his twentieth win of the season. The 7–3 loss reduced the Dodgers' lead to 2½ games.[6]

	W	L	Pct.	*
Los Angeles	90	48	.652	
San Francisco	87	50	.635	2½
Cincinnati	84	55	.604	6½

On September 4, the Dodgers jumped out to an early 5–1 lead against Giants left-hander Billy Pierce with three singles, a double, two triples, and a steal of home by catcher John Roseboro in the first four innings. Their own left-hander, rookie Pete Richert, lasted only 4⅓ innings due to wildness. Ron Perranoski took over in the fifth and went all the way into the ninth inning protecting a 5–2 lead. The lead shrunk to 5–4 after he gave up a single to Harvey Kuenn followed by a home run to Jose Pagan. With one out, and right-handed sluggers Mays and Cepeda coming up, Alston held a summit at the mound. He had right-handed starters Don Drysdale and Stan Williams warming up in the bullpen, but decided to stay with Perranoski. Perranoski came through to strike out both Mays and Cepeda, and the Dodgers escaped with a 5–4 win. The lead was restored to 3½ games.[7]

	W	L	Pct.	*
Los Angeles	91	48	.655	
San Francisco	87	51	.630	3½
Cincinnati	85	55	.607	6½

Sandy Koufax caused a sensation before the game of September 5. He threw for twenty minutes in the bullpen, then asked pitching coach Joe Becker to catch a few pitches. Becket was so encouraged by the velocity and spin on his fast ball that he asked Koufax if he wanted to finish up batting practice. As Koufax approached the mound, the crowd—that would eventually reach 54,395—spotted number 32 and burst into wild applause. The fans were on their feet, rapt in pure joy, as Koufax threw the last six minutes of batting practice. Though he had thrown occasionally on the sidelines, this was the most rigorous test of his index finger since his last start of July 17. Hopes escalated further when the understated Koufax described his session as "real good."[8] Juan Marichal was about to put a damper on things as he prepared to take on Johnny Podres in the vital Game 3.

Mays pounded Podres for two run-scoring doubles and Davenport knocked in another run with a single to give the Giants a 3–0 lead in the middle of the fifth. At the same time the Dodgers had stopped hitting. Marichal shut them out on four singles through the first six innings. He neutralized Maury Wills by picking him off first base in the first inning. It was an all-around bad night for Wills, who went on to commit two of the Dodgers' four errors. The Giants got a scare in the sixth when Marichal twisted his right instep while fielding a swinging bunt by the lightning Willie Davis. After he made the inning-ending unassisted putout on Davis, he slumped to the ground, his face contorted in pain. He had to be carried off the field. The Giants' flame-throwing right-hander, Bob Bolin, inherited the 3–0 lead and took over for Marichal in the seventh inning. The Marichal-Bolin tandem retired 14 Dodgers in a row until Jim Gilliam singled with one out in the ninth inning. Tommy Davis singled with two out, bringing Ron Fairly to the plate as the potential tying run. But the game ended when Bolin got

Fairly on a weak ground ball to first base. It was a disappointing 3–0 defeat for the Dodgers, who could manage only two singles after Marichal exited. Their lead was again just 2½.

	W	L	PCT.	*
Los Angeles	91	49	.650	
San Francisco	88	51	.633	2½
Cincinnati	87	55	.613	5

The series finale of September 6 was huge for both teams. A win for the Dodgers would give them a split and restore the teams to the same place in the standings they were in before the series began. A win for the Giants would enable them to take the series, three games to one, and reduce the Dodgers' lead to 1½ games. It would all come down to a contest between Don Drysdale (23–7) and Billy O'Dell (16–12). From the start it was evident that Drysdale was not on his game. The Giants got to him early, with two runs in the first and two more in the third to jump out to a 4–0 lead. By then he had already given up three singles and two doubles, had walked two, and had thrown a wild pitch. The Dodgers came back to tie the game, 4–4, in the fourth on a home run by Frank Howard. Drysdale hung on with the game tied 4–4 until the eighth, when he gave up a double to Mays, a single to McCovey, and walked Cepeda to load the bases—his fourth walk of the game. With one out, Alston brought in Perranoski. Perranoski, working his third game of the series, got Harvey Kuenn to hit a double play ground ball to third base that should have ended the inning. But Kuenn beat the throw to first, enabling Felipe Alou to score the go-ahead run. In the bottom of the eighth, the Dodgers tied the game again with a home run—this time by Tommy Davis.

The game went to the ninth, tied 5–5, with Perranoski still on the mound for the Dodgers. He came within one pitch of holding the Giants scoreless when the roof caved in. With two out and the bases loaded, he missed on a close 3–2 pitch to Cepeda and walked in the tie-breaking run. With the bases still loaded, Kuenn followed with a crushing, base-clearing double to break the game open. Behind 9–5, the Dodgers tried to mount a rally in the bottom of the ninth. With the bases loaded, Tommy Davis—already with a double and a home run—came to the plate against Stu Miller as the potential tying run. Davis drove in his 132nd run of the year with a sacrifice fly to cut the Giants' lead to 9–6. Miller then turned out the lights by getting Frank Howard to foul out to end the game. The ninth-inning collapse would have enormous consequences for the Dodgers. Again, they let the Giants back in the race. The 3½-game lead they enjoyed at the beginning of the series was reduced to a game and a half. They could not depend on their 23-game-winner, Don Drysdale, to come through in a crucial stopper role.

The Dodgers won eight of the first eleven meetings between the two clubs—two by Sandy Koufax. Without having to face Koufax, the Giants won six of the last seven to even the season series at 9–9. With Koufax gone, the momentum had clearly changed. Fortunately for the Dodgers, September 6 was their last regularly scheduled game for the year with the Giants. Alvin Dark would call it "the biggest game I've ever managed."[9]

The Wills Distraction

With a tighter enforcement of the balk rule against pitchers in 1962, Alston decided from the beginning of the season to give Wills the green light to steal on his own. On September 7, the day after the Giants left town, Maury Wills stole four bases against the Pirates at Dodger Stadium to set a new National League record with 82. The old record of 80 was established by Bob Bescher of the Cincinnati Reds in 1911 in 159 games.[10] This was only game number 142 for the Dodgers. Ominously, Stan Williams and the Dodgers—who committed five errors including two by Tommy Davis at third base—were routed 10–1. A disgusted Walter Alston called it "just about the worst exhibition I've ever seen."[11]

To accommodate Wills in his quest to break the base-stealing records, the Dodgers were beginning to do things that distorted the offense. With leadoff batter Wills on first base, they were increasingly reluctant to have second-hole batter Jim Gilliam sacrifice. But with Wills successful nearly 90 percent of the time, why bunt? What's more, Gilliam, instead of feeling free to choose the best pitch to hit, was taking pitches to allow Wills to choose the best one to take off on.

The Dodgers took the last two games of the series with the Pirates on September 8 and 9 with Wills adding four more stolen bases. They closed out their home stand by sweeping a 2-game series with the Cubs. Supported by four hits and three steals by Maury Wills and a grand slam home run by Tommy Davis, Drysdale won his twenty-fourth game on September 10. Before the game, Sandy Koufax pitched batting practice for 22 minutes, only to leave the Dodgers up in the air with the ambiguous comment, "I didn't feel great out there, but I felt better than I thought I would."[12] The next day Stan Williams and Ron Perranoski beat the Cubs 3–1 despite two near-fatal throwing errors by Maury Wills in the ninth inning. Wills had two more hits to raise his average to .300, and another stolen base to give him 90. He was now within six of Ty Cobb's major league record 96, set in 1915. While the baseball world was fixated on Maury Wills over the last week with his 17 hits and 14 stolen bases, the Giants were quietly putting together a 7-game winning streak. At the end of play on September 11, as both teams prepared to go out on the road, the Dodgers clung to a razor-thin half-game lead over the Giants. Earlier that day a confident Sandy Koufax told the press, "I'm certain in my own mind that I will be able to pitch on this road trip, possibly this weekend in Chicago."[13] The Dodgers held their breath as they began printing World Series tickets.

The first stop for the Dodgers on their final road trip of the season was Houston on September 12. Rookie Pete Richert made his ninth start of the season against journeyman right-hander Ken Johnson. A standing-room-only crowd of 28,669 turned out on a sweltering evening at Colts Stadium, principally to see Maury Wills. Johnson, who surprised the Dodgers with a strong 9-inning performance in his Houston debut back on June 8, again proved to be a handful. He retired 13 men in a row before Frank Howard hit a 2–2 pitch into the left-field stands for a solo home run in the fifth inning. Johnson and reliever Don McMahon disappointed the fans by keeping Wills off the bases. It was the first time in seven games that he did not steal a base. With two strikeouts and two ground-outs, his 19-game hitting streak was over. Halfway through the game, the scoreboard showed that the Giants had lost their game in Cincinnati. In the third inning at

Crosley Field, Willie Mays had to be taken to the hospital after he collapsed from exhaustion in the dugout.[14]

Richert lasted only three innings in the heat before Ed Roebuck had to take over for five innings. After he walked the tying run in the ninth, the wilting Roebuck had to be relieved by Perranoski. The tenuous 1–0 lead was further imperiled when Perranoski wild-pitched the tying run into scoring position. But he got Billy Goodman to pop out and froze ex–Dodger Bob Lillis with a called-third-strike curve ball to end the game.[15] Roebuck, who got the win in relief, was now 10–0. The Dodgers, who could manage only two singles after Frank Howard's home run, got out of town with 1–0 win and a 1½-game lead. It was their last game in Houston for the year.

An Opportunity Missed in Chicago

On September 13, while the Dodgers were off traveling to Chicago, the Giants—with Willie Mays still in the hospital—dropped another game in Cincinnati to fall another half-game behind in the standings. The Dodgers led by two as they prepared to open a 3-day weekend series with the Cubs.

On Friday, September 14, Johnny Podres (13–11) and Don Cardwell (7–15) opened the series at Wrigley Field. With the wind blowing out to Lake Michigan, their chances of being around at the end were not good. Maury Wills led off the game with a walk, and promptly stole his 91st base on Cardwell's next pitch. Cardwell lasted a third of an inning with the Dodgers jumping out to a 7–0 lead in the first against a combination of four Cub pitchers. The Cubs knocked Podres out of the game in the fourth. But the Dodgers went on to rout the Cubs 13–7, powered by Frank Howard's 28th home run, 3 singles, and 4 runs batted in. The Dodger pitching staff got a lift when Larry Sherry, who hadn't saved a game since August 2, pitched 4-hit ball over the last 5⅔ innings to pick up his seventh win. It was the sixth straight win for the Dodgers.[16] That night the Giants lost in Pittsburgh to fall to an even three games behind Los Angeles. Willie Mays had rejoined the team, but was still unable to play.

On Saturday, September 15, Don Drysdale (24–7) went for his twenty-fifth win against rookie Cal Koonce (9–9). Drysdale held the Cubs hitless through the first three innings before the defense collapsed behind him. In the fourth, errors by Wills and Roseboro allowed the Cubs to score four unearned runs to turn Drysdale's 1–0 lead into a 4–1 deficit. In the fifth, Maury Wills singled, stole his 92nd base, and scored on Ron Fairly's sacrifice fly to cut Chicago's lead to 4–2. Still behind 4–2, with two runners on in the eighth, Alston pulled Drysdale and brought in Wally Moon to pinch hit against Don Cardwell, pitching in relief of Koonce. Moon's 2-run double tied the game, 4–4. Drysdale was off the hook for a loss, but he now had no chance to win number twenty-five. The Dodgers pulled the game out in the ninth when the league's leading batter and RBI man, Tommy Davis, surprised everyone in the ballpark when he scored the winning run by stealing home as the lead runner in a triple steal—in which Maury Wills was not involved.[17] The 6–4 win was the seventh in a row for the Dodgers and increased their lead to 4 games over the Mays-less Giants, who lost their fourth straight in Pittsburgh. The loss of Willie Mays for four games in the pennant stretch that looked like a fatal knockout blow to the Giants was a surprise gift to the Dodgers. With Mays out of the San Francisco lineup, the Dodgers were able to increase their lead from a half game to four full games. After September 15, the term "magic number"—which was now ten—began to appear in the papers. From here on, any combination of Los Angeles wins + San Francisco losses equaling ten would result in the Giants' being eliminated and the Dodgers' advancing to the World Series.

On the day the Chicago series concluded, Sunday, September 16, the Dodgers had a chance to pull away from the Giants in the pennant race. A Dodger win and a Giant loss would grow the lead to five games, and reduce the magic number to eight with twelve games to go. The Giants did their part, losing their fifth straight in Pittsburgh in extra innings after Willie Mays—playing for the first time in four days—tied the game with a 3-run homer in the eighth. But the Dodgers ran into a human roadblock named Bob Buhl. Buhl, who had not beaten the Dodgers in 17 straight tries dating back to 1960 as a member of the Milwaukee Braves, got the starting assignment against Stan Williams. The first sign of trouble appeared in the first inning, when Maury Wills led off the game with a bunt, but was thrown out trying to steal second. He would not reach base again. Williams could retire only one batter in the bottom of the first, exiting the game after giving up a grand slam home run to an unknown rookie outfielder named Nelson Mathews. Mathews's first home run, and second hit of his career, gave the Cubs an insurmountable 4–0 lead.[18] All weekend the media had anticipated an appearance by Sandy Koufax. But Alston brought in Koufax's principal replacement, Jack Smith. Koufax continued to sit on the bench as Alston called on Phil Ortega in the fifth and Larry Sherry in the eighth. Buhl went on to pitch a complete-game, 5–0 shutout. Stan Williams absorbed the loss after pitching just a third of an inning. The Dodger offense could produce only three singles after the first inning bunt by Wills.

The potential break-away weekend that began with such promise ended in disappointment as the Dodgers missed an opportunity to put the Giants away. Their lead remained frozen at four games. The erratic Dodger defense that prevented Drysdale from winning his 25th, was still a problem. Sandy Koufax never threw a pitch, and remained a question mark as the team moved on to Milwaukee.

Drysdale Stops the Slide in Milwaukee

Twenty-four hours after being blanked by Bob Buhl in Wrigley Field, the Dodgers arrived in Milwaukee for a 3-game series with his former team, the Braves. Two left-handers with 18½ years difference in their ages, 41-year-old Warren Spahn and 23-year-old Pete Richert, opened the series at County Stadium the night of September 17. The Braves scored two runs off Richert in the second inning with an RBI triple by Henry Aaron's brother, Tommy, and a run-scoring groundout by Spahn. Spahn shut out the Dodgers until the seventh, when Frank Howard lined a solo home run over the left field fence to cut Milwaukee's lead to 2–1.

But for a rookie base running blunder by Dick Tracewski, the Dodgers would have tied the game in the eighth. Tracewski came in to run for Ron Fairly, who opened the inning with a walk. When Maury Wills lined Spahn's first pitch into the right field corner, Tracewski was determined to score. As he approached third base, a frantic Leo Durocher jumping up and down with his arms stretched to the sky, implored him to stop at third. But Tracewski blew past Leo, only to be thrown out at the plate.[19] The Dodgers left Wills stranded at second base. Their last chance to get to Spahn came in the ninth when Tommy Davis doubled with one out. But again, they left the tying run stranded. Warren Spahn's 5-hit, 2–1 win would have shaved a full game off the Dodgers' lead had the Giants not dropped their sixth game in a row in Pittsburgh. By sheer luck their lead was still four and the magic number was reduced to eight.

The next night, September 18, the Aaron brothers pounded the Dodgers 10–5. Henry had a double and a home run, and Tommy drove in three runs with two singles and a double. After his chronic stiff back forced Dodger starter Johnny Podres to leave the game in the sixth inning with the score tied, 4–4, the roof fell in on three successive reinforcements from the bullpen. The lone bright spot was the 93rd stolen base by Maury Wills in the third inning. Since the Giants were off traveling to St. Louis, the Dodgers' lead was only reduced by a half game, to 3½. With ten games left, the magic number remained at eight.[20]

On Wednesday afternoon, September 19, Alston called on Don Drysdale to stop the 3-game losing streak and salvage the last game of the series in Milwaukee. Drysdale responded with a clutch 5-hit, 4–0 shutout. The game was loaded with individual accomplishments. Drysdale's twenty-fifth win was the most by a Dodger starter since Don Newcombe's 27 in 1956. Maury Wills began the game with a single off Braves starter Bob Henley. When a sprinkling of 6,339 fans in County Stadium began their chant of "Go!-Go!-Go!," Wills obliged by stealing second base to pull to within two of Cobb's record. Wills came around to score the first and only run the Dodgers would need on a double-play grounder by Tommy Davis, albeit not an RBI under the rules. But Davis later drove in his 142nd and 143rd runs of the season to break Roy Campanella's 1953 club record of 142. Big Frank Howard hit his 30th home run in the ninth.[21] All the Dodgers needed to make the day complete was for the Giants to continue their losing streak that night in St. Louis. But their luck with the Giants ran out. The rejuvenated Willie Mays and Tom Haller knocked Larry Jackson out the game in the third inning with home runs on their way to a 7–4 San Francisco win. With nine games to go, the Dodgers' lead remained at 3½, and the magic number was still seven.

From the sidelines in Milwaukee, Sandy Koufax told reporters of his frustration: "Walt Alston's got four starters, and he doesn't seem anxious to use me. But I'm very anxious to try my arm under game conditions, even in a mop-up job."[22] Koufax, who had now not thrown a live pitch for over two months, raised more than a few eyebrows when he confessed, "It's a question, though, if I still have my good stuff, since I'm still not putting my index finger on the seams when I throw in practice."[23] In 48 hours the Dodgers would have their answer.

A Ford Frick Surprise

September 20 was a travel day for the Dodgers. As they were on their way to St. Louis, Commissioner Ford Frick made an announcement effecting Maury Wills and his pursuit of Ty Cobb's base stealing record. Although Cobb stole his record 96 bases in 156 games in 1915, Wills would have to break the record within the first 154 games of the 1962 season. Frick justified his ruling by pointing out that Cobb's record was based on a 154-game schedule. He ignored the fact that Cobb had actually played in 156 games, the two extra games resulting from ties.[24]

The year before, Frick had inserted himself into the Mantle & Maris race for Babe Ruth's home run record, thereby creating the infamous "asterisk" controversy. Now, at the last minute, Frick arbitrarily put Wills in a near-impossible situation. Since Wills had accumulated his 94 stolen bases through the Dodgers' 153rd regularly scheduled game, Wills would have to steal at least three bases in the game to begin in 24 hours in St. Louis to break the record. Moments after being caught off guard by the ruling, a disheartened, tired, and bruised Wills told reporters, "As far as I'm concerned, I might as well forget trying to break Ty Cobb's record. I wish I'd known earlier. I figured I had three games with the Cardinals to steal three bases."[25]

That night in St. Louis, they received a gift from the Cardinals, who came from behind with two runs in the bottom of the ninth to beat the Giants, 5–4.

The Ill-Fated Return of Sandy Koufax

Things were looking up on September 21 when the Dodgers came into St. Louis to begin a 3-game weekend series with the Cardinals. They had a 4-game lead with nine games to play. While the Dodgers expected to face Bob Gibson (15–12) on this Friday night, the announcement of Sandy Koufax as his opponent caught everyone by surprise. Walter Alston had given no previous indication that his return was imminent. "Starting Koufax is not an experiment; it's a necessity," Alston confessed to the press before the game. "Johnny Podres' back ailment flared up again in Milwaukee, and we need all the help we can get for the stretch run."[26] An hour before game time the Dodgers were handed another gift when Bob Gibson broke the fibula in his right leg after his spikes caught in the dirt during his turn in batting practice. Instead of facing the ferocious Gibson, they would face veteran left-hander Curt Simmons (8–9).

The stage was set for a momentous 154th game of the season. Koufax would be on the mound for the first time in 66 days. Maury Wills was prepared for a record-breaking performance—provided he could get on base. But it soon turned into a disaster. In the bottom of the first, a rusty and erratic Koufax walked the first two batters, retired Stan Musial and Ken Boyer, and then walked Bill White to load the bases for right fielder Charlie James. Koufax would later recall, "It was like pitching for the first time in spring training. I had good stuff, but my control was off."[27] James fouled off several pitches before connecting on a high outside fast ball, driving it onto the top of the right-field pavilion at old Busch Stadium for a grand slam home run—a ball Koufax would later say was a routine out in Dodger Stadium. After he walked the next batter on four pitches, Koufax was done. With the Dodgers already in a 4–0 hole, Alston brought in Ed Roebuck. Koufax would later recall just how pivotal this moment was: "I still think that if I had been able to get Charlie James, I might have been able to settle down and pitch a fair game."[28]

Roebuck helped the Dodgers get out of the first inning without further damage, and then held the Cardinals scoreless for the next five innings. In the top of the sixth he gave way to a pinch hitter to allow the Dodgers to chip away at a 4–1 deficit. Wills worked Simmons for an 8-pitch walk. Simmons had a reputation for being an easy pitcher to steal on, and one pitch later Wills was standing on second base with his 95th steal of the season. He scored on a 2-out single by Lee Walls to make the score 4–2, but would not reach base again. With Roebuck out of the picture, the Cardinals resumed the onslaught by scoring seven more runs in the bottom the sixth off three different Dodger pitchers to put the game away. Staked to a comfortable 9-run lead, Curt Simmons shut out the Dodgers over the final three innings.

It was an ugly 11–2 rout with multiple implications—all negative. Though the Dodgers escaped having to face Bob Gibson, they could produce only five hits against Curt Simmons. After 154 games, Maury Wills was still one stolen base short of Ty Cobb's record of 96. Under the Ford Frick formulation, the record was thus rendered unassailable. But the feisty Wills refused to accept the ruling: "I figure I've got 156 games to break the record, and I'm right on schedule."[29] Sandy Koufax came into the game as a big question mark for the Dodgers. After surviving for just two thirds of an inning, it was evident that they could not count on him for the remainder of the regular season—or the World Series, for that matter. After admitting to reporters in the clubhouse after the game that he still could not grip the ball tightly, Koufax tried to put a positive spin on the situation: "My finger doesn't feel 100 percent, but it does feel as good as it did two or three games before I went under the doctor's care."[30] No one in the room was convinced.

While the Dodgers were going down in St. Louis, Willie Mays and the Giants were beating up on the Colt .45s in Houston. A 4-for-4 performance by Mays led the Giants and their 24-year-old rookie right-hander, Gaylord Perry, to an easy 11–5 win. As a result, the Dodgers' lead was reduced to three with eight games to play. The magic number was six.

	W	L	Pct.	*
Los Angeles	99	55	.643	
San Francisco	96	58	.623	3
Cincinnati	94	62	.603	6

❊ ❊ ❊

The Defense Intelligence Agency learned of a first-hand sighting in Havana, Cuba, "of a truck convoy of 20 objects 65 to 70 feet long which resembled large missiles." But because earlier reports of a similar nature proved false, the DIA dismisses the information as only "potentially significant."[31]

❊ ❊ ❊

Rolling the Dice with Podres

The next day, Saturday, September 22, Alston rolled the dice and started Johnny Podres. The situation with Podres was touch-and-go ever since his back forced him to leave the game early in his last start in Milwaukee. He had failed to complete his last five games dating from September 1, but had won his last four starts in Busch Stadium. Today, he was in constant trouble, giving up nine hits—but only one run—in 6⅓ innings. He was handed a 4–0 lead when the Dodgers scored four runs in the fourth on an RBI single by Duke Snider and a 3-run home run by Tommy Davis, both off Cardinal starter Ray Washburn. The three runs batted in for Davis increased his season total to 146, already the most in the National League since 1937.

After Curt Flood and Stan Musial singled in the seventh off Podres, who was struggling to hold on to a 4–1 lead, Alston brought in Larry Sherry to pitch to Ken Boyer, representing the tying run at the plate. Sherry got Boyer to ground into a force play, then walked Bill White to load the bases for Charlie James. James launched a screaming line drive into center field that looked like a sure base-clearing, game-tying, extra-base hit until Willie Davis ran it down for the third out.

Sherry took the 4–1 lead to the bottom of the ninth. After Curt Flood led off with an infield single, Sherry struck out Musial and got Boyer to line out to Willie Davis. With two out, Bill White lined a single into center field to again bring up the dangerous Charlie James—this time as the potential tying run. On the first pitch Sherry got James on a pop up to Maury Wills, and the Dodgers ran off the field with a 4–1 win.[32]

That night in Houston the Giants lost, 6–5, to the Colt .45s after blowing another 1-run lead in the bottom of the ninth inning. Two outs away from a 5–4 win, they brought in their best left-handed starter, Billy Pierce, to pitch to Terry Pendleton with the tying and winning runs on base. After Pierce hit Pendleton with a pitch, they brought in their best right-handed starter, Jack Sanford, to pitch to Ramon Mejias with the bases loaded. Mejias promptly rocked Sanford with a walk-off 2-run single. It was a devastating loss for the Giants. They lost a full game in the standings to fall to four behind the Dodgers with seven games to go. The magic number for the Dodgers was reduced to four. And now it was just the two of them, as the defending NL champion Cincinnati Reds were eliminated in Philadelphia.

	W	L	Pct.	*
Los Angeles	100	55	.645	
San Francisco	96	59	.619	4
Cincinnati	94	63	.599	7

A Triumph for Wills, a Disaster for the Dodgers

In the series finale on Sunday, September 23, the Dodgers had a chance to move a step closer to the World Series with Don Drysdale on the mound seeking his 26th win on the heels of his shutout of the Braves. But the attention of the 20,743 people at Busch Stadium was on Maury Wills. Contrary to Commissioner Ford Frick's ruling, Wills entered the game—number 156 on the schedule—believing that this was his final chance to break Ty Cobb's record. Not only was he fighting the commissioner, he had to face Cardinals right-hander Larry Jackson, considered one of the hardest pitchers in the league to steal on. Jackson got Wills to ground out in the first inning. In the third, Wills hit a grounder through the hole between first and second for a single. The fans were on their feet chanting "Go!-Go!-Go!" as Wills took his lead. One of the Cardinal coaches even began taking movies. On Jackson's third pitch Wills stole number 96 with a belly-flop slide into second base. By this point in the season his hips were so bruised that he could no longer execute a conventional slide. But he was even with Cobb.

In the fifth, Wills tried to bunt to get on base, but was thrown out by the nimble Jackson, who fielded it in front of the mound. With two out in the seventh, Wills hit another single through the hole into right field off Jackson. On Jackson's first pitch to Jim Gilliam, Wills hesitated, then broke for second base, catching Cardinal shortstop Dal Maxville napping. Carl Sawatski's throw bounced past Maxville, who was late to the bag. The rare "delayed" steal was his 97th of the season. Head umpire Augie Donatelli confiscated the baseball from the Cardinals, and turned it over to the Dodgers for Wills. After the inning the grounds crew ran onto the field, unfastened the second base bag, and installed a new white one. When Wills came to the plate in the ninth the Cardinal management halted the game. Public address announcer Charlie Jones came onto the field and presented the record-breaking base to Wills with the admonition, "And you won't have to steal this one because we're giving it to you."[33] Maury Morning Wills was now the greatest base stealer in modern times—or was he? It would be up to Commissioner Frick to decide whether it was all a meaningless exercise. Lost in the excitement were the pennant race, and the fact that the Dodgers were being soundly trounced, 12–2, by the Cardinals.

It had all started on such a hopeful note. Drysdale was staked to a 2–0 lead after a half inning of play as the Dodgers got to Larry Jackson with two doubles and a single. But they failed to put him away. In the bottom of the inning the Cardinals jumped on Drysdale for consecutive singles by Javier and Flood, a walk to Musial, and a bases-loaded double to Bill White, all before he could get anyone out. By the end of the first the Cardinals were ahead, 3–2, and never looked back. After surviving the first inning, Jackson shut out the Dodgers the rest of the way. In the fourth inning, after Drysdale walked Javier to load the bases, and hit Flood with a pitch to force in the Cardinals' fifth run, he was gone. Drysdale's run for win number 26 was painfully brief: 8 runs (6 earned), 6 hits, in 3⅓ innings. The overworked Perranoski came in to try to keep the game within reach, but was cuffed around for another three runs.[34]

After Sandy Koufax's catastrophic performance of September 21, Alston was anxious to evaluate him further under game conditions. With the game out of reach at 11–2, he brought in Koufax to mop up the final two innings. The results were inconclusive. Koufax walked three batters, struck out two batters looking, gave up two singles, and allowed one run. He made 47 pitches, 24 for strikes.

After the game, Commissioner Ford Frick issued an ambiguous press release: "It's a record. Whether we say it's a record in 162 games or not, there's no question it's a record—the most bases ever stolen in a season."[35]

Of more importance was the news from Houston, where the Giants routed the Colt .45s 10–3 to cut the Dodgers' lead to three games.

	W	L	PCT.	*
Los Angeles	100	56	.641	
San Francisco	97	59	.622	3

That day in St. Louis the Dodgers concluded a rocky 10-game road trip—their last of the year. Despite lurching through it with a so-so 5–5 record, they actually picked up 2½ games on the Giants, who stumbled through the same 12-day period, September 12 to September 23, with a miserable 3–8 record. The Dodgers would finish the season with six games at Dodger Stadium, the final three with these same troublesome Cardinals. As Alston prepared the team for the final stretch run, question marks abounded: Could the Dodgers depend on Koufax? Would Podres's back hold up? Could Drysdale get beyond win number 25? Would the Dodgers start hitting again?

The Fatal Mistake of Looking Past the Colts

When the Dodgers arrived back in Los Angeles on September 24, they had one day to regroup after their disastrous weekend in St. Louis in which Koufax and Drysdale were routed, and the team was outscored 24–8. The good news was, they had a 3-game lead over the Giants with 6 games to play—all at Dodger Stadium. There would be three "easy" games with the eighth-place Colt .45s before they would have to take on the Cardinals again over the final weekend.

Alston went with Drysdale to open the series with the Colt .45s on September 25, even though he had made 61 pitches in his 3⅓ innings of work two days before in St. Louis. The plan was to start Drysdale followed by Podres—his back willing—so that both would be rested and ready to go on the weekend.[36] Ex-Dodger Turk Farrell, with an unimpressive 9–19 record, started for Houston.

Maury Wills continued to be the center of attention as he relentlessly drove himself toward a personal goal of 100 steals. He singled in the third, but was thrown out at second base, thereby removing the potential tying run. He singled again in the sixth and promptly stole second off Farrell, even though feisty Ex-Dodger Norm Larker, now playing first base for Houston, did his best to obstruct his path. Wills advanced to third on an infield single, then caught Farrell unaware in the middle of his windup and streaked home to tie the game at 1–1. It was the first career steal of home for Wills, and number 99 for the season. But it was his error at shortstop in the first inning that would come back to haunt the team.

Drysdale was making his third appearance in five games in a heroic effort to rally the team. Alston would have Ed Roebuck (10–0) waiting in the wings in case Drysdale's arm did not respond in pre-game warmups. But it was Drysdale who plunged into the first inning by walking the first batter, ex–Dodger Carl Warwick. He got Milwaukee Braves castoff Al Spangler to bunt into a fielder's choice before the Dodger defense let him down. Dave Roberts reached base on Larry Burright's error. Lumbering Norm Larker hit a sure inning-ending double play grounder to Wills. But Wills threw it away, enabling Spangler to score. Bobby Aspromonte, the fourth ex–Dodger in the Houston lineup, lined out to Willie Davis in center field. Drysdale survived the first inning down 1–0, then settled down to shut out the Colt .45s for the next five innings.

In the seventh, Drysdale was one out away from getting out of the inning with a 1–1 tie when Spangler tripled home shortstop J.C. Hartman to put Houston ahead, 2–1. The Dodgers came right back to tie the game 2–2 in the bottom of the seventh on a sacrifice fly by Johnny Roseboro. After 101 pitches, the overstretched Drysdale was done for the night. Perranoski came in to pitch the eighth and ninth, holding Houston to a mere single and no runs. But for the Wills error in the first inning, the Dodgers would be in the clubhouse with a win. Instead the game went to the tenth inning as a 2–2 tie. Alston finally brought in Roebuck, who had been ready since before the first pitch of the game. By then the scoreboard reflected the results from Candlestick: Jack Sanford and the Giants had beaten the Cardinals, 4–2. With one away the irrepressible Al Spangler reached out and drove Roebuck's 1–2 pitch into the left-field pavilion for what proved to be the game-winning home run. Turk Farrell closed out the Dodgers in the bottom of the tenth for a 3–2, complete-game win. It was Roebuck's first loss since August 8, 1960.[37] Maury Wills had 99 stolen bases, but the Dodgers' lead was sliced to two games and the magic number was still 4.

	W	L	Pct.	*
Los Angeles	100	57	.637	
San Francisco	98	59	.624	2

The Dodgers had a much-needed 13–1 "laugher" the next night at Dodger Stadium. And it was indeed a much-needed laugher. The Giants had already beaten the Cardinals, 6–3, in a matinee game at Candlestick. By the time the Dodgers took the field they were haunted by the specter of a mere one-game lead if they could not control an incorrigible eighth-place expansion team. But a laugher it was. Maury Wills stole his 100th base.[38] Johnny Podres's back held up for seven innings to enable him to post his 15th win. Frank Howard hit his 31st home run and drove in five runs. Tommy Davis went 3 for 3 to raise his league-leading batting average to .346. Clearly the Al Spangler debacle must have been an aberration. Tonight, after scoring a lone run in the first inning, Houston behaved by effectively disappearing for the last two and a half hours.

At the end of play on September 26, the Dodgers still had a 2-game lead with four to play. The magic number was reduced to three.

	W	L	Pct.	*
Los Angeles	101	57	.639	
San Francisco	99	59	.627	2

The morning of September 27 in the *Los Angeles Times*, a triumphant Maury Wills sat cross-legged on a white base. Behind him was a mountain of 99 bases, making a total of 100. That night the Dodgers would conclude their series with the upstart Colt .45s, who were presumably chastened by the 13–1 thumping of 24 hours before.

The Dodgers knew when they arrived at the ballpark that the Giants had already lost, 7–4, to the Cardinals at Candlestick courtesy of a 5-for-5 performance by Stan

Musial. The implications were huge: with a win the Dodgers could clinch a tie for the pennant and reduce the magic number to 1.

In desperate straits due to his depleted pitching staff, Walter Alston gambled by starting Sandy Koufax despite his two un–Koufax-like performances in St. Louis. Koufax would later recall that he had great stuff for the first four innings. He retired the first eleven batters in order, striking out four of them, and took a 3–0 lead into the fifth. It was there that he issued his only walk to leadoff batter Bobby Aspromonte. Ramon Mejias, the Colts' leading power hitter, was next. Koufax had struck him out on three pitches the first time up. This time Mejias hit his first pitch over the left-center-field fence for his 24th home run to cut the Dodger lead to 3–2. Koufax completed the fifth without further damage. The Dodgers bounced back to score their fourth run off Houston starter, and ex–Dodger, Jim Golden.

The Dodgers still had a 4–2 lead as the game moved to the sixth. Koufax had thrown 76 pitches, 47 for strikes. But having to effectively start over after being sidelined for 66 days, he was still in spring training mode as far as endurance was concerned. The press reported that it was at this point that Koufax told Alston that he had "run out of gas."[39] In arguably the key game of the season, Alston, fearing that Koufax was tiring, decided to take him out and bring in Ed Roebuck.

With Koufax out, the complexion of the game changed. Roebuck promptly blew the 4–2 lead by walking Johnny Temple, then giving up a triple to Norm Larker, followed by a single to Mejias. After just two-thirds of an inning, the score was tied 4–4 and Roebuck was gone. Larry Sherry came in to pitch to former Pirates catcher Hal Smith, of 1960 World Series Game 7 fame. Smith singled to left field, sending Mejias to third. Sherry and J.C. Hartman engaged in a 7-pitch battle that ended with Hartman's ripping a line drive into left field, on which Tommy Davis nearly made a brilliant shoestring catch. But when Davis could not hold on to the ball, it turned into a crushing 2-run double that put Houston ahead for the first time, 6–4. Again, the Dodgers bounced back in the bottom of the sixth to tie the game at 6–6 on singles by Fairly, Roseboro, and Wills.

Houston was ninth in the league in hitting, and they had already finished off Koufax and Roebuck. An increasingly desperate Alston brought in Perranoski to pitch the seventh. Perranoski, who was making his major-league-record 66th appearance for a left-hander, got no support from the Dodger defense. Leadoff batter Carl Warwick hit a sharp, but completely playable, grounder to Wills that he could not handle. With Warwick—credited with a hit—on first, Dodger third baseman Daryl Spencer threw away Johnny Temple's double-play ground ball. And when Perranoski was unable to field Al Spangler's bunt, the bases were loaded with none out. Perranoski bore down to get three consecutive groundouts, but two of them scored runs to put Houston ahead for good, 8–6. Big Colts right-hander Jim Umbricht shut out the Dodgers over the final three innings on two singles.

September 27 was a rude shock for the Dodgers. Even with Sandy Koufax pitching, they blew an opportunity to clinch a tie. They lost the series to the expansion Colt .45s, two games to one. The stolen base euphoria was over. Maury Wills had three hits, but never attempted to steal. The lead and magic number remained frozen at two.

	W	L	PCT.	*
Los Angeles	101	58	.635	
San Francisco	99	60	.623	2

With no more off days to regroup in a rapidly deteriorating season, the Dodgers had less than 24 hours to prepare for the Cardinals—the only team with a winning record against them for the year and the team that had already beaten them in four of the six games played at Dodger Stadium.

Lost Weekend at Dodger Stadium

A turn-away crowd of 51,064 (paid) squeezed into Dodger Stadium for the September 28 opener of the Cardinal series to witness the Dodgers' second attempt to clinch a tie. Even before the game began, the tension in the air was palpable. The Dodgers would have to face the same premier right-hander, Larry Jackson, who shut them down five days before in St. Louis and who had pitched a complete game to beat them in his only appearance at Dodger Stadium back in May. Alston had no one but rookie left-hander Pete Richert to put up against Jackson. Richert had pitched one complete game in his 78 innings in the major leagues.

The Dodgers knew the key to defeating Jackson was to get to him early. In the first inning Wills led off with a single and Gilliam reached base safely on an error by Bill White. Tommy Davis gave them a 1–0 lead by driving in Wills with his 150th run batted in. But just as they did in St. Louis, they went on to blow their best chance to put Jackson away. With one out and runners at first and third, an anxious Frank Howard struck out on a ball well out of the strike zone. When Ron Fairly, mired in a 1-for-30 slump, popped out leaving the runners stranded, the veteran Jackson was off the hook.

By the fourth inning the Dodgers were already into their bullpen. With one out and the bases loaded they had to remove Richert and bring in Ed Roebuck. Roebuck got the next two batters to keep the game tied at 1–1, then allowed the Cardinals to go ahead, 2–1, in the fifth when Musial lined an RBI single off him. Larry Sherry took over for Roebuck to begin the sixth and proceeded to pitch two scoreless innings.

After Wills tied the game, 2–2, in the seventh by driving in Roseboro with a single off Jackson, the overworked Ron Perranoski was brought in from the bullpen to begin the eighth. Perranoski was making his fourth appearance in the last five games. He retired the Cardinals in order in the eighth and ninth innings. The game went to the tenth tied, 2–2. Alston had no choice but to stay with Perranoski, who had already been stretched to his limit. Curt Flood and Musial led off the inning with singles. Dodger third baseman Jim Gilliam fielded Ken Boyer's sharp ground ball headed for left field and threw Flood out at the plate. Perranoski got Bill White on a force play for the second out. Then White pulled off a surprise steal of second to put two Cardinal runners in scoring position. Charlie James, whose grand slam home run ruined the return of Sandy Koufax in St. Louis, was next. In a controversial move, Alston decided to pitch to James even with first base open. Just as he had against Koufax, James went the other way against Perranoski, ripping his fourth pitch into right field for a base hit. The runner from third scored easily to break the tie, but Frank Howard's laser throw nailed Bill White at the plate. Howard's nineteenth outfield assist of the season kept the Dodgers within one run.[40]

In the bottom of the tenth, the Dodgers left the tying run on base as Larry Jackson got major league baseball's top run producer, Tommy Davis, to ground out to end the game. While the Dodgers had to burn through four pitchers, the Cardinals got a 10-inning complete game from Jackson. Since the Giants' game in San Francisco was rained out, the Dodgers' lead was cut by only a half game. But there was a sense of fatalism in the crowd as it filed out of Dodger Stadium in silence.

	W	L	PCT.	*
Los Angeles	101	59	.631	
San Francisco	99	60	.623	1½

The Dodgers gave the ball to Don Drysdale in their third attempt to clinch a tie on Saturday night, September 29, before another turn-away crowd at Dodger Stadium. It would also be Drysdale's third attempt to win his 26th game. Cardinal manager Johnny Keane named Ernie Broglio (11–9) as his starting pitcher.

The game was all but decided in the top of the second inning. After the maddening Charlie James grounded a single past Drysdale, Dal Maxville came to the plate with two outs and a .220 batting average. Maxville was unable to get around on Drysdale's fast ball, but managed to loop a weak pop fly over first base and down the right field line. Frank Howard made a long run for the ball and gloved it just as he was crossing the foul line. Drysdale was headed for the dugout with his shutout intact when the ball popped out of Howard's glove for an error. James scored all the way from first base, touching off a firestorm. Walter Alston, joined by General Manager Buzzie Bavasi, maintained that Howard had dropped the ball in foul territory. But they were overruled by first base umpire Chris Pelekoudas. An aggravated Drysdale then made a bad pitch to Cardinal pitcher Ernie Broglio, who lined it into center field to score Maxville. After an inning and a half, Drysdale and the Dodgers were down, 2–0, on two unearned runs.

The luckless Drysdale shut out the Cardinals for the next six innings before being removed for a pinch hitter in the eighth. Meanwhile the Dodgers had produced only two singles against Broglio as he took the 2–0 lead to the bottom of the ninth. Duke Snider, who had been put into the lineup to add some pop to the Dodgers' foundering offense, led off the inning with a walk. Tommy Davis, who had been moved in from left field to third base to make room for Snider, flied out to complete an 0-for-4 night. Frank Howard, with three strikeouts to go along with his colossal error, came to the plate as the tying run. Howard's nightmare continued as he grounded into a game-ending double play on Broglio's first pitch, thereby igniting a chorus of boos from an angry crowd.[41] Abandoned by both the Dodger offense and defense, Drysdale failed in his final attempt to win number 26. He would finish the year at 25–9. One of the five hits Drysdale gave up was a line-drive single by the 41-year-old Stan Musial in the third inning. It would be Musial's last hit of his last great season.

In San Francisco, the Giants pounded the Colt .45s 11–5 in the first game of a double-header on Jack Sanford's 24th victory of the year. The Dodgers were only able to hold onto their 1-game lead when old friend Norm "Dumbo" Larker beat Juan Marichal in the second game with a 2-run home run.

	W	L	PCT.	*
Los Angeles	101	60	.627	
San Francisco	100	61	.621	1

On Sunday, September 30, the Dodgers and Cardinals met for the third and final time on the last day of the season at Dodger Stadium. Alston's money pitcher, Johnny Podres, was asked to break the Dodgers' 3-game losing streak and prevent a complete collapse. Podres had won eight of his last nine home decisions. Today was his 30th birthday. He would be opposed by fellow left-hander Curt Simmons, the winning pitcher in the ill-fated return of Sandy Koufax on September 21 in St. Louis.

The desperate and pressing Dodgers drew the wrath of the less-than-capacity crowd as they committed a series of base-running blunders. In the second inning, Lee Walls was thrown out trying to stretch a lead-off, bloop single. In the third, the Cardinals embarrassed Willie Davis with a minor league decoy play, doubling him off first base as he took off on a steal attempt on Podres's foul pop fly. In the seventh, Tommy Davis was picked off first base by Simmons after he singled.

Left: Johnny Podres gets the call from Walter Alston to pitch the final regular season game of the 1962 season at Dodger Stadium. *Right:* Cardinals catcher Gene Oliver hit an eighth inning solo homer to beat Johnny Podres and the Dodgers 1–0 on September 30, 1962, to force a playoff with the Giants (both, George Brace photographs).

Podres had given up only two singles as he began the eighth inning of a scoreless tie. The problematic Charlie James led off the inning with a line shot to center field—but right at Willie Davis. With one out, Podres quickly got ahead of St. Louis catcher Gene Oliver with a 1–2 count. But Oliver connected on Podres's fourth pitch, hooking a long drive down the left-field line that he managed to keep fair. When the ball landed deep in the lower box seats between the foul pole and the bullpen, the crowd, sensing the Dodgers were doomed, fell silent. By then the news that Willie Mays had broken out of a 1-for-16 slump to single-handedly beat the Colt .45s, 2–1, with a late home run at Candlestick Park had been flashed on the message board.[42]

The Dodgers squandered their last two chances against Simmons, passively going down in order in both the eighth and ninth innings. After just an hour and 51 minutes, it was over. As the crowd of 42,325 left Dodger Stadium, it tried to come to grips with the events of the last week. The Dodgers had just lost 7 of their last 9 games to second-division teams. On September 22, after Podres beat these same Cardinals in St. Louis, the Dodgers had a four-game lead with seven games to play. Today's 1–0 shutout by Curt Simmons extended their scoreless streak to 21 consecutive innings. And if that wasn't enough, they just ended the season in a dead heat with the Giants, who caught them on the last day of the season to force a 3-game playoff to begin in less than 24 hours in San Francisco.

	W	L	PCT.	*
Los Angeles	101	61	.623	
San Francisco	101	61	.623	

After the last Dodger left the clubhouse, an elaborately decorated—but uncut—birthday cake for Johnny Podres remained on the table with its 30 candles still unlit.

❊ ❊ ❊

That same Sunday, President Kennedy spoke to the nation on television less than an hour after Mississippi Governor Ross R. Barnett of Mississippi announced that he would no longer attempt to block the enrollment of James Meredith, a 29-year-old Negro, at the University of Mississippi. Kennedy told the nation and the people of Mississippi, "The eyes of the nation and all the world are upon you and upon all of us, and the honor of your university and your state are in the balance."[43] That night in Oxford, Mississippi, James Meredith was admitted to the University of Mississippi, touching off a riot in which six United States marshals were shot.

❊ ❊ ❊

Fifteen

Left Behind in October

It was the worst inning I ever saw in my life.[1]—Leo Durocher
on the ninth inning of October 3, 1962

I don't like to be around drunks. So I got dressed and left.
It was the worst scene I ever saw with the Dodgers.[2]—John
Roseboro on the post-game scene in the locker room

On the plane trip to San Francisco on Sunday night, September 30, Alston and
pitching coach Joe Becker asked Koufax if he thought he could pitch the next day at
Candlestick. Koufax would later recall that it was obvious to him that they had nobody
else.[3] The plan was to cross their fingers and hope he could give them four or five
innings, and then turn it over to the bullpen.

The parallels with 1951 were unsettling. In that year, the Brooklyn Dodgers built
up a 13½-game lead, only to have the New York Giants catch them on the last weekend
to force a 3-game playoff that did not end well for the Dodgers. The 1962 playoff would
be packed with ghosts from 1951. Four San Francisco Giants were in New York Giants
uniforms eleven years before. The great Willie Mays was a rookie center-fielder; manager Alvin Dark was the shortstop; third base coach Whitey Lockman was the first
baseman; and first base coach Wes Westrum was the catcher. Current Los Angeles
Dodgers third base coach Leo Durocher was the New York Giants' manager. Duke
Snider was the 25-five-year-old center-fielder of the Brooklyn Dodgers.

Destroyed by Mr. Mays

The good soldier Koufax agreed to go in the first playoff game against the Giants
on the following afternoon, October 1, at Candlestick. He would be opposed by Giants
left-hander Billy Pierce (15–6). In hindsight, the idea of depending on Koufax was unre-
alistic from the start. He knew he was at a low point in a conditioning schedule that he
had to restart after the long layoff.

The great Willie Mays destroyed the Dodgers with 2 home runs, 3 runs scored, and 3 runs batted-in, in the first game of the playoff series at Candlestick Park October 1, 1962 (National Baseball Hall of Fame Library, Cooperstown, New York).

After the quagmire incident in August, the umpire crew was wary of further mud malfeasance by the Candlestick grounds crew. The Giants and their groundskeepers, expecting heightened scrutiny, went to a new weapon to neutralize the Dodgers' running game: sand. The night before, they turned the skin part of the infield into a virtual sandbox. The Dodgers were incensed when they arrived to see the condition of the field. Acting through their publicity director, Red Patterson, they attempted to lodge a protest with National League President Warren Giles. Unable to locate Giles an hour before the game, Patterson—with Leo Durocher safely muzzled in the clubhouse—went to head umpire Jocko Conlon. Conlon conducted an "inspection" of the field by sticking his toe in the sand around first base, then announced the verdict: "They've got to put this field in regulation condition."[4] Alvin Dark went ballistic. Nose to nose with Conlon, he screamed, "This is our park and we'll do whatever we want with it!"[5] After Dark refused Conlon's order to summon head groundskeeper Matty Schwab, Conlon personally tracked him down and ordered him to undo his handiwork. Several wheelbarrows of sand were removed. Conlon also forbade Schwab from wetting down the field before the game. Schwab maintained his innocence to the end: "All we did was run the harrows over it a little."[6] In what would turn out to be a brutal day for the Dodgers, at least they could say they won the argument over the field.

In the first inning it was obvious to Koufax that he did not have a fast ball. The *Los Angeles Times* even speculated that he may have been "trying to fake the Giants out with soft and breaking stuff."[7] But even with his un–Koufax-like stuff, he was able to retire the first two batters, Harvey Kuenn and Chuck Hiller, before his luck ran out. Felipe Alou lined one of his lame-duck fast balls down the left-field line for a double. Then up came Mr. Mays, who had been studying Koufax as he threw 10 pitches without a single legitimate fast ball. Mays tied into a 2–1 pitch and drove it over the right-center-field fence. After falling behind in the count 3–0 to Orlando Cepeda, Koufax got him to ground out to first baseman Lee Walls to get out of the inning, fortunate to be down only 2–0. In the bottom of the second, Jim Davenport led off with a home run, setting off a flurry of activity in the Dodger bullpen. After Giants' catcher Ed Bailey rifled a single into right field, Koufax was done for the day—and for the season. In facing just seven batters, he gave up two home runs, a double, a single, and three earned runs. Ed Roebuck came in to retire the next three batters in order. Roebuck went on to shut out the Giants over the next three innings to hold the score at 3–0, Giants, after five. At the same time the Dodgers could produce just a mere single against Billy Pierce.[8]

After the Dodgers were forced to remove Roebuck for a pinch hitter in the sixth inning, it got ugly. Larry Sherry came in to pitch the bottom of the sixth and lasted a third of an inning, giving up another home run to Mays, a home run to Cepeda, and a line drive single to Davenport. It was 5–0, Giants, after six. In the eighth, the Dodgers walked the bases loaded. Shortstop Jose Pagan unloaded on the Dodgers' sixth pitcher, Ron Perranoski, with a base-clearing double to make the final score 8–0, Giants.

Billy Pierce pitched a brilliant 105-pitch, 3-hit shutout. The Dodgers had now not scored a run in 30 innings. But it was Willie Mays who destroyed them. Mays had a perfect 3-for-3 day, with two home runs, three runs scored, and three runs batted in. After a demoralizing day at Candlestick Park in front of 32,660 merciless Giant fans, the Dodgers had to get right back on the plane to Los Angeles and try to put it behind them. Playoff game number two would begin at Dodger Stadium in less than 24 hours.

A Schizophrenic Game 2

The next afternoon, at a half-empty Dodger Stadium, Don Drysdale's assignment was to keep the Dodgers alive by winning Game 2 of the best-of–3-game series. Drysdale (25–9) would be pitching on two days' rest in front of a dispirited crowd of only 25,321 against the formidable Jack Sanford (24–7). In the Dodgers' third base coaching box, a superstitious—and desperate—Leo Durocher would wear the same T-shirt, socks, and underwear he wore on the day his New York Giants won Game 3 of the 1951 playoff with the Brooklyn Dodgers.

The Giants jumped out to a 1–0 lead in the second when Felipe Alou doubled home Orlando Cepeda. After five innings, Jack Sanford was pitching a 2-hit shutout to stretch the Dodgers' scoreless streak to 35 innings.

The Giants knocked Drysdale out of the game in the top of the sixth with a walk, a double, and two singles. Drysdale, who was pitching for the fourth time in nine days, lasted only 5⅓ innings. When a tired Ed Roebuck came in to give up a run-scoring base hit to Willie McCovey to increase the Giants' lead to 5–0, Dodger fans headed for the exits in droves. The matter appeared to be settled: Sanford would tie Drysdale for most wins, with 25, and the Giants would sweep the playoff series to advance to the World Series against the Yankees. But in the bottom of the sixth, after Sanford, battling a cold, walked leadoff batter Jim Gilliam, the cautious Alvin Dark surprised everyone when he went to the mound and motioned to the bullpen for Stu Miller. It all began to unravel for the Giants. It was as if Sanford had completed one game—a brilliant 5–0 shutout—and a second, completely different, game began. After Miller gave up a line-drive double to Duke Snider, Tommy Davis woke up what was left of the crowd with a sacrifice fly that scored the first Dodger run in four days. Wally Moon walked, Frank Howard singled home Snider, and Miller was done. Dark brought in Billy O'Dell, who started and won the game on Sunday that forced the playoff. But today, O'Dell could get nobody out. He gave up a single to Doug Camilli and hit Andy Carey with a pitch to load the bases. Lee Walls, pinch hitting for Roebuck, followed with a base-clearing double off the left-center-field wall to give the Dodgers a 6–5 lead and drive the revived crowd into a frenzy. Out went O'Dell, and in came Don Larsen. With Walls on third base, Maury Wills hit a ground ball to first base that Orlando Cepeda fielded and threw home. In a collision at the plate, Walls scored by causing Giants catcher, and former Illini football player, Tom Haller to drop the ball by slashing him with his spikes. Haller had to come out of the game with spike wounds on both hands, each requiring three stitches.[9] By the end of the sixth—a bizarre inning that took one hour and 18 minutes—the Dodgers had scored seven runs off four different Giants pitchers to take a 7–5 lead.

An overworked Ron Perranoski took over for Roebuck as the "new" Game 2 moved into the seventh inning. Perranoski staggered through the seventh without giving up a run despite two hits by the Giants. But when the first two Giants singled off him in the eighth, he got the hook from Alston, who brought in Jack Smith to face Ed Bailey. After Bailey singled home the Giants' sixth run and Cepeda reached base on Frank Howard's error in right field, Stan Williams was brought in to replace Smith. Williams promptly walked Felipe Alou to load the bases. The Giants' third-string catcher, Johnny Orsino, then tied the game, 7–7, with a sacrifice fly.[10]

The strategy wheels were spinning furiously for Walter Alston and Alvin Dark as the game moved to the bottom of the ninth tied, 7–7. When Maury Wills led off with a walk against Bob Bolin, Dark brought in left-hander Dick LeMay to pitch to Junior Gilliam. LeMay, with a good pick-off move, was able to keep Wills from stealing, but lost his concentration on the batter and walked Gilliam. With two on, Alston brought in right-handed-batting Daryl Spencer to pinch hit for lefty Duke Snider. Dark countered by bringing in his prize rookie right-hander, Gaylord Perry, to pitch to Spencer. Spencer advanced the runners to second and third with a sacrifice bunt. The Giants wanted no part of Tommy Davis, with his .344 batting average and 151 runs batted in. Dark ordered his eighth pitcher, left-hander Mike McCormick, to walk Tommy intentionally and pitch to the left-handed-hitting, slump-ridden Ron Fairly with the bases loaded. Fairly, who came to the plate with one hit in his last 31 at bats, fell behind, 0–2, before hitting a semi-line drive into medium center field. This game was now reduced to a 2-second contest between MVP rivals Willie Mays and Maury Wills. Wills tagged at third and headed for home. Mays, who was due to bat first for the Giants in the tenth, fielded the ball and unleashed a throw that was high and to the third base side of the plate. Wills slid under Orsino's tag to keep the Dodgers alive with an 8–7 win. A mob of teammates hoisted Wills on their shoulders and carried him into the clubhouse.

At the time, the 4-hour and 18-minute marathon was the longest 9-inning game in major league history. The two teams used a major league record 42 players: 23 for the Giants and 19 for the Dodgers. Maury Wills set a third record in the wild sixth inning when he stole his 101st base. Both teams were exhausted, but at least they didn't have to rush to the airport. Game 3 would be played on the same field the next afternoon.

Apocalypse in Chavez Ravine

The season came down to a sudden-death Game 3 on October 3. The National League's first 162-game season would end on game number 165. The difference in the mood of the crowd on this Wednesday afternoon at Dodger Stadium was like night and day compared to the previous day. In stark contrast to the half-empty morgue of yesterday, 45,693 fully-engaged fans—including Hollywood stars Frank Sinatra and Doris Day—showed up at Dodger Stadium in shirtsleeves and sun dresses. The scoreless streak was over. A new 1-game season would be played in bright sunshine, Johnny Podres (15–13) versus Juan Marichal (18–11).

Both Podres, pitching on two days' rest, and Marichal, pitching on three days' rest, sailed through the first two innings without being scored upon. In the third, the Dodgers' season-long Achilles heel—defense—reared its ugly head. Jose Pagan opened the inning with a line single to left field. As everyone in the park expected, Juan Marichal laid down a sacrifice bunt in front of the plate. Podres fielded the ball with enough time to force Pagan at second and double up Marichal, but he threw the ball into center field. With runners on first and third, Harvey Kuenn singled to drive in Pagan. The Dodgers had Marichal picked off second base, but John Roseboro threw another errant ball into center field, allowing Marichal to advance to third. Chuck Hiller lifted a fly to Duke Snider in left field. Snider, with no play on Marichal at the plate, had Kuenn thrown out at second until Jim Gilliam dropped the ball for the Dodgers' third error of the inning. Podres walked Mays intentionally to load the bases for Orlando Cepeda. With Cepeda at the plate with 35 home runs and 113 runs batted in, the Giants were in a position to break the game wide open. But Podres was able to escape by getting Cepeda to ground into an inning-ending double play and hold the score at 2–0, Giants.

The Dodgers got to Marichal for a run in the fourth with a double by Snider, a single by Tommy Davis, and a run-scoring ground ball by Frank Howard. The game remained 2–1, Giants, through the first five innings.

In the top of the sixth, Podres gave up singles to the first two hitters, Cepeda and Ed Bailey. When Jim Davenport's sacrifice bunt morphed into an unplayable infield single, the bases were loaded, prompting Walter Alston to come out to the mound. Podres was working on two days' rest for the first time in his career. After giving up 9 hits and a walk, and having thrown 71 pitches in five innings, he had clearly hit a wall. Alston motioned to the bullpen for his workhorse, Ed Roebuck. Though he was inheriting a bases-loaded-no-outs situation in the biggest game of the year, it took Roebuck all of four pitches to get out of the inning unscathed, thanks to the play of Maury Wills behind him. Wills threw out a runner at the plate, then started a double play to end the inning. In the bottom of the sixth, Snider led off with a line single against Marichal. After Marichal fell behind, 3–1, to Tommy Davis, Davis hit his next pitch over Mays's head and into the left-center field stands at the 390-foot sign to give the Dodgers their first lead of the day, 3–2. Tommy Davis now had 27 home runs, a .346 batting average, and an eye-popping 153 runs batted in.

Roebuck held the Giants scoreless in the top of the seventh. With one out in the bottom of the inning, Wills singled for the fourth time off Marichal. He stole second on Marichal's first pitch to Jim Gilliam. After Marichal got Gilliam to fly out, Wills stole third on his first pitch to Larry Burright. When Tom Haller's hurried throw skipped past Jim Davenport, Wills broke for the plate with Leo Durocher running with him down the third base line. As Wills slid safely into home, the 57-year-old bald wild man slid alongside him and got up laughing, thereby infuriating the Giants. At the end of seven innings the Dodgers had a 4–2 lead, and Maury Wills had a once-unimaginable 104 stolen bases.

Roebuck breezed through the top of the eighth by retiring the Giants in order on four pitches. But as he came off the mound, Leo Durocher asked him how he was feeling. Roebuck's answer stunned Durocher: "My arm feels like lead. Man, I'm tired."[11]

The Dodgers got their own chance to break the game open in the bottom of the eighth. After falling behind 3–0 to the red-hot Tommy Davis, Marichal, who was nursing a sore ankle, was taken out mid-batter by Alvin Dark. With his bullpen depleted, Dark had to bring in Don Larsen, who hadn't won a game since July 1. Larsen completed the job of walking Tommy D. Ron Fairly sacrificed Davis to second. After Davis stole third base as Frank Howard swung and missed a third strike, Dark forced Alston's hand by ordering Larsen to intentionally walk the next two batters, John Roseboro and Willie Davis, to load the bases with two outs and the pitcher's spot next. Now the question for Alston was: what to do with Roebuck? Roebuck had shut out the Giants for three innings, but he was also pitching his seventh game in the last nine days. Further, even a pinch single would likely score both Tommy D. and Roseboro to give the Dodgers a 4-run lead with three outs to go. Durocher tried to warn Alston about Roebuck's condition: "Walt, he told me he was tired. He's through."[12] Alston, determined to show he was in charge, brushed him off: "I'm going to win or lose with Roebuck. He stays right there."[13] Alston let Roebuck hit for himself, and Larsen promptly disposed of him on three pitches. When Durocher returned to the dugout from the third base coaching box, Drysdale, Koufax, and Podres all pleaded with him, "Don't let them send Roebuck back out. Tell him [Alston] he's got to make a change. Don't let him do it, Leo."[14] But the decision had been made.

The game went to the ninth with Roebuck back on the mound and the Dodgers ahead, 4–2. The crowd was standing in anticipation not only the clinching of the pennant, but one of the great comebacks. The Dodgers were about to overcome losing Sandy Koufax, blowing a 4-game lead in the last week of the season, being humiliated by Mays and the Giants on Monday at Candlestick Park, and being buried for dead midway through Game 2. What's more, the *TV Guide*—in black and white—guaranteed that the Dodgers and Yankees would begin the 1962 World Series tomorrow on this very field. A chill went through the crowd when Felipe's little brother, Matty, ripped Roebuck's first pitch into right field for a single to lead off the inning. Harvey Kuenn followed with a sharp ground ball to Wills—a perfect double play ball given Kuenn's lack of running speed. The Dodgers were about to have two out with no one on base, but Larry Burright was caught out of position. Right before the pitch, someone on the Dodger bench had signaled for Burright to move well over into the first base hole.[15] By the time he reached second base to catch the throw from Wills to force Matty Alou, it was too late to throw Kuenn out at first. Audible groans rippled through the crowd as number 44, Willie McCovey, came out of the Giants' dugout to pinch hit for Chuck Hiller. The exhausted Roebuck walked him on four pitches. If there was any doubt that Roebuck was out of gas, it was removed when he next walked Felipe Alou on a 3–2 pitch to load the bases. Inexplicably, Alston left him in to pitch to Willie Mays. Hoping

to induce a game-ending double play, Roebuck's first pitch was a tough-to-handle low and inside sinker ball. But Mays went down to get it, lashing a vicious line drive back through the box. Roebuck had no chance to react to this missile. The force of the ball tore his glove off as it caromed off him. Kuenn scored, and Mays was safe at first with his howitzer infield single to keep the bases loaded. With the Dodger lead cut to 4–3, the crowd stood in stunned silence as Roebuck walked off the mound and Durocher—on orders from Alston—signaled to the bullpen for Stan Williams. It was a risky move. With 107 walks and 6 wild pitches in 185 innings, Williams's control was erratic and unpredictable. Why did Alston not bring in Drysdale, who had only pitched 5⅓ innings the day before? As the frustrated Drysdale watched hopelessly from the bench, Cepeda drove in the tying run from third with a line-drive sacrifice fly to Ron Fairly in right field on the second pitch from Williams with Felipe Alou advancing to

Stan Williams walked in the winning run in the ninth inning of the Dodgers' disastrous 4–2 loss to the Giants in the third playoff game at Dodger Stadium October 3, 1962 (National Baseball Hall of Fame Library, Cooperstown, New York).

third. With two out, Williams's next offering to Ed Bailey was a wild pitch to the backstop, sending Mays to second. Alston ordered Williams to walk Bailey intentionally to reload the bases for Jim Davenport. The chaos continued as Williams walked in the go-ahead run. The desperate Alston removed Williams and brought in Perranoski. With the Dodgers in free-fall, the mood in Dodger Stadium turned ugly. The fans booed Williams as he walked into the dugout. Perranoski, pitching in his third straight playoff game and his fifth game in seven days, should have gotten out of the inning on three pitches. But Larry Burright committed the Dodgers' fourth error when he bobbled Jose Pagan's grounder, allowing Mays to score from third base with the Giants' fourth run of the inning. As a deadly quiet Dodger Stadium emptied, Perranoski struck out Bob Nieman to bring the top of the ninth to a merciful end. In his autobiography, Leo Durocher called it the "worst inning I ever saw in my life."[16]

In a flash, the Dodgers' 2-run lead had vanished. Now they were the ones who were behind by two runs and down to their last three outs. The Giants were not willing to take any chances with their gift 6–4 lead. Alvin Dark brought in his star left-hander, Billy Pierce, to pitch the bottom of the ninth inning. Maury Wills, 4-for-4 on the day, appeared to be a defeated player as he stepped into the batter's box. He fell behind 0–2, then went out on the next pitch with a weak ground ball to third. Pierce and Junior Gilliam engaged in a 6-pitch battle that ended with a harmless fly-out to Willie Mays in shallow center field. Down to his last out, Alston brought in the hero of yesterday's game, Lee Walls, to pinch hit for the goat, Larry Burright. In another heroic effort, Walls hit Pierce's third pitch on a line into center field. But the head-and-shoulders outstanding player of the series—and arguably the Most Valuable Player of the league—Willie Mays caught the baseball chest-high. The clock on the message board read 5:00 p.m. The 3-hour struggle was over, but not the suffering. The Dodgers were forced to watch the Giants celebrate at their mound in the middle of a nearly-deserted Dodger Stadium.

The sense of déjà vu was palpable. Eleven years before to the day, October 3, 1951, the Dodgers were in a similar situation: one out away from a date with the Yankees in the World Series. At the Polo Grounds on Coogan's Bluff they blew a 3-run lead in the ninth inning of the third play-off game on the Shot Heard Around the World, Bobby Thomson's 3-run home run off Ralph Branca that eliminated the Dodgers and propelled the Giants into the World Series with the Yankees.

The Giants' raucous celebration migrated to the clubhouse, where it became a champagne free-for-all. Walter Alston pulled himself together to make a brief visit to congratulate Alvin Dark. After Alston left, a calculating Richard Nixon—now a candidate for California governor—moved in to tell Dark, "I had a slight feeling for the Giants because they have more Californians on their team."[17] The door of the Dodger clubhouse was barred for an hour. When the doors were finally opened, reporters witnessed groups of dazed players—many in tears—in a room strewn with empty whiskey bottles and ripped-up Dodger uniforms. One half-full bottle was still being passed around. Years later, Johnny Roseboro recalled, "I don't like to be around drunks. So I got dressed and left. It was the worst scene I ever saw with the Dodgers."[18] The champagne was already on its way back to the caterer.

The 1962 World Series

When the Giants' DC-7 approached San Francisco International Airport on the night of October 3, 50,000 people were waiting for them. And these were just the lucky ones. Cars were backed up for miles along the Bayshore Freeway approach to the airport trying to get in. Some people even abandoned their vehicles and set off on foot for the airport. The pilot was told to circle the field "due to the riotous conditions at the airport."[19] In fact, the crowd was completely out of control, blocking the runway. Two earlier jets were stalled on the runway, unable to taxi in to unload their passengers. When the Giants' plane finally landed—after circling for an hour and twenty minutes—it had to be diverted to an old UAL maintenance depot a mile away. From there the Giants tried to escape in a bus. But they were mobbed by fans who broke through the police barricades, smashed windows, and climbed in over luggage to get to them. It would not be a good night to sleep for either team. The Yankees were staying at co-owner Dell Webb's Town House on Market Street, where a mob burst in and began throwing furniture around before police could restore order.

Nineteen hours after the Giants clinched the pennant at Dodger Stadium, they had to be ready to play the New York Yankees in Game 1 of the World Series at Candlestick Park. Several ardent Giant fans even made arrangements for Cardinals catcher Gene Oliver—who beat the Dodgers with a home run on the last day of the season to force the playoff—to fly to San Francisco from his home in Molina, Illinois, to attend the first two games of the World Series, all expenses paid.

On October 4, 43,852 at Candlestick saw Whitey Ford beat Billy O'Dell and the Giants 6–2 in Game 1. Ford was spotted a 2–0 lead when Roger Maris doubled home two runs in the first. Felipe Alou leaped high above the right-center-field fence to rob Maris of a 3-run home run, but couldn't hold onto the ball. The Giants ended Ford's World Series scoreless streak at 33⅓ innings when Jose Pagan bunted home Willie Mays from third in the second inning. The Giants tied the game, 2–2, in the third on an RBI single by Mays. Jim Coates was up in the bullpen, but Ford survived by getting Cepeda to hit into a double play.[20]

Clete Boyer broke the 2–2 tie in the seventh with a solo home run off O'Dell. The Yankees knocked O'Dell out of the game with two more runs in the eighth. They scored their sixth and final run off Don Larsen in the ninth. Ford pitched a complete game, scattering 10 hits—including 3 singles by Willie Mays—and walking 2.

The next day, Jack Sanford shut out the Yankees 2–0 on three hits before 43,910 at Candlestick to even the Series at one game apiece. The Giants jumped out to a 1–0 lead in the first. Chuck Hiller lined a Ralph Terry pitch down the right field line. Roger Maris came a long way to make what appeared to be a brilliant shoe-top catch until the ball popped out of his glove.[21] Hiller had a double, and was driven in on Matty Alou's groundout to second base. In the seventh, McCovey hit a tremendous home run to right field off Terry to make the score 2–0, Giants. Though Terry pitched a strong seven innings, allowing only 5 hits, his World Series record fell to 0–4.

The Series moved to New York for Game 3 on October 7. Both Bill Stafford and Billy Pierce had shutouts going through the first six innings in front of 71,434 at Yankee Stadium. After being shut out for fifteen straight innings, the Yankees broke finally through in the seventh. Roger Maris knocked Pierce out of the game with a two-run single. After Don Larsen replaced Pierce, Clete Boyer drove in Maris on a force play to make the score 3–0, Yankees. Stafford took a 3–0 shutout to the ninth. Mays opened with a double. With two out, Ed Bailey hit a 2-run homer to make the score 3–2, Yankees. Stafford got Davenport to fly out to end the game and put the Yankees up two games to one.

Whitey Ford and Juan Marichal met in Game 4 on October 8 before 66,607 at Yankee Stadium. Marichal lasted only four innings, Ford just six. Chuck Hiller broke a 2–2 tie in the seventh with a grand slam home run off left-handed reliever Marshall Bridges. It was the first World Series grand slam by a National League player. Both teams scored a run in the ninth. The Giants' 7–3 win evened the Series at two games apiece. Don Larsen won the game in relief, with Coates taking the loss.

After being rained out on October 9, Game 5 was played the next day in front of 63,165 at Yankee Stadium. Starters Ralph Terry and Jack Sanford were locked in a 2–2 tie as the game moved to the bottom of the eighth inning. After Kubek and Richardson singled, Tom Tresh hit Sanford's second pitch just beyond Matty Alou's reach and into the right-field seats for a 3-run home run. The blow gave the Yankees a 5–2 lead and brought Stu Miller in to relieve Sanford. Ralph Terry went on to record a complete-game 5–3 victory to give the Yankees a three-games-to-two lead in the Series.

Game 6 was rained out for three consecutive days, October 12 through 14, as a huge Pacific storm, originally Typhoon Freda, battered San Francisco with gale-force winds. After the rains finally stopped, and the Giants were able to dry off the field by using three helicopters, left-handers Whitey Ford and Billy Pierce were able to face off on October 15 in front of 43,948 at Candlestick Park. The layoff negatively affected Ford. He left before he could finish the fifth inning, down 5–1. Orlando Cepeda broke out of an 0-for-12 World Series slump with 2 singles, a double, and 2 runs batted in to lead the Giants to a 5–2 win. It took Billy Pierce an even 2 hours to pitch a complete-game 3-hitter to tie the Series at three games apiece and force a sudden-death seventh game. One of the Yankee hits was a fifth-inning solo home run by Roger Maris.

For Game 7 on Tuesday, October 16, at Candlestick Park, Ralph Terry and Jack Sanford met for the third time in the Series. As we have seen, Sanford shut out the Yankees 2–0 in Game 2, and Terry beat the Giants 5–3 in Game 5. Ralph Terry was 23–12 on the regular season to lead the American League in wins. But for two years he had been living with the stigma of being the pitcher who served up the winning home run ball to Bill Mazeroski in Game 7 of the 1960 World Series.

Terry and Sanford were locked in a scoreless tie through the first four innings. Bill Skowron and Clete Boyer hit consecutive singles off Sanford to open the fifth. Sanford then walked Terry on four pitches to load the bases for Tony Kubek with none out. Kubek hit a perfect double play ball to Giants shortstop Jose Pagan. Pagan didn't throw to the plate to force Skowron because, as he later explained, "it was too early in the game."[22] Instead, Pagan threw to second to start a 6-4-3 double play that allowed Skowron to score what would turn out to be the only run of the game.

Ralph Terry was pitching a perfect game until Jack Sanford singled with two out in the bottom of the sixth. With one out in the seventh, Willie Mays hit a long drive to left field off Terry that would have been a game-tying home run in any other park. But the wind held it up, allowing the racing Tom Tresh to make a one-handed "snow-cone" catch.[23] Willie McCovey followed with a booming triple to the 410-foot sign in center field, but was left stranded on third base when Orlando Cepeda struck out.

The game went to the bottom of the ninth with Ralph Terry and the Yankees clinging to a fragile 1–0 lead. Matty Alou dragged a bunt single past Terry to lead off the inning. Both Felipe Alou and Chuck Hiller struck out in consecutive futile attempts to bunt the runner to second base. Willie Mays, 0-for-3 on the day, came to the plate with the Giants down to their last out. Knowing Mays would be looking for a pitch to pull out of the park to win the game, Terry jammed him on two inside pitches. Terry's third pitch was away and out of the strike zone. But Mays reached out and lined it down the right-field line for extra bases. On the dead run, Roger Maris made a great play to cut the ball off in the right-field corner before it went to the fence, and threw a perfect strike to cut-off man Bobby Richardson in shallow right field. In a decision des-

Ralph Terry, scarred by giving up Bill Mazeroski's walk-off home run in Game 7 of the 1960 World Series, narrowly escaped a similar fate in Game 7 of the 1962 World Series. (National Baseball Hall of Fame Library, Cooperstown, New York).

tined to be second-guessed in perpetuity, Giants third base coach Whitey Lockman threw up his hands to hold Matty Alou—representing the tying run—at third base. With Alou on third and Mays—representing the winning run—on second with a double, and Willie McCovey coming to the plate, a grim Ralph Houk went to the mound. Houk gave Terry the option of pitching to McCovey, or walking him to load the bases for Orlando Cepeda, who was 3 for 19 in the Series. Despite having given up a tape-measure home run to McCovey in Game 2, and having just been rocked by his triple in the eighth, Terry told Houk he wanted to pitch to him.

McCovey pulled Terry's first pitch for a long, loud foul down the right-field line. McCovey took the second pitch for a ball. Then McCovey ignited a seismic roar from the capacity crowd of 43,948 when he connected on Terry's third pitch, sending a rocket toward right field. Since the ball had topspin on it, it was not going to be a home run. But a single would score both runners. Positioned perfectly, deep in the hole, Bobby Richardson made a staggering, shoulder-high catch of the ball. Like throwing a switch, in a split second Richardson ended the game, ended the World Series, and silenced the crowd. Two feet—either way—and the Giants would have been World Champions. Now they had to endure the same humiliation they visited upon the Dodgers on October 3

On October 16, 1962, at Candlestick Park, Willie McCovey's potential Series-winning laser shot was caught by Bobby Richardson for the final out to give the Yankees a 1–0 victory and another World Championship (National Baseball Hall of Fame Library, Cooperstown, New York).

at Dodger Stadium as they watched the Yankees celebrate at the center of their own infield.

❊ ❊ ❊

In Washington, D.C., on the day the World Series concluded, National Security Advisor McGeorge Bundy presented President Kennedy with photographic evidence from a U-2 spy flight of Soviet offensive missiles under construction in western Cuba.[24] They were identified as SS-24 Scalpels, medium-range ballistic missiles with a range of a thousand miles. While it was clear that they could reach well into the United States, what was not clear was how rapidly they could be equipped with nuclear weapons.[25] Thus the clock began to tick on the 13-day Cuban Missile Crisis.

❊ ❊ ❊

Dodgers 1962—An Index Finger Away

Until July 17—the day the Dodgers lost Sandy Koufax—this was arguably the best team in the history of the Los Angeles Dodgers. Even without Koufax for 66 days, and with a shadow, ineffectual Koufax for the last 10 days of the season, the Dodgers were in first place, or tied for first, for 111 days of the 175-day season. They were in sole possession of first place from July 8 until the last pitch of the regular season on September 30. They won 102 games, and set a new major league attendance record of 2,755,184 in their first year in Dodger Stadium.

The 1962 season was a year of great individual accomplishments. Tommy Davis had one of the greatest offensive years in National League history. He won the batting title with a .346 batting average, and led the league in hits with 230 and runs batted in with 153—the most in the NL since 1937. Don Drysdale had the best year of his career. He led the league in wins with 25, in strikeouts with 232, and won the Cy Young Award as the best pitcher in the majors. Even with his sub-par performance after his return in late September, Sandy Koufax led the league with a 2.54 earned run average, and had 216 strikeouts in only 184⅓ innings. As a team, the Dodgers led the league in strikeouts for the fifteenth consecutive season with 1,104.

Twenty-two-year-old Willie Davis blossomed into one of the league's top center fielders in his second full year in the major leagues with 21 home runs, 85 runs batted in, 103 runs, 32 stolen bases, and a league-leading 10 triples. Batting third in the lineup ahead of Tommy D., Willie D. was batting .303 through August. But he hit .192 and drove in only 3 runs for the remainder of the season. He was 1 for 18 in the critical period spanning the final weekend with the Cardinals and the 3-game playoff series with the Giants, during which he was moved down to eighth in the batting order.

Until the team's collapse at the end, the story of the year in major league baseball was the revolutionary base stealing of Maury Wills. Wills broke Ty Cobb's record of 96 stolen bases set in 1915. He became the first player to eclipse the 100 mark with an amazing 104. He won the Most Valuable Player award by a narrow 209 to 202 vote over Willie Mays, igniting a controversy between Dodger and Giant fans that exists to this day. He also set a new major league record by playing in every regular-season game and all three playoff games for a total of 165. But his personal stolen base feat came at a cost. The players batting behind Wills had to take good pitches to allow him to steal. Second-hole batter Jim Gilliam, batting .292 through July, hit only .228 the rest of the way. After the season, Duke Snider disclosed, "I think Jim would have hit over .300 if he hadn't sacrificed so much to help Maury."[26] As we have seen, third-hole batter Willie Davis slumped severely during Wills's record-breaking month of September. The intense media attention on Wills proved to be a distraction for the entire team, as the Dodgers seemed to lose focus on their main objective: winning the pennant. In the last week of the season, as Wills was busy chasing and surpassing Ty Cobb, the Dodgers blew a 4-game lead and found themselves in a playoff with the Giants. Dusty Boggess, the 20-year veteran umpire who called Wills safe on the play that broke Cobb's record, offered this candid post-season comment right after he announced his retirement: "All the Dodgers were unconsciously pulling for Wills. They thought more about the record than they did about the pennant."[27]

Frank Howard had his finest year as a Dodger with 31 home runs, 119 runs batted in, and a .296 batting average. But he virtually disappeared in the final six games, going 2 for 22.

Ed Roebuck was the star of the Dodger bullpen with a perfect 10–0 record and a 2.77 earned run average until he collapsed from overwork in the last week of the season. In the critical series with the Colt .45s of September 25–27, he lost game number 157 and blew a save in game number 159. As we have seen, he was the losing pitcher in the disastrous final playoff game with the Giants. Ron Perranoski had a 1.89 earned run average through September 4. But after being used in 7 of the last 9 games—2 of which he lost—it had ballooned to 2.85 by the end of the year.

The Dodger defense was a major liability that was particularly costly down the stretch. They were ninth in the league in fielding percentage. Only Casey Stengel's Amazin' Mets committed more errors. The base-stealing accomplishments of Maury Wills masked his 36 errors, the second-highest total for a major league shortstop in 1962.

In the aftermath of the year-end collapse, speculation was rampant that Leo Durocher would replace Walter Alston as manager of the Los Angeles Dodgers. But at a hastily arranged press conference the day after the World Series ended, the Dodgers announced that Alston would be retained. Even after Durocher was accused in the press of the incendiary comment, "The Dodgers would have won if I had been managing that last game,"[28] Leo was retained as third base coach. The 1962 season was a rocky year for Durocher and Alston, and one that stretched their relationship to the breaking point. Durocher survived a life-threatening medical emergency in September and a charge of disloyalty in October. Alston survived one of the most notorious collapses in baseball history with perhaps the best Los Angeles Dodger team ever. The Odd Couple would be back in 1963.

Bavasi's Purge

At the Winter Meetings at the end of November in New York, Buzzie Bavasi conducted what appeared to be a purge of two scapegoats from the October collapse. Though the Dodgers were in need of right-handed pitching, on November 26 he traded 26-year-old Stan Williams to the New York Yankees for power-hitting first baseman Bill "Moose" Skowron. As we have seen, Williams walked in the winning run and was the losing pitcher in the October 3 game that sent the Giants to the World Series. Williams had never had a losing season in the majors, winning 14, 15, and 14 games respectively over the last three seasons. But his unpredictable wildness proved to be his undoing.

On November 30, the Dodgers traded second baseman Larry Burright and first baseman Tim Harkness to the New York Mets for Bob Miller, a 23-year-old right-hander with a 1–12 record in 1962. Burright was the Dodgers' starting second base until he slumped with a .141 month of July, after which he started only six games. After his grievous error in the ninth inning of the October 3 holocaust at Dodger Stadium, his days were numbered. What's more, the Dodgers already had big plans for their 23-year-old "can't miss" second baseman, Nate "Pee Wee" Oliver. Oliver put together a .317 season in 124 games at Spokane, and was ranked as one of the fastest men in the entire Dodger organization.

Bob Miller was signed as a Bonus Baby by the Cardinals in 1957 at the age of 17. After four limited-service seasons in St. Louis, he was the number one pick in the 1961 expansion draft. Bavasi, who had been high on Miller for years, had to outbid the Giants and Tigers to land him. Miller was destined to play a key role for the Dodgers in 1963.

Koufax at 27

Sandy Koufax turned twenty-seven on December 30. He had just been declared "completely healed" by Dr. Travis Winsor, the nationally recognized authority on vascular ailments who treated him from the beginning of the crisis in July.

The Dodgers picked up the Mets' 1–12 right-hander Bob Miller in an off-season trade. Miller would play a key role for the 1963 Dodgers (National Baseball Hall of Fame Library, Cooperstown, New York).

Though his first monster season was derailed on July 17, the date his finger split open in Cincinnati, it was a great abbreviated season—even with his last five outings negatively affected by the injury.

	G	W	L	IP	H	SO	ER	HR	BB	ERA
Season up to July 17	23	14	4	174⅔	121	208	40	9	49	2.06
July 17 + (Sep 21–Oct 1)	5	0	3	9⅔	13	8	12	4	8	11.17
Year	28	14	7	184⅓	134	216	52	13	57	2.54

His rapidly escalating improvement was reflected in the statistics. His control—as measured by walks per 9 innings—was substantially better than in his breakout season of 1961.

	IP	BB	BB/9
1961	255⅔	96	3.38
1962	184⅓	57	2.78
Change		−39	−0.60
% Change			−17.8%

His strikeouts-to-walks ratio jumped by more than 35 percent.

	STRIKEOUTS	BB	SO/BB
1961	269	96	2.80
1962	216	57	3.79
Change			+.99
% Change			+35.4%

There was a significant improvement in his earned run average as well as in the modern Sabermetric, WHIP (Walks + Hits per Innings Pitched).

	ERA	H	BB	WHIP
1961	3.52	212	96	1.205
1962	2.54	121	57	1.036
Change	−0.98			−.169
% Change	−27.8%			−14.0%

Koufax continued to put up ever-more-amazing strikeout numbers. He had 209 on July 17. Don Drysdale, who led the league with 232, didn't reach that number until September 15. Koufax led the league for the third consecutive year with a career-best 10.5 strikeouts per 9 innings.

	IP	SO	SO/9
1961	255⅔	269	9.5
1962	184⅓	216	10.5
Change			+1.0
% Change			+10.5%

At the end of 1962, his career 9.29 strikeouts-per–9-innings mark was a major league record.

On Christmas Eve, Koufax had begun a 30-day engagement with Milton Berle at the Desert Inn in Las Vegas as part of the 6-man Dodger Chorus that included Don Drysdale, Willie Davis, Maury Wills, Frank Howard, and Duke Snider. With two months to go before spring training and unsure of his future in baseball, he was pursuing outside business interests. In January, he planned to open a new radio station in Thousand Oaks, 29 miles from his home in Studio City. He would be the president and program director of KNJO, the first all-stereo radio station in Southern California. He was also a part owner of Sandy Koufax's Tropicana Motor Hotel in Hollywood, where guests were frequently surprised to find him working behind the front desk when they registered for the night.[29] The "Trop" would become a favorite hangout for such rock and roll luminaries as Jim Morrison, Led Zeppelin, and The Clash.

※ ※ ※

The day after Sandy Koufax turned 27 was the last day of 1962. The country and the world had survived the 13-day Cuban Missile Crisis of October. President Kennedy was about to enter the third and final year of his presidency. The number of U.S. "military advisors" in Vietnam was now 12,000.

※ ※ ※

Part IV

1963:
Return to the Summit

Sixteen

A Season Hanging on a Finger

Sandy Koufax is our main concern. I know that's putting a
lot of pressure on one man, but you can't replace a man like
Koufax.[1]—Walter Alston the first day of Spring Training

While the Dodgers entered the new year haunted by the question of whether they could ever recover from the collapse of 1962, the real key to the 1963 season was Sandy Koufax. Could he come back from the injury that cost them the pennant and nearly cost him his index finger? They had been assured by the doctors that the finger was completely healed, but they were still uneasy because there was no guarantee the circulatory ailment would not recur. They were not concerned about his fast ball. The test would be his ability to spin the curve ball off that index finger.[2]

In the country, JFK, with the Cuban Missile Crisis behind him, began what would be the final year of his brief presidency. It would be a tumultuous year in the civil rights struggle in America. It would also be the year in which the U.S. involvement in Vietnam reached a point of no return.

A "New" Strike Zone

Meeting in New York City on January 26, Major League Baseball's Official Rules Committee voted to expand the strike zone, effectively reinstituting the pre–1950 definition: "The strike zone is that area over the plate 'which is between the top of the batter's shoulders and his knees when he assumes his natural stance.'"[3] This had been the strike zone for 75 years until 1950, when it was reduced under a new definition: "The strike zone is that area over the plate 'which is between the batter's arm pits and the top of his knees when he assumes his natural stance.'"

After 13 years of play under the reduced strike zone, and facing mounting competition for fans from the National Football League, Major League Baseball acted. The stated rationale for the rule change was to increase the speed of the game by reducing

the number of walks without reducing the action. It was estimated that the new definition would expand the strike zone by 10 to 12 inches for the average batter. Reaction
was mixed, with pitchers generally in favor and hitters generally opposed. An unen-
thused Mickey Mantle saw himself striking out 400 times.[4] Sandy Koufax reacted favor-
ably: "The higher strike zone will save me about 20 pitches a game. I wish they'd have
done this about eight years ago when I was breaking in and had a lot of trouble keeping
the ball down."[5] The new rule was to take effect immediately, with umpires expected
to enforce it beginning with the spring exhibition games in March.

On February 9, Koufax signed a new contract for $32,000 (a $7,000 increase) as
he and his fellow Dodger Chorus members prepared to continue the Milton Berle Show
with an 11-night stand in Las Vegas from February 14 through February 24. Chorus
members planned to bring their baseball gear for light workouts during the day. It was
Koufax's practice to not throw during the off season. He had not picked up a baseball
since the previous October 1 at Candlestick Park.

Spring Training—The Moment of Truth

The Dodgers reported to Vero Beach on February 25. On March 1 the entire
Dodgers organization held its breath as Koufax threw 20 minutes of batting practice.
Despite Moose Skowron's bombing his first pitch over the fence, there was a collective
sigh of relief as he finished with no sign of a problem. This was followed by 2 innings
in a camp inter-squad game the next day for his first "official outing." The Dodgers continued to be encouraged by the results. He was spinning the ball, throwing curves without feeling any ill effects.[6] Koufax also put their minds to rest on the question of a
possible recurrence of the "circulatory ailment." He made clear that in fact it was an
injury (a blood clot caused by being jammed by Earl Francis on April 28), and not a *circulatory disease*, that forced him to the sidelines on July 17. Walter Alston, who at the
start of spring training called Koufax "our biggest concern," could now rest easy. It was
a trifecta: there was no sign of any trouble with Sandy's pitching hand, no chance of a
recurrence, and he was spinning his devastating twelve-to-six curve ball just like before
the injury.

On March 10, Koufax pitched 3 innings against the Braves, striking out 3 and allowing 2 singles. On March 19 in Sarasota he dispelled any lingering doubts that his index
finger was healed by striking out 13 White Sox in 7 innings of work, including the last
5 batters he faced.

An Uneasy Troika

Manager Walter Alston, the "Quiet Man from Darrtown," was about to begin his
tenth season at the helm of the Dodgers.[7] At 51, he was now the National League's
senior manager. Though Alston was promptly retained after the October collapse, he
would be working under Walter O'Malley's not-so-subtle ultimatum: "Win or else." The
volatile Alston-Durocher relationship would be further complicated by the hiring of

another ex–Dodger manager, Chuck Dressen, as "special advisor" to General Manager Buzzie Bavasi, Alston's boss. The Dodgers would begin the 1963 season with what was essentially a "troika" of managers with a combined 39 years of experience: Durocher (17) with the Dodgers and Giants; Dressen (12) with the Reds, Dodgers, Senators, and Braves; and Alston (10), all with the Dodgers.

The Selling of the Dook

On April 1, after 16 years in his familiar number 4 Dodger uniform, 36-year-old Duke Snider, aka the Dook of Flatbush, was sold to the Mets for a mere $40,000 in cold cash. Everyone knew it was coming. The air around the team had been thick with rumors for weeks. He played in only 80 games the year before, and his salary had eroded to $34,000 from $44,000 in 1958. Mets 73-year-old manager Casey Stengel, whose Yankees had been hurt by Snider's 10 World Series home runs in the 1950s, had long coveted him. Waivers were asked on March 22. By the time they expired on March 25, Stengel's Mets had claimed him. He left the Dodgers with 389 home runs and a lifetime .300 batting average.

Edwin Donald Snider was born in Los Angeles on September 19, 1926, the only child of Ward and Florence Johnson Snider. He grew up in Compton, and was a standout athlete at Compton High School. He was the leading scorer on the same basketball team with future NFL commissioner Pete Rozelle, and quarterback of the football team. He had only one year of varsity baseball as a pitcher-outfielder-cleanup batter as a junior. He was signed by Brooklyn Dodgers scout Tom Downing for $750 after his junior year in 1943, thus ending his high school eligibility.[8]

Most Dodgers were given nicknames when they established a place on the team. Snider was already "The Duke" when he arrived as a 17-year-old at spring training at Bear Mountain, New York, in March 1944. His father gave him the nickname at age five for his self-assured swagger. After camp, he was assigned to Newport News in the Class-B Piedmont League, where he batted .294 and threw out 25 runners from the outfield in 131 games. He enlisted in the Navy that fall after turning 18.

Upon discharge from the service on the 4th of July of 1946, Snider played 68 games for the Fort Worth Cats in the Class-AA Texas League. At spring training in 1947, Branch Rickey was so impressed by the gifted but temperamental Snider that he found a place for him on the roster as backup outfielder on the team that made history with the first Negro player, Jackie Robinson. On April 17 he hit a pinch single off the Boston Braves' Si Johnson for his first major league hit in his first major league at bat. After spending most of the first three months on the bench, Snider was sent down to St. Paul in the Triple-A American Association for July and August, where he hit .316 with 12 home runs in 66 games. He returned to the Dodgers for the September pennant stretch. While he did not appear in the 1947 World Series, which the Dodgers lost in 7 games to the Yankees, he was voted a quarter share of the Series money. After the 1947 season he married his high school sweetheart, Beverly Null.

During spring training in 1948, Snider worked with Branch Rickey and batting coach George Sisler to correct his tendency to lunge and overswing—to "learn the strike zone." As he did in 1947, Snider made the big club at the start of 1948, but was shipped out to Triple-A Montreal in June for more seasoning. He lit it up in his two months at Montreal with 17 home runs and 77 runs batted in in 77 games. By the end of July, it was evident to Branch Rickey that he had a classic 5-tool player in Duke Snider, a fleet, elegant young center fielder who hit .322 with 29 home runs and 18 outfield assists in his last 143 games at the Triple-A level. The Duke returned to Ebbets Field on August 6, 1948, and never left the majors again.

The 1949 season was Snider's first full year as the Brooklyn Dodgers' center fielder. He batted .292 with 23 home runs and 92 runs batted in, but hit a disappointing .143 with 8 strikeouts in the 1949 World Series, which the Dodgers lost in five games to the Yankees. Snider had a breakout year in 1950, batting .321 with a league-leading 199 hits, including 10 triples and 31 home runs. On the last day of the season the Dodgers missed a chance to force a pennant playoff with the Phillies. In the Dodgers' ill-fated 1951 season, Snider slipped to .277 with an anemic .157 September as the team blew a 13½-game lead to the Giants. The devastated Snider asked to be traded. After he had weathered criticism from his teammates for his pouting, the crisis passed. In 1952 Snider's home run total fell to 21, but he distinguished himself in the World Series against the Yankees with 4 home runs, 10 hits, and 8 runs batted in.

Duke Snider entered his prime in 1953—the first of his five straight seasons with 40 or more home runs. He hit .336 with 42 home runs and 126 runs batted in and was third in the MVP voting. The Dodgers under Chuck Dressen won 105 games, but lost again to the Yankees in the World Series, four games to two. The 1954 season was Snider's first year under manager Walter Alston. While the Dodgers finished second to the World Champion Giants, Snider had a career best .341 batting average with 40 home runs and 130 runs batted in.

In the Brooklyn Dodgers' first and only World Championship year of 1955, Snider hit .309 with 42 home runs and led the league in runs scored with 126 and in runs batted in with 136. In the World Series against the Yankees, he hit 4 home runs for the second time. In Game 6 he tripped on a wooden sprinkler cover in Yankee Stadium and twisted his left knee, causing an injury that would haunt him for the rest of his career. In a controversial MVP vote, Snider finished second to teammate Roy Campanella, 226 to 221.

Snider hit a career-best 43 home runs and drove in 101 runs in 1956. But the knee contributed to a decline in batting average to .292. The Dodgers lost again to the Yankees in the World Series, 4 games to 2, as Snider could produce just 1 home run and 4 runs batted in. The knee continued to get worse in 1957, the Dodgers' last year in Brooklyn. The center of power in the National League had moved from New York to Milwaukee, with the Dodgers falling to third place. Snider hit 40 home runs, but his batting average further declined to .274. He finally had surgery on the knee in the off season.

The 1958 season was Dodgers' first year on the West Coast. Before the inaugural game with the San Francisco Giants on April 18 at the Los Angeles Memorial Coliseum, Willie Mays pointed to the 440-foot power alley in right center field and taunted Snider, "Duke, they killed you!"[9] Mays was right. As the Dodgers barely escaped last place, Snider's power numbers took a precipitous drop: home runs from 40 to 15, and runs batted in from 92 to 58. In the Dodgers' unlikely World Championship year of 1959,

Snider began playing right field and left field to take the stress off his knee. Cortisone helped him to play in 126 games with 23 home runs and a team-best 88 runs batted in. Snider's 11th and final World Series home run, a 2-run bomb in Game 6 off the White Sox' Early Wynn, was the deciding blow in the clincher at Comiskey Park.

Snider's career declined rapidly after 1959. He was utilized less and less as Tommy Davis, Willie Davis, and Frank Howard took over the Dodger outfield. As we have seen, he hit only .243 in 1960, and his promising 1961 start was derailed when Bob Gibson fractured his arm with a pitch in April, limiting him to only 85 games. The Dodgers honored his 16 years of service by making him captain of the team in 1962. A year later all the Boys of Summer[10] were gone.

JFK's Last Pitch

On the afternoon of Monday, April 8, 1963, John F. Kennedy, accompanied by a battery of secret service agents, made his way down the tunnel leading from the umpires' room to the Washington Senators' dugout and on to his seat in the Presidential Box at Griffith Stadium as the Marine Band played "Hail to the Chief." It was a routine security maneuver that went off without a hitch. He was even spared the embarrassment of having to walk through the ballpark vendors' picket line when Secretary of Labor Willard Wirtz got the Café and Restaurant Workers Union to agree to withdraw their pickets an hour before Kennedy's arrival. From his box the bare-headed and top-coatless Kennedy made his last ceremonial pitch into a cluster of Washington Senators and Baltimore Orioles players. Senators catcher Ken Ketzer, who had discarded his catcher's mitt in favor of a 5-fingered glove, elbowed Orioles center fielder Jackie Brandt out of the way to spear the ball. Ketzer and the baseball were beckoned to the Presidential Box for the presidential autograph.

Kennedy enjoyed his role as Baseball-Fan-in-Chief in the flag-bedecked box as he puffed on cigars and talked animatedly with his neighbors, who included Vice President Lyndon Johnson and Speaker of the House John McCormick, the first two in the line of succession in the event of the death or inability of the president to discharge his duties. Kennedy leaped to his feet twice in the second inning when the Orioles' first baseman, Jim Gentile, and their giant 245-pound left fielder, Boog Powell, each hit home runs. Otherwise, it was a quiet day for the humble Senators, who went down to a 3–1 defeat. In an effort to improve the frosty U.S.-Cuba relations six months after the Cuban Missile Crisis, JFK sought out Havana-born outfielder Minnie Minoso, complimenting him on his 2-hit debut with the Senators. Minoso, who was the last player to leave the field and close to the president as he dashed back through the tunnel, remarked, "The President see me and say, 'nice work'!"[11]

The National League held its opener on the same day in Cincinnati, where the Reds hosted the Pittsburgh Pirates, two teams that first met in 1882. In the bottom of the first inning the Reds' 21-year-old rookie second baseman, Pete Rose, drew a walk in his first major league plate appearance. To everyone's amazement, he just didn't trot to first base; he sprinted full bore like a man with his hair on fire. After an 0-for-12 start, his first hit—a triple—would come five days later against Bob Friend. Rose would go on to become the NL Rookie of the Year.

Opening Day in Chicago

The 1963 season opened April 9 at Wrigley Field on a frigid 33-degree day in Chicago. Coming off his greatest season, Don Drysdale was honored with the start. Dodger nemesis Larry Jackson started for the Cubs. Pitching for the Cardinals in 1962, Jackson beat the Dodgers twice in the last 7 games as they blew a 4-game lead. But today the Dodgers chased him after 7 innings. Drysdale won his third opener in four years with a 5–1 complete-game victory. It was so cold that he had to wear gloves in the dugout while the Dodgers were at bat.[12] There were several new faces in the starting lineup.

The same day in Cincinnati a young dynamo second baseman named Pete Rose made his major league debut (National Baseball Hall of Fame Library, Cooperstown, New York).

	APRIL 9, 1963		APRIL 10, 1962	
1	Maury Wills	SS	Maury Wills	SS
2	Nate Oliver	2B	Jim Gilliam	2B
3	Willie Davis	CF	Wally Moon	LF
4	Tommy Davis	LF	Duke Snider	RF
5	Bill Skowron	1B	John Roseboro	C
6	John Roseboro	C	Ron Fairly	1B
7	Ron Fairly	RF	Daryl Spencer	3B
8	Ken McMullen	3B	Willie Davis	CF
9	Don Drysdale	P	Johnny Podres	P

Nate "Pee Wee" Oliver took over second base, sending Jim Gilliam back to his familiar role as "utility man." The 22-year-old Oliver was born and raised in St. Petersburg, Florida. His father, Jimmy Oliver, was a star shortstop for the famed Indianapolis Clowns in the Negro American League, where in 1946 he played against Gilliam, then with the Baltimore Elite Giants.[13] Jimmy tutored Pee Wee on playing the infield from the time he could walk. At Gibbs High School in St. Petersburg, Nate was a 9.7 sprinter on the track team, quarterback of the football team, and a standout on the baseball and basketball teams.[14] He was signed by the Dodgers as a free agent in June of 1959. In Oliver's first three years in the Dodger farm system he committed a whopping 113 errors as a shortstop. He was moved to the more comfortable position of second base at Triple-A Spokane in 1962, where he blossomed with a .317 batting average. Durocher and Bavasi were high on Oliver from the time he arrived at Vero Beach. He was the starting second baseman from the first exhibition game. The Dodgers already had outstanding team speed, but it went up a notch with Oliver—only Willie

Davis was faster. Oliver hit two singles off Larry Jackson in his first two big league at bats.

Twenty-year-old Ken McMullen was the new Dodger third baseman. Third base was a trouble spot for the Dodgers, with five players sharing the position in 1962. Alston planned to have Tommy Davis take over the position in 1963. The experiment ended in Florida on March 20 when Davis committed his eighth error in twelve games—most of them wild throws.[15] The next day Davis and McMullen traded places: Davis back to left field; and McMullen from left field to third. McMullen doubled home two runs in the eighth off a Barney Schultz knuckle ball.

Bill "Moose" Skowron, who came over from the Yankees in the Stan Williams trade, was the starting first baseman. Skowron, a former Purdue fullback, was a 4-time All-Star with a career .300 batting average and 7 World Series home runs in

Nate "Pee Wee" Oliver (National Baseball Hall of Fame Library, Cooperstown, New York).

First baseman Bill "Moose" Skowron, a former Purdue fullback, came over from the Yankees in the Stan Williams trade (National Baseball Hall of Fame Library, Cooperstown, New York).

Ken McMullen (National Baseball Hall of Fame Library, Cooperstown, New York).

his nine years in New York. He hit 23 homers and drove in 80 for the 1962 World Champions. But there was a downside to Skowron: he was also 32 years old with a well-known history of back problems.[16]

Sporting new eyeglasses behind his catcher's mask, John Roseboro made his sixth straight opening-day start behind the plate. In 1962 Roseboro led the league with 14 errors and hit only .249 with 7 home runs, after hitting 18 the year before. After a poor performance in the playoff series with the Giants (0-for-8 with a costly error), he was put on the trading block during Bavasi's fall purge. Though there were several interested teams, a deal never materialized.[17] When Alston's highly publicized first choice for catcher, Doug Camilli, didn't pan out in the spring exhibition season, Roseboro was given another chance.

Before the season was an hour old, the Dodgers suffered their first setback when Maury Wills sprained his right ankle in a collision at the plate with Cubs catcher Dick Bertell. The National League MVP was thrown out at home plate trying to score from second base on an infield topper by Willie Davis. After setting a major league record by playing in all 165 games in 1962, he would be lost for a week. The Dodger defense was one of the biggest question marks coming into the season. They played error-free baseball on opening day. But the biggest question mark was Sandy Koufax. While he was impressive during the exhibition season, it was not the same as the heat of regular competition. His first real test would come the next day at Wrigley Field.

The First Test of Sandy Koufax

On April 10 Sandy Koufax made his first non-exhibition appearance since October 1, 1962. His opponent was Bob Buhl, with 25 career victories over the Dodgers. A crowd of 2,673 hearty souls showed up on a 34-dgree day at Wrigley Field to see Koufax beat the Cubs 2–1 with a complete-game 5-hitter. He gave up 5 singles, walked 2, and struck out 10.

Willie Davis was implicated in both of the unearned runs given up by Buhl. Davis, replacing Wills in the leadoff spot, was hit on the foot by Buhl's first pitch of the game. Though hobbled by a muscle pull, the fastest man in baseball still managed to steal second and third, and then score when Dick Bertell's throw sailed into left field. In the fifth, Davis singled home Dick Tracewski, playing shortstop in place of Wills, with the deciding run. The only run off Koufax came in the bottom of the eighth. Lou Brock struck out on three pitches, but reached base when the third pitch eluded John Roseboro. Koufax then gave up back-to-back singles to Andre Rodgers and Billy Williams to score Brock.

In the clubhouse after the game, Koufax jangled a few nerves when told reporters, "There was still some numbness in the tip of my index finger."[18] But with the first win by Sandy Koufax since July 12, 1962, Walter Alston could sleep easier.

Throwing Zeroes Again

The Dodgers were one game under .500 as they went into a 3-game weekend series with the Colt .45s at Dodger Stadium. Sandy Koufax started in the April 19 Friday night opener against Turk Farrell. Koufax had never completed a game against the Houston expansion team in five previous starts, the latest being a pounding he took in Houston on April 14. The 15,564 people who turned out on a threatening night were treated to a gem as Koufax threw a 2-hit, 2–0 shutout with 14 strikeouts. He disposed of Houston in a mere one hour and 48 minutes to improve his season record to 2–1.

Jim Gilliam was back at third base for the Dodgers. The third base "problem" resurfaced after the first week. When rookie third baseman Ken McMullen got off to a .174 start (4-for-23), the Dodgers turned to the trusty Gilliam to take over the position.

Turk Farrell matched Koufax, with a 2-hit shutout through the first six innings. In the bottom of the seventh, Gilliam got to him with a leadoff double. After Nate Oliver sacrificed Gilliam to second, Frank Howard followed with a tremendous 450-foot home run to the back of the bullpen in left field to give Koufax an insurmountable 2–0 lead.

After Sandy Koufax's first win over Houston brought the Dodgers back to .500, they went on to take three out of four from the Colts with a double-header sweep on Sunday, April 21. The Milwaukee Braves came into town the next night for a 2-game series. In the opener, Hank Aaron and Eddie Mathews homered off Dodger stopper Don Drysdale in a 10–2 loss.

The First Koufax Crisis

On Tuesday night, April 23, Alston called on Sandy Koufax to give the Dodgers a split in their 2-game series with the Braves. His opponent was big right-hander Bob Shaw. Shaw and Koufax had a history. It was Shaw who beat Koufax and the Dodgers 1–0 in Game 5 of the 1959 World Series on a run-scoring double play ground ball. Last season Shaw was 15–9, second only to Warren Spahn in wins on the Braves staff.

Koufax took a 1–0 lead into the seventh inning. Though he had given up only 2 singles and struck out 5, he appeared to be laboring as he bounced several pitches in front of home plate. After retiring the first two batters, he suffered what appeared to be a muscle spasm, and had to be removed from the game. Koufax had been bothered by muscle spasms in spring training. Ron Perranoski came in to strike out Dennis Menke to end the inning.

On the Braves side, Bob Shaw had a 1-hitter through the first seven innings, allowing an unearned run in the second. The Braves removed Shaw for a pinch hitter in the eighth, and replaced him with Claude Raymond. Koufax was in line for his third win as Perranoski carried the 1–0 lead into the ninth inning. But when Hank Aaron hit Perranoski's first pitch 420 feet over the center field fence to tie the game, Koufax had to settle for a no decision. In the bottom of the inning, Frank Howard, who was playing the game with eyeglasses for the first time, won it with a home run into the upper reaches of the left field pavilion.[19]

When Koufax revealed after the game that he had "felt something tear in his shoulder,"[20] he was sent to the hospital for X-rays. The next day the Koufax situation rose to the level of a full-blown crisis when the X-rays revealed that the problem was not a muscle spasm, but an injury to the posterior capsule of the left shoulder joint.[21] He would be out for a minimum of ten days—at least two starts. It was devastating news for the Dodgers. A year ago, the loss of Koufax—first estimated to be 30 days, that turned into 66 days, and was effectively the rest of the season—cost them the pennant. Now, after a great start, he was lost again—and for exactly how long was anyone's guess.

Sinking Without Koufax

After sweeping two games from the Reds on April 24–25, the Dodgers prepared to meet the St. Louis Cardinals for the first time since the catastrophic final weekend of 1962. They would be without the services of Sandy Koufax. The surprising 10–6 Cardinals were tied with the Giants for first place, with the Dodgers a half game behind with a 10–7 record.

An Encounter with the New Cardinals

In 1962 the Cardinals finished sixth, 17½ games behind the Giants. In the off season, Manager Johnny Keane and General Manager Bing Devine took action to improve the team. They picked up big power-hitting outfielder George Altman from the Cubs and premier shortstop Dick Groat from the Pirates.[22] With Groat providing the much-needed leadership, the entire Cardinal infield (White, 1B; Javier, 2B; Groat, SS; Boyer, 3B) would make the All-Star team. In the flurry of off-season trading they gave up prematurely on two veteran pitchers: starter Larry Jackson and reliever Lindy McDaniel. At 42, Stan Musial was in his last season. He was 25 when the Cardinals won their last pennant in 1946.

The 3-game weekend series with the Cardinals at Dodger Stadium began Friday, April 26, with a Bob Gibson-Don Drysdale matchup. Gibson (0–0) was coming off a 15–13 season cut short by a broken ankle on September 21. Drysdale (2–2) had lost his last two starts. Neither pitcher was on his game this night. In the first three innings the Dodgers roughed up Gibson for 7 runs on 6 hits, including home runs by Howard and Roseboro. Gibson exited in the fourth without retiring a batter. Drysdale took a 7–3 lead to the eighth before Boyer and Musial drove him to the showers with run-scoring singles to make it 7–5. In a disastrous ninth inning, Ron Perranoski blew the save by giving up 5 hits and 3 runs as the Cardinals came from behind to win, 8–7. It would be the only game in 1963 for which Perranoski was charged with a blown save and a loss.

April 27 would have been Koufax's turn to start. Instead, Larry Sherry got his first start of the year against the Cardinals' Ray Washburn. Coming into spring training, Sherry was Alston's top choice to replace Stan Williams as the fourth starter. But when he failed miserably in his pre-season audition, he was once again relegated to the bullpen. Sherry shut out the Cardinals on three hits through the first five innings, while Washburn was pitching a no-hitter for St. Louis. It all fell apart for Sherry in the sixth when the Dodgers committed 3 errors, allowing 3 unearned runs to score. Washburn went on to pitch a 3-hit, 3–0 shutout to improve his record to 4–0 and reduce his ERA to 1.25. The 24-year-old right-hander, who was once turned down at a Dodger tryout camp, called the game "my best ever."[23]

Johnny Podres attempted to salvage the third game on Sunday, April 28. But he could get only three batters out as the Cardinals jumped out to an insurmountable 7–1 lead after an inning and a half. With two home runs by Ken Boyer and a 3-for-3 performance by the irrepressible Charlie James, St. Louis won the game, 9–5, to complete a 3-game sweep. The game marked the end of the Dodgers' 14-game home stand. They left town with a 10–10 record.

There would be no day off for the trip to New York. The next night at the Polo Grounds, Bob Miller faced his old Mets team and Roger Craig, who was coming off a 10–24 season with the hapless 1962 Mets. Miller was pitching well with a 2–1 lead going into the seventh inning before he hit a wall. He gave up two singles and a double, and allowed a run to score on a wild pitch—all without retiring another batter. By the time Ed Roebuck came in to put out the fire, the Mets had wiped out the lead and gone ahead by 2 runs. Craig's complete-game, 4–2 win was an isolated bright spot in what would be a 5–22 season. With the solo game in New York, the Dodgers ended the month of April in fifth place, one game under .500.

	W	L	PCT.	*
St. Louis	14	6	.700	
Pittsburgh	11	5	.688	1
Milwaukee	12	9	.571	2½
San Francisco	11	9	.550	3
Los Angeles	10	11	.476	4½

*Games behind leader

By now Walter Alston was under withering criticism. The besieged Dodger manager was improvising with an injury-depleted lineup. Not only had he lost Koufax, he lost MVP Maury Wills for a week from an ankle sprain on opening day, batting champ Tommy Davis for 15 games when his pulled hamstring muscle hemorrhaged and landed him in the hospital, and his other premier left-hander, Johnny Podres, to a shoulder injury.

The Dodgers began May with another solo game in Philadelphia on May 2 after a rainout the night before. In a pitchers' duel between Don Drysdale and Art Mahaffey at Connie Mack Stadium, Ron Fairly's 2-run homer in the ninth gave the Dodgers a come-from-behind 3–2 win. Ron Peranoski picked up another win in relief of hard-luck Drysdale, whose one mistake was lined by Wes Covington into the upper deck in right field in the sixth.

Rumors about the demise of Walter Alston were swirling as the team moved on to Pittsburgh for a 4-game series with the second-place Pirates. Larry Sherry opened the series on May 3 in place of Koufax. For the first time in 17 games, Tommy Davis was back in the starting lineup at third base, with Gilliam taking over second base for the faltering Nate Oliver, whose batting average had plummeted to .218. Rookie Ken McMullen was on his way back to the minors after batting a disappointing .205 and driving only 1 run after opening day.[24] The game was a scoreless tie through the first three and a half innings with Sherry and Pirates starter Al McBean throwing matching shutouts. In the bottom of the fourth, Sherry came within one pitch of matching McBean's four consecutive scoreless innings until Dick Schofield, the first new Pirate shortstop in eight years, started a landslide. Schofield lined Sherry's 3–2 pitch into right field to score the first 2 runs of the game. This was followed by a run-scoring single by Bill Virdon and a crushing RBI triple by Bob Skinner that brought Alston out of the dugout. With the Dodgers suddenly down 4–0, he took Sherry out and brought in 23-year-old left hander Pete Richert. Richert struck out rookie first baseman Willie Stargell, looking, on three pitches, but he was not the answer. The Pirates put the game out of reach in the fifth as Richert handed them 4 more runs with a balk, a wild pitch, 2 singles, a double, and a triple. Down 8–0, Alston brought in Jack Smith, in what was essentially mop-up duty. In Smith's one inning the Pirate lead ballooned to 12–0. In what ended as a 13–2 beating, the Dodgers again fell a game below .500. Larry Sherry would not get another start until the last weekend of the season.

The next day at Forbes Field, Alston gave the ball again to Bob Miller. But Miller could last only three innings, and the Dodgers could manage only four singles as they were shut out 5–0 by the Pirates' 6-foot, 6-inch right-hander Don Schwall.

With Johnny Podres sidelined, the Dodgers' chances were slim on Sunday, May 5, as they had to go up against Vernon Law with the winless Pete Richert and his grotesque 12.15 ERA. But Richert gave them five solid innings. In fact, he was pitching a 3-hit, 2–0 shutout before he fell apart in the sixth. After he retired the first two batters, he gave up a walk, 2 singles, and a 2-run triple, and allowed a third run to score on a wild pitch. The Pirates were on top, 3–2, and Richert was out of the game. The game was tied 3–3 as it moved to the ninth with Law still on the mound for the Pirates. Both Roseboro and Skowron singled with one out to force Pittsburgh manager Danny Murtaugh's hand. Murtaugh brought in Harvey Haddix to face to pinch hitter Lee Walls. Walls, who had a .316 lifetime batting average against Haddix, lined his first pitch over the clock atop the scoreboard in left field for a 3-run homer. Gilliam doubled home Walls. With four runs in the ninth, the Dodgers came back to win 7–3. Ron Perranoski pitched the last three scoreless innings to pick up his fourth win of the season in relief.

On Monday, May 6, Don Drysdale tried to give the Dodgers a split in the series and bring them back to .500 for the season. He got off to a shaky start in the first inning by giving up a walk, three singles, and a triple. Only a gift double-play ground ball by the Pirates' slothful catcher, Smokey Burgess, held the score to 2–0. The Dodgers came back with 4 runs off Pittsburgh's starter Bob Friend to take a 4–2 lead, but Drysdale couldn't hold it. He was chased in the sixth after a throwing error by Junior Gilliam opened up the floodgates for four more Pirate runs—three of them unearned. The Pirates won the game, 7–4, to take the series three games to one. The win put the Pirates in first place by percentage points ahead of the Cardinals and Giants, who were tied for second. The Dodgers had fallen to seventh place, 2 games under .500. After being shelled with 10 hits and 6 runs in 5⅔ innings, their Cy Young winner, Don Drysdale, was off to a 2–3 start. They had to be in St. Louis the next night for a 3-game series with the high-flying Cardinals.

The Bus Incident

Nerves were frayed on the bus ride to the Pittsburgh airport after the team had blown the lead and the series at Forbes Field. Since the players couldn't undo the results on the field, they decided to take it out on the bus. No sooner had they gotten on board than several of them began to complain vociferously to traveling secretary Lee Scott about the cramped seating conditions. A stressed-out Walter Alston, now in fear of losing his job, ordered Scott and the others to "knock it off"![25]

A few miles later the simmering Alston blew his top. He told the driver to pull the offending bus over to the side of the road and stop. The quiet man from Darrtown rose to his feet to ask, "Can everybody in the back hear me?"[26] There was not a peep. He probed, "Does anyone want to volunteer to book the bus we get in St. Louis?" Again, there was not a peep. After Alston told them that he would personally take over the job, he issued a stern warning: "If any of you don't like the bus I get, you can come to me, and we'll step outside and discuss it among ourselves."[27] With that, Alston sat down shaking with anger as the subdued busload continued on its merry way to the airport.

The next day from Los Angeles, Dodger owner Walter O'Malley squelched the rumors of an impending takeover of the team by Leo Durocher: "Alston is my manager, and I have no intention of making a change."[28] In St. Louis, Alston could breathe easier as he prepared to take on the Cardinals with Sandy Koufax on the mound.

Seventeen

Life Is Good on Planet Koufax

In the no-hitter I didn't have overpowering stuff.[1]—Sandy
Koufax, May 11, 1963

"I'm too old to fight." That's what Walter Alston told reporters when they pressed him about the bus incident before the opening game of the Cardinal series on May 7 at Busch Stadium in St. Louis. Much was riding on the game. The seventh-place Dodgers limped into the series after losing seven of their last nine games. What's more, they had lost seven straight to the Cardinals dating back to the end of the last season. Sandy Koufax was making his first appearance after missing three turns in his two-week stint on the sidelines. And they would face the red-hot Ray Washburn, who came into the game with a 5–0 record and a 1.61 ERA.

Koufax's Trial

While the Dodgers desperately needed a stop from Koufax, no one knew how his shoulder would respond. They soon got their answer. But for two errors by the Dodger infield, he retired the Cardinals in order in the first three innings. At the same time, the Dodger hitters knocked Washburn out of the game by pounding him for 7 hits and 5 runs. By the end of the seventh, the Dodgers had staked Koufax to a 9–0 lead while he held the Cardinals to two infield singles. In the eighth an unknown pinch hitter, Leo Burke, hit a high fly ball that cleared the left field fence for a solo home run—his only home run in his brief 53-game stay with the Cardinals. Rookie relief pitcher Ken Rowe took over for Koufax to pitch the ninth with a lead that had grown to 11–1. Rowe, who was unceremoniously optioned out to Spokane after the game, held the Cardinals scoreless to save the win for Koufax.

May 7 was a turning point in the season. Koufax passed through that trial with a strong 8 innings in which he allowed 5 hits and 1 run, while striking out 5 and walking only 1. He was now 3–1 for the season and would not miss another start for the rest of the year. The Dodger offense responded with 11 runs and 13 hits, including 3 by Ron Fairly, who had to take over first base on short notice when Moose Skowron pulled a hamstring muscle in pre-game warmups. Tommy Davis hit his first home run of the season. It was the beginning of a momentum shift for the Cardinals. They committed 5 errors and were knocked out of first place. Ray Washburn would not win another game for the rest of the season.

The next night the Dodger offensive again scored 11 runs on 13 hits to beat St. Louis, 11–5. Ron Perranoski won his fifth game in relief of Bob Miller. Willie Davis had two home runs, a triple, and three runs batted in. The Dodgers had a chance to sweep the series on May 9 with young Pete Richert facing Bob Gibson. Willie Davis gave the Dodgers a 2–0 lead with another triple to drive in two runs off Gibson in the fourth. After shutting out the Cardinals for the first four innings, Richert left the game with the bases loaded and none out in the fifth. The Cardinals pounded his replacements, Dick Scott and Larry Sherry, for a grand slam home run, a 2-run home run, and an RBI single to take an insurmountable 7–2 lead. The Cardinals went on to win a seesaw game, 10–7. Gibson won his first game of the year despite giving up 5 runs on 11 hits in 6⅔ innings. With the loss, the Dodgers closed out their 9-game road trip at 4–5. The next night the Dodgers had a date with the first-place Giants at Dodger Stadium.

On Friday night, May 10, the Dodgers opened a 3-game weekend series with the Giants at Dodger Stadium. The Giants, who were leading the league in home runs, had been in first place for a week. Felipe Alou was the league's leading hitter with a scorching .384 average. Tonight it would be Don Drysdale against Jack Sanford, two pitchers with 49 wins between them last season. Coming into the game, Drysdale was 2–3 and Sanford 5–1.

In the third inning, Tommy Davis broke a 1–1 tie with a 2-out, run-scoring double off Sanford to put Los Angeles in front, 2–1. It was the last run of the evening. Drysdale went on to beat Sanford and the Giants, 2–1, on a complete-game 6-hitter with 11 strikeouts. Tom Haller's solo home run in the second inning off Drysdale was the Giants' only run.

The Second Koufax No-Hitter

On Saturday night, May 11, a turn-away crowd of 55,530 filled Dodger Stadium to see a highly anticipated meeting between Sandy Koufax and Juan Marichal. Dodger officials had to go on the air an hour before game-time to tell people to stay home unless they already had a ticket. While warming up, Koufax realized that he didn't have great stuff, but that it was "good enough."[2] As he walked out to the mound to start the game, he yelled a warning to his third baseman, Tommy Davis: "Hang loose!"[3] From the beginning the stars were aligned for Koufax. The first Giants batter, Harvey Kuenn, hit a line shot to center field—right at Willie Davis. Years later Koufax would recall, "Twenty feet in either direction, and the no-hitter would have been gone before I had out number one."[4] He then got Felipe Alou on an infield pop-up and Willie Mays on another fly ball to Willie Davis in center field. Already it was noticeable that the Giants were hitting the ball in the air.

Koufax retired the Giants in order in the second, third, and fourth innings. Wally Moon hit a solo home run off Marichal in the second inning to put the Dodgers up, 1–0.

In the top of the fifth, lead-off batter Orlando Cepeda hit a swinging-bunt topper past Koufax—a likely infield single. Shortstop Dick Tracewski charged the ball, picked it up with his bare hand, and threw off balance to nip Cepeda at first base. Koufax then got both Ed Bailey and Jim Davenport to pop out to first baseman Ron Fairly.

After Koufax retired the side in order again in the sixth, it was 18 batters up and 18 batters down for the Giants, a perfect game through six innings. In the bottom half of the inning, the Dodgers knocked Marichal out of the game with 5 singles for 3 more runs to increase their lead to 4–0. With Koufax pitching a perfect game, Alston moved the erratic Tommy Davis out to left field, switched Gilliam from second to third, and brought in Nate Oliver from the bench to play second.

In the top of the seventh, Felipe Alou tied into a Koufax 2–2 pitch, sending it soaring toward the left-field foul pole. Sandy's reaction at the crack of the bat was, "Oh God, it's a home run."[5] But the newly inserted Tommy Davis hauled it in with his back against the left-field railing at the 360-foot mark.[6] Willie Mays followed with a scream-

ing line drive that the new third baseman, Gilliam, stabbed behind the third base bag to preserve the perfect game. Out in the right-field bullpen, Giants reliever Don Larsen—the last man to throw a perfect game, in Game 5 of the 1956 World Series—watched the proceedings through a chain-link fence.[7]

Cepeda led off the top of the eighth with a sharp ground ball that caromed off Koufax's glove. Fortunately, the ball rolled right to Nate Oliver at second base. After Oliver threw out Cepeda, Koufax had retired twenty-two consecutive batters. But the eighth continued to be a problematic inning as he then threw three straight pitches out of the strike zone to Ed Bailey, the only left-handed batter in the Giants' starting lineup. Bailey then took two strikes and fouled off a fast ball to run the count to 3–2. On the seventh pitch, Bailey took a low fast ball for ball four to break up the perfect game. Koufax regrouped to get Jim Davenport on an inning-ending double play ground ball. Through eight innings he still had a no-hitter after facing the minimum 24 batters. Koufax had to sit in the dugout for nearly a half hour in the bottom of the inning while the Dodgers pounded Giants reliever John Pregerizer for four more runs to increase their lead to 8–0.

By 1963, Dodger Stadium fans were already

Giants right fielder Felipe Alou nearly broke up a Sandy Koufax no-hitter on May 11, 1963. Alou's seventh-inning home run bid was hauled in at the left field barrier by Tommy Davis (George Brace photograph).

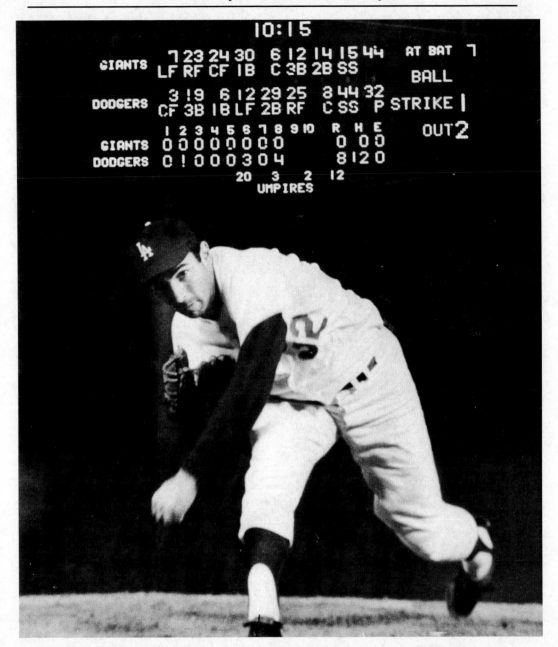

Sandy Koufax making the last pitch of his second no-hitter May 11, 1963 (National Baseball Hall of Fame Library, Cooperstown, New York).

famous for leaving early. But tonight it seemed as if all 55,530 were present and on their feet as Koufax walked out to the mound to pitch the ninth inning. He began by getting lead-off batter Joey Amalfitano to pop out on a 2–0 pitch. Next, he got Jose Pagan to fly out to Willie Davis in center field. Down 8–0, and one out away from being no-hit, Alvin Dark sent Willie McCovey up to the plate to pinch hit for the pitcher. With the perfect game gone, Koufax walked the dangerous McCovey on four pitches, making it necessary to face Harvey Kuenn for the fourth time. Kuenn took the first pitch for a strike, then hit a fast ball on one hop back to Koufax. To make sure he didn't throw it away, Koufax ran almost all the way to first base hugging the ball before lobbing it underhanded to Ron Fairly for the final out and leaped into the air touching off pandemonium at Dodger Stadium. For the next ten minutes, the fans showered the field with seat cushions, cheered, and stomped as the Dodgers mobbed and mauled Koufax.[8]

After this game, it was clear that 1963 was going to be a special season for Sandy Koufax. He had come back from a season-ending finger injury and his recent shoulder injury—later diagnosed as a torn adhesion. Without his best stuff, he pitched a no-hit, no-run game against the league's top power team. While he made 111 pitches, 72 for strikes, he struck out only 4 batters. No longer relying exclusively on the fast ball, he was using his curve more frequently to keep the hitters off balance. Koufax had now thrown 24⅔ innings for the season at Dodger Stadium without allowing a run. His record was 4–1 and the league was batting .122 against him.

In a Sunday afternoon game the next day at Dodger Stadium, Walter Alston asked Johnny Podres to complete a sweep of the Giants against right-hander Jack Fisher. Fisher had come over from Baltimore in an off-season trade in which the Giants gave up Mike McCormick and Stu Miller. Podres was making his first start since April 28, the day he hurt his shoulder in the first inning against the Cardinals. Desperate to solve his third base problem, Alston made Maury Wills his new third baseman—the team's fifth in 32 games. Dick Tracewski became the new .179-hitting shortstop.

Orlando Cepeda, who homered off Podres in the second inning, knocked Podres out of the game in the fourth with a run-scoring double to tie the game at 2–2. McCovey and Cepeda roughed up Bob Miller with a triple and a single for two more runs in the fifth to give the Giants a 4–2 lead. Down 5–2 in the eighth, the Dodgers scored 4 runs for a come-from-behind 6–5 win. With the 3-game sweep of the Giants, the Dodgers moved up to fourth place at 17–15, 2 games behind the first-place Giants.

The Phillies came into town for a 2-game series beginning May 14. Philadelphia and Cal McLish beat Don Drysdale and the Dodgers 5–1 the first night. The second night Koufax squared off against the Phillies' ace left-hander, Chris Short. Short lasted only 4⅔ innings. Koufax took a 2–1 lead to the ninth. Former Dodger Don Demeter led off with a double. Three batters later, Phillies shortstop Bobby Wine singled home Demeter to tie the game at 2–2 and send it into extra innings. Koufax shut out the Phillies for the next three innings. With the score still tied, 2–2, in the bottom of the twelfth, Alston took Koufax out for a pinch hitter. Unless the Dodgers pulled it out before the inning was over, he would have a no decision to show for twelve innings of work. With two out, Junior Gilliam singled off another former Dodger, Johnny Klippstein. After Klippstein wild-pitched him into scoring position, Ron Fairly hit a single to right field to score Gilliam with the game-winning run. Koufax got his fifth win, a Herculean 12-inning complete game in which he made 164 pitches, struck out 12, walked none, and scattered 11 hits.

The Dodgers swept a 3-game series from the Pirates May 16 through May 18—including a 1–0 shutout by Podres in the first game—to move into second place. They would close out a 12-game home stand with a 4-game series with the Mets beginning with a Sunday double-header on May 19.

Sandy Koufax and Roger Craig met in the first game of the double-header. Koufax retired the Mets in order in the top of the first. With one out in the bottom of the inning, Gilliam walked and advanced all the way to third on a single by Fairly. He scored what would be the only run of the game on a sacrifice fly by Tommy Davis. Koufax breezed the rest of the way to a 2-hit, 1–0 shutout in one hour and fifty-seven minutes. The only hits by the Mets were singles by Ron Hunt in the fourth and Craig in the sixth. With his third shutout, Koufax, now 6–1, reduced his ERA to a stunning 1.06.

Left-handers Pete Richert and Al Jackson matched up in the second game. After Tommy Davis tied the game, 2–2, with an RBI single in the sixth inning, no runs were scored for the next two hours. In the top of the thirteenth, Ron Hunt led off with a line shot into the right-center-field gap off Ron Perranoski. The ball looked like a sure triple until Frank Howard made a sensational one-handed catch. It turned out to be a pivotal play. The next batter, Jim Hickman, lined a double to left field. He was left stranded on second as Perranoski settled down to retire the next two batters. Howard won the game in the bottom of the thirteenth with a tape-measure 2-run homer into the pavilion in left center off reliever Ken MacKenzie.[9] Perranoski pitched seven shut-out innings in relief to win his sixth game. It was the sixth straight win for the Dodgers.

The winning streak reached eight as the Dodgers completed a 4-game sweep of the Mets with complete-game wins by Podres on May 21 and Drysdale on May 22. As they prepared to fly to San Francisco to begin a 15-game road trip, they were in second place, just one game behind the Giants. After the bus incident in Pittsburgh, they had gone on a 13–2 run to climb five places in the National League standings ignited by the May 7 return of Sandy Koufax, who was 4–0 during that period with two shutouts.

Return to Candlestick

In the Koufax-Marichal rematch of Friday, May 24, the Dodgers made their first appearance in Candlestick Park since the ill-fated Monday afternoon of October 1, 1962. It was on that day that Sandy Koufax lasted just one inning in the first post-season playoff game. Tonight he would last one-*third* of an inning. After Juan Marichal blanked the Dodgers in the top of the first, the Giants went to work on Koufax in the bottom of the inning. He gave up singles to Jose Pagan and McCovey, and walked Willie Mays to load the bases for Orlando Cepeda. Cepeda ripped his first pitch into the right-center-field gap between Wally Moon and Willie Davis for a base-clearing double. Felipe Alou followed with a crushing 2-run homer to make the score 5–0 before Koufax

Nineteen sixty-three was the first super season for Juan Marichal. He would tie Koufax with 25 wins and go 4–2 against the Dodgers with a 1.96 ERA (National Baseball Hall of Fame Library, Cooperstown, New York).

could get anyone out. After he struck out Jim Davenport with Larry Sherry frantically warming up in the bullpen, Koufax gave up a line-drive single to Ed Bailey, then wild-pitched him to second base. When Koufax fell behind 3–0 on Joey Amalfitano, Alston had seen enough. He took out Koufax and brought in Sherry, mid-batter. Sherry finished walking Amalfitano before retiring the next two Giants.

Marichal went on to pitch a brilliant 4-hit, 7–1 complete game. Don Zimmer prevented a shutout with a solo pinch-hit home run in the sixth inning that struck the left-field foul pole before caroming into left-center.[10] Marichal was now 6–3 in what would be his first super season. Koufax was 6–2. His 5 earned runs in a third of an inning made his ERA jump from 1.06 to 1.71.

The next day, Billy O'Dell beat Johnny Podres and the Dodgers, 6–2. Tommy Davis had a double and two singles off O'Dell, who was now a perfect 7–0 for the year. On Sunday afternoon, May 26, Drysdale pitched a gutty 10-inning complete game to beat Jack Sanford and the Giants, 4–3, and salvage the final game of the series. Tommy Davis won it with a run-scoring single in the tenth. It was the 19th RBI in the last 18 games for the red-hot Davis. With two more hits, he raised his average to .305.[11] As the Dodgers left San Francisco for the Midwestern leg of their road trip they were in second place, 2 games behind the Giants.

A Lone Bright Spot in Milwaukee— Another Koufax Shutout

On May 28 in Milwaukee, Sandy Koufax shut out the Braves, 7–0, on 6 hits—all singles. The game was a scoreless pitcher's duel between left-handers Koufax and Denny Lemaster until Frank Howard hit a solo home run off Lemaster with one out in the seventh inning. It was not one of Howard's prodigious blasts. He got under a 3–2 pitch and lofted it down the left-field line until it barely cleared the fence at the 320-foot mark. One run was more than enough for Koufax, but the Dodgers scored six more runs in the ninth off a trio of Braves relievers. Even with the best pitcher in baseball on the mound for the visiting team, only 4,573 fans showed up at County Stadium to support the eighth-place Braves.[12] Koufax improved his record to 7–2, and reduced his ERA to 1.51. He threw 111 pitches, walked 2, and struck out 8.

The next night the Braves and Dodgers played to a rain-shortened, 7-inning, 3–3 tie game. The series in Milwaukee concluded on May 30 with Warren Spahn beating Don Drysdale 7–4 in an afternoon game.

A Low Point in Cincinnati

The Dodgers ended the month of May with 7–4 loss at Crosley Field in Cincinnati. Dodger starter Bob Miller lasted only an inning and two thirds against the Reds. Their 22-year-old right-hander, Jim Maloney, won his seventh game of what would be a 23-win season. The loss dropped Los Angeles into third place in the standings at the end of play on May 31:

	W	L	Pct.	*
San Francisco	30	18	.625	
St. Louis	29	21	.580	2
Los Angeles	27	20	.574	2½

*Games behind leader

On the first day of June, Sandy Koufax suffered a tough 1–0 loss in his first start at Crosley Field in Cincinnati since the fateful day of July 17, 1962, when he walked off the same field with a split index finger. On this night he pitched well enough to win, giving up only 3 hits. But one of them, off the bat of an ex-teammate, cost him the game. The Reds' new 34-year-old third baseman, Daryl Spencer, released by the Dodgers just two weeks before, lined a single off Koufax in the fourth inning that scored the game's only run. At the same time, Koufax was getting no support from the Dodger offense. Their catalyst, Maury Wills, missed his eighth straight game due to calcium deposits on the bottom of his left foot, a condition that was making surgery more likely every day. Cincinnati's big right-hander, Joey Jay, shut them out on 4 singles.

The series concluded on June 2 with a Podres versus O'Toole battle of left-handers. The Reds jumped out to an insurmountable 5–0 lead with five unearned runs off Podres in the second inning. The Dodgers could muster only 5 hits against Jim O'Toole through the first eight innings, and eventually went down to a 5–2 defeat. It was the Dodgers' fourth straight loss, and the first time they had been swept in Cincinnati since 1952.

In disarray without Wills, the Dodgers tried putting Wally Moon in the leadoff spot in Houston on June 3. It was futile, as the Dodgers could produce only two hits. Turk Farrell went all the way to beat them, 2–1. Wasted was a fine performance by Don Drysdale, who struck out 13 Colts in his seven innings. The Dodgers had now lost five games in a row to fall into a third-place tie with the Cubs, four games behind the league-leading Giants.

In 10 games on the road without Maury Wills, the Dodgers had used four different leadoff men, losing seven games and tying one. They were fortunate that Wills finally responded to treatment and avoided surgery.[13] Things began to turn around for the team when he returned to the lineup the night of June 4 at Colts Stadium in Houston. The Dodgers' Bob Miller turned in a strong 8-inning performance to beat the Colt .45s, 2–1, and snap the losing streak. Back in the lead-off spot, Wills scored both runs and stole a base.

Sandy Koufax was scheduled to start on the night of June 5 to close out the Houston series. And he came through with a complete-game, 5–1 victory. He even played a key role with a bat in his hand. With two runners on in the sixth inning, he came to the plate with a batting average—albeit .034 (1 for 29). He looped Ken Johnson's 0–1 pitch into center field to score both runs. It was Koufax's seventh complete game in twelve starts. He scattered 8 hits and struck out 8 batters. The game would mark the beginning of one of his most prodigious winning streaks. The Dodgers picked up a game and a half on the first-place Giants, who lost a double-header at Wrigley Field.

On the same night in Baltimore, Mickey Mantle fractured a bone in his left foot, and suffered ligament and cartilage damage to his left knee crashing into a chain link center-field fence in a futile attempt to chase down a Brooks Robinson home run in the sixth inning. The Memorial Stadium outfield had no warning track.[14] Thinking he had a play, Mantle jumped high for the ball as he raced toward the 8-foot fence. The ball evaded his reach and just cleared the fence for a game-tying home run. As he came down, his spikes caught in the mesh wiring, severely twisting his left foot and causing a break to his third metatarsal bone. Mantle had to be carried off the field on a stretcher by his teammates.[15]

Triumph at Wrigley Field

The last leg of the road trip was a 3-game weekend series in Chicago. Twenty-five years before they installed lights in Wrigley Field, the series opened on a Friday afternoon, June 7. Don Drysdale pitched a complete-game 7-hitter to beat the Cubs, 4–1. Frank Howard tripled and homered. The next day the Dodgers, behind Johnny Podres, were leading 3–1 until Podres ran out of gas, walking his third batter with two outs in the sixth. Larry Sherry was brought in against pinch hitter Merrit Ranew to get the final out. Ranew hit Sherry's 2–0 pitch over the ivy-covered right field wall to tie the game at 3–3. With six runs in the final three innings, the Dodgers pulled the game out, 9–5. Perranoski won his seventh game in relief. The win put them into a virtual tie for first place with three other teams.

When the Dodgers arrived at Wrigley Field for the final game of the series on Sunday, June 9, there were mixed signs. The good news was that they would have Sandy Koufax on the mound; the bad news was the wind that was blowing straight out to Lake Michigan. A capacity crowd of 35,743 turned out in anticipation of a pitchers' duel between the league's two leading left-handers. Koufax was 8–3, with a 1.45 ERA. His opponent, Dick Ellsworth, was 8–3 with a 1.51 ERA.

But it was anything but a pitchers' duel. Koufax was shelled for six earned runs on eight hits, including two home runs by Ernie Banks and one by Ron Santo in 4⅔ innings. After he gave up a single, two doubles, and two home runs before he could complete the fifth inning, he was done. The Dodgers pounded Ellsworth for eight runs on seven hits in his 5⅔ innings. In the top of the sixth, Lee Walls drew a bases-loaded walk from Ellsworth to cut Chicago's lead to 6–5 and drive him from the game. The next batter, Maury Wills, hit a base-clearing, 3-run double off reliever Don Elston to put the Dodgers in the lead, 8–6.

Despite giving up Ernie Banks's third home run of the game with two out in the ninth inning, Larry Sherry pitched the last four innings to pick up an 11–8 win. Koufax escaped with a no decision, though his ERA took a 48-point jump to 1.93. By sweeping the series in Chicago, the Dodgers took over sole possession of first place, with the Cardinals a half game behind. They were 5–0 since the return of reigning MVP Maury Wills. During the 5-game winning streak, Wills hit .500 (11 for 22), reached base 15 times, stole 4 bases, scored 6 runs, and drove in 5.[16] Tommy Davis had also caught fire. He was 8 for 13 with 2 home runs in the weekend series with the Cubs. During the 15-game road trip concluded on this day, he hit .414 to raise his season batting average from .277 to .329.

Derailed Again by the Giants

After winning their last five games on the road to move into first place, the red-hot Dodgers returned to Los Angeles on June 10 to meet the Giants in a 2-game series at Dodger Stadium. The Giants were reeling, having just lost the last seven games on the road to fall from first place to third. Bob Miller and Billy Pierce met in the Monday night opener before 52,993, to date the largest major league attendance. After a 16–6 season in 1962, Pierce came into the game with a 1–4 record. Relegated to a spot-starter role, he was making only his fifth start of the year. Miller was 4–2, coming off a fine 8-inning performance in Houston. Neither starter lasted past the sixth inning, nor figured in the decision. The Giants won the game 7–3 on home runs by Cepeda, McCovey, and Ed Bailey. Giants' reliever Don Larsen pitched the last 3⅓ innings to pick up the win. Ron Perranoski was ineffective in relief of Miller, giving up 3 walks, 2 singles, and a home run over two innings. He was charged with his second loss of the year.

An even bigger crowd, 53,436, turned out the next night to see Don Drysdale against Juan Marichal. With two runners on in the sixth inning, Willie McCovey broke up a scoreless tie with a towering shot into the left-field bullpen off Drysdale. It was the first ball ever hit there by a left-handed batter.[17] Marichal coasted to a 3–0 shutout on 7 singles and no walks. With their second straight loss, the Dodgers slid back into a second-place tie with the Giants, one game behind St. Louis.

On June 12, Johnny Podres (4–5) pitched a complete game to beat the visiting Colt .45s, 9–1. Losing Houston starter Don Nottebart (5–4) exited after the fourth inning with the Colt .45s down, 5–1. Maury Wills had 4 hits to raise his batting average to .323. With a perfect 3-for-3 night, Tommy Davis raised his average to .341.

The next night, Sandy Koufax (9–3) shut out Houston 3–0 on 3 hits with 10 strike-outs. Batting against Houston starter Bob Bruce in the fourth inning, Willie Davis singled home two runs to give Koufax a 2–0 lead to work with. In the sixth, John Roseboro lined Bruce's 0–1 pitch into right field for a single to score Tommy Davis with the Dodgers' third run. With another 2 hits in 4 at bats, Tommy Davis took over the National League batting lead at .345, 2 points higher than the Cardinals' Dick Groat.[18] At the end of play on June 13, there was a 3-way tie in the National League standings, with the Dodgers mere percentage points in front.

	W	L	Pct.	*
Los Angeles	34	25	.576	
San Francisco	35	26	.574	
St. Louis	35	26	.574	

*Games behind leader

In between Koufax starts, the Dodgers split a 4-game series with the Cubs to close out the home stand with on June 16 in third place, one game behind the first-place Giants and a half game behind the second-place Cardinals. The Dodgers' 22-year-old left-hander, Nick Willhite, made his major league debut with a 5-hit shutout of the Cubs in the second game of the June 16 double-header. When Bavasi was unable to put together a deal for a pitcher at the trade deadline, he brought Willhite up from Spokane.[19]

Koufax Prevents a Sweep at Candlestick

On Monday night, June 17, at frigid Candlestick Park in San Francisco, Sandy Koufax shut out the Giants, 2–0, on 4 singles. Koufax's sixth shutout of the year dislodged the Giants from first place, with the Cardinals moving up to fill the vacuum. At the end of the night the Giants and Dodgers were both a half game back in a tie for second.

Many of the 36,818 Giants fans wore winter clothes to withstand the 58-degree cold and omnipresent wind blowing off the Pacific Ocean. With two out in the top of the third inning of a scoreless tie, Bill Skowron came to the plate with Wills and Fairly on base to face Giants starter Billy O'Dell. Skowron sent O'Dell's first pitch deep into the right-center field gap. When Willie Mays and Felipe Alou got tangled up chasing the ball in the blustery wind, it rolled all the way to the chain-link fence to score both runners with the only two runs of the game.[20] Koufax's curve ball cutting through the wind was so "live" that it was impossible for the hitters—or John Roseboro—to handle. In the bottom half of the third, as McCovey struck out on a darting 12-to-6 curve, Roseboro injured his left palm when he misjudged the ball and had to catch it with his bare hand. He was forced to leave the game to have two stitches sewn in.

Even though he walked four batters for the first time since his abortive return of September 21, 1962, Koufax became the league's first 10-game winner at 10–3. His earned run average fell to 1.63. As it turned out, Koufax prevented the Dodgers from being swept as they were soundly beaten the next two nights at Candlestick. On June 18, Jack Sanford went all the way to beat them, 9–3. The next night Don Drysdale gave up a 2-run homer to Willie McCovey in the first inning, and never recovered. Juan Marichal, with help from Billy Pierce, beat the Dodgers, 8–3. As they got on the plane for St. Louis they were back in third place, 2½ games behind the Cardinals.

	W	L	Pct.	*
St. Louis	40	27	.597	
San Francisco	40	28	.588	½
Los Angeles	37	29	.561	2½

*Games behind leader

Koufax Sets the Stage in St. Louis

On Friday night, June 21, Sandy Koufax came within one pitch of his third straight shutout as the Dodgers began a 3-game weekend series at Busch Stadium in St. Louis with a 5–3 win. Curt Simmons started for the first-place Cardinals, who came into the series with a 4-game winning streak.

In the top of the first, a throwing error by Cardinals' shortstop Dick Groat allowed the Dodgers to score 2 unearned runs off Simmons on a 2-out, bases-loaded single by Bill Skowron. Both Simmons and Koufax threw shutout ball through the next five innings. In the seventh, Maury Wills stretched his hitting streak to 17 games by singling home Dick Tracewski to make it 3–0, Dodgers. In the eighth, Willie Davis led off with a "bunt" single. By now the Dodgers had given up on teaching Davis the art of the drag bunt. Instead, like a conventional sacrifice bunt, Willie squared around with his hands repositioned near the trademark of the bat in anticipation of Simmons's delivery. When the pitch arrived, he merely jabbed at it, rolled the ball toward second base, and outran Julian Javier's throw to first. Tommy Davis hit Simmons's next pitch into the left-field pavilion for a 2-run home run to increase the lead to 5–0.

Through the first eight scoreless innings, Koufax had given up just four singles. But on this humid night he was laboring noticeably as he began the ninth. He got leadoff batter Ken Boyer to ground out to shortstop Tracewski. The ever-troublesome Charlie James lined his next pitch into left field for the Cardinals' fifth single. Koufax then struck out an overmatched Leo Burke for the third time. He ran the count to 3–2 on Javier before walking him to put runners on first and second for the Cardinals' rookie catcher, Tim McCarver. The 22-year-old McCarver came into the game hitting .352. After again running a count to 3–2, Koufax was forced to throw the next pitch down the middle to avoid loading the bases. McCarver jumped on it, driving the ball over the right-field fence for a 3-run homer to ruin the shutout. As he watched the ball disappear into the stands, Koufax picked up the rosin bag and slammed it to the mound in disgust. When Koufax walked pinch-hitter Stan Musial on his third straight 3–2 count to advance his pitch count to 138, Alston came out of the dugout to get him. Perranoski had to come in to retire Curt Flood on a ground ball to Wills for the final out.

It was the fourth straight win for Koufax, who was now 11–3. He had been one pitch away from his third straight shutout and a 1.51 earned run average, but McCarver's home run made his ERA jump to 1.73. He struck out 9 batters and walked 3 in 8⅔ innings. With the 5–3 win the Dodgers picked up a full game on the Cardinals to move to within a game and a half of the lead.

The next afternoon at Busch Stadium, young Nick Willhite made his second major league start. His opponent was Bob Gibson. Tommy Davis hit a solo home run off Gibson in the top of the second to stake Willhite to a 1–0 lead. It would be the only run the Dodgers would score off Gibson. Willhite got away with a balk in the second inning, but his second balk in the fifth with runners on second and third allowed the tying run to score. Charlie James delivered the fatal blow to Willhite with a solo home run in the sixth to put the Cardinals in front for good, 2–1. Gibson won his sixth game with a save from Ron Taylor.

Johnny Podres got the call for the series finale on Sunday, June 23. but could get only one batter out. Podres, who was having problems

The Cardinals' 22-year-old rookie catcher, Tim McCarver, hit a 3-run homer off Sandy Koufax with two outs in the bottom of the ninth at Busch Stadium on June 21, 1963. Koufax came within one pitch of his third consecutive shutout (George Brace photograph).

with his elbow, was taken out of the game after giving up a 2-run home run to Dick Groat in the first inning, and flown back to Los Angeles for cortisone treatments. Alston brought in Bob Miller, who got Charlie James on an inning-ending double play, and then went on to pitch five more strong innings. The Dodgers were trailing, 2–1, with two on and two out in the fifth when Jim Gilliam hit an Ernie Broglio pitch onto the right-field roof for a 3-run home run.[21] It was the deciding blow. Perranoski shut out the Cardinals over the last three innings to save the 4–3 win for Miller.

By winning the series two games to one, the Dodgers cut the Cardinals' lead to a half game. Los Angeles moved back to within a game and a half of the lead, even though they were now technically in fourth place. The surging Cincinnati Reds moved into third in the congested NL upper division after winning their seventh straight game, and nine of their last ten. Cincinnati was the Dodgers' next stop.

	W	L	Pct.	*
St. Louis	41	29	.586	
San Francisco	41	30	.577	½
Cincinnati	40	30	.571	1
Los Angeles	39	30	.565	1½

*Games behind leader

A Sweep in Cincinnati

The Dodgers arrived in Cincinnati on June 24 to conclude the road trip with a 3-game series with the red-hot Reds. Don Drysdale (8–8) went up against a rapidly declining Joey Jay in the Monday night opener. A 21-game winner in both 1961 and 1962, Jay came into the game with a 3–10 record. Already behind, 1–0, after two innings, Jay disintegrated in the third. After retiring Drysdale, he walked Wills and Gilliam, gave up a 3-run home run to Willie Davis, then gave up consecutive singles to Tommy Davis, Wally Moon, and Ron Fairly. Fairly's run-scoring hit made it 5–0, Dodgers, and ended Jay's evening after only 2⅓ innings.

Drysdale shut out the Reds through the first seven innings on two hits. But he was unable to get anyone out in the eighth as the Reds got to him for four runs. Perranoski had to come in from the bullpen to put out the fire. Perranoski retired the final three batters in the ninth on just four pitches to save a 5–4 win for Drysdale.

Earlier that day, Don Zimmer, who had only 5 hits in 23 at bats primarily as a pinch hitter, was sold to the Washington Senators, where he would play third base for his old Brooklyn teammate, Gil Hodges.[22]

The night of June 25, Sandy Koufax (11–3) and the Dodgers took on Cincinnati's own premier left-hander, Jim O'Toole (13–3) who came into the game with seven straight wins. Koufax got off to a shaky start with a 22-pitch first inning, walking two batters and giving up a run-scoring triple to Vada Pinson to fall behind, 1–0. He settled down to shut out the Reds on five singles the rest of the way. With a 4–1, complete-game win—his fifth straight victory in the month of June—Koufax improved his record to 12–3, and lowered his ERA to 1.68. His nine strikeouts gave him a league-leading 129 in 134 innings.

The Dodgers closed out the Cincinnati series and the road trip on Wednesday night, June 26. Nick Willhite (1–1) got the start against the Reds' 23-year-old star right-hander from Fresno, Jim Maloney. The fireballing Maloney was 11–2 with 99 strikeouts in 102 innings. With the game tied, 2–2, in the top of the eighth, Jim Gilliam won it with a 2-run double to right-center off Maloney, then scored on a single by Tommy Davis. With a 5–2 lead, Perranoski shut out the Reds over the final two innings to win his eighth game in relief and give the Dodgers a sweep. Gilliam was 5 for 10 with 3 doubles and 3 runs batted in for the series. The Dodgers would return to Los Angeles in second place, a half-game behind the Cardinals.

	W	L	Pct.	*
St. Louis	43	30	.589	
Los Angeles	42	30	.583	½
San Francisco	42	32	.568	1½

*Games behind leader

The Problematic Braves

The Milwaukee Braves would be problematical for the Dodgers—and for Sandy Koufax—the entire season. When the Braves came into Dodger Stadium for a 4-game series on June 28, they were a .500 team in sixth place. But in their first five games with the Dodgers they had two wins and a tie. Warren Spahn (10–3) and Don Drysdale (9–8) put on a pitching clinic in the Friday night opener. In the first inning, though, it appeared that Drysdale would not last long. He gave up a single to lead-off man Lee Maye, walked Eddie Mathews, and was ripped for a line-drive single by Hank Aaron to load the bases with nobody out. The Braves' 22-year-old catcher, Joe Torre, launched Drysdale's 1–0 pitch to the deepest part of the park before Willie Davis could haul it in on the warning track in center field. Maye scored on the play to make it 1–0, Milwaukee. Drysdale settled down to get the next two batters on pop flies, and then shut out the Braves over the next eight innings. His only mistake came in the top of the fifth, when with two out he tried to buzz Hank Aaron with a high, inside fast ball. With his lightning wrists, Aaron fought the off ball by lining it against the center-field fence for a triple. After the game Aaron told reporters, "The pitch was coming right at my chin, so I hit it before it hit me."[23] Though Drysdale went on to pitch a complete-game 7-hitter, his first inning proved to be fatal. Spahn was even better, shutting out the Dodgers, 1–0, on three singles with no walks. It was the first time since 1948 that Spahn had beaten the Dodgers on the road.[24]

The next start for Sandy Koufax (12–3) was Saturday night, June 29, in front of a crowd of 50,148 at Dodger Stadium. His opponent, Braves right-hander Denny Lemaster, was 4–4 with a 1.73 earned run average. Koufax appeared to be headed for another shutout when he retired the Braves in order in the first inning on only seven pitches. But then he began to lose command. He gave up a 400-foot home run to Joe Torre leading off the second to fall behind, 1–0. After Hank Aaron hurt him with a 2-run double in the third, he was down, 3–1. The Braves finished him off in the fifth with four singles and two more runs. Alston took him out with two out, two runners on base, and the Dodgers down, 5–1. Larry Sherry had to come in to get the third out. In 4⅔ innings, Koufax had given up 5 earned runs on 8 hits—albeit with 8 strikeouts. His ERA spiked from 1.68 to 1.95. In three starts against the Braves he had one win and two no decisions.

With two out in the bottom of the seventh with the Dodgers still behind, 5–1, Alston sent Moose Skowron in to pinch hit for Sherry with a runner on second. Skowron, who averaged 26 home runs a year in his last three years with the Yankees, came to the plate with a .216 average and the one homer he hit back on April 28. He worked the count to 3–2, then hit Lemaster's next pitch over the center-field fence to cut the Braves' lead to 5–3. Jim Gilliam led off the eighth inning with a home run to bring the Dodgers to within one run of Milwaukee. Down 5–4 with two out in the bottom of the ninth and Tracewski on second base, Gilliam looped a single along the left-field foul line off Braves reliever Bob Shaw to tie the game at 5–5 and send it into extra innings.[25]

The game moved to the bottom of the eleventh, tied 5–5. With two out, Gilliam again came to the plate against Shaw with Tracewski in scoring position—this time on third base. Gilliam, whom Alston called the best bunter he ever had, dragged an unplayable bunt past Shaw to score Tracewski to win it. It was the fourth time in the last five Dodger victories that Gilliam had driven in the winning run. Perranoski won his ninth game in relief. Koufax escaped with his third no decision.

The great Henry Aaron hit .406 with 8 home runs against the 1963 Dodgers. They passed on him as a skinny 16-year-old shortstop at their Mobile, Alabama, tryout camp in 1950 (National Baseball Hall of Fame Library, Cooperstown, New York).

On Sunday afternoon, June 30, Tony Cloninger shut out the Dodgers, 7–0. The 22-year-old, $100,000 bonus baby from Iron Mountain, North Carolina, faced only 28 batters—one over the minimum. Two Dodger singles prevented a no-hitter. The game was all but decided in the first inning when Hank Aaron hit a Nick Willhite pitch over the left-center field fence for a solo home run. Aaron also singled off Willhite in the fifth to raise his season average against the Dodgers to .533. Bad Henry's 16 hits in 8 games included 4 home runs, 3 doubles, and a triple. Back in the summer of 1950 the Brooklyn Dodgers sponsored a 3-day tryout camp in Mobile, Alabama. A skinny 16-year-old shortstop named Henry Aaron was given short shrift. "They only let me on the field once in three days," recalled Aaron.[26] By the sixth inning Willhite had been knocked out of his third straight game since his shutout debut.

In the series finale on Monday night, the Dodgers got a lift from Johnny Podres, who was making his first start since undergoing eight days of Dr. Robert Kerlan's cortisone treatments on his elbow. Podres pitched a complete-game, 2–1 gem to give the Dodgers a split with the Braves. With the score tied 1–1 in the bottom of the ninth, pinch hitter Wally Moon doubled home Maury Wills with the winning run. It was the best game of the season so far for Podres. He struck out 12, gave up 5 hits, and gave Hank Aaron a rare 0-for-4 night. At the end of play on July 1 the Dodgers were within a half game of the Cardinals, who were on their way to Los Angeles to begin a big 3-game series the next night. It would be the last time in 1963 that the Cardinals held first place.

	W	L	Pct.	*
St. Louis	45	32	.584	
Los Angeles	44	32	.579	½
San Francisco	44	34	.564	1½

*Games behind leader

Sweeping the Cardinals to Take Over First Place

Don Drysdale and Curt Simmons worked the July 2 Tuesday night opener in front of 39,824.[27] The last time the Dodgers beat the Cardinals at Dodger Stadium was June 19, 1962, when Drysdale beat Simmons, 3–2. Tonight, both pitchers were on their game. Drysdale had a 2-hit shutout through the first seven innings. Simmons had a 4-hit shutout until Ron Fairly singled home Frank Howard with the only run of the game with two out in the bottom of the seventh. Drysdale cruised to a 5-hit, 1–0 masterpiece in one hour and forty-eight minutes in which he threw only ninety pitches—sixty-seven for strikes. He had a 3-ball count to just one batter, Curt Simmons, who drew Drysdale's only walk. With the win the Dodgers took over first place for the first time since June 13 by a half-game.[28]

More than four hours later, at midnight in San Francisco, the game between the Giants and Braves moved to the bottom of sixteenth inning as a scoreless tie. Remarkably, both starting pitchers were still in the game. Juan Marichal had just completed his sixteenth shutout inning. Warren Spahn began the bottom of the sixteenth by retiring Harvey Kuenn on a fly ball to center field. Willie Mays, whose first major league hit was a home run off Spahn in 1951, was next. At 12:10 a.m. on July 3, Mays hit Spahn's first pitch—a screwball that Spahn later said "didn't break worth a damn"[29]—over the left-field fence to win the game, 1–0.

A horde of 51,898 turned out on the night of July 3 to see Sandy Koufax against Bob Gibson. Gibson had won his last six decisions, and Koufax his last five. Wills led off the game with a single off Gibson, stole second, and came around to score on a sacrifice fly by Willie Davis to make it 1–0, Dodgers after one. Both Koufax and Gibson threw scoreless baseball for the next four innings. With two out in the sixth, Wills set off a rally when he bounced a ball over Gibson's head and beat out Julian Javier's throw. After Moon followed with a single, Willie Davis singled them both home to give Koufax a 3–0 lead. The Dodgers knocked Gibson out in the seventh with two more runs on three hits and a walk. Koufax mowed down the Cardinals over the last two innings by facing the minimum six batters for a 5–0 shutout—his seventh of the season. Of his 123 pitches, 85 were strikes. St. Louis could manage just three singles against him. No Cardinal runner reached second base.[30] Koufax walked no batters and struck out nine. This dominating performance against the league's top hitting team was over in one hour and fifty-three minutes. With his sixth straight win he was now 13–3 with a 1.83 ERA.

The 4th of July was a critical point in the season for the Cardinals. They had not scored a run since arriving in Los Angeles, and had been shut out in three of their last four games. After failing with their aces, Simmons and Gibson, they needed Ernie Broglio (9–3) to come through to salvage the final game and stay within a half-game of the Dodgers. Alston picked former Cardinal Bob Miller to start for the Dodgers.

But for a 2-out, 2-run single that he gave up to Jim Gilliam in the third, Broglio held the Dodgers in check for the first five innings. Having already disposed of Bob Miller and Larry Sherry, the Cardinals had a 4–2 lead as the game moved to the bottom of the sixth, when the floodgates opened. Tommy Davis led off with a bad-bounce single over third baseman Ken Boyer's head. Broglio began to fall apart when the next batter, Wally Moon, hit a routine fly ball to right field that George Altman lost in the lights and allowed to drop in for another single. The unnerved Broglio walked Fairly to load the bases for 21-year-old Ken McMullen. McMullen, recently recalled from Spokane to replace Don Zimmer, lined a 1–2 pitch into the left-field stands for a grand slam home run.[31] Suddenly on the ropes, behind 6–4, Broglio threw three straight balls to Ron Fairly before Cardinal manager Johnny Keane came out to replace him mid-batter with Ed Bauta from the bullpen. The sixth inning would prove to be fatal for St. Louis as the Dodgers went on to score 8 runs on their way to a wild 10–7 win.

The Dodgers' first series sweep of a Cardinal team since April of 1960 at the Memorial Coliseum put them on top in the National League by 2½ games. Having now lost five games in a row, the Cardinals were in free-fall.

	W	L	PCT.	*
Los Angeles	47	32	.595	
St. Louis	45	35	.563	2½
Chicago	44	35	.557	3
San Francisco	45	36	.556	3

*Games behind leader

Going into the All-Star Break on Top

The Reds came into Los Angeles on the last weekend before the All-Star break for a 4-game series that began with a Podres-O'Toole left-hander matchup on Friday night, July 5. With a record of 13–5, O'Toole was a leading candidate to start for the National League All-Stars in Cleveland in four days. The two left-handers put on a show for the

35,536 fans at Dodger Stadium. Podres, who was nearly written off two weeks before due to a bad elbow, came within two pitches of a perfect game as he shut out the Reds, 1–0, on two singles.[32] O'Toole matched Podres until the seventh inning, when leadoff batter Frank Howard drove his 0–2 pitch high into the left-field stands for a game-winning solo home run.[33] O'Toole threw 93 pitches, Podres only 90. It was over in a remarkable one hour and thirty-five minutes—the shortest game in the National League for 1963.

On Saturday, July 6, right-handers Don Drysdale (10–9) and Jim Maloney (12–3) held a duel in a blinding afternoon sun at Dodger Stadium. Hard-luck Drysdale, who retired the first ten Reds batters in order, was victimized by the sun in the fourth. With two out and Vada Pinson and Bob Skinner on base with bloop singles, Drysdale got Cincinnati first baseman Gordy Coleman to hit a harmless pop fly near second base. Running on the pitch, Pinson and Skinner scored easily when the ball landed five feet behind a blinded Jim Gilliam on the skin part of the infield.[34] A passed ball by John Roseboro allowed the Reds to score a third—unearned—run off Drysdale in the eighth. Maloney pitched a complete-game, 7-hit, 3–1 win to break the Dodgers' 5-game winning streak.[35]

The series concluded with a Sunday double-header on July 7. Sandy Koufax pitched the first game against Bob Purkey in front of a capacity crowd of 55,269. The Reds were no match for Koufax, who threw a 3-hit, 4–0 shutout. The game was essentially over in the first inning when Ken McMullen hit a 2-out, 2-run single off Purkey. Wally Moon finished Purkey in the seventh with a 2-run double to make it 4–0, Dodgers. Koufax gave up three singles, walked one batter, and struck out a modest four. Only one Cincinnati runner reached second base. Koufax threw just 99 pitches, 67 for strikes. With his seventh straight win he took over the league lead with fourteen. His second consecutive shutout lowered his earned run average to 1.73—it was now 0.81 at Dodger Stadium. His eighth shutout of the season broke the club record set by Burleigh Grimes in 1918 and tied by Whitlow Wyatt in 1941.[36]

Nick Willhite, with a save from Ron Perranoski, beat the Reds 3–1 in the second game to complete the double-header sweep. The Dodgers went into the All-Star break in first place by three games ahead of the Giants. The fading Cardinals, who had dropped eight of their last nine games, were now percentage points behind the Cubs in fourth place.

	W	**L**	**Pct.**	*
Los Angeles	50	33	.602	
San Francisco	48	37	.565	3
Chicago	45	37	.549	4½
St. Louis	46	38	.548	4½

*Games behind leader

Interlude in Cleveland

After four years of playing two All-Star games, Major League Baseball returned to the one-game format for the 34th classic in Cleveland on July 9. The Dodgers were represented by Tommy Davis, Sandy Koufax, Don Drysdale, and Maury Wills. Davis, the National League's leading batter at .327, was a late addition by manager Alvin Dark, who assigned him to the lead-off position in the batting order. But it was the great Willie Mays who led the Nationals to a 5–3 win. Mays stole 2 bases, scored 2 runs, drove in 2 more, and made a dazzling catch of Joe Peptone's long blast off Drysdale before crashing into the center-field wall in the eighth. Drysdale shut out the AL over the last two innings to save the win for Larry Jackson. The fifth inning saw 42-year-old pinch-hitter Stan Musial line out to Al Kaline in right field in his 24th and final All-Star Game appearance.[37]

The Dodger Shutout Machine Peaks in New York

The Dodgers' All-Star contingent joined the team in New York the next day to begin a 4-game series with the Mets at the Polo Grounds. The July 10 opener was a pitching gem between Podres and Carlton Willey. It was a scoreless tie after seven innings with Podres holding the Mets to three singles and Willey holding the Dodgers to four. In the top of the eighth, Roseboro lined a Willey pitch into the lower right-field stands for what turned out to be a game-winning solo home run. The game nearly got away from Podres in the bottom of the ninth. With one out and a runner on first, Mets slugger Frank Thomas drove a ball high and deep to left field. As the ball took off it looked like it would drop into the overhanging stands for a game-winning 2-run home run. But it began to lose momentum, and Tommy Davis was able to make a leaping one-handed catch against the concrete wall. The Mets' base runner, who was nearly at third base when the ball was caught, was easily doubled up at first to end the game.[38] With a 1–0 shutout and 11 strikeouts, Podres was now 3–0 since returning to the team. It was a bitter loss for Carlton Willey, who made only 69 pitches in his eight innings.

On July 11 Don Drysdale survived two home runs by Mets catcher Jessie Gonder to beat Roger Craig and the Mets, 4–3. Drysdale was done after seven innings and had to be bailed out by Perranoski for the eighth and ninth. Perranoski found himself in a jam in the ninth when Rod Kanehl and Jim Hickman singled with two out. But he struck out former Dodger Tim Harkness looking on a 3–2 curve ball to end the game and preserve Drysdale's eleventh win. It was the twelfth straight loss for poor Roger Craig.[39]

A total of 34,889 came out on a Friday night to see Sandy Koufax and little Mets left-hander Al Jackson pitch the July 12 game. The game was effectively over in the first inning when the Dodgers scored three runs off Jackson. Before the third inning was over, he was headed for the showers with the Dodgers ahead, 5–0. But the story was Koufax, who pitched his third consecutive 3-hit shutout. Remarkably, it was the sixth shutout in the last ten games for the Dodger pitching staff. Though Koufax struck out 13 batters to run his season total to a league-leading 163, he was still behind his 1962 strikeout pace. With his eighth straight win, he was 15–3 for the season with a 1.63 earned run average.[40]

Bob Miller completed a sweep of the New York series with a complete-game 11–2 win on Saturday, July 13. Miller, who gave the Mets their only win of the season series back on April 29, breezed through their inept batting order, allowing just 6 hits.[41] Going into the game, the Dodger pitching staff had allowed only 14 earned runs in its last 11 games—for a 1.27 earned run average. Only a 2-run home run by the Mets' left fielder, Frank Thomas, in the fourth inning prevented yet another shutout. The Mets' fourteenth loss in a row was the Dodgers' sixteenth win in the last nineteen games. They were now six games ahead of the second-place Giants.

	W	**L**	**Pct.**	*
Los Angeles	54	33	.621	
San Francisco	49	40	.551	6
Chicago	47	39	.547	6½
St. Louis	48	40	.545	6½

*Games behind leader

A Fortunate Split in Philadelphia

The Dodgers moved into Philadelphia on July 14 for a Sunday double-header with the Phillies. In the first game Podres survived solo home runs by Johnny Callison and Ruben Amaro to pitch his fourth straight complete game, a rain-shortened 3–2 win, to stretch his record to 8–6 and the Dodgers' win streak to seven games. The game was called after six innings, and the second game was also rained out.[42] With their twelfth win in the last thirteen games, the Dodgers took a 6½-game lead over the second-place Cubs. The Cardinals and Giants dropped into a tie for third, seven games back.

The next night Don Drysdale blew a 2–0 lead in the fifth. But it was reliever Ed Roebuck—making his first appearance in 10 days—who ultimately lost the game, 5–4, in the eleventh by giving up a walk-off single to Philadelphia's back-up catcher Bob Oldis.[43]

Sandy Koufax and Nick Willhite teamed up to pitch the series-concluding twinight double-header of July 16 in front of a turn-away crowd of 35,353 at tiny Connie Mack Stadium. Koufax took a perfect game and a 5–0 lead into the seventh inning before he began to labor on this muggy 86-degree night. Phils leadoff man Tony Taylor broke up the perfect game with a double. Taylor scored on a sacrifice fly by Tony Gonzalez that snapped Koufax's steak of 33⅓ scoreless innings. He gave up another run in the eighth on doubles by Don Hoak and Earl Averill. After retiring the first two batters in the ninth, Koufax began staggering to the finish. He gave up a line-drive double to Roy Sievers, followed by a line-drive single to Don Demeter before getting Hoak on a ground out to end the game with a 5–2 victory. The Koufax statistics were beginning to be positively mind-boggling. With his ninth straight win, he was major league baseball's first 16-game winner with a record of 16–3. He also led the majors with 14 complete games, 170 strikeouts, and a 1.65 earned run average.[44]

The Phillies trounced the Dodgers 10–2 in the second game. They drove Willhite from the game with four straight hits for three runs before he could anyone out in the first inning. Ed Roebuck took over for Willhite and retired the next three Phillies batters in order. Roebuck eventually succumbed to the heat in the third inning, giving up four runs on a walk, two singles, a double, and a home run. Before it was over, the Dodgers had burned through three more pitchers from the bullpen. Phillies right fielder Johnny Callison, who was blossoming into one of the league's top players, had a perfect 4-for-4 game with two home runs and three runs batted in.

It was clear that the Dodgers were fortunate to salvage a split, playing poorly in three of the four games in Philadelphia. They came into town with a 6-game lead, and left up 5½ games over the Cubs.

	W	L	Pct.	*
Los Angeles	56	35	.615	
Chicago	50	40	.556	5½
St. Louis	50	42	.543	6½
San Francisco	50	43	.538	7

*Games behind leader

Ending the Road Trip with a Double Loss in Milwaukee

The 14-game July road trip concluded with a 4-game weekend series in Milwaukee. In the July 19 Friday night opener, Drysdale beat the Braves, 4–2, with a complete-game 6-hitter with 11 strikeouts. Frank Howard hit solo home runs in the second and fourth innings off Braves starter Bob Hendley to stake Drysdale to a 2–0 lead. Ken McMullen increased the lead to 4–0 with a 2-run single in the top of the seventh. In the bottom of that inning, Hank Aaron led off with his 27th home run to ruin Drysdale's shutout. The win increased the Dodgers' lead to 7½ games. It was their largest lead since 1955.[45]

Koufax (16–3) pitched the following afternoon at County Stadium against Milwaukee's third left-handed starter in a 4-man rotation, Denny Lemaster (5–5).[46] Koufax, whose only career home run came off Warren Spahn the year before in the same park, hit his second and final one off Lemaster with two runners on in the fifth. But on the mound this was another disappointing performance for Koufax against the nettlesome eighth-place Braves. He took a 4–1 lead to bottom of the sixth despite having already given up two singles, two triples, and a solo home run. The Braves got to Koufax for another two runs on three singles and a walk before Perranoski could come in from the bullpen to put out the fire. Perranoski blew the save in the seventh, but was eventually credited with the win when Frank Howard won the game, 5–4, in the eighth with a solo home run—his third in less than 24 hours. It was the third no decision of the year against Milwaukee for Koufax. He gave up 3 earned runs on 8 hits and 2 walks in his 5⅓ innings. By now Milwaukee was a dying franchise. A paltry 11,804 came out to support their team against Koufax. Minutes after the last out, a solar eclipse blotted out the sun in Milwaukee.[47]

The Dodgers started Bob Miller and Nick Willhite in the get-away day doubleheader of Sunday, July 21. Both pitchers were routed by the Braves. In the first game, Miller left with one out and the bases loaded in the sixth inning with the Dodgers down, 2–1. Before Roebuck could get the final two outs, they were down, 5–1. Roebuck also served up a solo home run to Henry Aaron in the seventh. By now the handwriting was on the wall: Ed Roebuck's days with the Dodgers were numbered. The 7–2 Milwaukee win snapped the Dodgers' 4-game winning streak.

In the second game, Willhite was gone after coughing up 6 earned runs on 3 singles, 2 home runs, and a walk in the first three innings. Four successive Dodger relievers were then pounded for 11 hits and 7 more runs. Even Ron Fairly's breakout 4-for-4 performance—a single, a double, 2 home runs, and 6 RBIs—was not enough to counter the onslaught. The Braves won the game, 13–7, to sweep the double-header. Despite the final day that saw a frustrated Walter Alston ejected from both ends of a double loss, it was still a very successful 10–4 road trip for the Dodgers.[48] They left Milwaukee 6 games ahead of the Cardinals. The Giants had slid into a tie for fourth with the Reds.

	W	L	Pct.	*
Los Angeles	60	37	.619	
St. Louis	54	43	.557	6
Chicago	52	43	.547	7
Cincinnati	52	46	.531	8½
San Francisco	52	46	.531	8½

*Games behind leader

The Pirates Snap Koufax's 9-Game Win Streak

The Dodgers began a 9-game home stand on July 23 with a 3-game series with the Pirates. Johnny Podres shut them out, 6–0, that night on 7 hits. It was the sixth straight win for Podres since his July 1 return to the club, and his fifth shutout of the year.[49] Drysdale followed that up with an easy 106-pitch, 5–1, complete-game win the next night at Dodger Stadium. It was the third straight win for Drysdale, and his thirteenth of the season.[50] The Dodgers were now seven games ahead of the pack, and they had Sandy Koufax—with 9 straight wins—ready to close out the series.

But the series finale of July 25 was a strange game. Judging by his 12 strikeouts after six innings, Koufax should have been well on his way to his tenth straight win. He had command of his best pitch: "strike one." He threw a first-pitch strike to 22 of the first 27 batters he faced (81.5 percent). But he had also thrown 100 pitches—one being an 0–2 mistake that Roberto Clemente hit over the left-center field fence for a 3-run homer in the third.[51] Already down, 4–2, after allowing 4 earned runs on 8 hits and a walk, he would not be around to begin the seventh inning. Meanwhile the Dodger hitters had been given 7 bases on balls, a passed ball, and a gift throwing error on a double play ball to go with their 5 hits, but had only 2 runs to show for it. In the fifth they chased Pirates starter Joe Gibbon after he allowed the first four batters to reach base, only to be no-hit for the rest of the game by a 21-year-old rookie relief pitcher from Long Beach Poly named Tommie Sisk. The Pirates went on to win the game, 6–2, and Sisk was credited with his only win of the year.

It was ironic that Koufax's 9-game winning streak should end on a night where he appeared to be dialed in. In the clubhouse after the game, he told reporters, "I had the best stuff and felt better than at any time this season."[52] With his first loss since June 1, his record was now 16–4.

Koufax Prevents a 4-Game Sweep by the Phillies

On July 26 the Dodgers began a 4-game series with another problematic team: the Philadelphia Phillies. Nick Willhite got the start against fellow left-hander Chris Short. Six weeks after he had thrown a surprise shutout in his major league debut, the Dodgers' patience with Willhite was wearing thin. He had not pitched another complete game in his next six starts, and had only one win to show for it. On this night, Alston took him out of the game in the third inning with two runners on base and the team behind, 2–0. Bob Miller took over for the next four innings, followed by three other Dodger relievers in a futile attempt to hold off the sixth-place Phillies. The game ended with Philadelphia on top, 6–5. Two Cuban exiles drove in all 6 of the Phillies' runs: Tony Taylor, 5; and Tony Gonzalez, 1.[53] Miller was pinned with his sixth loss. Though Willhite escaped with a no decision, he was shipped back to the minors the next day for the remainder of the season.

Johnny Podres, seeking his seventh straight win, pitched Saturday night, July 27, in front of 36,262 at Dodger Stadium. Gene Mauch's red-hot Phillies knocked him out of the game before he could finish the sixth inning on their way to a 4–1 win. Podres gave up all of Philadelphia's 7 hits and all 4 runs.[54] Dennis Bennett (3–0), a 6'3" left-hander, won his third straight game for the Phillies. The Dodgers' lead was cut to four.

Drysdale tried to slow down the Phillies in the Sunday matinee game of July 28. He came into the game with a 3-game winning streak and was staked to a 3-run lead after two innings. But he began to fall apart in the sixth after Phillies' catcher Clayton Dalrymple rocked him with a 2-out, 3-run homer to put Philadelphia in the lead for the first time, 4–3. Tony Taylor knocked him out of the game in the seventh with an RBI single to make it 5–3. Perranoski was brought in to pitch to the dangerous Johnny Callison. Perranoski lost command of a 1–1 curve, and Callison hit a towering drive high off the right-field foul pole to put the game out of reach at 7–3. It was the first home run Perranoski had ever given up to a left-handed batter.[55] The Dodgers went down to a 7–4 defeat, their fourth loss in a row. The Phillies had now won 11 of their last 13 games, and were 20–8 for the month of July. The job of stopping them, and preventing a 4-game sweep, would fall on Sandy Koufax.

Koufax took on Cal McLish (10–5) and the Phillies in the series finale on Monday night, July 29. Even without his best stuff, he was able to stop the Dodgers' 4-game losing streak with a complete-game, 6–2 win—his seventeenth of the season. The line was unimpressive by Koufax standards: 138 pitches, 5 hits, 4 walks, and 7 strikeouts. But he had only one bad inning: the sixth. After Koufax retired the first two batters in order, Tony Gonzalez lined a 2–0 pitch into right field for a double. Koufax walked the next two batters to load the bases for third baseman Don Hoak. Hoak ripped the first pitch to left field to score two runs and ruin Koufax's bid for a tenth shutout. Cal McLish could not survive a pair of 2-run homers by the Davis boys, Tommy and Willie, and was gone after 5⅔ innings. The Dodgers' lead was 4½ over the surging second-place Giants—who had now won eight games in a row—and five over the Cardinals.[56]

Roebuck Is Exiled to the Washington Senators

Prior to the night game between the Dodgers and Mets of July 30 at Dodger Stadium, Dodger fans who arrived early witnessed a strange sight: Ed Roebuck, no longer in his familiar number 37 Dodger jersey, pitching batting practice for the Mets. Earlier in the day Roebuck had been traded to the Washington Senators for a utility infielder named Marv Breeding. Bavasi's purge was complete. All three of the goats from the October 3, 1962, collapse had now been severed from the team. Stan Williams was with the Yankees, Larry Burright was with the Mets, and Roebuck was on his way to baseball's version of Siberia: the last-place Washington Senators. On the bright side, he would be playing for his longtime pal and former teammate, Gil Hodges.

The 32-year-old Roebuck had been with the Dodger organization for his entire 14-year career. After making 14 appearances in the first 29 games of the 1963 season, he was effectively put on the shelf for two solid weeks and given the silent treatment. This coincided with the emergence of Ron Perranoski as *The Man* of the Dodger bullpen. Roebuck had clearly become superfluous. From there things turned ugly. On June 15, the deadline for making trades within the National League, Roebuck told Buzzie Bavasi that he wanted to be traded because "he wasn't pitching, and didn't want to be treated like cattle."[57] Bavasi sniped at the disgruntled Roebuck in the press: "If Walter [Alston] didn't pitch him, there must have been a reason. Maybe it was because he was out of shape due to his 'extracurricular' activities during spring training."[58] In fact, Roebuck had merely brought his wife with him to Vero Beach.

Alston tried to defend the trade by maintaining that "Breeding will give us a little more right-hand hitting."[59] Little, indeed. Marv Breeding had a lifetime .248 batting average with only 6 home runs in over 1,100 at bats. He would finish this season with the Dodgers and spend the remaining four years of his career in the minor leagues.

As Roebuck was clearing out his locker in the Dodger Stadium clubhouse before heading for LAX, he took his parting shot at Alston: "I'm going to be with a great man. He's a man I've always respected. I'm sort of sad to leave. But in another way, it's like getting out of prison getting away from Alston."[60] In eight seasons with the Dodgers, Ed Roebuck appeared in 332 games, including 29 in 1963. He had a record of 40–22, 43 saves, and a 3.45 earned run average. As we have seen, he was a perfect 10–0 with a 2.77 ERA in 1962 before he deteriorated from overwork in the last eight days of the season. Thus ended the topsy-turvy relationship between Walter Alston and Ed Roebuck that began with their time together at Triple-A Montreal in 1952.

Later that evening, the Mets responded to Roebuck's batting practice by thumping the Dodgers, 5–1, to snap their 22-game road losing streak. The Mets amassed 14 hits against four Dodger pitchers, including 7 off losing starter Bob Miller, who lasted just five innings. Mets starter Tracy Stallard pitched a complete-game 4-hitter. Only a 2-out, fifth-inning solo home run by Ken McMullen prevented an embarrassing shutout.

The Dodgers' lead was cut to 3½ games over the Giants—who won their ninth straight game that night in San Francisco—and four over the Cardinals.[61]

On the last night of July, a tender left elbow caused Podres to skip his turn in the rotation. Little left-hander Pete Richert, recently recalled from Spokane, took his place against Roger Craig, who came into came into the game with a 16-game losing streak. Richert and relievers Ken Rowe and Ron Perranoski cobbled together a 5–3 win. Perranoski's eleventh save gave Richert his first win since the previous September. Despite pitching a 6-hit complete game, the hard-luck Craig suffered his 17th straight loss.[62]

The win gave the Dodgers a 21–10 month of July. Ten minutes before midnight the Giants' winning streak ended as the Phillies scored 4 runs in the 14th inning to beat them, 7–4, at Candlestick. As July ended the Dodgers led the National League by 4½ games.

	W	L	Pct.	*
Los Angeles	64	42	.604	
San Francisco	60	47	.561	4½
St. Louis	59	47	.557	5

*Games behind leader

Eighteen

An August Lull Becomes a September Fight

That morning in St. Louis we were one game ahead of the Cardinals. "There go the Dodgers, choking again," they said.[1]—Sandy Koufax September 16, 1963

In order to throw 87 pitches in a game your stuff cannot be too good.[2]—Sandy Koufax on blanking St. Louis on 87 pitches, September 17, 1963

The Dodgers began the month of August on the road. On the second in Houston, the Colt .45s' 21-year-old rookie center fielder, Jimmy Wynn, pounded Don Drysdale for a single, a double, and a home run in a 4–1 pasting. The loss—the sixth in the last eight games—reduced their lead to 3½.[3]

Koufax Stops Another Dodger Tailspin

Koufax pitched the next game with the Dodgers in need of a stop. On a humid Houston night, in front of 25,473 hostile fans—the largest crowd of the year at Colts Stadium—he came through with another 3-hit shutout. The game was all but over in the top of the first after a walk to Gilliam, Tommy Davis's RBI triple, and Ron Fairly's run-scoring single—all off Houston starter Bob Bruce—gave Koufax a 2–0 lead to work with. Koufax retired the first 12 batters in order before Carl Warwick beat out an infield single to lead off the fifth. But for two other singles and an error by Ron Fairly, he would have had a perfect game.[4] After striking out the side in the second, he struck out just one other batter. It was clear by this point in the season that with pinpoint control and devastating stuff, Koufax was now able to retire batters without striking them out. With his tenth shutout of the season he lowered his ERA to 1.81 and improved his record to 18–4, already matching his career high in wins. Making his Dodger debut, Marv Breed-

221

ing played second base and went 0-for-4 at the plate. In Boston, Ed Roebuck pitched four innings of 2-hit ball for Gil Hodges and the Senators.

Ed Roebuck in a Washington Senators uniform. Roebuck was traded July 30, 1963, thus ending his topsy-turvy relationship Walter Alston (George Brace photograph).

Johnny Podres, with help from Larry Sherry, shut out the Colt .45s for the second straight night. Podres pitched eight strong innings before succumbing to the humidity in the ninth. After he gave up a line-drive single to Johnny Temple, and hit Bob Aspromonte with a pitch, Alston brought in Sherry to get the final three outs in the 4–0 win. The Dodgers left Houston 4½ games ahead of the Giants and 5 ahead of the Cardinals.

That same night at Yankee Stadium, Mickey Mantle caused two seismic events. The first occurred at 7:31 p.m. (EDT) when he came out of the dugout to pinch hit in the second game of a double-header with the Baltimore Orioles. Mantle, who had missed 61 games after breaking his left foot in Baltimore on June 5, was sent up to bat for the pitcher in the seventh inning with the Yankees trailing, 10–9. His unexpected appearance set off a prolonged, thunderous ovation from the crowd of 38,555. Mantle would later say, "The ovation really chilled me. I was shaking, and I could feel the goose bumps rising on my arms."[5] Batting right-handed against Orioles left-hander George Brunet, Mantle took the first pitch for a strike. When Mantle lined Brunet's second pitch into the lower left-field stands to tie the game, the crowd noise reached a deafening roar as he trotted around the bases favoring his left leg. His teammates engulfed him as he returned to the dugout.[6] The Yankees went on to win the game, 11–10, in extra innings.

Sandy Lets One Slip Away in Chicago

August 5 was a travel day for the Dodgers as they moved on to Chicago. After Drysdale beat the Cubs, 4–1, in an hour and 58 minutes on August 6, Sandy Koufax and Dick Ellsworth hooked up in a brilliant pitchers' duel the next afternoon in front of 27,184 at Wrigley Field. Both pitchers threw shutouts for the first nine innings. The Dodgers broke the scoreless tie when Wills singled home Marv Breeding with two out in the tenth off Ellsworth. Already with a high pitch count, Koufax was staggering as he took a 5-hit shutout to the bottom of the tenth. He walked leadoff man Andre Rodgers on 5 pitches. But he got Alex Grammas, pinch hitting for Ellsworth, to ground out to shortstop on the first pitch. After he gave up a line drive single to Leo Burke and Ellis

Burton ruined his shutout with a line drive RBI single, his pitch count had reached 141. Alston brought in Perranoski to pitch to Billy Williams with the winning run on second base. It took Perranoski three pitches to dispose of Williams and Ron Santo and send the game to the eleventh.

Leadoff batter Tommy Davis broke an 0-for-11 slump by hitting Lindy McDaniel's first pitch over the ivy-covered wall in left field to break the 1–1 tie. Five batters later, Marv Breeding drove in Willie Davis with a ground out to make the score 3–1, Dodgers. Perranoski held the Cubs scoreless in the bottom of the eleventh to win his eleventh game in relief.[7]

Koufax had 11 strikeouts to give him a league-leading 210 for the season; but the game went into the record book as a 9⅔-inning no decision. His third straight year of more than 200 strikeouts tied a record set by Christy Mathewson in 1903–1905.[8]

On August 8 Ron Santo, who hit a solo home run off Dodger reliever Larry Sherry to tie the game in the fifth, hit a second one off Sherry—a line drive walk-off—in the bottom of the tenth to salvage the last game of the series for the Cubs.

Koufax Is Routed at Crosley Field as the Dodgers Drop a Series

On Sunday, August 11, Koufax, with a 7-game road win streak, pitched the rubber game of a 3-game series in Cincinnati. After the Reds beat Podres in the Friday night opener, Drysdale had evened the series with a clutch complete-game, 13-strikeout performance on Saturday. The Reds' Don Pavletich was a stocky little catcher-first baseman utilityman who came into the game with a .195 batting average. But he would give Koufax problems his entire career. Koufax's curve ball was not working on this day,[9] and Pavletich hit a 2-out solo home run off a flat Koufax curve in the second inning to tie the game, 1–1. Frank Howard saved Koufax in the third by making a leaping inning-ending catch of Gene Freese's line drive in the right field gap with the bases loaded.

Don Pavletich, the Reds' catcher–first baseman utilityman, would surprisingly give Sandy Koufax problems his entire career (National Baseball Hall of Fame Library, Cooperstown, New York).

Koufax made it to the sixth with a 4–1 lead when the roof fell in. Frank Robinson, having an off year batting .259, led off the inning with a home run. Gene Freese lined a double into center field, and Mr. Pavletich promptly singled him home. After Cincinnati's shortstop, Leo Cardenas, followed with a line single to right field—the ninth hit off Koufax—Alston came out with the hook. Perranoski was brought in, but even he couldn't stop the onslaught. Perranoski blew his fifth save as the Reds got to him for 3 hits and 4 more runs in his two thirds of an inning to take a 7–4 lead. Four of the six runs were charged to Koufax. In the last two innings the Reds continued to pound Larry Sherry for another 4 hits and 2 runs.

Koufax lost his fifth game of the year, giving up 5 earned runs in 5⅓ innings. His record now stood at 18–5, and his ERA jumped from 1.77 to 1.94. The 9–4 defeat caused the Dodgers to lose the series, two games to one. Coupled with the Giants' win in Philadelphia, their lead was cut to 3½ games over San Francisco.[10]

The Braves Cause More Trouble for Koufax and the Dodgers in Milwaukee

On August 13 at County Stadium in Milwaukee, Warren Spahn beat the Dodgers, 4–3, in the opening game of a 3-game series. The next night, Drysdale took a 3-hit, 1–0 shutout into the bottom of the seventh, only to have Henry Aaron destroy it with a grand slam homer. The Dodgers went on to lose the game, 5–3, to a rookie right-hander named Bob Sadowski. Their fifth loss in the last six games reduced their lead to three over the Giants. It would be up to Sandy Koufax, who hadn't picked up a baseball in three days due to a sore elbow, to prevent a sweep and a further deterioration of the lead.

The series finale was held on Thursday afternoon, August 15. The Dodgers gave Koufax a 3–0 lead in the top of the first on an RBI single by Tommy Davis and a 2-run home run by Frank Howard off Braves starter Bob Hendley—Howard's fourth home run in four appearances against Hendley.[11] But Koufax couldn't hold it; in fact, he lasted only a third of an inning. He retired the leadoff batter, Lee Maye, then gave up successive singles to Frank Bolling, Hank Aaron, and Eddie Mathews. When Gene Oliver—who would bat .429 against him in 1963 after being traded from St. Louis and .392 against him over his career—followed with a 3-run home run, the Dodgers were behind, 4–3, and Koufax was out of the game.

Tommy Davis finished off Hendley in the third inning with a 2-run homer to put the Dodgers back in front, 5–4. The Dodgers broke a 5–5 tie with 2 runs in the seventh. The game came down to a head-to-head battle between Ron Perranoski and Hank Aaron with two outs in the bottom of the ninth with the Dodgers clinging to a 7–5 lead. With a runner on first, Aaron came to the plate representing the potential tying run. Perranoski had never gotten Aaron out in 11 tries, walking him 3 times and giving up 5 singles, 2 doubles, and a home run.[12] Perranoski finally got Aaron on a fly out to deep right field to end the game. He pitched 1–hit ball over the last 3⅔ innings to win his twelfth game in relief.

It was Koufax's fourth no decision of the year against the Braves. By giving up 4 earned runs in his ⅓ inning of work, his ERA moved above 2.00 for the first time since April. The Dodgers thus salvaged the last game of the series to preserve their 3-game over the Giants. They pulled to an even 6–6 on a difficult road trip.

Antidote for a Tough Road Trip—
A 4-Game Series with the Mets

New York was the last leg of the trip. Johnny Podres and Roger Craig squared off in the first game on Friday night, August 16, at the Polo Grounds. After a 6–1 month of July, Podres had his third straight sub-par outing in August. Despite hitting a 2-run home run off Craig in the top of the second, he blew a 3–1 lead in the bottom of the inning, exiting before he could complete it, down 4–3. In the third, the Dodgers hit two more home runs off Craig—by Moon and Howard. Howard's monstrous home run completely cleared the left field roof. Leo Durocher would later say it was the longest he ever saw at the Polo Grounds.[13] They went on to score 3 runs in the ninth for a 9–7 come-from-behind victory. Perranoski, the fourth of five Dodger pitchers, won his 13th game in relief. Mets' reliever Larry Bearnarth was the losing pitcher, thus sparing the beleaguered Roger Craig from a 21st loss.

Sandy Koufax pitched the Saturday afternoon game against Tracy Stallard. Stallard achieved instant immortality two years before by serving up Roger Maris's 61st home run six blocks away in Yankee Stadium. Today, the Dodgers hit three solo home runs off him: Howard in the second; Roseboro in the third; and Moon in the fifth to give Koufax a 3–0 lead after five. At the same time, Koufax was turning in another dominating performance. After eight innings, he had a 4-hit, 3–0 shutout with 9 strikeouts. Two of the hits were infield singles.[14] He was on the verge of setting a new National League single season shutout record for left-handers when things got complicated in the ninth.[15]

Leadoff batter Ron Hunt, a .264 hitter, lined his first pitch off the upper deck façade in left-field for a home run to ruin the shutout. When Frank Thomas followed with a sharp line single to center field, Koufax had thrown 118 pitches and Alston was on his way to the mound. Bob Miller was brought in to pitch to Mets third baseman Jim Hickman. Miller got Hickman to hit a double play ground ball to Gilliam at third. But they could only get one out when Tracewski was declared off the second base bag when he caught Gilliam's throw. Perranoski came in to pitch to pinch hitter Tim Harkness. After Perranoski struck out Harkness, he got first baseman Duke Carmel to hit what looked to be an inning-ending ground ball to Tracewski at second. But Ron Fairly dropped Tracewski's throw for an error, allowing Carmel to reach base and pinch runner Al Jackson to go to third. It was bedlam at the Polo Grounds when Duke Snider—with 14 home runs in only 290 at bats—came to the plate as the potential winning run. Perranoski's first offering was a wild pitch that scored Jackson and moved Carmel up to second as the tying run. Snider, who delivered a 2-run single as a pinch hitter the night before, went down swinging to end the game. It was Perranoski's twelfth save of the year.

Despite losing the shutout, Koufax now had a career-best nineteen wins. The next day the Dodgers wrapped up the series and the road trip with Sunday double-header that drew a crowd of 46,184. Drysdale threw a dazzling 3-hit, 7–0 shutout in the first game. He threw only 97 pitches, gave up 3 singles, struck out 8, and walked none to improve his record to 16–13. At the plate he drew two walks and helped knock Mets starter Al Jackson out of the game in the seventh inning with a line-drive RBI single.

The Dodger youngsters took over in the second game. Pete Richert got the start against the Mets' Carlton Willey. In four innings of work Richert gave up 2 runs on 4 hits and walked 2 batters. He was pulled for a pinch hitter in the fifth inning with the Dodgers behind, 2–1. Before the inning was over Tommy Davis had put the Dodgers in front, 3–2, with a 2-run single off Willey. Nineteen-year-old Dick Calmus took over the pitching duties from Richert. The string bean 6'4" 187-pound right-hander shut out the Mets on one hit over the last five innings to pick up his second major league win. The 3–2 victory gave the Dodgers a 4-game sweep.

After losing six of the first eleven games on the road, the Dodgers won the last five to finish the road trip at 10–6 thanks in large part to the awakened bats of Frank Howard and Tommy Davis. In the last nine games Howard hit 5 home runs and Tommy Davis drove in 14 runs.[16] As they prepared to fly back to Los Angeles to begin an 18-game home stand including a big series with the Cardinals, the Dodgers were 6 full games ahead of the Giants and the Cardinals, who ended the day locked in a tie for second.

	W	L	Pct.	*
Los Angeles	74	48	.607	
San Francisco	68	54	.557	6
St. Louis	68	54	.557	6

*Games behind leader

The Last Trip to Los Angeles for The Man and His Cardinals

Monday, August 19, was an off day for the Dodgers. In St. Louis the Cardinals scored three runs in the bottom of the ninth to beat the Giants, 9–7, and pick up a half game on the Dodgers.

On August 20, Johnny Podres and the 36-year-old ex–Brave and longtime Dodger nemesis, Lew Burdette, met in the opening game of a 3-game series in Dodger Stadium. Both pitchers were routed. The Dodgers knocked Burdette out of the game with one out in the bottom the fourth. By the time Ray Sadecki could complete the inning, the Dodgers were ahead, 7–4, and Burdette had been charged with 7 runs on 9 hits. In the top of the fifth, the Cardinals scored their fifth run off Podres and chased him before he could get anyone out. But Bob Miller came in from the bullpen to hold St. Louis scoreless for the last 5 innings for a 7–5 win. He retired pinch hitter Stan Musial—on his farewell tour of the western ballparks—on a ground out to first to end the game.

Sandy Koufax, seeking his twentieth win, went up against Curt Simmons the next night. The 54,125 at Dodger Stadium were treated to a twin pitching masterpiece. The Dodgers went up 1–0 in the third on a double by Gilliam and a bloop single by Howard off Simmons. In the sixth, Koufax gave up singles to Ken Boyer and George Altman to put runners on first and third. The Cardinals tied the game at 1–1 when the speedy Julian Javier beat out a potential inning-ending double play ground ball to score Boyer from third. From there Koufax shut them out for the next 6⅓ innings. He left for a pinch hitter in the twelfth inning after throwing 165 pitches.[17] The 34-year-old Simmons left for a pinch hitter in the fourteenth inning after throwing 177 pitches.

The game moved to the sixteenth still tied, 1–1. With two out and the winning run on first base, Cardinal manager Johnny Keane sent Musial to the plate as a pinch hitter. Larry Sherry, the Dodgers' third pitcher, got Musial on a pop fly to end the inning. In the bottom of the inning the Cardinals' third pitcher, Ron Taylor, quickly retired the first two Dodger batters. Ken McMullen then lined a ball over Curt Flood's head that landed on the warning track and bounced over the center field fence for a ground-rule double. Ten minutes before midnight, John Roseboro, 0-for-6 for the night, lined a ball past a diving Ken Boyer and down the left field line to score McMullen to end it.[18] The Dodgers had a 2–1 win to go 7½ games ahead of the Cardinals, and 8½ ahead of the Giants—who two hours before had lost their fifth game in a row in San Francisco at the hands of the Braves. Sherry was credited with his second win. Koufax was stuck with a tough 12-inning no decision in which he struck out 10, walked 2, and gave up 9 hits and 1 earned run.

The Dodgers had a chance to bury the Cardinals by sweeping them the next night with Don Drysdale on the mound. Drysdale had a rocky 25-pitch first inning in which he walked a batter, hit another with a pitch, and gave up two hits and two runs. The Dodgers tied the game, 2–2, in the third on three singles and two walks off Broglio. In top of the sixth, the Dodgers fell behind for good, 3–2, as the Cardinals got to Drysdale with a leadoff double by Boyer and a run-scoring single by Javier. The seventh inning saw Drysdale retire Stan Musial on an inning-ending double play. It was The Man's last at bat in Los Angeles. Broglio and two Cardinal relievers shut out the Dodgers over the last three innings on their way to a 3–2 win. By salvaging the final game of the series, the Cardinals managed to stay within 6½ games of the Dodgers. The Giants snapped their losing streak to move back to within 7½.

	W	L	Pct.	*
Los Angeles	76	49	.608	
St. Louis	70	56	.556	6½
San Francisco	69	57	.548	7½

*Games behind leader

Avoiding a Braves Sweep Thanks to Koufax

The day after the Dodgers took two out of three from the Cardinals, the Braves came into town looking to cause them more trouble. On Friday, August 23, 19-year-old Dick Calmus made his first major league start against Warren Spahn, the Braves' 42-year-old veteran, who was making his 601st. The nervous Calmus never made it out of the first inning. After the first two batters greeted him with sharp singles, he had to face the great Henry Aaron, who was having a typical Aaron year: 32 home runs, 104 runs batted in, and a .315 batting average in the first 126 games. Calmus paid the price for falling behind in the count, 2–0, on Aaron. His third pitch—that everyone in the park knew was going to be a fast ball—was hit like a rocket down the third base line.

But Tommy Davis was able to snare the ball behind the bag and throw it to Gilliam at second base for a double play. It made for a strange result: three line drives, two outs. It was a short-lived reprieve as Eddie Mathews hit a 2–1 pitch into the right field pavilion for a 2-run home run. When Joe Torre followed with a vicious line drive off Calmus's left shin, the shell-shocked rookie had made his last pitch.[19] Alston mercifully brought in Ken Rowe to finish the inning.

Rowe held the Braves to five hits and one run over the next six innings. But after the Dodgers had to take him out for a pinch hitter, behind 3–1 in the seventh, Milwaukee shelled Larry Sherry for three runs in the ninth, capped by a 2-run home run by the inescapable Mr. Aaron. Wily Spahn scattered nine singles for a 6–1 win. It was his sixteenth victory on the way to an amazing 23–7 season, his nineteenth in the major leagues.

On Saturday, August 24, Denny Lemaster beat Podres and the Dodgers, 2–1. The Braves scored both of their runs off Podres in the third inning; and, of course, Henry Aaron was implicated in both. He drove in the first run with a double, and scored the other on a sacrifice fly by Joe Torre. Alston took Podres out in the fourth inning after he had loaded the bases for Aaron. Bob Miller came in to get Aaron to line into an inning-ending double play. Miller went on to shut out the Braves over the last five innings on two singles. But Lemaster and Bob Shaw held the Dodger offense to only six hits and one run. Podres, who was now 0–2 with 3 no decisions in his last 5 starts, exploded in frustration in the clubhouse after the game when a reporter asked him about the condition of his shoulder: "I'll tell you why I've been losing. I've been losing because I'm a s_____ pitcher!"[20] The Dodgers were now 7–10, with 1 tie, in 18 games with the infuriating sixth-place Braves.

The Dodgers looked to Koufax to avert a sweep on Sunday afternoon. His opponent was Bob Sadowski, the same rookie right-hander who beat them in Milwaukee on the 14th. Both pitchers threw blanks through the first six innings. Koufax would later reveal that he began to tire in the seventh—the result of throwing 165 pitches in 12 innings four days before.[21] But he still managed to retire the side in order. In the bottom of the inning the Dodgers jumped in front, 1–0, on doubles by Frank Howard and Willie Davis off Sadowski.

Koufax made it to the ninth inning with a 3-hit, 1–0 shutout. Henry Aaron led off by sending Koufax's second pitch to the deepest part of the park before Willie Davis hauled it in with his back against the 410' sign in center field. Bob Miller began warming up hurriedly in the Dodger bullpen. Dodger right fielder Lee Walls barely missed making a diving catch of Ed Mathews's line double. Joe Torre followed with a long fly ball to Walls in deep right field to move Mathews to third. With the tying run 90 feet away, Alston made the mistake of leaving Koufax in to face the troublesome Gene Oliver. Oliver promptly doubled in the tying run to give him 6 hits and 7 runs batted in for the year in 14 at bats against Koufax. Miller was on his way in from the bullpen. Koufax, who had lost his shutout and the chance for his twentieth win, was furious with Alston for taking him out. It was his fifth no decision of the year against Milwaukee. Alston heard an angry chorus of boos as he made his way back to the dugout.

The Dodgers pulled the game out in the bottom of the ninth with a bases-loaded single by their .177-hitting reserve catcher, Doug Camilli, off Braves reliever Bob Shaw.

With a 2–1 win, the Dodgers gained a full game on both the Cardinals and the Giants. Even better, they were finally done with Aaron and the Braves for the year.

	W	L	Pct.	*
Los Angeles	77	51	.602	
St. Louis	71	58	.550	6½
San Francisco	71	58	.550	6½

*Games behind leader

Like Podres, Koufax had hit a lull. In his last six starts—from August 7 to August 25—he had one win, one loss, and four no decisions.

On August 26 the Cincinnati Reds came into Los Angeles to take another 3-game series from the Dodgers, two games to one. The series was decided when the Reds handed Podres his third consecutive loss in the August 28 rubber game. At Candlestick Park in San Francisco the Giants moved to within 5½ games of the Dodgers by beating Bob Gibson to take two out of three from the Cardinals. It was the fourth loss in five games for the Cardinals, who appeared to be fading fast as they dropped back into third place. The 3-team pennant race was beginning to look like a 2-team West Coast pennant race as the Giants and Dodgers prepared to close out the month of August with a big 4-game series in Los Angeles.

* * *

Earlier that day in Washington, D.C., Martin Luther King stood in front of the Lincoln Memorial to deliver an address to conclude the "March for Justice and Jobs." There was a 7-minute limit placed on all the speeches. About halfway through his address, Mahalia Jackson called out from behind the podium, "Tell 'em about the dream, Martin!"[22]

* * *

Finishing off the Giants in L.A.

Sandy Koufax (19–5) and Bobby Bolin (8–4) opened the series on a Thursday night, August 29, before a new Dodger Stadium record crowd of 54,978. It took Koufax 108 pitches to beat the Giants, 11–1, in another dominating complete-game performance to become Major League Baseball's first 20-game winner.[23] Because the Giants were popping up his rising fast ball all night, the Dodger infielders made just four assists.[24] Only Orlando Cepeda's leadoff home run in the second inning prevented a shutout. Just three other Giants reached base: Jim Davenport's ground ball found its way through the infield in the first; Jose Pagan beat out a swinging bunt in front of the mound in the fifth; and Cap Peterson walked on a 3–2 pitch in the eighth. Though Koufax struck out only seven, he had good command, falling behind in the count on only five of the thirty-one batters he faced. He became the first Dodger left-hander to win twenty games since Preacher Roe in 1951, and was now the major league leader in strikeouts (246), complete games (17), shutouts (10), and earned run average (1.93). In the clubhouse after the game, Koufax told reporters that winning his twentieth was a bigger thrill than pitching a no-hitter, "because it was so long in coming. It took me nine years to win twenty—and three tries before I finally made it."[25] For once, he didn't have to worry about run support, as the Dodgers pounded Bolin and three other Giants pitchers for 11 runs on 15 hits, and drew 8 walks.

Drysdale (16–15) and Marichal (19–7) met the next night in front of 54,843. In a shaky 29-pitch first inning, Drysdale fell behind, 1–0, on an RBI single by Mays. He settled down to hold the Giants scoreless the rest of the way. The Giants had to remove Marichal for a pinch hitter in the seventh. Drysdale threw a complete game with nine strikeouts, and drove in the Dodgers' second run with a single in the fifth inning. Jim Gilliam—an emerging MVP candidate—doubled and tripled in the other two runs.

On Saturday afternoon, August 31, another huge crowd of 54,858 packed Dodger Stadium for the third game, between Jack Sanford and Bob Miller. By the end of the third inning the Dodgers had taken a 3–0 lead with a home run and three singles off Sanford. Miller held the Giants to one unearned run on four singles through the first six innings. But Perranoski had to relieve him in the seventh after he gave up a home run to Pagan that cut the Dodgers' lead to 3–2. Perranoski blew the lead in the ninth inning when Orlando Cepeda tied the game with a home run to send the game into extra innings. The Giants pulled it out, 4–3, in the twelfth on a 2-out RBI single by Felipe Alou off Larry Sherry.[26]

Left-handers Billy O'Dell and Pete Richert closed out the series on Sunday, September 1, in front of a fourth straight sellout crowd of 54,263. It would be the final meeting of the year in Los Angeles between the two teams. O'Dell took a 3–2 lead to the bottom of the eighth. He had retired ten batters in a row until Gilliam led off the inning with a single. Alvin Dark brought in Dan Larsen, who gave up a single to Tommy Davis and a 2-run double to pinch hitter Wally Moon. Billy Hoeft was brought in to pitch to pinch hitter Ron Fairly. Fairly lined Hoeft's first pitch into left field to score Davis with the Dodgers' third run of the inning. The 3-run eighth-inning rally—all resulting from pinch hits—proved fatal as the Dodgers went on to win the game, 5–3, and the series, three games to one. Johnny Podres, who came in to get the last three outs in the ninth, was credited with a rare save—his first since 1958. At the end of the first day of September, the Dodgers led the second-place Cardinals by 6 games. This series—played before 218,942 people—broke the back of the Giants. They came into Los Angeles behind by 5½ games in second place, and left town in third place, behind by 7½.

	W	**L**	**Pct.**	*****
Los Angeles	81	54	.600	
St. Louis	75	60	.556	6
San Francisco	74	62	.544	7½

*Games behind leader

On Monday, September 2, the Dodgers continued their 18-game home stand with a Labor Day double-header with Houston. Koufax pitched a complete-game 7-hitter in the first game to beat Turk Farrell and the Colt .45s, 7–3, for his 21st win. He struck out 13 and walked none. While he threw first-pitch strikes to 25 of the 36 batters he faced (69.4 percent), the Colts jumped on two of those pitches to drive in runs: Ernie Fazio's RBI double in the fifth, and Bob Aspromonte's solo home run leading off the seventh.[27] Farrell, who had already beaten the Dodgers three times that season, was chased in the fourth inning.

In the second game, Podres collaborated with Perranoski on a 5-hitter to beat Houston, 7–1. Podres's first win since August 4 broke a six-start drought. Perranoski shut out the Colts on one hit over the last two innings for his fourteenth save.

The next night at Dodger Stadium, the Dodgers scored two runs in the bottom of the tenth to beat Houston, 4–3, and sweep the series. The Colts' 19-year-old rookie first baseman, Rusty Staub, put them in front, 3–2, in the top of the inning with a double off Perranoski. The baseball gods were kind to Perranoski. He retired only one of the two batters he faced, yet was credited with his fourteenth win of the year. They were not kind to the Dodgers' starter, Don Drysdale, who pitched eight innings of 6-hit baseball with a no decision to show for it.

The home stand concluded with a 2-game series with the Cubs. Bob Miller took on the Cubs' Cal Koonce in the first game. Both starting pitchers had shutouts through the first five innings. Ron Santo broke the scoreless tie in the top of the sixth with a sacrifice fly. Tommy Davis tied the game, 1–1, in the bottom of the inning with an RBI double off Koonce. Both pitchers were removed for pinch hitters: Miller in the seventh, and Koonce in the tenth. Perranoski took over for Miller in the eighth and shut out the Cubs over the next three innings on one hit. The game remained a 1–1 tie as it moved to the eleventh inning. The Cubs won it in the top of the inning on a 2-out single by Ken Hubbs off Ken Rowe.

On September 5, Pete Richert and Larry Sherry shut out the Cubs, 4–0. It was the third win of the year for Richert, who gave up 5 hits and struck out 7 in 7⅓ innings. Sherry picked up his third save by throwing 1⅔ innings of hitless ball.

By winning five of the last six games, the first-place Dodgers ended their 18-game home stand with a record of 11–7. As they prepared to meet the Giants over the weekend in San Francisco, they led the Cardinals—who had come back from the dead to win their last 8 games in a row—by 5 games, and the Giants—who had dropped 6 of their last 9—by 9½.

	W	**L**	**Pct.**	*
Los Angeles	85	55	.607	
St. Louis	80	60	.571	5
San Francisco	76	65	.539	9½

*Games behind leader

But for Koufax, It's a Giants Sweep at Candlestick

On Friday night, September 6, Koufax was on the mound as the Dodgers and Giants began a 3-game weekend series at Candlestick Park in San Francisco. The

Dodgers jumped on Giants starter Billy O'Dell for 4 runs on 7 hits in the first seven innings, including home runs by Jim Gilliam and Frank Howard. Though Koufax took a 4–1 lead to the eighth inning, he had what he would describe after the game as "lousy stuff."[28] He had already thrown 108 pitches, with 2 doubles, 5 singles, and a walk charged against him. In the eighth he got the first two batters out: Willie McCovey on a fly out, and Orlando Cepeda on a pop foul. But then in succession he gave up a home run to Mays and a double to Felipe Alou, and walked Jim Davenport on four pitches. With the tying runs on base and Perranoski warming up in the bullpen, he managed to escape by getting Jose Pagan on an infield pop-up. That was his last batter. Alston brought in Perranoski to close down the Giants in the ninth. Koufax ended up making 136 pitches—90 for strikes—in his eight innings, striking out eight batters and walking two. His fourth win in a row brought his record to 22–5. Gilliam, who had 3 hits and scored 4 of the Dodgers' 5 runs, had now hit safely in nine straight games.

The Dodgers went on to drop the last two games in San Francisco. Marichal beat Drysdale, 5–3, on Saturday for his 21st win of the season. Drysdale had another tough day at Candlestick. In six innings of work, he gave up 4 runs on 7 hits, including home runs by Cepeda, Mays, and, of course, McCovey. On Sunday, September 8, Perranoski, pitching in relief of Bob Miller, blew a 3–2 lead in the bottom of the eighth when Cepeda hit his 0–2 pitch for a crushing 3-run homer. The Dodgers lost the game, 5–4, with Perranoski charged with his third and final loss of the season. As the Dodgers said goodbye to Candlestick for the year, they saw their lead shrink to 3½ games over St. Louis, who split a double-header in Pittsburgh.[29] The Giants, who pulled to an even 9–9 in the season series with the Dodgers, remained buried in fourth.

	W	L	Pct.	*
Los Angeles	86	57	.601	
St. Louis	83	61	.576	3½
Milwaukee	78	65	.545	8
San Francisco	78	66	.542	8½

*Games behind leader

Run-Up to the Showdown in St. Louis

The Dodgers bounced back from their unpleasant weekend in San Francisco by sweeping a 3-game series in Pittsburgh. In the September 10 opener, Koufax pitched a complete game 6-hitter at Forbes Field to beat the Pirates, 4–2. His fifth straight win gave him twenty-three for the season. He stuck out nine batters and walked none. In the third inning, when he struck out opposing pitcher Don Cardwell, he raised his season total to 270, thereby breaking his own National League record of 269 set in 1961.

Koufax's chances for an eleventh shutout were killed in the seventh inning due to a defensive lapse by Tommy Davis. With two out, Pirates left fielder Ted Savage hit a ground ball that found its way through the infield and into left field. Davis, who had been moved out to left for "defensive purposes" after making yet another throwing error from third base, let the ball roll through his legs, allowing Savage to advance all the way to third. When the .228-hitting Bob Bailey followed with another ground single into left field, the shutout was gone. Koufax kicked the dirt and slammed the rosin bag to the ground in frustration.[30] Half of the 6 hits he gave up came off the bat of Roberto Clemente: 2 singles and a 420-foot solo home run hit with two out in the eighth. Clemente would finish with a .545 batting average for the season against Koufax.

Roberto Clemente hit .545 against Sandy Koufax in 1963 (George Brace photograph).

The next night, Don Drysdale, who flew in from Los Angeles after being treated for shingles, got the start. He lasted just three innings. But Pete Richert and Ron Perranoski took over and pitched the Dodgers to a 9–4 win. On September 12, Podres beat Bob Friend and the Pirates, 5–3, to complete the sweep. Despite the sweep, their lead was now only three games over the torrid Cardinals, who beat the Cubs in St. Louis that day for their sixth straight win.

On September 13 the Dodgers arrived in Philadelphia for a 4-game weekend series with the Phillies. This team, a year away from their breakout season under Gene Mauch, would be the most troublesome opponent for the 1963 Dodgers. The series began with a twi-night double-header on Friday night, September 13. Koufax pitched the first game against the Phillies' star left-hander, Chris Short. Both were working on two days' rest. Koufax held Philadelphia scoreless through the first six innings. The Phillies cobbled together a run off him in the seventh with a single, a wild pitch, and a squeeze bunt to take a 1–0 lead. Alston was forced to remove Koufax for a pinch hitter in the top of the eighth with the team down to its last six outs. Short continued on to the ninth with the 1–0 lead, having struck out 14 Dodgers in the first eight innings. After Tommy Davis led off the inning with a line single, a hitless Frank Howard came to the plate. Short, who had already struck out Howard three times, hung a 1–1 curve ball that Howard hit into the upper deck in left field to put the Dodgers ahead, 2–1.[31]

In the bottom of the ninth, Larry Sherry, pitching in relief of Koufax, gave up a single to leadoff man Tony Gonzalez and hit Roy Sievers with a pitch. When Gene Mauch brought in the sensational 21-year-old rookie, Dick "Ritchie" Allen, to pinch run for Sievers, Alston countered by bringing in Perranoski to pitch to Ruben Amaro. Amaro promptly advanced both runners with a sacrifice bunt. After Perranoski intentionally walked Don Hoak to load the bases, he got the Phillies' slothful catcher, Bob Oldis, to hit a perfect double play ball to Gilliam at second. Gilliam threw to Wills for the force out at second. But the hard-nosed Hoak barreled into Wills, causing his relay to sail over Ron Fairly's reach at first base to allow Gonzalez and Allen to score the winning runs. The tough 3–2 loss went into the record books as a loss for Sherry and another no decision for Koufax. In seven innings he made 102 pitches, gave up the 1 tainted run and 4 hits, walked 1, and struck out 8.

The Dodgers won the nightcap, 2–1, with Ron Perranoski picking up his fifteenth win in relief of Bob Miller. Perranoski shut out the Phillies over the last three innings on three singles to lower his ERA to 1.84. The same night in Minnesota, Jim Bouton shut out the Twins, 2–0, to clinch the American League pennant for the Yankees. It was the twentieth win of the year for Bouton, and the twenty-eighth pennant for the Yankees.

After Pete Richert pitched a complete-game 5-hitter to beat the Phillies, 5–1 on Saturday, September 14, Alston gave the ball to Drysdale with a chance to win the series on Sunday. But errors by Wills and McMullen, and three passed balls by Roseboro, caused him to exit the game after the seventh inning, down by four runs. Future Phillies manager Dallas Green pitched a complete-game 5-hitter to beat the Dodgers, 6–1. Only a fourth inning solo home run by Tommy Davis kept the Dodgers from being shut out. While the Dodgers were losing two out of four in Philadelphia, the Cardinals continued to roll, sweeping a 4-game series from the Braves in St. Louis. They had now won an incredible 19 out of their last 20 games—one of the best late-season surges in league history. While the Dodgers played .700 ball (14–6) during the same period, their lead—a comfortable seven at the start of the Cardinals' 19–1 run on August 30—was now only one at the end of play on September 15, 1963. And they had a date with the Cardinals the next night in St. Louis. Talk of another L.A. "choke" began to swirl in the media.

	W	L	PCT.	*
Los Angeles	91	59	.607	
St. Louis	91	61	.599	1
San Francisco	81	69	.540	10

*Games behind leader

❊ ❊ ❊

That morning in Birmingham, Alabama, a bomb exploded in the basement of the Sixteenth Street Baptist Church, killing four young black girls dressed in white dresses and white shoes who had left their Bible classes early.[32] The next day on the front page of the *New York Times*, the country was forced to stare at a picture of rescue workers searching through the rubble for survivors. In addition to the four dead, twenty surviving church members had to be rushed to a local hospital. Two black boys were killed in the violence that ensued. A 16-year-old was shot in the back by a Birmingham policeman. A 13-year-old was shot while riding his bicycle just outside Birmingham. "There apparently was no reason at all," was the Jefferson County Sheriff's Office explanation.[33]

❊ ❊ ❊

Showdown in St. Louis

The specter of the disastrous final weekend of the 1962 season hung over the Dodgers as they arrived in St. Louis on Monday, September 16, along with over 60 sportswriters from all over the country. As they surrounded Walter Alston in the clubhouse that afternoon, one confronted him with the inevitable question, "Do you think you're going to blow the pennant again?"[34] The largest crowd of the season, 32,442, packed Busch Stadium that night for the opener. The Cardinals had won their last 16 games in a row in that park. Johnny Podres (13–10), the player Walter Alston called the "key to his pitching,"[35]got the start for the Dodgers. St. Louis manager Johnny Keane chose right-hander Ernie Broglio (16–8).

Podres retired the first sixteen batters in a row, and had a no-hitter for the first five innings. In the top of the sixth, Tommy Davis singled home Wills from third base to break a scoreless tie. It was the first time the Cardinals had trailed in a game since September 7 in Pittsburgh. With one out in the bottom of the seventh, Stan Musial drove a Podres fast ball onto the top of the right-field pavilion roof to tie the game at 1–1. It was the 475th and last home run of Musial's career.[36]

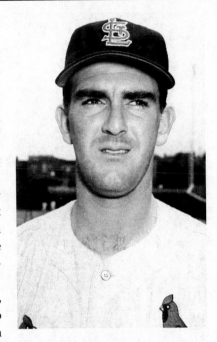

Right-hander Ernie Broglio, 18–8 for the 1963 Cardinals, started the first game of the crucial 3-game series in St. Louis September 16, 1963 (George Brace photograph).

Though Broglio pitched eight solid innings of 6-hit ball, Keane had to remove him for a pinch hitter to try to make something happen in the bottom of the eighth. But the game remained a 1–1 tie through eight. In the ninth, Keane brought in little left-hander Bobby Shantz when it started to unravel for the Cardinals. Fairly hit his first pitch for a double. Shantz struck out Roseboro, but Willie Davis lined his next pitch into right field for a single to drive in Fairly, who beat Charlie James's throw to the plate by

Stan Musial hit the 475th and last home run of his career off Johnny Podres at Busch Stadium on September 16, 1963 (George Brace photograph).

a whisker to break the tie. When Shantz walked McMullen, Ron Taylor was brought in from the bullpen to pitch to Moose Skowron, pinch hitting for Podres. Skowron hit Taylor's first pitch sharply up the middle. Second baseman Julian Javier made a tumbling stop, but his throw to Dick Groat sailed into left field, allowing the mercurial Willie D. to score uncontested. Taylor walked Wills to load the bases, then retired the next two batters to get out of the inning without further damage.

With a 3–1 lead, Perranoski was brought in to face the heart of the St. Louis order in the bottom of the ninth. He got the first two batters—Groat and Musial—on infield ground outs, and struck out Ken Boyer to end the game.

The clutch 8-inning, 3-hit gem by Podres gave him his fourteenth win of the season. He threw only 88 pitches—64 for strikes—with 6 strikeouts and no walks. Other than the seventh-inning bomb to Musial, he allowed just 2 singles. When Perranoski retired the side in order in the ninth, he recorded his eighteenth save. The National League batting race tightened as Dick Groat, who came into the game leading with a .327 average, dropped to .325 after going 0-for-4. Clemente was now second at .324. Tommy Davis went 1-for-4 to finish the night at .320, tied for third with Henry Aaron.

With this victory not only did the Dodgers break the Cardinals' 10-game winning streak—their longest since 1952—they broke their momentum.[37] The Dodgers now led by two full games with Koufax scheduled to go the next night.

On Tuesday night, September 17, Koufax (23–5) and Curt Simmons (15–7) squared off

Top: **Long-time Pirates shortstop Dick Groat donned a Cardinals uniform in 1963. He and Tommy Davis would compete down the stretch for the NL batting title.** *Bottom:* **Cardinals' premier left-hander Curt Simmons locked horns with Sandy Koufax on September 17, 1963, at Busch Stadium. Simmons came into the game with three consecutive shutouts (both photographs, National Baseball Hall of Fame Library, Cooperstown, New York).**

in front of 30,450. Simmons, who had thrown shutouts in his last three starts, fell behind, 1–0, in the first inning when Wills led off the game with a single, stole second, and scored on a double down the left-field line by Gilliam.[38]

With one out in the bottom of the third, Koufax gave the Cardinals their first base runner when he hit Tim McCarver with a pitch. Simmons laid down a sacrifice bunt in front of the mound that Koufax threw into right field. The Cardinals now had the tying run on third base and the go-ahead run on second. The next batter, Julian Javier, hit a ground ball to Wills near second base. Koufax's mind flashed on Game 5 of the 1959 World Series, when Wills had gone for the double play, allowing Nellie Fox to score from third base with the game's only run.[39] On this night Wills chose to throw home with a throw that sailed up the third base line. But the agile Roseboro managed to block the plate, reach for the ball, and put the tag on McCarver. On the next pitch, when Dick Groat hit a harmless bouncer back to the mound, Koufax escaped unscathed. He would later call the play at the plate the key play of the game.[40]

Simmons had retired 17 batters in a row until Tommy Davis singled with two out in the top of the sixth inning.[41] When Koufax retired the Cardinals in order in the bottom of the inning, he still had a no-hitter.

Koufax took the no-hitter to the bottom of the seventh with the Dodgers clinging to a 1–0 lead. Stan Musial led off the inning for the Cardinals. Musial was several years past his prime, but he had hit a game-tying home run in a similar situation the night before. Koufax, determined to keep Musial from pulling the ball, pitched him outside. Musial went with the pitch and lined it into left center for a single to break up the no-hitter. As Musial's pinch runner was left stranded at first base, a hushed Busch Stadium crowd could sense the inevitable.

With two out in the top of the eighth, Tommy Davis hit a 3–2 pitch from Simmons through the right side of the infield for a single. Frank Howard came to the plate with no hits in 19 at bats for the year at Busch Stadium. The drought came to an end when Howard reached out and drove a 0–2 pitch onto the roof in right field to increase the Dodger lead to 3–0. Simmons completed the inning, but was done for the evening.

The Dodgers added a run in the top of the ninth on an RBI double by Roseboro off a Barney Schultz knuckle ball. Koufax took the 4–0 lead to the bottom of the ninth. He had made only 74 pitches through the first eight innings, and it took him just 12 more to close out the Cardinals. His eleventh shutout of the year broke the Major League record for left-handers set by the New York Giants' Carl Hubbell in 1936— when Koufax was a year old. It was a stunning performance at the most critical point in the season. He struck out only four batters because he didn't *need* strikeouts. He shut out the league's top hitting team on four singles in an hour and fifty-four minutes on 86 pitches—67 for strikes. He was behind in the count on only 5 of the 33 batters he faced, and walked none. He threw a total of two balls to the last fourteen batters. "I probably had the best control of my life,"[42] was how Koufax described the game in his autobiography. Koufax was now 24–5 with a 1.87 ERA. The Dodgers' magic number was seven. With a 2-for-3 night, Tommy Davis raised his average to .322, one point behind Dick Groat, who drew an 0-for-4 collar against Koufax.

The suffocating pitching by Podres and Koufax set up a desperation game for the Cardinals the next night. They called on their ace right-hander, Bob Gibson, to right the ship. Gibson came into the game with an 18–8 record, having won his last four consecutive starts. Young Pete Richert made the start for the Dodgers.

By the end of the third inning the Cardinals had scored five runs off Pete Richert and Bob Miller. After getting through the third, Miller settled down to pitch four scoreless innings. Gibson gave Johnny Keane seven strong innings. The Dodgers cobbled together a run off him in the second inning on 3 singles, and then could manage only one other hit until the eighth.

Gibson entered the eighth inning with a 5–1 lead and nine strikeouts. The Dodger leadoff batter was a 23-year-old rookie first baseman named Dick Nen. The strapping 6'3" 200-pound Nen arrived just before the game from Oklahoma City, where he played in a Pacific Coast League playoff game for Spokane the night before. The left-handed-batting Nen battled Gibson to a 2–2 count before lining out to Curt Flood in center field.[43] The Cardinal bench took notice. After Wills and Gilliam hit successive singles off Gibson, he walked Moon to load the bases. Tommy Davis followed with a 2-run single to knock Gibson out of the game. Before the inning was over, the Dodgers had scored another run on a sacrifice fly by Willie Davis to cut the Cardinals' lead to 5–4. Nen stayed in the game to play first base. Ron Perranoski took over for Miller in the bottom of the eighth and set down the Cardinals in order.

The Cardinals went to the ninth inning with a 5–4 lead and ace reliever Ron Taylor on the mound. Taylor got the leadoff batter, Ken McMullen, on a pop fly to second

Unknown 23-year-old rookie first baseman Dick Nen tied the pivotal game of September 18, 1963, at Busch Stadium with a home run in the eighth inning. The Dodgers won the game in the thirteenth inning to sweep the series. The Cardinals would never recover (George Brace photograph).

base. Dick Nen, who hit 288 with 9 home runs and 88 RBIs for Spokane, came to the plate for the second time seeking his first major league hit. Nen took a strike, then delivered a crushing blow to the Cardinals' pennant hopes by sending Taylor's second pitch into orbit. When the ball landed on top of the right-center field roof, the game was tied, 5–5. The 25,975 at Busch Stadium sat in stunned silence as Nen touched home plate. Back in Los Angeles, Dodger fans were in hysterics in front of their television sets. Perranoski continued to pitch brilliantly in relief. In the bottom of the ninth, he again retired the Cardinals in order to send the game into extra innings.

The game went to the thirteenth inning tied, 5–5. Lew Burdette, who came in from the St. Louis bullpen to begin the tenth, was still on the mound for the Cardinals. On the opening night of the series, Burdette had taunted the Dodgers by giving them the "choke" sign as he strutted in the Cardinal dugout.[44] Willie Davis led off with a ground single into left field. After Perranoski struck out attempting to bunt, Dick Tracewski hit a hot smash on the ground to Julian Javier at second base. Javier went to his knees to stop it, but threw wildly past first base and into the Dodger dugout. The third Cardinal error of the game put Davis on third and Tracewski on second. The Cardinals had learned their lesson with Nen; Keane ordered Burdette to walk him to load the bases for Wills. Burdette got Wills to hit a ground ball right to Javier at second base. But Javier had no chance to get Willie Davis—the fastest man in baseball—at home plate. Instead, he threw to first as Davis scored the tie-breaking run. Like a machine, Perranoski mowed down the Cardinals in order in the bottom of the thirteenth to give the Dodgers a dramatic come-from-behind 6–5 victory and a sweep of the series. He shut out the Cardinals over the last six innings on three hits. With a record of 16–3 and an ERA of 1.73, he was clearly the best relief pitcher in baseball. After a 1-for-5 night, Tommy Davis left St. Louis batting .321, tied for second with Roberto Clemente in the NL batting race, and 2 points behind the leader, Dick Groat.

The sweep in St. Louis was a triumph for the Dodgers and a devastating blow to the Cardinals. The fragile single game that separated the two teams before Friday night's opener had ballooned to a commanding 4-game lead for the Dodgers. When the team arrived at LAX at 4:08 the next morning after a tiring 5-hour flight, they found a large crowd of Dodger fans on hand despite a heavy downpour of rain. A homemade sign read, "Today St. Louis, Tomorrow the World Series!"[45] Koufax, who had left St. Louis immediately after Tuesday night's game to spend Yom Kippur at home, didn't know anything about the dramatic final game until he read about it in the papers later that morning.[46]

	W	L	Pct.	*
Los Angeles	94	59	.614	
St. Louis	91	64	.587	4
San Francisco	83	70	.542	11

*Games behind leader

The Final Home Stand

The final home stand of the year began with a 3-game weekend series with the eighth-place Pirates. On September 20, Drysdale threw a 7-hit, 2–0 shutout. Tommy Davis had three hits to take over the batting lead from Dick Groat, .324 to .322.

Koufax went for his 25th win the next night in front of a Dodger Stadium crowd of 55,100. Though he struggled with sub-par stuff, he made it into the eighth inning with the game tied, 2–2, and retired the first two batters. After that, the Pirates jumped on him for three successive singles. The last one, by Ted Savage, put Pittsburgh ahead, 3–2. Alston had Koufax walk Bill Mazeroski intentionally to load the bases before bringing in Ron Perranoski to pitch to Pirates center fielder Bill Virdon. It took Perranoski three pitches to end the inning on a come-backer to the mound.

Koufax was on the hook for the loss when the Dodgers pulled the game out in the bottom of the ninth on a 3-run home run by Willie Davis. Koufax was lucky to escape with a no decision. In 7⅔ innings, he gave up three earned runs on eight hits, including a fourth-inning home run by Donn Clendenon. He had an usually high pitch count of 134, and was able to get the first pitch over the plate to only 18 of the 33 batters he faced. On an off night, Koufax still managed to strike out 10.[47]

Bob Veal and Elroy Face shut out the Dodgers, 4–0, on Sunday afternoon, September 22, to salvage the third game. Podres, who turned in a decent 6-inning, 6-hit performance with 7 strikeouts, was charged with his eleventh loss. Tommy Davis went 5-for-12 in the series to take a 3-point lead over Dick Groat, .323 to .320. Since the Reds had already beaten Curt Simmons and the Cardinals in Crosley Field earlier that day, the Dodgers' magic number was reduced to one. While they had a seemingly comfortable 5½-game lead over St. Louis, there were still six games left to play. As the Dodgers and their fans were painfully aware, another collapse was still mathematically possible.

That possibility was rendered moot the afternoon of the 24th when the Cardinals, who delivered the dagger that prevented them from clinching the pennant on the final weekend of 1962, were eliminated at Wrigley Field when the Cubs scored three runs off Bob Gibson in the bottom of the eighth inning to beat them, 6–3.[48]

With the pennant in the bag, the Dodgers breezed through a 3-game series with the tenth-place Mets. On September 24, Walter Alston—with the luxury of eight days to get his pitching staff ready for the World Series—let Drysdale go seven innings before bringing in Perranoski to complete an easy, 4–1 win. The next night Alston let Koufax pitch the first five innings in 87-degree heat to allow him to win his twenty-fifth game. The combined Koufax-Miller-Perranoski 4–0 shutout was the twenty-fourth of the season for the Dodgers. Of the 66 pitches Koufax threw, 53 were for strikes. He struck out eight, walked none, and was behind in the count on not one of the nineteen batters he faced. The Dodgers shut down Koufax for the remaining three games. With their minds on the Yankees, the Dodgers were swept by the Phillies on the final weekend of the regular season. Podres lasted only 1⅔ inning in the 12–3 rout of September 28. On September 29, the final day of the season, Drysdale left after five innings with a 1–0 lead and a chance to win his twentieth game. But the bullpen collapsed, allowing the Phillies to come back to win the game, 3–1. With the sweep, Philadelphia won the 18-game season series, 11–7. Tommy Davis, who sat out the game, won his second straight batting title with an average of .326. Clemente finished second at .320. In St. Louis, Dick Groat—who, as we have seen, edged out Norm Larker on the last day of the 1960 season—went 0-for-4 to finish tied with Henry Aaron for third at .319. In the bottom of the sixth inning in the same game at Busch Stadium, Stan Musial delivered his 3,630th and last major league hit: an RBI single off the Reds' Jim Maloney. When Johnny Keane sent in a pinch runner for Musial, the crowd of 27,576, who were there mainly to say goodbye to The Man, rose in a tumultuous tribute as number 6 trotted off the field for the last time.[49]

The Dodgers won the pennant by six games over the Cardinals and eleven games over the Giants.

	W	L	Pct.	*
Los Angeles	99	63	.611	
St. Louis	93	69	.574	6
San Francisco	88	74	.543	11

*Games behind leader

The *TV Guide* said that the 1963 World Series between the Los Angeles Dodgers and the New York Yankees would begin on Wednesday, October 3, at Yankee Stadium in New York. This time it would not be wrong.

Nineteen

Four Days in October

I can see how he won 25 games during the season. What I
don't understand is how he lost five.—Yogi Berra

October 2, 1963: Game 1—Yankee Stadium

The 1963 World Series opened on Wednesday, October 2, at Yankee Stadium. Stan
Musial wanted to be with his Cardinals in left field on this day with a chance of ending
his 22-year career with a World Series championship. Instead, Musial—in a coat and
tie—threw out the first ball as Yankee great Joe DiMaggio stood beside him. The 69,000
fans were there to see the much-anticipated matchup between baseball's two premier
left-handers, Whitey Ford (24–7) and Sandy Koufax (25–5)—a matchup postponed for
a year as the result of Ed Roebuck's inability to hold onto a 2-run lead in the bottom of
the ninth at Dodger Stadium on October 3, 1962. Had it taken place the year before,
Yankee fans would have seen a sub-par Koufax still in the early stages of his second
spring training. But by the end of the first inning on this day at Yankee Stadium—after
he had blown away the first three Yankee batters on strikes—it was clear that this was
a different Sandy Koufax.

With the exception of Moose Skowron, the Yankee lineup was unchanged from
Game 1 of the 1962 Series:

	YANKEES		**DODGERS**	
1	Tony Kubek	SS	Maury Wills	SS
2	Bobby Richardson	2B	Jim Gilliam	3B
3	Tom Tresh	LF	Willie Davis	CF
4	Mickey Mantle	CF	Tommy Davis	LF
5	Roger Maris	RF	Frank Howard	RF
6	Elston Howard	C	Bill Skowron	1B

	YANKEES			DODGERS	
7	Joe Pepitone	1B		Dick Tracewski	2B
8	Clete Boyer	3B		John Roseboro	C
9	Whitey Ford	P		Sandy Koufax	P

Elston Howard, who would be voted the American League MVP, had a career-high 28 home runs. Mickey Mantle hit .314 with 15 home runs in only 172 at bats. Joe Pepitone hit 27 home runs, Tom Tresh 25, and Roger Maris 23 in 312 at bats. A late-season injury to Dodger third Ken McMullen caused Alston to move Gilliam to third base and Dick Tracewski to second.

When Ford pitched in his first World Series game in 1950, Koufax was a student at Lafayette High School in Brooklyn. Now making his twentieth Series start and seeking his eleventh Series win, Ford retired the Dodgers in order in the first inning.[1] But he

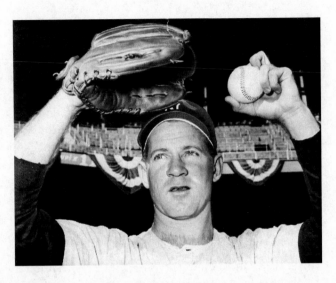

Whitey Ford was 24–7 for the 1963 New York Yankees (National Baseball Hall of Fame Library, Cooperstown, New York).

ran into trouble in the second. With one out, Ford made the mistake of throwing Frank Howard a fast ball that he turned into a low line drive that carried over center fielder Mickey Mantle's head. Like a 1-iron shot, the ball seemed to never reach more than 25 feet off the ground before it ricocheted off the black protective screening around the public-address amplifiers in front of the center-field bleachers.[2] The crowd sat in stunned disbelief as the 6'7", 255-pound Howard rumbled into second base with a 460-foot double. The next batter was Bill Skowron, a Yankee for nine years before he was traded to the Dodgers the previous

Elston Howard, who was the Yankees' first black player in his rookie year of 1955, was the American League's Most Valuable Player in 1963 (National Baseball Hall of Fame Library, Cooperstown, New York).

November. Though Skowron had been a major disappointment during the regular season with his .203 batting average, 4 home runs, and 19 RBIs, Alston put him in the lineup at first base on the hunch that he could produce in his old stadium. And it paid off as Skowron singled up the middle to score Howard with the first run of the Series. Second baseman Dick Tracewski, who later admitted to feeling "kind of sick and afraid"[3] as he walked to the plate for the first time in a World Series, followed with a looping single into center field to bring up John Roseboro with runners on first and third. Roseboro, the bespectacled Dodger catcher, who had not hit a home run all season against a left-handed pitcher, hit a towering fly ball down the right-field line that landed just inside the foul pole in the tenth row of the lower stands for a 3-run home run. At the end of the second inning, Whitey Ford walked off the mound, behind 4–0. It was the most runs he had ever given up in a single inning in the World Series. When Skowron hit another RBI single off Ford in the third to make it 5–0, the game was—for all practical purposes—out of reach for the Yankees against Sandy Koufax.

Before Elston Howard eked out an opposite field single with two out in the bottom of the fifth, Koufax had retired the first 14 batters in a row—10 on strikeouts. After Joe Pepitone followed that with a single to right and Clete Boyer got on with an infield single, the bases were loaded. Ralph Houk brought in Hector Lopez to pinch hit for Ford. The Yankees left all three runners stranded as Lopez struck out swinging.

In the sixth, Bobby Richardson walked on a close 3–2 pitch. The call appeared to upset Koufax, and he walked Tom Tresh on four pitches in front of Maris & Mantle. But Koufax got Maris to pop out to Tracewski, and Mantle to pop out to Wills to end the threat.

Koufax took a 5–0 shutout to the bottom of the eighth. With one out, Tony Kubek beat out an infield single. Bobby Richardson, who had struck out only 22 times in 630 at bats during the regular season, went down on strikes for the third time in the game. Tom Tresh, batting right-handed, lined a ball into the left-field seats for a 2-run homer to ruin the shutout. After Mantle walked, Alston came out to the mound to slow Koufax down and tell him to "not be too fine" when pitching to Roger Maris. Koufax got Maris to ground out to second base to end the inning. Alston told reporters after the game that he would have brought in Drysdale to pitch to Elston Howard had Maris reached base.[4]

With one out in the bottom of the ninth, Joe Pepitone lined a single off Koufax into right field. Clete Boyer flied out to Willie Davis in center for the second out. By now the crowd—sensing history in the making—was rooting for Koufax. The Yankees' .234-hitting utilityman, Harry Bright, came up to bat for relief pitcher Steve Hamilton. When Bright trickled a roller down the third base line the crowd groaned, then cheered when it veered foul. They then let out a seismic roar when Koufax blew a third strike past Bright to end the game and set a new World Series record of 15 strikeouts. Carl Erskine, who set the old record by striking out 14 Yankees in the 1953 Series—exactly ten years to the day before Koufax's performance—was the first to congratulate him in the Yankee Stadium clubhouse.

With Koufax's dominating 5–2 win, the Dodgers jumped out to a 1-game lead in the Series with Podres scheduled for Game 2 the next day at the Stadium.

October 3, 1963: Game 2—Yankee Stadium

The second game was played on Thursday afternoon, October 3, before 66,455 under perfect conditions at Yankee Stadium. The job of evening the Series fell on the Yankees' 5'11" 22-year-old rookie left-hander, Al Downing (13–5). Alston went with his 10-year veteran, Johnny Podres (14–12), already with two World Series wins under his belt.

It was a nervous Al Downing who gave up a leadoff single to Maury Wills in the first inning. Then the pick-off play the Yankees had been working on to shackle Wills backfired. When Downing fired the ball to first baseman Joe Pepitone it looked like the start of a perfectly timed pickoff play: Wills was caught leaning the wrong way, trapped in no-man's land. But Maury's natural ability to improvise was something the Yankees couldn't prepare for. He made no attempt to get back to first. Instead, he took off for second. Left-handed Pepitone made a rushed throw to the infield side of second base that Bobby Richardson had to lunge across the bag to catch. Wills, still 15 feet from the base, went into a headfirst slide angling away from the base at a 45 degree angle. Richardson's momentum had carried him too far away from the base to be in position to execute the play. By the time he reversed direction and applied the tag, Wills was already hugging the bag.[5] The botched pickoff play was a turning point. It rattled young Downing. Gilliam exploited the opening with a line-drive single to right sending Wills to third. Willie Davis hit a sinking line drive to right field that Roger Maris, an excellent outfielder, misjudged in the haze that frequently enshrouded Yankee Stadium at this time of year. The disoriented Maris' first step was in. Then, realizing the ball was going to go over his head, he tried to turn back, slipped, and fell to his knees. The ball got by him and rolled all the way to the fence. By the time Maris chased it down and got it back to the infield, two runs had scored and Davis was standing at second base with a double.[6] Already down, 2–0, before he could get anyone out, Downing somehow managed to settle down and retire the next three batters in order to escape the inning without further damage.

The Yankees started a 22-year-old rookie lefthander, Al Downing, in Game 2 of the 1963 World Series October 3, 1963 (National Baseball Hall of Fame Library, Cooperstown, New York).

In the top of the third, with two out and the bases empty, Tommy Davis sliced an outside pitch from Downing down the right field line. In the right field corner, Maris plunged headlong after the ball and crashed into the box seat railing as Davis stretched the play into a triple. The game was stopped as Maris had to be led off the field with a badly bruised left arm. Davis was left at third base as Downing struck out Frank Howard. In the top of the fourth, Bill Skowron ripped another Downing pitch down the right field line. This one cleared the wall at the 314-foot sign to make the score 3–0. It was Skowron's eighth World Series homer.

Podres was a different pitcher with money on the line. Five days before, with the pennant sewn up, he had been routed early by the Phillies. Today, with a chance to put the Yankees in a deep hole, he blanked them through the first seven innings on four hits—at one point retiring 13 batters in a row.

The Dodgers increased their lead to 4–0 in the top of the eighth inning when Willie Davis hit a double off Ralph Terry, now in his third inning of relief of Downing, and scored when Tommy Davis drove him in with his second triple of the game. After Podres held the Yankees scoreless on one hit in the bottom of the inning, he told Alston that he was tired. But Alston stayed with his "money pitcher" and allowed him to take a 6-hit shutout into the bottom of the ninth. Mantle led off with a long drive to the cavernous "death valley" section of left-center field for a load out. After Maris's replacement, Hector Lopez, followed that with a line-drive, ground rule double into the left-field seats, Alston had seen enough. Perranoski was brought in to pitch to Elston Howard. Perranoski proceeded to lose the shutout by allowing Howard to line a single into right field to score Lopez. He then retired the next two batters, Joe Pepitone and Clete Boyer, to end the game.

The 4–1 loss put the Yankees in a precarious position. They were now down two games to none in the Series. While they had come back from this position twice before—in 1956 and 1958—both times, they were able to recover at Yankee Stadium and go on to win the Series after falling behind 2–0 on the road.[7] This time they would have to do it at Dodger Stadium against Drysdale and Koufax. It was a daunting challenge. And they would be without Roger Maris, who was lost for the Series.

October 5, 1963: Game 3—Dodger Stadium

Game 3 was played Saturday afternoon, October 5, a bright 75-degree day, at Dodger Stadium. For the first time in the Series, both teams went with right-handed starters: Don Drysdale (19–17) for the Dodgers and Jim Bouton (21–7) for the Yankees. Twenty-seven-year-old Drysdale, who hadn't pitched since his brief 5-inning appearance six days before against the Phillies, beat the White Sox at the Coliseum in his only other World Series start in 1959. This was the first Series start for the 24-year-old Bouton.

The game was all but decided in the bottom of the first inning before many in the record crowd of 55,912 had ever found their seats. After throwing out lead-off man Maury Wills on a failed bunt attempt, Bouton walked Jim Gilliam on a close 3–2 pitch, then got Willie Davis to fly out to right field for the second out. Bouton's sharp-breaking curve ball was his best pitch. He lost control of one against Tommy Davis that exploded in the dirt in front of Elston Howard. Howard could only partially block it before it went to the backstop. The wild pitch moved Gilliam into scoring position. Tommy D. then hit a bullet up the middle. In the millisecond Bouton had to stop the ball, it shot under his glove, and glanced off the left side of the pitching rubber toward second baseman Bobby Richardson. At first, Richardson lost sight of the ball in the white shirts behind home plate.[8] When it entered his vision, he was able to get in front of it, but it took two bad hops on the notoriously hard Dodger Stadium infield. The last one caused the ball to ricochet off his shin and into right field, allowing Gilliam to score easily from second base.[9] Bouton got Ron Fairly to foul out to end the inning. But the damage was done. On a freak single, the Dodgers scored what would be the only run of the game.

Drysdale was pitching what he would call in his autobiography "the best game I ever pitched."[10] The slumping Yankees created only two serious threats for him. In the second inning, Mickey Mantle lobbed a bunt over third baseman Gilliam's head for his first Series hit. Drysdale then grazed Joe Pepitone with a pitch to put runners on first and second. After Elston Howard struck out on three pitches and John Blanchard rolled out weakly to second, Drysdale walked Clete Boyer to load the bases with the pitcher's spot up next. The threat ended when Bouton was blown away on strikes. In the sixth, Tony Kubek singled to right field and was advanced to third base on a sacrifice bunt and an infield out. Mantle, who struck out staring at an odd-looking pitch in the fourth, came to the plate. When he took a strike on another suspicious pitch, the Yankees went ballistic, certain that Drysdale was throwing a spitball, the pitch that was outlawed in 1920. Third base coach Frankie Crosetti charged plate umpire Larry Napp, frantically pointing at Drysdale. Napp calmly instructed Drysdale to make sure to wipe off his fingers after sticking them in his mouth.[11] Two pitches later, Mantle froze on another third strike, leaving the tying run at third base.

Though the Dodgers had managed only four singles and one tainted run against Bouton through the first seven innings, the Yankees, trailing 1–0, had to bring in Yogi Berra to pinch hit for him with one out in the eighth. The 38-year-old Berra, who had only 147 at bats during the regular season, was making his first appearance in the Series. Berra, a great clutch hitter, hit the ball on a line to deep right field—only it was right at Ron Fairly. It would be Berra's last major league at bat. After Kubek followed with his second single, Drysdale got Richardson to ground out to end the inning.

Drysdale had to face the heart of the Yankee order as the game moved to the ninth inning with the score still 1–0. With the crowd on its feet, he began by striking out Tom Tresh for the second time on three pitches. When Mantle grounded out to Moose Skowron on the first pitch, the Yankees were down to their last out. Joe Pepitone took Drysdale's first pitch for a ball, then made the crowd gasp as he sent a towering drive heading for the right-field fence. It looked like a game-tying home run until it began to lose carry as it approached the Yankee bullpen. Fairly was able to catch it with his back against the bullpen gate. The Dodgers raced out to the mound to mob Drysdale, who had just thrown a brilliant 3-hit, 1–0 shutout to put the Dodgers up three games to none in the Series. At the post-game press conference, Alston told reporters, "Without taking away anything from Koufax or Podres, this was the outstanding pitching job of the Series so far."[12]

The Yankees, who had never been swept in a World Series, were now staring that possibility in the face, with Koufax scheduled to come at them again the next day.

October 6, 1963: Game 4—Dodger Stadium

Koufax and Ford met for the second and last time on Sunday, October 6, before another capacity crowd of 55,912 at Dodger Stadium. On this day both pitchers were superb. Koufax, who was pitching with an ulcerated foot only made tolerable with a shot of morphine[13] from team physician Dr. Robert Kerlan, didn't allow a hit until the top of the fourth inning—and a questionable hit at that. With one out and the score tied, 0–0, Bobby Richardson hit a high pop fly into short center field. Maury Wills, Dick Tracewski, and Willie Davis all converged on the ball. It looked like Davis would make the play until he lost it in the sun at the last moment. Wills lunged for the ball, got his glove on it, but dropped it. When the smoke cleared, Richardson was standing on second base. The official scorer had no choice but to rule it a "double."[14]

Ford shut out the Dodgers on one hit through the first four innings, facing the minimum of 12 batters thanks to a double play. In the bottom of the fifth, Frank Howard broke the scoreless tie with a monumental home run. In an awesome display of strength, Howard took a one-handed swing at a waist-high Ford curve ball and launched a towering drive down the left-field line. It came down inside the foul pole eight rows deep in the second tier mezzanine section, 450 feet from home plate. It was the first time a fair ball had ever been hit into the second tier.[15]

The game was still 1–0 as it moved to the seventh. Koufax got leadoff batter Tom Tresh to foul out. Mickey Mantle was 1-for-11 for the Series when he stepped into the batter's box batting right-handed. He was looking for a fast ball, and he got one on the first pitch. From the instant the ball left Mantle's bat, Koufax, the crowd, the national television audience—everyone—knew that he had just tied the game. The post-contact sights were almost anticlimactic: the ball clearing the left-field wall at the 380-foot sign and landing in the back of the bleachers. The tie lasted only a few minutes. On Ford's first pitch in the bottom of the inning, leadoff batter Junior Gilliam hit a high bounding ball off home plate and down the third base line. It looked like it would bounce over Clete Boyer's head and into the left-field corner for extra bases. But Boyer timed his leap perfectly, speared the ball, and threw a bullet across the diamond to Joe Pepitone at first base. What happened next was emblematic of the Yankees' luck. Pepitone lost the ball in the white-shirted background of the left field stands. In rapid-fire succession, the ball glanced off his wrist, his forearm, and his chest, and ended up in the right-field corner. Before it could be retrieved, Gilliam had made it all the way to third base. Willie Davis followed with a fly ball into deep center field. Mantle caught the ball, and made a fine throw to the plate. But Gilliam scored standing up to put the Dodgers in front, 2–1. Pepitone's 3-base error—the Yankees' only error of the Series—not only knocked them out of a tie, it forced Houk to pull Whitey Ford for a pinch hitter in the eighth. To this point, many thought Ford had outpitched Koufax. Through 7 innings, he had given up just 2 hits and 1 earned run, and walked 1 batter.

Koufax went to the ninth with a 2–1 lead. After Richardson opened the inning with a single to center field, he struck out Tresh and Mantle, looking at change-up curves.[16] Elston Howard hit a ground ball to shortstop that should have ended it: all Wills had to do was to flip the ball to second base for the force out on Richardson. But rookie second baseman Tracewski dropped it. Had Roger Maris not gone down in Game 2, the Yankees would have had him at the plate with the tying and winning runs on base. Instead, they had to use Hector Lopez. Lopez could only manage a halting half-swing at Koufax's first pitch—a searing inside fastball. The result was a jam-shot dribbler to Wills, who threw him out to end the game.[17] The New York Yankees, who had a 14-game lead on September 13—the day they clinched the American League pennant—were swept for the first time in a World Series.

It was the second complete game victory for Koufax in the Series. He pitched a 6-hitter with 8 strikeouts and no walks. His 23 strikeouts in two games set a new World Series record. He would be named the Most Valuable Player of the Series. In the chaotic champagne-drenched clubhouse after the game, the entire national media contingent—radio, television, press, and photographers—converged on Koufax. The soft-spoken Koufax, in typical understatement, told them, "I thought I had pretty good stuff."[18] Down the hall in his office, Walter Alston, the quiet man from Darrtown, Ohio, who took the brunt of the abuse for blowing the pennant in the last week of 1962, told reporters, "This makes up for everything."[19] In a dramatic one-year turnaround, the Los Angeles Dodgers went from choke artists to World Champions.

Great Dodger Pitching

The story of the 1963 World Series was the great Dodger pitching. The Yankees were the top power team of the era. While they were not the 1961 Yankees, they were still second in the American League in home runs and runs scored. They were shut out only eight times in the regular season. But against the Dodger pitching staff they batted .171 and scored only 4 runs. They struck out 37 times in four games, an average of over 9 per game. The great Mickey Mantle was 2 for 15 with one run batted in. He stuck out five times—four times looking.

The Yankees knew they would have their hands full with Koufax. When he set a new strikeout record to beat them in Game 1, they counted on being able to bounce back the next day. But when they could score only one run against Podres and Perranoski, they were suddenly down two games to none and having to play the next three games in Los Angeles—without Roger Maris. Being shut out 1–0 by Drysdale in Game 3 put them in an impossible situation: they would have to beat Sandy Koufax in Game 4 to survive. As we have seen, though Ford pitched brilliantly for seven innings, the Yankees could do nothing against Koufax. But for a heroic seventh-inning home run by Mickey Mantle, he would have shut them out. The Yankees never recovered from the shock of the first game. Remarkably, the Dodgers used only four pitchers in the Series. Simply put, the Koufax-Drysdale-Podres-Perranoski strikeout machine overwhelmed the Yankees. It is still considered one of the most dominating pitching performances in World Series history.

Twenty

The Apotheosis of Sandy Koufax

apo•the•o•sis *n* Gk: elevation to divine status[1]

Trying to hit him was like trying to drink coffee with a fork.[2]—Willie Stargell (who was given the day off in Koufax's three starts against the Pirates)

The 1963 Dodgers were sixth in the National League in run production, scoring 202 fewer runs than the year before. They hit 30 fewer home runs to finish seventh in the league, and had only two .300 hitters: batting champion Tommy Davis, .326, and Maury Wills, .302. Tommy led the team with an unremarkable 88 runs batted in after his Hall-of-Fame number of 153 the previous year. The Dodgers stole 74 fewer bases than in 1962, mainly attributable to a more restrained—but more effective—Maury Wills. Though his output dropped from 104 to 40, it was still enough for him to lead the league in stolen bases for the fourth straight year. Despite their efforts to shore up their defense, the Dodgers still committed the fourth-most errors in a 10-team league. How did such a punchless, porous Dodger team win the pennant by six games and sweep the mighty New York Yankees in the World Series? In a word: Pitching.

Koufax on Another Planet

As we have seen, at the end of 1960 Sandy Koufax was an unfulfilled Bonus Baby with a losing record. If 1961 was a career turnaround season, and 1962 was an unfinished question mark, 1963 was the first season that he seemed to be pitching on a different planet. He won 25 games and lost only 5; set a new major league record for left-handers with 11 shutouts; broke his own NL record with 306 strikeouts; and led both leagues with an ERA of 1.88. His WHIP (Walks plus Hits per Innings Pitched) of 0.875 was the lowest in Major League Baseball since Grover Cleveland Alexander's 0.842 in 1915.

	W	L	W–L %	IP	SO	ERA	SHO	WHIP
1955–1960 AVG	6	6.7	.474	115	113.8	4.11	0.8	1.447
1961	18	13	.581	255.2	269	3.52	2	1.205
1962	14	7	.667	184.1	216	2.54	2	1.036
1963	25	5	.833	311	306	1.88	11	0.875

Wildness had always been Koufax's downfall as a young pitcher. But by 1963 he had pinpoint control, walking only one more batter than he had in 1962 even though he pitched nearly 127 more innings. With a strikeout-to-walk ratio of 5.28, he was now striking out over five times more batters than he was walking.

	IP	BB	BB/9	SO	SO/BB
1955–1960 AVG	115	67.5	5.2	113.8	1.60
1961	255.2	96	3.4	269	2.80
1962	184.1	57	2.8	216	3.79
1963	311	58	1.7	306	5.28

Koufax led a Dodger pitching staff that was first in the National League with a team Earned Run Average of 2.85, compared to 3.62 the year before. Thanks to his 11 shutouts, they led the majors with 24 (including 4 combined efforts). For the sixteenth consecutive year they led the league in strikeouts. As a team, the Dodgers walked 186 fewer batters than in 1962.

Though Ed Roebuck departed at mid-season, Ron Perranoski emerged as the premier relief pitcher in baseball with a record of 16–3 and an ERA of 1.67. Larry Sherry, hero of the 1959 World Series, was 2–6 with only three saves out of the bullpen after failing his April audition for the fourth starting spot. A major factor in the team's success was Johnny Podres's response to cortisone treatments on his elbow at the end of June. After a 4–6 start, he won six straight games in July to help the Dodgers take over first place, and finished the regular season with a record of 14–12 and 5 shutouts. Despite a chronic lack of run support, Don Drysdale was 19–17 with a career-best 251 strikeouts and a 2.63 ERA. After a 1–12 season with the Mets in 1962, Bob Miller came through with a surprise 10 wins as the Dodgers' fourth starter and middle reliever.

On October 24 a select committee of the Baseball Writers' Association of America made Sandy Koufax the first unanimous winner of the Cy Young Award.[3] Six days later, the BWAA also named him the National League's Most Valuable Player. Koufax's stunning per-

Relief pitcher Ron Perranoski was 16–3 with a 1.67 ERA. He finished fourth in the MVP voting (National Baseball Hall of Fame Library, Cooperstown, New York).

formance in the World Series did not influence the voting, since the ballots for both awards were cast before the Series began. He became the second pitcher to win both awards in the same year. Brooklyn Dodger right-hander Don Newcombe swept both in 1956, the first year of the Cy Young Award.[4] Ron Perranoski finished fourth in the MVP balloting; Jim Gilliam finished sixth and even received one of the twenty first-place votes (Koufax captured fourteen).[5] The 34-year-old 11-year veteran Gilliam, who began another season in Los Angeles as a utilityman, ended up playing in 148 games as a combination second baseman-third baseman, timely filling the vacuums created when highly touted rookies Nate Oliver and Ken McMullen were sent down to the minors. He batted a solid .282, stole 19 bases, and was far and away the team's best clutch hitter, batting .333 in Late & Close plate appearances. (Late & Close plate appearances are those in the 7th inning or later with the batting team tied, ahead by one, or the tying run at least on deck.) Gilliam hit .319 against the Giants, and .311 against the Cardinals with 14 runs batted in. When Koufax was notified about the MVP award at his golf club in Los Angeles, he deflected the attention away from himself: "I'm amazed that Junior Gilliam didn't finish higher than sixth. Junior never gets what he deserves."[6] Despite his modesty, there was no doubt that Sandy was the key to the season.

The 1963 Los Angeles Dodgers approached the season with two lingering questions from the prior year: 1. Could Koufax's pitching hand ever recover from the injury that cost them the pennant and nearly cost him his index finger? and 2. Could they as a team shake the stigma of blowing a 4-game lead in the final week of the season? Sandy Koufax provided an affirmative answer to both questions: the first in April, the second in October.

❈ ❈ ❈

On November 1, South Vietnam's President Ngo Dinh Diem was overthrown in a military coup in Saigon. While it was initially reported that Diem committed suicide,[7] it would later be revealed that he was assassinated. The number of American "military advisors" in Vietnam would reach 16,300 by the end of the year. What would President Kennedy do about Vietnam? What would he do about civil rights? Three weeks later, he and Jackie boarded Air Force One for Dallas on a trip to build Southern support for his reelection campaign against his likely opponent, Barry Goldwater. America would never know the answer to these questions.

❈ ❈ ❈

Epilogue

Before the 1963 season began, a sportswriter bet Leo Durocher two neckties that he would be the Dodger manager by the Fourth of July. It never happened. Walter Alston survived the collapse of 1962 and its aftermath; he then went on to win his third World Championship—his second in Los Angeles. In late November, he signed a new contract for the upcoming 1964 season. His eleventh consecutive one-year contract came with a $7,500 raise, making his $52,500 salary the highest to date in club history. Alston and the 1964 Dodgers would face challenges from a St. Louis team greatly improved despite being without the services of Stan Musial for the first time since 1941, and from Gene Mauch's new powerhouse in Philadelphia. But the biggest challenge for the Dodgers would come from the ever-present risk of injury from within.

On December 6, after a brief and disappointing stint in the National League, the Dodgers sold Bill Skowron to the Washington Senators for an estimated $25,000 twelve days before his 34th birthday. He would end his career in 1967, splitting that season with his hometown Chicago White Sox and the California Angels.

December 30, 1963, was Sandy Koufax's twenty-eighth birthday. It was on this day four years before that he decided to "give it one more year" after struggling with the idea of quitting the game. As he approached his tenth season he was considered baseball's greatest pitcher. Koufax would separate himself even further from his peers for the next three seasons. During this period the Dodgers' fortunes would continue to rise and fall with the health of his left arm.

Appendix:
Sandy Koufax Statistics

*The tables on the following 11 pages run
across the two-page spreads left to right.*

Career

Year	W	L	PCT	ERA	G	GS	GF	CG	SHO	SV	IP	H	R	ER	HR	BB ➤
1955	2	2	.500	3.02	12	5	4	2	2	0	41.2	33	15	14	2	28
1956	2	4	.333	4.91	16	10	1	0	0	0	58.2	66	37	32	10	29
1957	5	4	.556	3.88	34	13	12	2	0	0	104.1	83	49	45	14	51
1958	11	11	.500	4.48	40	26	7	5	0	1	158.2	132	89	79	19	105
1959	8	6	.571	4.05	35	23	6	6	1	2	153.1	136	74	69	23	92
1960	8	13	.381	3.91	37	26	7	7	2	1	175	133	83	76	20	100
1961	18	13	.581	3.52	42	35	2	15	2	1	255.2	212	117	100	27	96
1962	14	7	.667	2.54*	28	26	2	11	2	1	184.1	134	61	52	13	57
1963	25*	5	.833	1.88*	40	40	0	20	11*	0	311	214	68	65	18	58
1964	19	5	.792*	1.74*	29	28	1	15	7*	1	223	154	49	43	13	53
1965	26*	8	.765*	2.04*	43	41	2	27*	8	2	335.2*	216	90	76	26	71
1966	27*	9	.750	1.73*	41	41*	0	27*	5*	0	323*	241	74	62	19	77
12 Yrs	165	87	.655	2.76	397	314	44	137	40	9	2,324.1	1,754	806	713	204	817

*League leader

1955– 1960	36	40	.474	4.10	174	103	37	22	5	4	691.2	583	347	315	88	405
6-YR AVG	6.0	6.7	.474	4.10	29.0	17.2	6.2	3.7	0.8	0.7	115.1	97.2	57.8	52.5	14.7	67.5
1961– 1966	129	47	.733	2.19	223	211	7	115	35	5	1,632.2	1,171	459	398	116	412
6-YR AVG	21.5	7.8	.733	2.19	37.2	35.2	1.2	19.2	5.8	0.8	272.1	195.2	76.5	66.3	19.3	68.7

Source: Sports Reference LLC. "Players—Sandy Koufax."
Baseball-Reference.com—Major League Statistics and Information.
http://www.baseball-reference.com/players/k/koufasa01.shtml (Accessed June 2014).

1961

Date	Loc	Opp	Result	Innings	Decision	IP	H	R	ER	BB	SO	HBP
Apr 14		PIT	L,3–6	GS-5	L(0–1)	5	5	4	3	1	3	0
Apr 21		CIN	W,5–3	CG	W(1–1)	9	6	3	3	3	11	0
Apr 30(2)@		CHC	L,5–10	4–4		1	1	1	1	1	1	0
				April	**1–1**	**15**	**12**	**8**	**7**	**5**	**15**	**0**
May 2	@	MLN	W,11–9	GS-4		3.333	6	5	2	2	6	0
May 4	@	MLN	L,6–10	9–9		0	1	1	1	1	0	0
May 7	@	PIT	W,4–2	GS-7	W(2–1)	6.333	8	2	2	0	3	0
May 12		CHC	W,4–2	GS-9	W(3–1)	8.667	4	2	2	5	11	0
May 16		MLN	L,3–5	GS-5	L(3–2)	4	7	5	5	3	3	0
May 21	@	SFG	W,3–2	CG	W(4–2)	9	4	2	2	2	6	0

➤ IBB	SO	HBP	BK	WP	Batters	AVG	WHIP	H/9	HR/9	BB/9	SO/9	SO/BB
1	30	1	1	2	183	.216	1.464	7.1	0.4	6	6.5	1.07
0	30	0	2	1	261	.286	1.619	10.1	1.5	4.4	4.6	1.03
1	122	2	0	5	444	.216	1.284	7.2	1.2	4.4	10.5	2.39
6	131	1	0	17*	714	.220	1.494	7.5	1.1	6	7.4	1.25
4	173	0	1	5	679	.235	1.487	8	1.4	5.4	10.2	1.88
6	197	1	0	9	753	.207	1.331	6.8	1	5.1	10.1*	1.97
6	269*	3	2	12	1,068	.222	1.205	7.5*	1	3.4	9.5*	2.80*
4	216	2	0	3	744	.197	1.036*	6.5*	0.6	2.8	10.5*	3.79
7	306*	3	1	6	1,210	.189	0.875*	6.2*	0.5	1.7	8.9	5.28*
5	223	0	0	9	870	.191	0.928*	6.2*	0.5	2.1	9.0*	4.21
4	382*	5	0	11	1,297*	.179	0.855*	5.8*	0.7	1.9	10.2*	5.38*
4	317*	0	0	7	1,274*	.205	0.985	6.7	0.5	2.1	8.8*	4.12
48	2,396	18	7	87	9,497	.205	1.106	6.8	0.8	3.2	9.3	2.93
18	683	5	4	39	3,034	.225	1.428	7.6	1.1	5.3	8.9	1.69
3.0	113.8	0.8	0.7	6.5	506	.225	1.428	7.6	1.1	5.3	8.9	1.69
30	1713	13	3	48	6,463	.197	0.970	6.5	0.6	2.3	9.4	4.16
5.0	285.5	2.2	0.5	8.0	1,077	.197	0.970	6.5	0.6	2.3	9.4	4.16

ERA	Pitches	Strikes	Batters	1st pitch K	AB	1B	2B	3B	HR	AVG
5.40	79	50	23	16	21	4	1	0	0	.238
3.86	123	79	34	22	31	5	0	0	1	.194
4.20	19	11	4	2	3	0	0	1	0	.333
4.20	**221**	**140**	**61**	**40**	**55**	**9**	**1**	**1**	**1**	**.218**
4.42	86	51	19	8	16	4	2	0	0	.375
4.91	12	7	2	1	1	0	0	1	0	1.000
4.38	102	73	25	15	24	7	0	0	1	.333
3.78	152	97	36	18	31	2	1	1	0	.129
4.58	81	49	22	15	19	5	1	0	1	.368
4.08	129	87	33	23	30	2	1	0	1	.133

1961

Date	Loc	Opp	Result	Innings	Decision	IP	H	R	ER	BB	SO	HBP
May 25	@	STL	W,1–0	SHO	W(5–2)	9	3	0	0	3	8	0
May 29		STL	W,2–1	CG	W(6–2)	9	3	1	1	5	13	0
May					**5–1**	**49.333**	**36**	**18**	**15**	**21**	**50**	**0**
Jun 3		SFG	W,4–3	CG	W(7–2)	9	7	3	3	5	7	0
Jun 7		PIT	W,7–3	CG	W(8–2)	9	7	3	3	2	7	0
Jun 11		PHI	W,6–3	CG	W(9–2)	9	5	3	3	2	10	0
Jun 16		MLN	L,1–2	GS-7	L(9–3)	6.333	8	2	2	4	8	0
Jun 20	@	CHC	W,3–0	SHO	W(10–3)	9	2	0	0	2	14	0
Jun 24	@	CIN	W,9–7	GS-3		3	5	5	5	1	3	0
Jun 25	@	CIN	L,2–3	5–6		2	1	0	0	0	3	0
Jun 29	@	PIT	L,2–4	GS-8	L(10–4)	7.667	7	3	3	1	11	0
June					**4–2**	**55**	**42**	**19**	**19**	**17**	**63**	**0**
Jul 3	@	MLN	W,3–2	GS-8	W(11–4)	8	3	2	2	6	7	0
Jul 7(1)		CIN	L,7–11	GS-4	L(11–5)	3.667	7	8	4	3	4	0
Jul 9		CIN	L,3–14	3–5		2	3	2	2	1	2	0
Jul 15		PHI	L,2–7	GS-8	L(11–6)	7.333	8	5	5	1	7	0
Jul 17		PIT	W,6–4	8–GF	S(1)	2	0	0	0	0	2	0
Jul 20	@	CIN	W,10–1	CG	W(12–6)	9	7	1	1	1	7	0
Jul 25	@	PHI	W,7–2	CG	W(13–6)	9	6	2	2	1	10	0
Jul 29	@	PIT	W,5–4	GS-6		6	8	2	2	4	7	0
July					**3–2**	**47**	**42**	**22**	**18**	**17**	**46**	**0**
Aug 4		CHC	L,2–4	GS-7	L(13–7)	7	4	4	4	3	7	0
Aug 8		MLN	W,7–3	GS-6		5.333	8	3	3	1	4	0
Aug 15		CIN	L,2–5	GS-7	L(13–8)	6	8	5	4	3	6	1
Aug 20	@	SFG	L,8–11	GS-4	L(13–9)	3	8	6	6	2	3	0
Aug 25	@	CIN	W,7–2	CG	W(14–9)	9	5	2	2	5	6	1
Aug 29	@	CHC	W,2–1	CG	W(15–9)	9	2	1	0	5	12	0
August					**2–3**	**39.333**	**35**	**21**	**19**	**19**	**38**	**2**
Sep 2	@	MLN	L,0–4	GS-7	L(15–10)	7	7	4	2	1	2	0
Sep 6		SFG	W,9–5	GS-5		4.667	8	5	5	2	10	0
Sep 10	@	SFG	L,1–7	5–6		2	2	3	3	1	5	0
Sep 12		PHI	L,10–19	GS-2	L(15–11)	1.333	5	6	6	1	4	0
Sep 15		MLN	W,11–2	CG	W(16–11)	9	5	2	1	3	10	0
Sep 17		MLN	W,4–3	10–GF(11)	W(17–11)	2	4	1	1	0	1	0
Sep 20		CHC	W,3–2	CG(13)	W(18–11)	13	7	2	2	3	15	1
Sep 24	@	STL	L,7–8	GS-3	L(18–12)	3	4	4	2	3	3	0
Sep 27	@	PHI	L,1–2	CG(8)	L(18–13)	8	3	2	0	3	7	0
September					**3–4**	**50**	**45**	**29**	**22**	**17**	**57**	**1**
Year					**18–13**	**255.67**	**212**	**117**	**100**	**96**	**269**	**3**

ERA	Pitches	Strikes	Batters	1st pitch K	AB	1B	2B	3B	HR	AVG
3.42	131	83	31	16	28	3	0	0	0	.107
3.08	145	90	35	23	30	1	1	1	0	.100
2.74	**838**	**537**	**203**	**119**	**179**	**24**	**6**	**3**	**3**	**.201**
3.07	144	88	35	23	30	5	1	0	1	.233
3.06	139	88	35	17	33	4	1	0	2	.212
3.05	122	76	34	20	31	3	1	0	1	.161
3.04	116	75	30	20	26	7	0	0	1	.308
2.78	131	77	30	15	28	2	0	0	0	.07
3.12	51	36	15	9	14	2	2	0	1	.357
3.06	29	19	7	6	7	1	0	0	0	.143
3.09	127	88	30	20	29	5	2	0	0	.241
3.11	**859**	**547**	**216**	**130**	**198**	**29**	**7**	**0**	**6**	**.212**
3.04	135	72	33	16	26	1	2	0	0	.115
3.23	87	50	22	11	19	4	1	0	2	.368
3.32	38	24	10	8	9	3	0	0	0	.333
3.46	107	69	31	21	27	6	1	1	0	.296
3.41	26	17	6	3	6	0	0	0	0	.000
3.27	125	84	36	18	35	5	2	0	0	.200
3.20	139	87	34	15	33	5	1	0	0	.182
3.19	111	67	29	15	24	6	2	0	0	.333
3.45	**768**	**470**	**201**	**107**	**179**	**30**	**9**	**1**	**2**	**.235**
3.27	113	66	28	15	25	2	0	0	2	.160
3.32	97	61	25	14	24	6	1	0	1	.333
3.41	128	82	31	17	27	6	1	0	1	.296
3.64	69	44	18	13	16	5	1	0	2	.500
3.57	132	80	37	14	30	3	1	0	1	.167
3.41	136	79	34	24	29	2	0	0	0	.069
4.35	**675**	**412**	**173**	**97**	**151**	**24**	**4**	**0**	**7**	**.232**
3.39	85	67	29	23	28	5	1	0	1	.250
3.52	106	64	25	12	23	3	2	0	3	.348
3.61	37	22	9	4	8	1	0	0	1	.250
3.83	45	30	11	9	10	3	0	1	1	.500
3.72	133	84	34	23	31	4	0	0	1	.161
3.73	34	21	10	5	10	4	0	0	0	.400
3.60	205	128	50	23	44	6	0	0	1	.159
3.63	60	32	16	9	12	4	0	0	0	.333
3.52	115	74	30	18	26	2	1	0	0	.115
3.96	**820**	**522**	**214**	**126**	**192**	**32**	**4**	**1**	**8**	**.234**
3.52	**4,181**	**2,628**	**1,068**	**619**	**954**	**148**	**31**	**6**	**27**	**.222**
		62.9%	Strikes	58.0%	1st pitch K					

1962

Date	Loc	Opp	Result	Innings	Decision	IP	H	R	ER	BB	SO	HBP
Apr 11		CIN	W,6–2	CG	W(1–0)	9	4	2	2	3	7	0
Apr 15		MLN	L,3–6	GS-7	L(1–1)	6.333	8	5	4	3	7	0
Apr 19	@	CIN	W,4–3	GS-8	W(2–1)	7.667	7	3	3	3	9	0
Apr 24	@	CHC	W,10–2	CG	W(3–1)	9	6	2	2	4	18	0
Apr 28		PIT	W,2–1	CG	W(4–1)	9	6	1	1	1	6	0
				April	**4–1**	**41**	**31**	**13**	**12**	**14**	**47**	**0**
May 2		CHC	L,1–3	GS-7	L(4–2)	6.333	8	3	1	1	8	0
May 8	@	HOU	W,9–6	GS-6		5.667	7	4	2	2	8	1
May 12	@	STL	L,5–6	GS-6		6	9	4	3	0	7	0
May 17		HOU	W,5–4	GS-6		6	8	4	4	1	4	1
May 21		SFG	W,8–1	CG	W(5–2)	9	5	1	1	1	10	0
May 26		PHI	W,6–3	CG	W(6–2)	9	5	3	2	2	16	0
May 30(1)	@	NYM	W,13–6	CG	W(7–2)	9	13	6	6	3	10	0
				May	**3–1**	**51**	**55**	**25**	**19**	**10**	**63**	**2**
Jun 4	@	PHI	W,6–3	CG	W(8–2)	9	3	3	3	2	13	0
Jun 5 susp	@	PIT	W,8–3	9-GF	S(1)	1	0	0	0	0	2	0
Jun 8	@	HOU	W,4–3	GS-6		5.333	2	2	2	3	6	0
Jun 13	@	MLN	W,2–1	CG	W(9–2)	9	3	1	1	2	6	0
Jun 18		STL	W,1–0	SHO	W(10–2)	9	5	0	0	0	9	0
Jun 22		CIN	L,3–4	GS-8	L(10–3)	8	5	2	1	3	11	0
Jun 26		MLN	L,1–2	GS-8	L(10–4)	8	6	2	1	1	13	0
Jun 30		NYM	W,5–0	SHO	W(11–4)	9	0	0	0	5	13	0
				June	**4–2**	**58.333**	**24**	**10**	**8**	**16**	**73**	**0**
Jul 4(1)		PHI	W,16–1	CG	W(12–4)	9	5	1	1	3	10	0
Jul 8	@	SFG	W,2–0	GS-9	W(13–4)	8.333	3	0	0	3	9	0
Jul 12	@	NYM	W,3–0	GS-7	W(14–4)	7	3	0	0	3	6	0
Jul 17	@	CIN	L,5–7	GS-1	L(14–5)	1	3	2	2	0	1	0
				July	**3–1**	**25.333**	**14**	**3**	**3**	**9**	**26**	**0**
Sep 21	@	STL	L,2–11	GS-1	L(14–6)	0.667	1	4	4	4	1	0
Sep 23	@	STL	L,2–12	7-GF(8)		2	2	1	1	3	2	0
Sep 27		HOU	L,6–8	GS-5		5	3	2	2	1	4	0
				September	**0–1**	**7.667**	**6**	**7**	**7**	**8**	**7**	**0**
Oct 1	@	SFG	L,0–8	GS-2	L(14–7)	1	4	3	3	0	0	0
				October	**0–1**	**1**	**4**	**3**	**3**	**0**	**0**	**0**
				Year	**14–7**	**184.333**	**134**	**61**	**52**	**57**	**216**	**2**

ERA	Pitches	Strikes	Batters	1st pitch K	AB	1B	2B	3B	HR	AVG
2	124	77	34	20	31	2	2	0	0	.129
3.52	98	66	32	21	27	6	1	0	1	.296
3.52	125	77	32	16	29	7	0	0	0	.241
3.09	143	95	36	24	32	3	2	0	1	.188
2.63	144	92	33	21	32	5	1	0	0	.188
2.63	**634**	**407**	**167**	**102**	**151**	**23**	**6**	**0**	**2**	**.205**
2.47	92	61	27	12	25	6	2	0	0	.320
2.55	104	61	27	14	24	5	1	1	0	.292
2.75	102	72	27	18	27	8	1	0	0	.333
3.05	99	61	28	14	25	7	0	0	1	.320
2.8	127	89	33	21	32	4	0	0	1	.156
2.71	132	89	35	20	33	2	2	0	1	.152
3.03	159	99	43	24	40	10	2	0	1	.325
3.35	**815**	**532**	**220**	**123**	**206**	**42**	**8**	**1**	**4**	**.267**
3.03	131	88	33	25	31	2	0	0	1	.097
3	11	7	3	1	3	0	0	0	0	.000
3.02	93	55	22	7	19	2	0	0	0	.105
2.86	123	73	32	19	30	2	0	0	1	.100
2.66	122	83	31	17	31	5	0	0	0	.161
2.56	143	85	32	16	29	3	2	0	0	.172
2.48	116	77	31	17	29	5	1	0	0	.207
2.33	138	80	30	15	25	0	0	0	0	.000
1.23	**877**	**548**	**214**	**117**	**197**	**19**	**3**	**0**	**2**	**.122**
2.26	150	96	35	21	32	2	2	0	1	.156
2.15	136	85	30	15	27	3	0	0	0	.111
2.06	104	68	28	17	25	2	1	0	0	.120
2.15	25	16	6	3	6	2	1	0	0	.500
1.07	**415**	**265**	**99**	**56**	**90**	**9**	**4**	**0**	**1**	**.156**
2.35	33	13	7	3	3	0	0	0	1	.333
2.37	47	24	11	4	8	2	0	0	0	.250
2.41	74	46	19	9	18	2	0	0	1	.167
8.22	**154**	**83**	**37**	**16**	**29**	**4**	**0**	**0**	**2**	**.207**
2.54	30	18	7	1	7	1	1	0	2	.571
27.00	**30**	**18**	**7**	**1**	**7**	**1**	**1**	**0**	**2**	**.571**
2.54	**2,925**	**1,853**	**744**	**415**	**680**	**98**	**22**	**1**	**13**	**.197**

63.4% Strikes   **55.8% 1st pitch K**

1963

Date	Loc	Opp	Result	Innings	Decision	IP	H	R	ER	BB	SO	HBP
Apr 10	@	CHC	W,2–1	CG	W(1–0)	9	5	1	1	2	10	0
Apr 14	@	HOU	L,4–5	GS-6	L(1–1)	5.333	6	5	4	2	4	0
Apr 19		HOU	W,2–0	SHO	W(2–1)	9	2	0	0	2	14	0
Apr 23		MLN	2–1	GS-7		6.667	2	0	0	2	5	0
April					**2–1**	**30**	**15**	**6**	**5**	**8**	**33**	**0**
May 7	@	STL	W,11–1	GS-8	W(3–1)	8	5	1	1	1	5	0
May 11		SFG	W,8–0	SHO	W(4–1)	9	0	0	0	2	4	0
May 15		PHI	W,3–2	CG(12)	W(5–1)	12	11	2	2	0	12	0
May 19(1)		NYM	W,1–0	SHO	W(6–1)	9	2	0	0	1	5	0
May 24	@	SFG	L,1–7	GS-1	L(6–2)	0.333	5	5	5	2	1	0
May 28	@	MLN	W,7–0	SHO	W(7–2)	9	6	0	0	2	8	0
May					**5–1**	**47.333**	**29**	**8**	**8**	**8**	**35**	**0**
Jun 1	@	CIN	L,0–1	GS-7	L(7–3)	7	3	1	1	1	10	0
Jun 5	@	HOU	W,5–1	CG	W(8–3)	9	8	1	1	2	8	0
Jun 9	@	CHC	W,11–8	GS-5		4.667	8	6	6	1	6	0
Jun 13		HOU	W,3–0	SHO	W(9–3)	9	3	0	0	2	10	1
Jun 17	@	SFG	W,2–0	SHO	W(10–3)	9	4	0	0	4	9	0
Jun 21	@	STL	W,5–3	GS-9	W(11–3)	8.667	6	3	3	3	9	0
Jun 25	@	CIN	W,4–1	CG	W(12–3)	9	6	1	1	3	9	0
Jun 29		MLN	W,6–5	GS-5		4.667	8	5	5	1	8	0
June					**5–1**	**61.001**	**46**	**17**	**17**	**17**	**69**	**1**
Jul 3		STL	W,5–0	SHO	W(13–3)	9	3	0	0	0	9	0
Jul 7(1)		CIN	W,4–0	SHO	W(14–3)	9	3	0	0	1	4	0
Jul 12	@	NYM	W,6–0	SHO	W(15–3)	9	3	0	0	1	13	0
Jul 16(1)	@	PHI	W,5–2	CG	W(16–3)	9	6	2	2	0	7	0
Jul 20	@	MLN	W,5–4	GS-6		5.333	8	3	3	2	6	0
Jul 25		PIT	L,2–6	GS-6	L(16–4)	6	8	4	4	1	12	0
Jul 29		PHI	W,6–2	CG	W(17–4)	9	5	2	2	4	7	0
July					**5–1**	**56.333**	**36**	**11**	**11**	**9**	**58**	**0**
Aug 3	@	HOU	W,2–0	SHO	W(18–4)	9	3	0	0	0	4	0
Aug 7	@	CHC	W,3–1	GS-10		9.333	7	1	1	3	11	0
Aug 11	@	CIN	L,4–9	GS-6	L(18–5)	5.333	9	5	5	1	4	0
Aug 15	@	MLN	W,7–5	GS-1		0.333	4	4	4	0	0	0
Aug 17	@	NYM	W,3–2	GS-9	W(19–5)	8	6	2	1	2	9	0
Aug 21		STL	W,2–1	GS-12		12	9	1	1	2	10	0
Aug 25		MLN	W,2–1	GS-9		8.667	5	1	1	2	6	1
Aug 29		SFG	W,11–1	CG	W(20–5)	9	3	1	1	1	7	0
August					**3–1**	**61.666**	**46**	**15**	**14**	**11**	**51**	**1**

ERA	Pitches	Strikes	Batters	1st pitch K	AB	1B	2B	3B	HR	AVG
1.00	159	107	35	21	33	5	0	0	0	.152
3.14	96	64	25	20	22	5	1	0	0	.273
1.93	123	84	31	22	29	2	0	0	0	.069
1.50	95	60	24	14	22	2	0	0	0	.091
1.50	**473**	**315**	**115**	**77**	**106**	**14**	**1**	**0**	**0**	**.142**
1.42	101	63	32	17	31	4	0	0	1	.161
1.15	111	72	28	14	26	0	0	0	0	.000
1.22	164	118	47	32	45	10	1	0	0	.244
1.06	119	79	30	18	29	2	0	0	0	.069
1.71	25	14	8	5	6	3	1	0	1	.833
1.51	111	74	34	19	32	6	0	0	0	.188
1.52	**631**	**420**	**179**	**105**	**169**	**25**	**2**	**0**	**2**	**.172**
1.49	113	72	25	12	24	2	1	0	0	.125
1.45	137	92	36	23	33	5	2	1	0	.242
1.93	71	49	23	18	22	1	4	0	3	.364
1.77	121	80	32	19	28	2	0	1	0	.107
1.63	138	94	35	19	31	4	0	0	0	.129
1.73	138	95	36	20	33	5	0	0	1	.182
1.68	129	86	36	20	32	5	0	1	0	.188
1.95	73	51	23	14	21	4	3	0	1	.381
2.51	**920**	**619**	**246**	**145**	**224**	**28**	**10**	**3**	**5**	**.205**
1.83	123	85	29	20	29	3	0	0	0	.103
1.73	99	67	31	18	30	3	0	0	0	.100
1.63	129	92	31	18	30	2	0	1	0	.100
1.65	108	76	33	22	32	2	4	0	0	.188
1.75	86	61	26	17	24	5	0	2	1	.333
1.89	100	67	27	22	26	7	0	0	1	.308
1.9	138	88	36	25	32	4	1	0	0	.156
1.76	**783**	**536**	**213**	**142**	**203**	**26**	**5**	**3**	**2**	**.177**
1.81	122	80	31	13	31	3	0	0	0	.097
1.77	141	99	38	23	34	7	0	0	0	.206
1.94	79	57	26	14	25	6	1	0	2	.360
2.1	16	12	5	4	5	3	0	0	1	.800
2.06	118	82	31	19	29	5	0	0	1	.207
2	165	104	47	24	45	8	1	0	0	.200
1.96	117	85	33	24	28	3	2	0	0	.179
1.93	108	74	31	23	30	2	0	0	1	.100
2.04	**866**	**593**	**242**	**144**	**227**	**37**	**4**	**0**	**5**	**.203**

1963

DATE	LOC	OPP	RESULT	INNINGS	DECISION	IP	H	R	ER	BB	SO	HBP
Sep 2(1)		HOU	W,7–3	CG	W(21–5)	9	7	3	3	0	13	0
Sep 6	@	SFG	W,5–2	GS-8	W(22–5)	8	9	2	2	2	8	0
Sep 10	@	PIT	W,4–2	CG	W(23–5)	9	6	2	1	0	9	0
Sep 13(1)	@	PHI	L,2–3	GS-7		7	4	1	1	1	8	0
Sep 17	@	STL	W,4–0	SHO	W(24–5)	9	4	0	0	0	4	1
Sep 21		PIT	W,5–3	GS-8		7.667	8	3	3	2	10	0
Sep 25		NYM	W,1–0	GS-5	W(25–5)	5	4	0	0	0	8	0
				September	**5–0**	**54.667**	**42**	**11**	**10**	**5**	**60**	**1**
				Year	**25–5**	**311**	**214**	**68**	**65**	**58**	**306**	**3**

ERA	Pitches	Strikes	Batters	1st pitch K	AB	1B	2B	3B	HR	AVG
1.97	125	92	36	25	36	5	1	0	1	.194
1.98	136	90	34	21	32	5	3	0	1	.281
1.94	132	85	34	17	33	5	0	0	1	.182
1.93	102	71	26	14	24	2	2	0	0	.167
1.87	86	66	33	23	31	4	0	0	0	.129
1.91	134	86	33	18	31	7	0	0	1	.258
1.88	66	53	19	14	19	4	0	0	0	.211
1.65	781	543	215	132	206	32	6	0	4	.204
1.88	4,454	3,026	1,210	745	1,135	162	28	6	18	.189

67.9% Strikes   61.6% 1st pitch K

Chapter Notes

Prologue

1. Brian Endsley, *Bums No More: The 1959 Los Angeles Dodgers, World Champions of Baseball* (Jefferson: McFarland, 2009), 158.
2. Bob Hunter, "Buzzie Will Buzz Three A.L. Clubs," *The Sporting News*, November 18, 1959, 2.
3. Robert Burnes, "Majors Toe Mark for Inter-Loop Swaps," *The Sporting News*, November 18, 1959, 2.
4. Shirley Povich, "Scouts Tips Sold Nats on Nabbing Lees," *The Sporting News*, December 9, 1959, 19.
5. Bob Hunter, "Buzzie Chills Sievers Swap When Nats Get Hot on Lillis," *The Sporting News*, December 16, 1959, 8.
6. Oscar Kahan, "Bargain Hunters Baffled," *The Sporting News*, December 16, 1959, 7.
7. Shirley Povich, "Nats Plug 2 Holes with Pair of Swaps," *The Sporting News*, April 13, 1960, 10.

Chapter One

1. Bob Hunter, "1,200 Serenade Dodgers at L.A. Writers," *The Sporting News*, April 20, 1960, 11.
2. Bob Hunter, "Fast-dealing Bavasi Shuffles Dodgers to Flag-fighting Size," *The Sporting News*, April 20, 1960, 11.
3. Clifton Daniel, ed., *The 20th Century Day by Day* (New York: DK, 1999), 844.
4. Michael Gavin, "A Whole Family Goes to the Mound," *Baseball Digest*, June 1955, 30.
5. Ibid., 31.
6. Ibid.
7. Frank Finch, "Roebuck Put on Retired List in Six-Player L.A. Shuffle," *The Sporting News*, August 6, 1958, 8.
8. Bob Hunter, "Roebuck's Dead Arm Rated No. 1 Rally-Killer," *The Sporting News*, January 11, 1961, 5.
9. Ibid.
10. Ibid., 18.
11. Ibid.
12. Ibid.
13. Ibid.
14. Art Ryon, "Thousands Cheer Parading Players During Civic Salute to Champions," *Los Angeles Times*, April 13, 1960.
15. Ibid.
16. Frank Finch, "FINCH PICKS BRAVES FIRST," *Los Angeles Times*, April 10, 1960.
17. Art Ryon, "Thousands Cheer Parading Players During Civic Salute to Champions," *Los Angeles Times*, April 13, 1960.
18. Paul Zimmerman, "Dodgers Win Opener Before 67,550," *Los Angeles Times*, April 13, 1960.
19. Don Drysdale and Bob Verdi, *Once a Bum, Always a Dodger* (New York: St. Martin's Press, 1990), 18.
20. Ibid., 23.
21. Ibid., 44.
22. Frank Finch, "ESSEGIAN'S HOMER IN 11TH BEATS CUBS," *Los Angeles Times*, April 13, 1960.
23. Bob Hunter, "Shortstop Battle Spices Dodger Training Tilts," *The Sporting News*, March 23, 1960, 7.
24. Frank Finch, "ESSEGIAN'S HOMER IN 11TH BEATS CUBS."
25. Paul Zimmerman, "Dodgers Win Opener Before 67,550."
26. Ibid.

27. Frederick G. Lieb, "Powerful N.L. Looks for Banner Year," *The Sporting News*, April 6, 1960, 1.

28. United Press International, "President Closes a Career as Opening-Day Pitch," *New York Times*, April 19, 1960.

29. Bob Addie, "Pascual and Pals Rock Bosox in Opener," *Washington Post*, April 19, 1960.

30. Associated Press, "Eisenhower and Nixon Root Williams Around," *New York Times*, April 19, 1960.

31. Shirley Povich, "This Morning with Shirley Povich," *Washington Post*, April 19, 1960.

32. Phil Casey, "He Makes It Four Wins," *Washington Post*, 4–19–60.

33. Frank Finch, "Cincy Wins on Dodger Errors," *Los Angeles Times*, May 3, 1960.

34. Harry Keck, "FAT-FREE BUCS GREASE PLANK FOR RIVALS," *The Sporting News*, May 11, 1960, 1–2.

35. Robert A. Rosenbaum, *The Penguin Encyclopedia of American History* (New York: Penguin Reference, 2003), 392.

36. Daniel, *The 20th Century Day by Day*, 84.

Chapter Two

1. F. Scott Fitzgerald, *The Last Tycoon* (New York: Scribner's, 1941), 176.

2. Frank Finch, "Roger Craig Optimistic, Eager to Start," *Los Angeles Times*, June 19, 1959.

3. Frank Finch, "Cincy Wins on Dodger Errors."

4. Ibid.

5. Bob Hunter, "Craig Out for Two Months After Collision with Pinson," *The Sporting News*, May 11, 1960, 19.

6. Edward Gruver, *Koufax*. (Dallas: Taylor Publishing, 2000), 123.

7. Sandy Koufax and Ed Linn, *Koufax* (New York: Viking Press, 1966), 144.

8. Ibid.

9. Frank Finch, "DODGERS RECALL FRANK HOWARD," *Los Angeles Times*, May 13, 1960.

10. Paul Zimmerman, "Furillo, Dodgers Part on Sour Note," *Los Angeles Times*, May 18, 1960.

11. Roger Kahn, *The Boys of Summer* (New York: Harper & Row, 1972), 333.

12. Don Drysdale and Bob Verdi, *Once a Bum, Always a Dodger*, 116.

13. Bob Hunter, "Muscle Injury Casts Doubt on Future of Veteran Furillo," *The Sporting News*, April 13, 1960, 11.

14. Charlie Park, "This Howard Has 50 Coat, Bat to Match," *Baseball Digest*, March 1961, 57.

15. The Website of South High School, http://www.southbulldogs.com.

16. Tom Murphy, "Modest Howard Brash Belter as L.A. Farmhand," *The Sporting News*, June 18, 1958, 38.

17. Charlie Park, "This Howard Has 50 Coat, Bat to Match," 57.

18. Ibid., 58.

19. Frank Finch, "Dodgers Send Howard, Fairly to Farm Clubs," April 12, 1960.

20. Paul Zimmerman, "Furillo, Dodgers Part on Sour Note."

21. Edgar Munzel, "For Shame!" *The Sporting News*, June 1, 1960, 14.

22. Paul Zimmerman, "Furillo, Dodgers Part on Sour Note."

23. Roger Kahn, *The Boys of Summer*, 336.

24. Frank Finch, "Dodgers Stun Braves, 6–4, on Howard Grand-Slammer," *Los Angeles Times*, May 18, 1960.

25. Bob Hunter, "Howitzer Howard Puts Hefty Charge in Dodger Attack," *The Sporting News*, May 25, 1960, 16.

26. Jane Leavy, *Sandy Koufax: A Lefty's Legacy* (New York: HarperCollins, 2002), 28–29.

27. Ibid., 30.

28. Ibid., 38.

29. Ibid., 49–50.

30. Bob Hunter, "Dodgers Weed Out Vets— Clear Decks for Kid Stars," *The Sporting News*, October 26, 1960, 20.

31. Jane Leavy, *Sandy Koufax: A Lefty's Legacy*, 56.

32. Ibid.

33. Don Drysdale and Bob Verdi, *Once a Bum, Always a Dodger*, 136.

34. Bill Fleischmann, "Many Veterans Included in Majors' Cut-Down," *The Sporting News*, May 21, 1958, 7.

35. Jane Leavy, *Sandy Koufax: A Lefty's Legacy*, 92.

36. Frank Finch, "KOUFAX'S ONE-HITTER BLANKS BUCS, 1–0," *Los Angeles Times*, May 24, 1960.

37. Ibid.

38. Ibid.

Chapter Three

1. Frank Finch, "Burning Alston Roasts Dodgers," *Los Angeles Times*, June 23, 1960.

2. Frank Finch, "Listless Dodgers Absorb 6–4 Beating from Cincy," *Los Angeles Times*, June 22, 1960.

3. Paul Zimmerman, *The Los Angeles Dodgers* (New York: Coward-McCann, 1960), 121.

4. Ibid., 121.

5. Bob Hunter, "Smokey Locks Doors, Takes Cut at Ragged Dodger Play," *The Sporting News*, June 29, 1960, 6.

6. Frank Finch, "Burning Alston Roasts Dodgers," *Los Angeles Times*, June 23, 1960.

7. Ibid.

8. Ibid.

9. Arthur M. Schlesinger, Jr., *A Thousand Days* (Boston: Houghton Mifflin, 1965), 39.

10. Ibid., 56.

11. Ibid., 60–61.

12. Frank Finch, "Dodgers Win Fog-Delayed Game, 5–3," *Los Angeles Times*, July 16, 1960.

13. Dave Anderson, "The Dodgers' Tommy Gun," *Baseball Digest*, January 1963, 31.

14. Bob Hunter, "Mom Made Big Decisions—Steered Tommy to Dodgers," *The Sporting News*, March 28, 1962, 9.

15. Ibid.

16. Oscar Kahn, "Kids Shine on Every Club in Big Time," *The Sporting News*, April 13, 1962, 14.

17. Frank Finch, "DAVIS' HOMER IN THE 11TH BEATS BUCS, 7–5," *Los Angeles Times*, July 21, 1960.

18. Bob Hunter, "Handcuffed Hitters Bust Loose, Dodgers Out of Doldrums," *The Sporting News*, July 13, 1960, 26.

19. Buzzie Bavasi and John Strege, *Off the Record* (New York: Chicago: Contemporary Books, 1987), 96.

20. Frank Finch, "Dodgers Trade Lillis for Spokane Shortstop Wills," *Los Angeles Times*, June 2, 1959.

21. Frank Finch, "Maury Wills from Spokane Joins L.A.," *Los Angeles Times*, June 6, 1959.

22. Buzzie Bavasi and John Strege, *Off the Record*, 96.

23. Charlie Park, "The Versatile Maury Wills," *Baseball Digest*, February 1962, 35.

24. Zimmerman, *Dodgers*, 143.

25. Ibid., 140.

26. Bob Hunter, "Shortstop Battle Spices Dodger Training Tilts," *The Sporting News*, March 23, 1960, 7.

27. Bob Hunter, "Base Burglar Wills Preparing to Swipe Mays' Theft Crown," *The Sporting News*, August 17, 1960, 17.

28. Oscar Kahan, "Groat Third Buc Shortstop to Cop Bat Title," *The Sporting News*, December 21, 1960, 19.

Chapter Four

1. Les Biederman, "'Profit' Bragan Labeled Bucs 'Team of Destiny' Back in June," *The Sporting News*, October 26, 1960, 14.

2. Rick Cushing, *1960 Pittsburgh Pirates, Day by Day* (Pittsburgh: Dorrance Publishing, 2010), 377.

3. Arthur Daley, "Sports of the Times," *New York Times*, May 1, 1961.

4. Bob Hunter, "Dodgers Wheel Out Flashy Youngsters," *The Sporting News*, September 14, 1960, 8.

5. Bob Hunter, "Willie Nixed Track Career," *The Sporting News*, March 28, 1962, 9.

6. Bob Hunter, "Fast-Stepping Davises—Dodger Jet Jobs," *The Sporting News*, March 28, 1962, 9.

7. Ibid.

8. Frank Finch, "Rookies Star in 7–4 Dodger Win," *Los Angeles Times*, September 9, 1960.

9. Ibid.

10. Frank Finch, "Cardinal Pitchers End Reign of Dodgers, 1–0," *Los Angeles Times*, May 24, 1960.

11. Bob Hunter, "Dodgers Wheel Out Flashy Youngsters, Size Up Coast Pair," *The Sporting News*, September 4, 1960, 8.

12. Frank Finch, "DUMBO—The Dodgers' Newest Star," *Baseball Digest*, October 1958, 25.

13. Frank Finch, "Larker Big Blaster with Borrowed Bats," *The Sporting News*, October 12, 1960, 3.

14. Frank Finch, "Larker Big Blaster with Borrowed Bats."

15. Don Drysdale and Bob Verdi, *Once a Bum, Always a Dodger*, 98.

16. Ibid.

17. Ibid.

18. John Kuenster, "Milwaukee's Return to the National League Revives Fond Memories," *Baseball Digest*, March 1998, 21.

19. Jerry Holzman, "Fiber of the Pirates," *Baseball Digest*, October 1960, 23–24.

20. Tim Horgan, "How Bucs Beat Senators to Groat," *Baseball Digest*, April 1961, 38.

21. Les Biederman, "Dick Groat's First Big Time Hit Sets off Wild Rhubarb," *The Sporting News*, June 25, 1952, 21.

22. Jerry Holzman, "Fiber of the Pirates," 28.

23. Ibid., 29.

24. Les Biederman, "Swap Groat? Very Thought Jars Buc Fans," *The Sporting News*, January 13, 1960, 20.

25. Jerry Holzman, "Fiber of the Pirates," 24.

26. Bob Hunter, "Bavasi, Alston Start Desperate Search for Slugger at Series," *The Sporting News*, October 5, 1960, 42.

27. Bob Hunter, "Dodgers Set Trap Early, Hoping to Land Big Belter," *The Sporting News*, September 28, 1960, 20.

28. Bob Hunter, "Red-Hot Dodgers Stomp and Fidget at All-Star Break," *The Sporting News*, July 20, 1960, 12.

29. Bob Hunter, "Bad News for N.L. Hurlers—Snider's Knee Improved," *The Sporting News*, April 20, 1960, 11.

30. Theodore H. White, *The Making of the President 1960* (New York: Atheneum, 1961), 323.

31. Robert A. Rosenbaum, *The Penguin Encyclopedia of American History* (New York: Penguin Reference, 2003), 294.

32. Sandy Koufax and Ed Linn, *Koufax* (New York: Viking Press, 1966), 142.

33. Ibid., 143

34. Sandy Koufax and Ed Linn, *Koufax*, 147.

35. Edward Gruver, *Koufax*, 124.

36. Sandy Koufax and Ed Linn, *Koufax*, 147.

37. Edward Gruver, *Koufax*, 124.

38. Sandy Koufax and Ed Linn, *Koufax*, 147.

Chapter Five

1. Frank Finch, "Lippy Officially Back in Dodger Camp as Coach," *Los Angeles Times*, January 10, 1961.
2. Leo Durocher and Ed Linn, *Nice Guys Finish Last* (New York: Simon & Schuster, 1975), 27.
3. Ibid., 30–32.
4. Ibid., 36–36.
5. Ibid., 42.
6. Ibid., 63.
7. Ibid., 114.
8. Ibid., 260.
9. Ibid., 317.
10. Frank Finch, "Lippy Officially Back in Dodger Camp as Coach."
11. Ibid.
12. Ibid.
13. Ibid.
14. Robert T. Hartmann, "Kennedy Urges New Quest for Peace," *New York Times*, January 21, 1961.

Chapter Six

1. Merriam-Webster's Collegiate Dictionary, 11th ed., s.v. "control."
2. Bob Hunter, "Wary Skipper Walt Warns of Pitfalls for Dodger Bandwagon," *The Sporting News*, April 12, 1961, 14.
3. Sandy Koufax and Ed Linn, *Koufax*, 148.
4. Walter Bingham, "Dodgers in Mufti," *Sports Illustrated*, August 15, 1960, 1.
5. Ibid., 149.
6. Sandy Koufax and Ed Linn, *Koufax*, 148.
7. Edward Gruver, *Koufax*, 125.
8. Jane Leavy, *Sandy Koufax: A Lefty's Legacy*, 102.
9. Edward Gruver, *Koufax*, 125.
10. Jane Leavy, *Sandy Koufax: A Lefty's Legacy*, 102.
11. Jane Leavy, *Sandy Koufax: A Lefty's Legacy*, 102.
12. Edward Gruver, *Koufax*, 125.
13. Edward Gruver, *Koufax*, 126.
14. Sandy Koufax and Ed Linn, *Koufax*, 150.
15. Sandy Koufax and Ed Linn, *Koufax*, 154.
16. Ibid.
17. Sandy Koufax and Ed Linn, *Koufax*, 156.
18. Bob Hunter, "Wary Skipper Walt Warns of Pitfalls for Dodger Bandwagon," *The Sporting News*, April 12, 1961, 14.

Chapter Seven

1. Sandy Koufax and Ed Linn, *Koufax*, 157.
2. Bob Hunter, "Wary Skipper Walt Warns of Pitfalls for Dodger Bandwagon," *The Sporting News*, April 12, 1961, 14.

3. Bob Hunter, "Roebuck on the Disabled List," *The Sporting News*, April 12, 1961, 14.
4. Ibid.
5. Shirley Povich, "Kennedy Sets Presidential Mark with Fireball Pitch," *The Sporting News*, April 19, 1961, 3.
6. W.H. Lawrence, "Right-Hander Kennedy Opens the Baseball Season," *New York Times*, April 11, 1961.
7. Frank Finch, "50,665 SEE DODGERS WIN OPENER, 6–2," *Los Angeles Times*, April 12, 1961.
8. Al Wolf, "Sherry Appears in 1959 Form—Alston," *Los Angeles Times*, April 12, 1961.
9. United Press International, "Yuri Gagarin, a Major Makes the Flight in 5-Ton Vehicle Russians Succeed," *New York Times*, April 12, 1961.
10. http://baseballhall.org/hof/conlan-jocko.
11. Durocher and Linn, *Nice Guys Finish Last*, 162.
12. Ibid.
13. Frank Finch, "'LEO THE TOE' LOSES KICKING DUEL," *Los Angeles Times*, April 17, 1961.
14. Frank Finch, "Lip Draws Three-Day Ban for Kicking Duel," *Los Angeles Times*, April 17, 1961.
15. Bob Hunter, "Slumps, Bumps Slow Dodgers' Swifties in Jump from Barrier," *The Sporting News*, April 26, 1961, 17.
16. Daniel, ed., *The 20th Century Day by Day*.
17. Rosenbaum, *The Penguin Encyclopedia of American History*, 32.
18. Edgar Munzel, "Scrappy Zim Fires Up Cubs at Hot Corner," *The Sporting News*, April 20, 1961, 29.
19. Bob Hunter, "Ron Idolized Yankees but Signed $21,000 Cub Pact," *The Sporting News*, June 29, 1963, 4.
20. Bob Hunter, "Ex-Spartan Sparkers Sponge Up Relief Honors," *The Sporting News*, June 29, 1963, 3.
21. Frank Finch, "KOUFAX BEATS REDS, 5–3; MOON HOMERS Wally's Blow No. 7—Sandy Steals Show," *Los Angeles Times*, April 22, 1961.
22. Frank Finch, DODGERS WIN, 2–1, THEN LOSE, 10–5, May 1, 1961.

Chapter Eight

1. Bill Becker, "Scatter-Arm Koufax Finds Plate," *New York Times*, June 11, 1961.
2. Taylor Branch, *The King Years: Historic Moments in the Civil Rights Movement* (New York: Simon & Schuster, 2013), 24.
3. Ibid., 34.
4. Bob Gibson and Ed Phil Pepe, *From Ghetto to Glory: The Story of Bob Gibson* (Englewood Cliffs: Prentice Hall, 1968), 13.
5. Ibid., 22.
6. Frank Finch, "Koufax Hurls 3-Hit, 1–0 Dodger Victory," *Los Angeles Times*, May 26, 1961.
7. Taylor Branch, *Parting the Waters: America*

in the King Years 1954–63 (New York: Simon & Schuster, 1988), 477.

8. Frank Finch, "Koufax Fans 13; Dodgers Win, 2–1," *Los Angeles Times*, May 30, 1961.

9. Frank Finch, "Spencer's Homer Punch Flattens Giants in 9th, 4–3," *Los Angeles Times*, June 4, 1961.

10. Nathan Thrall and Jessie James Wilkens, "Kennedy Talked, Khrushchev Triumphed," *New York Times*, May 22, 2008.

11. Frank Finch, "DODGERS WIN, 6–3—KOUFAX SPARKLES FOR SIXTH IN ROW," *Los Angeles Times*, June 12, 1961.

12. Al Wolf, "Lew Hit 'Perfect Pitch' Out of Park," *Los Angeles Times*, June 17, 1961.

13. Sandy Koufax and Ed Linn, *Koufax* (New York: Viking Press, 1966), 158.

14. Frank Finch, "KOUFAX FANS 14 CUBS IN 2-HIT, 3–0 WIN," *Los Angeles Times*, June 21, 1961.

15. Frank Finch, "Reds Top Dodgers in 9th," *Los Angeles Times*, June 24, 1961.

16. Frank Finch, "Dodgers' Homers in 9th Beat Reds," *Los Angeles Times*, June 25, 1961.

17. Frank Finch, "BUCS RALLY TO CHASE DODGERS, 4–2," *Los Angeles Times*, June 30, 1961.

18. Frank Finch, "Willie Runs Wild; Dodgers Beat Phils," *Los Angeles Times*, July 1, 1961.

19. Frank Finch, "Koufax Nabs 11th with Three Hitter," *Los Angeles Times*, July 4, 1961.

20. Tom Adelman, *Black and Blue: Sandy Koufax, the Robinson Boys, and the World Series That Stunned America* (New York: Little, Brown, 2006), 3.

21. Frank Robinson and Al Silverman, *My Life Is Baseball* (Garden City: Doubleday, 1968), 34.

22. Ibid., 4.

23. Ibid.

24. Steve Jacobson, *Carrying Jackie's Torch: The Players Who Integrated Baseball—and America* (Chicago: Lawrence Hill Books, 2007), 142.

25. Ibid., 5.

26. Frank Finch, "Reds Go on Rampage, 14–3, and Drysdale Follows Suit," *Los Angeles Times*, July 10, 1961.

27. C.C. Johnson Spink, "Writers Back Frick's Homer Decision," *The Sporting News*, August 2, 1961, 1.

28. Frank Finch, "Dodgers Win, Back on Top," *Los Angeles Times*, July 30, 1961.

Chapter Nine

1. Frank Finch, "Tail-Spinning Dodgers Invade Cincinnati," *Los Angeles Times*, August 25, 1961.

2. Frank Finch, "DODGERS CLOUT CARDS, 8–0; 6TH IN ROW," *Los Angeles Times*, August 14, 1961.

3. Frank Finch, "Dodgers Lack One Big Gunner," *Los Angeles Times*, August 14, 1961.

4. Daniel, *The 20th Century Day by Day*, 870.

5. Frank Finch, "REDS CHASE KOUFAX, BEAT DODGERS, 5–2," *Los Angeles Times*, August 16, 1961.

6. Frank Finch, "REDS SWEEP, TAKE LEAD BEFORE 75,364," *Los Angeles Times*, August 17, 1961.

7. Ibid.

8. Frank Finch, "Bavasi Absolves Alston of Blame for Dodgers' Disastrous Tailspin," *Los Angeles Times*, August 25, 1961.

9. Bob Hunter, "Dodger Flag Dream Wrapped Up in Stout Left Wing of Koufax," *The Sporting News*, December 13, 1961, 20.

10. Frank Finch, "Dodgers Rout Reds, 7–2, to End Slump," *Los Angeles Times*, August 25, 1961.

11. Frank Finch, "Reds Erupt too Late; Dodgers Win," *Los Angeles Times*, August 27, 1961.

12. Frank Finch, "Here We Go Again! Dodgers Lose Two," *Los Angeles Times*, August 27, 1961.

13. Frank Finch, "Injuries, Power Fizzles Helped to Paint...," *The Sporting News*, September 27, 1961.

14. Frank Finch, "KOUFAX'S 2-HITTER STOPS CUBS, 2–1," *Los Angeles Times*, August 30, 1961.

15. Jim Murray, "Sandy Rare Specimen," *Los Angeles Times*, August 30, 1961.

Chapter Ten

1. Bob Hunter, "Line-drive Hitters no Longer Penalized by Lofty Screen," *The Sporting News*, October 11, 1961, 16.

2. Frank Finch, "Spahn, Braves Shut Out Dodgers, 4–0," *Los Angeles Times*, September 7, 1961.

3. Frank Finch, "Dodgers-Koufax win final game in Coliseum," *Los Angeles Times*, September 21, 1961.

4. Bob Hunter, "Dodgers Say So-Long to Colossal Coliseum," *The Sporting News*, September 27, 1961.

5. Frank Finch, "Dodgers 'Is' Dead—Reds Win N.L. Flag," *Los Angeles Times*, September 27, 1961.

6. Robert Shelton, "Bob Dylan—A Distinctive Folk-Song Stylist," *New York Times*, September 27, 1961.

7. Ibid.

8. Frank Finch, "KOUFAX Sets Strikeout Mark, Loses," *Los Angeles Times*, September 28, 1961.

9. Robert Trumbull, "Ngo Says Struggle with Viet Nam Reds Is a 'Real War,'" *New York Times*, October 2, 1961.

10. Pat Harmon, "Queen City Flips Lid Over Prince Charmings," *The Sporting News*, October 4, 1961, 12.

11. Bob Hunter, "Buzzie Kayoes Rumors, Hands Dodger Reins to Alston for '62," *The Sporting News*, October 18, 1961, 6.

12. Les Biederman, "N.L. Player Draft Day After Series," *The Sporting News*, October 4, 1961, 40.

Chapter Eleven

1. Bob Hunter, "Line-drive Hitters No Longer Penalized by Lofty Screen," *The Sporting News*, October 11, 1961, 16.
2. Walter Bingham, "Boom Goes Baseball," *Sports Illustrated*, October 23, 1962, 18.
3. Paul Zimmerman, "At Last—It's Play Ball in Chavez Ravine Today," *Los Angeles Times*, April 10, 1962.
4. Sandy Koufax and Ed Linn, *Koufax*, 163.
5. Bob Hunter, "Fast-Stepping Davises—Dodger Jet Jobs," *The Sporting News*, March 28, 1962, 9.
6. Ibid.
7. Frank Finch, "REDS 'CRASH' DODGER STADIUM PARTY," *Los Angeles Times*, April 11, 1962.
8. Frank Finch, "Koufax Hurls 4-Hitter," *Los Angeles Times*, April 12, 1962.
9. Frank Finch, "KOUFAX FANS 18 CUBS, EQUALS RECORD," *Los Angeles Times*, April 27, 1962.
10. Bob Hunter, "Hats Off! Sandy Koufax," *The Sporting News*, May 2, 1962, 25.
11. Sandy Koufax and Ed Linn, *Koufax*, 173.

Chapter Twelve

1. Sandy Koufax and Ed Linn, *Koufax*, 171.
2. Frank Finch, "Koufax Fans 1,000th, But Loses, 3–1," *Los Angeles Times*, May 3, 1962.
3. Frank Finch, "DODGERS CONQUER COLTS IN 10TH," *Los Angeles Times*, May 9, 1962.
4. Frank Finch, "Javier Single Nips Dodgers in 15th," *Los Angeles Times*, May 13, 1962.
5. Sandy Koufax and Ed Linn, *Koufax*, 165.
6. Ibid.
7. Frank Finch, "DODGERS HAND GIANTS 8–1 THUMPING," *Los Angeles Times*, May 21, 1962.
8. Frank Finch, "Koufax Fans 16, Tosses 6–3 Victory-Over Phils," *Los Angeles Times*, May 27, 1962.
9. Joe King, "The Prodigals Return," *The Sporting News*, June 9, 1962, 8.
10. Koufax and Linn, *Koufax*, 167.
11. Koufax and Linn, *Koufax*, 165.
12. Ibid.
13. Frank Finch, "Wills Hits 2 Home Runs, Dodgers Sweep Met," *Los Angeles Times*, May 31, 1962.
14. Frank Finch, "KOUFAX (W) 3-HITTER CHILLS PHILS," *Los Angeles Times*, June 5, 1962.
15. Mickey Herskowitz, "Colt Fans Will Be Ushered to Seats by Trigger-Ettes," *The Sporting News*, April 4, 1962, 12.
16. Frank Finch, "Dodgers Lead Loop; Wills 'Steals' Game," *Los Angeles Times*, June 9, 1962.
17. Koufax and Linn, *Koufax*, 166.
18. Frank Finch, "Koufax Homer Gives Dodgers 2–1 Triumph," *Los Angeles Times*, June 14, 1962.
19. Frank Finch, "Sandy, Tommy Double-Deal Cards, 1–0," *Los Angeles Times*, June 19, 1962.
20. Koufax and Linn, *Koufax*, 167.
21. Ibid., 168.
22. Koufax and Linn, *Koufax*, 169.
23. Frank Finch, "'BIG D' SAVES KOUFAX," *Los Angeles Times*, July 9, 1962.
24. Koufax and Linn, *Koufax*, 170.
25. Frank Finch, "Koufax's Sore Finger Cause of Concern," *Los Angeles Times*, July 10, 1962.
26. Frank Finch, "Koufax Wins, Shelved by Injury," *Los Angeles Times*, July 13, 1962.
27. Koufax and Linn, *Koufax*, 172.
28. Frank Finch, "Koufax Hurts Finger Again as Reds Win," *Los Angeles Times*, July 18, 1962.

Chapter Thirteen

1. Koufax and Linn, *Koufax*, 174.
2. Koufax and Linn, *Koufax*, 172.
3. Ibid., 173–174.
4. Bob Hunter, "Index Finger Ailment Sideline Koufax for 30 Days," *The Sporting News*, July 28, 1962, 16.
5. Bob Hunter, "Howard Edges Out Drysdale for July Player of the Month," *The Sporting News*, July 28, 1962, 16.
6. Bob Hunter, "Don Hit 20 Mark Faster Than Any N.L. Ace Since '18," *The Sporting News*, August 18, 1962, 8.
7. Durocher and Linn, *Nice Guys Finish Last*, 8.
8. Ibid.
9. Koufax and Linn, *Koufax*, 174.
10. Bob Hunter, "Podres Johnny on the Spot in Jacking Up Dodger Staff," *The Sporting News*, August 18, 1962, 5.
11. Frank Finch, "Giants Erupt in 6th to Rip Dodgers, 11–2," *Los Angeles Times*, August 11, 1962.
12. Bob Hunter, "Shook Up Dodgers Count Welts, Scars After Frisco Quake," *The Sporting News*, August 25, 1962, 7.
13. Bob Hunter, "Alston Buttons Up the Lip," *The Sporting News*, September 1, 1962, 11.
14. Ibid.
15. Sandy Koufax and Ed Linn, *Koufax*, 174.
16. Bob Hunter, "Quick Work by Dodgers, Doc Save Lippy from Final Out," *The Sporting News*, September 8, 1962, 25.
17. Frank Finch, "Penicillin Shot Puts Durocher in Hospital," *Los Angeles Times*, August 25, 1962.
18. Frank Finch, "Frank Finch, 'MIGHTY METS STUN DRYSDALE,'" *Los Angeles Times*, August 25, 1962.
19. Associated Press, "Koufax Doubts He'll Pitch Again This Year," *Washington Post*, August 26, 1962.

Chapter Fourteen

1. Lee Allen, "Maury's Theft Feats Stir Record Ruckus," *The Sporting News*, October 6, 1962, 10.
2. Koufax and Linn, *Koufax*, 175.
3. Frank Finch, "Omaha Relief Ace Joins Dodgers," *Los Angeles Times*, September 5, 1962.
4. Paul Zimmerman, "Dodger Errors Mar Flag Bid," *Los Angeles Times*, September 5, 1962.
5. Ibid.
6. Frank Finch, "54,418 SEE MAYS, GIANTS MAUL DODGERS," *Los Angeles Times*, September 4, 1962.
7. Frank Finch, "51,567 SEE DODGERS HALT GIANTS, 5–4," *Los Angeles Times*, September 5, 1962.
8. Frank Finch, "Koufax Feels Good After Mound Chore," *Los Angeles Times*, September 6, 1962.
9. Frank Finch, "GIANT EXPLOSION IN 9TH RUINS DODGERS," *Los Angeles Times*, September 7, 1962.
10. Associated Press, "WILLS SETS MARK FOR STOLEN BASES," *New York Times*, September 8, 1962.
11. Frank Finch, "Smokey Sizzles as Dodger Bid Fizzles," *Los Angeles Times*, September , 1962.
12. Frank Finch, "What Keeps Dodgers' Pennant Drive Going," *Los Angeles Times*, September 11, 1962.
13. Frank Finch, "Koufax Expects to Pitch on Weekend," *Los Angeles Times*, September 12, 1962.
14. James S. Hirsch, *Willie Mays: The Life, the Legend* (New York: Scribner's, 2010), 355–356.
15. Frank Finch, "DODGERS NIP HOUSTON, 1–0; LEAD BY 1½," *Los Angeles Times*, September 13, 1962.
16. Frank Finch, "DODGERS ROUT CUBS, 13–7, PULL 3 AHEAD," *Los Angeles Times*, September 15, 1962.
17. Frank Finch, "DODGERS PULL TRIPLE STEAL, TOP CUBS 6–4," *Los Angeles Times*, September 16, 1962.
18. Frank Finch, "DODGERS BOW, 5–0, KEEP 4-GAME LEAD," *Los Angeles Times*, September 17, 1962.
19. Frank Finch, "SPAHN CHECKS DODGERS ON 5 HITS, 2–1," *Los Angeles Times*, September 18, 1962.
20. Frank Finch, "DODGERS TAKE 10–5 SCALPING BY BRAVES," *Los Angeles Times*, September 19, 1962.
21. Frank Finch, "DRYSDALE WINS 25TH; WILLS STEALS 94TH," *Los Angeles Times*, September 20, 1962.
22. Frank Finch, "ANXIOUS KOUFAX FRETS OVER DELAY," *Los Angeles Times*, September 20, 1962.
23. Ibid.
24. Bob Hunter, "Frick Puts 154-Game Limit on Wills' Record Theft Bid," *The Sporting News*, September 29, 1962, 7.
25. Frank Finch, "Frick: Wills Must Break Record Tonight," *Los Angeles Times*, September 21, 1962.
26. Frank Finch, "KOUFAX TO RETURN AS STARTER TONIGHT," *Los Angeles Times*, September 21, 1962.
27. Koufax and Linn, *Koufax*, 175.
28. Ibid.
29. Frank Finch, "WILLS GETS 95TH; KOUFAX ROUTED, 11–2," *Los Angeles Times*, September 22, 1962.
30. Bob Hunter, "Dodgers Eye Koufax Pitch for Comeback," *The Sporting News*, October 6, 1962, 6.
31. Robert Dallek, *An Unfinished Life: John F. Kennedy 1917–1963* (New York: Little, Brown, 2003), 542–543.
32. Frank Finch, "TOMMY DAVIS HITS HOMER TO WIN, 4–1," *Los Angeles Times*, September 23, 1962.
33. Associated Press, "Wills Sets Mark as Dodgers Lose," *Washington Post*, September 24, 1962.
34. Frank Finch, "Wills Steals 96th and 97th to Break Cobb's Record," *Los Angeles Times*, September 24, 1962.
35. Ibid.
36. Frank Finch, "Dodgers Open Crucial Home Stand," *Los Angeles Times*, September 25, 1962.
37. Frank Finch, "Dodgers, Wills (99) Still Sliding," *Los Angeles Times*, September 26, 1962.
38. Frank Finch, "DODGERS ROMP, 13–1, STAVE OFF GIANTS," *Los Angeles Times*, September 27, 1962.
39. Frank Finch, "DODGERS BOW, BLOW BID TO CLINCH TIE," *Los Angeles Times*, September 28, 1962.
40. Frank Finch, "51,094 SEE DODGERS FALL IN 10TH, 3–2," *Los Angeles Times*, September 29, 1962.
41. Frank Finch, "DODGERS BOOT CHANCE TO WRAP IT UP," *Los Angeles Times*, September 30, 1962.
42. Frank Finch, "CARDS SLAM BACK DOOR ON DODGERS," *Los Angeles Times*, October 1, 1962.
43. Anthony Lewis, "President Asks Mississippi to Comply with U.S. Laws," *New York Times*, October 1, 1962.

Chapter Fifteen

1. Durocher and Linn, *Nice Guys Finish Last*, 10.
2. Ibid.
3. Koufax and Linn, *Koufax*, 176.
4. Jack McDonald, "Jocko Shouts 'Foul' Over Giants' Sand Bar," *The Sporting News*, October 13, 1962, 7.

5. Ibid.

6. Ibid.

7. Paul Zimmerman, "MAYS, GIANTS ROUT FUTILE DODGERS, 8–0," *Los Angeles Times*, October 2, 1962.

8. Ibid.

9. Bob Hunter, "Giants Plunge L.A. Fans into Smog of Defeat," *The Sporting News*, October 13, 1962, 10.

10. Paul Zimmerman, "DODGERS BEAT GIANTS TO SQUARE SERIES," *Los Angeles Times*, October 3, 1962.

11. Leo Durocher and Ed Linn, *Nice Guys Finish Last*, 9.

12. Ibid.

13. Ibid., 10.

14. Ibid.

15. Bob Broeg, "Foul-up on DP Tabbed Key to Dodger Debacle," *The Sporting News*, October 20, 1962, 10.

16. Durocher and Linn, *Nice Guys Finish Last*, 10.

17. Hunter, "Giants Plunge L.A. Fans into Smog of Defeat," 10.

18. James S. Hirsch, *Willie Mays: The Life, the Legend* (New York: Scribner's, 2010), 367.

19. Jack McDonald, "50,000 Hail Heroes at 'Frisco Airport," *The Sporting News*, October 13, 1962, 7.

20. Bob Burnes, "Ford Tames Giants to log Tenth Series Win," *The Sporting News*, October 20, 1962, 19.

21. Bob Burnes, "Giants Pull Even on Classy 3-Hit Blank Job by Sanford," *The Sporting News*, October 20, 1962, 20.

22. Bob Burnes, "Terry Twirls 4-Hit Shutout as Yanks Cop World's Title," *The Sporting News*, October 27, 1962, 27.

23. Hirsch, *Willie Mays*, 372.

24. Chris Mathews, *Jack Kennedy: Elusive Hero* (New York: Simon & Schuster, 2011), 364.

25. Ibid., 365.

26. Bob Hunter, "'Dodgers Tired, We Didn't Fold' Snider Declares," *The Sporting News*, November 10, 1962, 19.

27. Bob Hunter, "Wills Cost L.A. Flag—Boggess," *The Sporting News*, March 23, 1963, 3.

28. Bob Hunter, "Dodger Yelpers to Face Bavasi's Pruning Shears," *The Sporting News*, October 27, 1962, 8.

29. Bob Hunter, "Sandy's Pinkie Give Dodgers Rosy Hue," *The Sporting News*, February 16, 1963, 3.

Chapter Sixteen

1. Associated Press, "Alston Terms Koufax Main Concern as Drills Start," *New York Times*, February 25, 1963.

2. Bob Hunter, "Sandy's Pinkie Give Dodgers Rosy Hue," *The Sporting News*, February 16, 1963, 3.

3. Bob Joyce, "Hurlers Hail New Strike Zone, Expanded by 10 to 12 Inches," *The Sporting News*, February 9, 1963, 4.

4. Joe Reichler, "Mantle Sees Himself Striking Out 400 Times," *Washington Post*, February 2, 63.

5. Bob Hunter, "Sandy's Pinkie Give Dodgers Rosy Hue," *The Sporting News*, February 16, 1963, 3.

6. Bob Hunter, "Dodger Spirits Soar in Wake of Koufax's Flying-Colors Start," *The Sporting News*, March 16, 1963, 17.

7. Frank Finch, "Alston Starts 10th Year as Dodger Boss," *Los Angeles Times*, February 24, 1963.

8. Barney Kremenko, "Duke of Dodgertown Still King in Gotham," *The Sporting News*, April 20, 1963, 3.

9. Ross Newhan, "The Coliseum Was Not Real Baseball," *Los Angeles Times*, March 29, 2008.

10. *The Boys of Summer* is a 1972 nonfiction book by Roger Kahn that tracks the lives of 13 Brooklyn Dodger players: Clem Labine, George Shuba, Carl Erskine, Andy Pafko, Joe Black, Preacher Roe, Pee Wee Reese, Carl Furillo, Gil Hodges, Roy Campanella, Jackie Robinson, Billy Cox, and Duke Snider.

11. Shirley Povich, "Kennedy's Quick Pitch Launches New Season," *The Sporting News*, April 20, 1963, 7.

12. Frank Finch, "Drysdale Stymies Cubs Again, 5–1," *Los Angeles Times*, April 10, 1963.

13. Bob Hunter, "Oliver Wraps Up Dodger Keystone with Tidy Show," *The Sporting News*, March 23, 1963, 30.

14. Frank Finch, "'Lip' Drools Over Dodger Rookie Oliver," *Los Angeles Times*, February 25, 1963.

15. Frank Finch, "T. Davis Benched; Experiment Over?," *Los Angeles Times*, March 22, 1963.

16. Bob Hunter, "Dodgers Expect Moose's Muscle to Pep Up Attack," *The Sporting News*, December 27, 1962, 11.

17. Bob Hunter, "Classy Kids Closing Dodger Infield Gap," *The Sporting News*, April 20, 1963, 18.

18. Frank Finch, "Koufax Posts 10 Strikeouts, Wills Out," *Los Angeles Times*, April 11, 1963.

19. Frank Finch, "HOWARD'S BLAST SINKS BRAVES, 2–1," *Los Angeles Times*, April 24, 1963.

20. Frank Finch, "Koufax Lost for 10 Days with Injury," *Los Angeles Times*, April 25, 1963.

21. Ibid.

22. Edward Prell, "HOWARD'S BLAST SINKS BRAVES, 2–1," *Chicago Tribune*, February 8, 1963.

23. Neal Russo, "Cautious Keane Eyes Cards' Comet," *The Sporting News*, May 11, 1962, 9.

24. Bob Hunter, "Tommy D 3-D Dandy in Delayed Debut at Dodgers' Hot Corner," *The Sporting News*, May 18, 1963, 7.

25. Frank Finch, "Dodgers Blow Decision, Take It Out on Bus," *Los Angeles Times*, May 7, 1963.

26. Ibid.

27. Ibid.

28. Bob Hunter, "O'Malley Stymies Rumors,

Says Alston's Job is Safe," *The Sporting News,* May 18, 1963, 8.

Chapter Seventeen

1. Koufax and Linn, *Koufax,* 181.
2. Koufax and Linn, *Koufax,* 182.
3. Ibid., 181.
4. Ibid.
5. Ibid., 182.
6. Bob Hunter, "Koufax's No-Hit Voodoo Kayoes Injury Hex," *The Sporting News,* May 25, 1963, 6.
7. Melvin Durslag, "Perfecto Larsen Viewed Sandy's Classic Curving," *The Sporting News,* May 25, 1963, 6.
8. Frank Finch, "SANDY'S FINGER, ARM OK—AND HOW!," *Los Angeles Times,* May 12, 1963.
9. Frank Finch, "DODGERS WIN PAIR, TRAIL BY ONE GAME 42,541 See Mets Bow, 1–0 and 4–2 DODGERS NIP METS TWICE," *Los Angeles Times,* May 20, 1963.
10. Frank Finch, "KOUFAX KO'D IN 1ST, GIANTS BREEZE, 7–1," *Los Angeles Times,* May 25, 1963.
11. Bob Hunter, "Tommy D Dents Fences, Powers Dodger Take-off," *The Sporting News,* June 8, 1963, 8.
12. Frank Finch, "Koufax Shuts Out Milwaukee, 7–0—Sandy Checks Braves on Six Hits," *Los Angeles Times,* May 29, 1963.
13. Bob Hunter, "Dodgers, in Throes of Injury Plague, Still Find Time to Grin," *The Sporting News,* June 15, 1963, 25.
14. Robert Creamer, "For the Want of a Warning a Pennant Was Lost," *Sports Illustrated,* June 17, 1993, 68.
15. Gordon S. White, Jr., "Mantle Fractures Left Foot in Yank Victory at Baltimore," *New York Times,* June 6, 1963.
16. Frank Finch, "Dodgers Survive 3 Banks Homers," *Los Angeles Times,* June 10, 1963.
17. Bob Stevens, "Traffic Boo-Boos Throw Brakes on Giants' Jitney," *The Sporting News,* June 22, 1963, 8.
18. Frank Finch, "KOUFAX SHOOTS BLANKS AT COLT 45'S," *Los Angeles Times,* May 14, 1963.
19. Bob Hunter, "Willhite Stirs Up Dodger Wind After Buzzie Whiffs on Trade," *The Sporting News,* June 29, 1963, 8.
20. Frank Finch, "KOUFAX BLANKS GIANTS ON 4 HITS, 2–0," *Los Angeles Times,* June 18, 1963.
21. Bob Hunter, "Gilliam Grabs Hero's Role with Storybook Socking for Dodgers," *The Sporting News,* July 13, 1963, 16.
22. Bob Hunter, "Dodgers Sniff Happy Hunting as Big Moose Starts to Stir," *The Sporting News,* July 6, 1963, 18.
23. Frank Finch, "GILLIAM'S BELT, BLOOP N' BUNT BEAT BRAVES—50,148 See Junior-Size Hit," *Los Angeles Times,* June 30, 1963.
24. Bob Wolf, "Spahn Ends a 15-Year Hex in Road Win Over Dodgers," *The Sporting News,* July 13, 1963, 18.
25. Bob Hunter, "Gilliam Grabs Hero's Role with Storybook Socking for Dodgers," *The Sporting News,* July 13, 1963, 16.
26. Frank Finch, "MOON SHOT CARRIES DODGERS TO 2–1 WIN," *Los Angeles Times,* July 1, 1963.
27. Associated Press, "Dodgers Win, 1–0, Lead League," *New York Times,* July 3, 1963.
28. Frank Finch, "DRYSDALE PITCHES DODGERS TO TOP, 1–0," *Los Angeles Times,* July 3, 1963.
29. Ron Fimrite, "July 2, 1963," *Sports Illustrated,* July 19, 1993, 44.
30. Frank Finch, "K-000-000-000-FAX DOES IT AGAIN, 5–0," *Los Angeles Times,* July 4, 1963.
31. Frank Finch, "M'MULLEN'S SLAM GIVES DODGERS SWEEP," *Los Angeles Times,* July 5, 1963.
32. United Press International, "DODGERS 2-HITTER TOPS REDS, 1 TO 0," *New York Times,* July 6, 1963.
33. Frank Finch, "Podres Pitches One, Tooo-ooo-ooo!," *Los Angeles Times,* July 6, 1963.
34. Frank Finch, "Red-faced Dodgers Burned by Sun Drysdale Drops 3–1 Duel," *Los Angeles Times,* July 7, 1963.
35. Associated Press, "Reds Top Dodgers by 3–1 on Fly Lost by Gilliam in Sun," *New York Times,* July 7, 1963.
36. Frank Finch, "55,269 SEE DODGERS BEAT REDS TWICE Koufax Twirls 8th Shutout," *Los Angeles Times,* July 8, 1963.
37. John Drebinger, "2 STOLEN BASES LEAD TO TALLIES," *New York Times,* July 10, 1963.
38. Frank Finch, "PODRES, ROSEBORO CUT DOWN METS, 1–0," *Los Angeles Times,* July 11, 1963.
39. Frank Finch, "Dodgers Barely Squeak by Spunky Mets, 4–3," *Los Angeles Times,* July 12, 1963.
40. Frank Finch, "Dodgers Lead by 5 Games KOUFAX AGAIN, 6–0," *Los Angeles Times,* July 13, 1963.
41. Leonard Koppett, "MILLER TRIUMPHS Pitches 6-Hitter and Sends Mets to 14th Straight," *New York Times,* July 14, 1963.
42. Associated Press, "DODGERS WIN, 3–2, FOR 7TH IN A ROW," *New York Times,* July 15, 1963.
43. Frank Finch, "DODGERS OUTFUMBLE PHILS, LOSE IN 11TH," *Los Angeles Times,* July 16, 1963.
44. Frank Finch, "KOUFAX NO-HITTER FOILED; DODGERS SPLIT," *Los Angeles Times,* July 17, 1963.
45. Frank Finch, "Dodgers Rolling, 7.5 Ahead Howard's 2 Homers Rip Braves," *Los Angeles Times,* July 20, 1963.

46. Associated Press, "Dodgers Win, 5–4, on Howard's Clout," *New York Times*, July 21, 1963.

47. Frank Finch, "HOWARD'S HOMER WINS ANOTHER, 5–4," *Los Angeles Times*, July 21, 1963.

48. Frank Finch, "Dodgers Lose Twice, and So Does Alston," *Los Angeles Times*, July 22, 1963.

49. Associated Press, "Dodgers Triumph Over Pirates, 6–0," *New York Times*, July 24, 1963.

50. Frank Finch, "DRYSDALE, DODGERS DO IT AGAIN Pirates Fall 5–1 Before 30,402," *Los Angeles Times*, July 25, 1963.

51. Frank Finch, "KOUFAX KO'D IN SIX—STREAK ENDS AT 9 Bucs Win, 6–2," *Los Angeles Times*, July 26, 1963.

52. Frank Finch, "Phillies' Cuban 'Army' Turns Back Dodgers, 6–5," *Los Angeles Times*, July 27, 1963.

53. Ibid.

54. Frank Finch, "DODGERS FAIL IN CLUTCH, LOSE AGAIN L.A. Lead Down to 4 Games," *Los Angeles Times*, July 28, 1963.

55. Frank Finch, "Phillies Pin 7–4 Setback on Dodgers," *Los Angeles Times*, July 29, 1963.

56. Frank Finch, "KOUFAX ENDS DODGER SLUMP," *Los Angeles Times*, July 29, 1963.

57. Frank Finch, "ROEBUCK DEPARTS WITH BLAST AT ALSTON," *Los Angeles Times*, July 31, 1963.

58. Ibid.

59. Bob Hunter, "Roebuck Sears Alston in Farewell," *The Sporting News*, August 10, 1963, 9.

60. Ibid.

61. Frank Finch, "Sad Sack Mets Wallop Slumping Dodgers, 5–1," *Los Angeles Times*, July 31, 1963.

62. Gordon S. White, Jr., "CRAIG IS DEFEATED 17TH TIME IN ROW," *New York Times*, August 1, 1963.

Chapter Eighteen

1. Koufax and Linn, *Koufax*, 177.

2. Koufax and Linn, *Koufax*, 179.

3. Associated Press, "KOUFAX SHUTS OUT COLTS WITH 3 HITS," *New York Times*, August 4, 1963.

4. Frank Finch, "Koufax Pulls Off Another Blank Job Against Colts," *Los Angeles Times*, August 4, 1963.

5. Associated Press, "Ovation 'Shakes' Mantle," *Chicago Tribune*, August 5, 1963.

6. United Press International, "Mickey Mantle Returns to an Ovation," *Chicago Tribune*, August 5, 1963.

7. Frank Finch, "Dodgers Beat Cubs, 3–1, on Davis' Homer in 11th," *Los Angeles Times*, August 8, 1963.

8. United Press International, "Dodgers Whip Cubs in 11th—Koufax Ties Strikeout Record," *Washington Post*, August 8, 1963.

9. Frank Finch, "EVEN KOUFAX BOMBED AS REDS RIP DODGERS," *Los Angeles Times*, August 12, 1963.

10. Associated Press, "KOUFAX IS ROUTED IN SIX-RUN SIXTH," *New York Times*, August 12, 1963.

11. Associated Press, "KOUFAX IS ROUTED, BUT DODGERS WIN," *New York Times*, August 16, 1963.

12. Frank Finch, "PERRANOSKI TO RESCUE; DODGERS WIN," *Los Angeles Times*, August 16, 1963.

13. Bob Hunter, "Dodgers' Bats Trip Critics Reaching for Panic Button," *The Sporting News*, August 31, 1963, 9.

14. Robert Lipsyte, "KOUFAX WINS 19TH," *New York Times*, August 18, 1963.

15. Frank Finch, "Koufax Loses Shutout in 9th but Wins, 3–2," *Los Angeles Times*, August 18, 1963.

16. Bob Hunter, "Dodgers' Bats Trip Critics Reaching for Panic Button," *The Sporting News*, August 31, 1963, 9.

17. Associated Press, "DODGERS TRIUMPH IN 16 INNINGS, 2–1" *New York Times*, August 22, 1963.

18. Frank Finch, "KOUFAX MISSES 20TH VICTORY—Dodgers Win in 16th, 2–1," *Los Angeles Times*, August 22, 1963.

19. Bob Hunter, "Tommy D Sounds Dodger 'Charge' with Sock Salvo," *The Sporting News*, September 7, 1963, 9.

20. Sid Ziff, "Dodgers on Edge," *Los Angeles Times*, August 27, 1963.

21. Frank Finch, "DODGERS WIN, 2–1 (BUT NOT FOR SANDY)," *Los Angeles Times*, August 26, 1963.

22. Taylor Branch, *Parting the Waters: America in the King Years 1954–63* (New York: Simon & Schuster, 1988), 882.

23. Associated Press, "KOUFAX WINS 20TH AS GIANTS LOSE," *New York Times*, August 30, 1963.

24. Frank Finch, "RECORD 54,978 SEE DODGERS ROMP, 11–1," *Los Angeles Times*, August 30, 1963.

25. Al Wolf, "20th Victory Bigger Thrill Than No-Hitter—Koufax," *Los Angeles Times*, August 30, 1963.

26. Bob Hunter, "L.A. Fans Have Circus Watching Dodger Feast," *The Sporting News*, September 14, 1963, 9.

27. Frank Finch, "DODGERS GUN DOWN COLT 45'S TWICE Koufax Wins 21st," *Los Angeles Times*, September 3, 1963.

28. Frank Finch, "GILLIAM, KOUFAX TEAM TO SINK GIANTS," *Los Angeles Times*, September 7, 1963.

29. Associated Press, "KOUFAX RECORDS HIS 22D TRIUMPH," *New York Times*, September 7, 1963.

30. Frank Finch, "KOUFAX TAMES BUCS, 4–2, FOR 23RD WIN," *Los Angeles Times*, September 11, 1963.

31. Frank Finch, "DODGERS SPLIT, LEAD CUT TO 2.5 GAMES," *Los Angeles Times*, September 14, 1963.

32. Branch, *Parting the Waters*, 899.

33. Claude Sitton, "Birmingham Bomb Kills 4 Negro Girls in Church," *New York Times*, September 16, 1963.

34. Robert Creamer, "Nothing Stopped the Dodgers," *Sports Illustrated*, September 30, 1993, 26.

35. Bob Hunter, "Dodgers Pluck Fine-Feathered Birds," *The Sporting News*, September 28, 1963, 5.

36. Frank Finch, "DODGERS BRING BIRDS BACK TO EARTH," *Los Angeles Times*, September 17, 1963.

37. Neal Russo, "Oh Wotta Spree Before Bubble Burst!," *The Sporting News*, September 28, 1963, 5.

38. Frank Finch, "IT'S ANOTHER DANDY FOR SANDY, 4–0," *Los Angeles Times*, September 18, 1963.

39. Koufax and Linn, *Koufax*, 179.

40. Ibid.

41. Leonard Koppett, "SHUTOUT IS 11TH FOR LEFT-HANDER," *New York Times*, September 18, 1963.

42. Sandy Koufax and Ed Linn, *Koufax*, 180.

43. Leonard Koppett, "WINNERS EXTEND LEAD TO 4 GAMES," *New York Times*, September 19, 1963.

44. Frank Finch, "DODGERS GIVE ST. LOOEY THE BLUES," *Los Angeles Times*, September 19, 1963.

45. Bob Hunter, "Dodgers Pluck Fine-Feathered Birds," *The Sporting News*, September 28, 1963, 5.

46. Koufax and Linn, *Koufax*, 181.

47. Frank Finch, "WILLIE DAVIS KO'S PIRATES IN 9TH, 5–3," *Los Angeles Times*, September 21, 1963.

48. Frank Finch, "FLAG'S IN THE BAG—DODGERS CELEBRATE," *Los Angeles Times*, September 25, 1963.

49. Lowell Reidenbaugh, "Stan Whacks Pair of Hits in Grande Finale," *The Sporting News*, October 12, 1963, 22.

Chapter Nineteen

1. Frank Finch, "SANDY SIZZLES, BOMBERS FIZZLE," *Los Angeles Times*, October 3, 1963.

2. John Drebinger, "Strike-out Mark Is Set by Koufax," *New York Times*, October 3, 1963.

3. William Leggett, "Koo-foo the Killer," *Sports Illustrated*, October 14, 1963, 21.

4. Bob Burnes, "Sandy Spins Strikeout Tale—15 Yankees Get Message," *The Sporting News*, October 19, 1963, 23.

5. Leggett, "Koo-foo," 21.

6. John Drebinger, "DODGERS DEFEAT YANKS AGAIN, 4–1; LEAD BY 2 GAMES," *New York Times*, October 4, 1963.

7. Bob Burnes, "Podres, Dodgers' Speedsters Pin Second Defeat on Yanks," *The Sporting News*, October 19, 1963, 25.

8. William Leggett, "Koo-foo the Killer," *Sports Illustrated*, October 14, 1963, 22.

9. John Drebinger, "BIG D CUTS OFF YANK POWER AGAIN, 1–0," *New York Times*, October 6, 1963.

10. Don Drysdale and Bob Verdi, *Once a Bum, Always a Dodger*, 173.

11. Leggett, "Koo-foo," 23.

12. Bob Burnes, "Drysdale Sparkles, Blanks Bombers with 3-Hit Gem," *The Sporting News*, October 19, 1963, 27.

13. Bob Hunter, "Couldn't Be Done—But Dodgers Did it," *The Sporting News*, October 28, 1963, 2.

14. John Drebinger, "DODGERS WIN, 2–1, SWEEPING SERIES AGAINST YANKEES," *New York Times*, October 7, 1963.

15. Leggett, "Koo-foo," 24.

16. Bob Burnes, "Ford Superb—But Not Good Enough to Turn Back Sandy," *The Sporting News*, October 19, 1963, 29.

17. John Drebinger, "DODGERS WIN, 2–1, SWEEPING SERIES AGAINST YANKEES."

18. Bob Burnes, "Ford Superb—But Not Good Enough to Turn Back Sandy," 30.

19. Paul Zimmerman, "SWEET VICTORY!," *Los Angeles Times*, October 7, 1963.

Chapter Twenty

1. *Merriam-Webster's Collegiate Dictionary*, 11th ed., s.v. "apotheosis."

2. Willie Stargell, "Quotes About Sandy Koufax," *Baseball Almanac*: http://www.baseball-almanac.com/quotes/quokouf.shtml.

3. Associated Press, "KOUFAX RECEIVES CY YOUNG AWARD," *New York Times*, October 25, 1963.

4. John Drebinger, "Koufax Picked as Most Valuable," *New York Times*, October 31, 1963.

5. Hy Hurwitz, "Sandy First Hill Ace to Win N.L. MVP Since 1956," *The Sporting News*, November 9, 1963, 8.

6. Frank Finch, "SANDY STRIKES AGAIN—WINS MVP AWARD," *Los Angeles Times*, October 31, 1963.

7. Hedrick Smith, "Rebels in Viet Nam Oust Diem," *New York Times*, November 2, 1963.

Bibliography

Books

Adelman, Tom. *Black and Blue: Sandy Koufax, the Robinson Boys, and the World Series That Stunned America*. New York: Little, Brown, 2006.

Bavasi, Buzzie, and John Strege. *Off the Record*. Chicago: Contemporary Books, 1987.

Branch, Taylor. *The King Years: Historic Moment in the Civil Rights Movement*. New York: Simon & Schuster, 2013.

_____. *Parting the Waters: America in the King Years 1954–63*. New York: Simon & Schuster, 1988.

Dallek, Robert. *An Unfinished Life: John F. Kennedy 1917–1963*. New York: Little, Brown, 2003.

Daniel, Clifton, ed. *The 20th Century Day by Day*. New York: DK, 1999.

Delsohn, Steve. *True Blue: The Dramatic History of the Los Angeles Dodgers, Told by the Men Who Lived It*. New York: HarperCollins, 2001.

Drysdale, Don, and Bob Verdi. *Once a Bum, Always a Dodger*. New York: St. Martin's Press, 1990.

Endsley, Brian. *Bums No More: The 1959 Los Angeles Dodgers, World Champions of Baseball*. Jefferson, NC: McFarland, 2009.

Finch, Frank. *The Los Angeles Dodgers: The First Twenty Years*. Virginia Beach: Jordan, 1977.

Gibson, Bob, and Phil Pepe. *From Ghetto to Glory: The Story of Bob Gibson*. Englewood Cliffs: Prentice Hall, 1968.

Gruver, Edward. *Koufax*. Dallas: Taylor, 2000.

Gulbrandsen, Don, ed. *Ballparks Yesterday and Today*. New York: Chartwell, 2007.

Hirsch, James S. *Willie Mays: The Life, the Legend*. New York: Scribner's, 2010.

Jacobson, Steve. *Carrying Jackie's Torch: The Players Who Integrated Baseball—and America*. Chicago: Lawrence Hill, 2007.

Kahn, Roger. *The Boys of Summer*. New York: Harper & Row, 1972.

Koufax, Sandy, and Ed Linn. *Koufax*. New York: Viking, 1966.

Leavy, Jane. *Sandy Koufax: A Lefty's Legacy*. New York: HarperCollins, 2002.

Mathews, Chris. *Jack Kennedy: Elusive Hero*. New York: Simon & Schuster, 2011.

Robinson, Frank, and Al Silverman. *My Life Is Baseball*. Garden City, NJ: Doubleday, 1968.

Rosenbaum, Robert A. *The Penguin Encyclopedia of American History*. New York: Penguin Reference, 2003.

Schlesinger, Arthur M., Jr. *A Thousand Days*. Boston: Houghton Mifflin, 1965.

Smith, Ron, ed. *Heroes of the Hall: Baseball's All-time Best*. St. Louis: The Sporting News, 2002.

Snider, Duke, and Phil Pepe. *Few and Chosen: Defining Dodgers Greatness Across the Eras*. Chicago: Triumph, 2006.

Snyder, John. *Dodgers Journal: Year by Year & Day by Day with the Brooklyn & Los Angeles Dodgers Since 1884*. Cincinnati: Clerisy, 2009.

Stout, Glenn, and Richard A. Johnson. *The Dodgers: 120 Years of Dodgers Baseball*. New York: Houghton Mifflin, 2004.

Travers, Steven. *Dodgers Past & Present*. Minneapolis: MVP Books, 2009.

Whittington, Richard. *Illustrated History of the Dodgers*. Chicago: Triumph Books, 2005.

Articles

Allen, Lee, "Maury's Theft Feats Stir Record Ruckus." *The Sporting News*, October 6, 1962: 10.

Anderson, Dave. "The Dodgers' Tommy Gun." *Baseball Digest*, January 1963: 31.

Biederman, Les. "Dick Groat's First Big Time Hit Sets off Wild Rhubarb." *The Sporting News*, June 25, 1952: 21.

_____. "Swap Groat? Very Thought Jars Buc Fans." *The Sporting News*, January 13, 1960: 20.

_____. "N.L. Player Draft Day After Series." *The Sporting News*, October 4, 1961: 40.

Bingham, Walter. "Dodgers in Mufti." *Sports Illustrated*, August 15, 1960: 1.

_____. "Boom Goes Baseball." *Sports Illustrated*, October 23, 1962: 18.

Broeg, Bob. "Foul-up on DP Tabbed Key to Dodger Debacle." *Sports Illustrated*, October 20, 1962: 10.

Burnes, Robert. "Majors Toe Mark for Inter-Loop Swaps." *The Sporting News*, November 18, 1959: 2.

_____. "Ford Tames Giants to Log Tenth Series Win." *The Sporting News*, October 20, 1962: 19.

_____. "Giants Pull Even on Classy 3-Hit Blank Job by Sanford." *The Sporting News*, October 20, 1962: 20.

_____. "Terry Twirls 4-Hit Shutout as Yanks Cop World's Title." *The Sporting News*, October 27, 1962: 27.

_____. "Drysdale Sparkles, Blanks Bombers with 3-Hit Gem." *The Sporting News*, October 19, 1963: 27.

_____. "Ford Superb—But Not Good Enough to Turn Back Sandy." *The Sporting News*, October 19, 1963: 29.

_____. "Podres, Dodgers' Speedsters Pin Second Defeat on Yanks." *The Sporting News*, October 19, 1963: 23.

_____. "Sandy Spins Strikeout Tale—15 Yankees Get Message." *The Sporting News*, October 19, 1963: 23.

Creamer, Robert. "For the Want of a Warning a Pennant Was Lost." *Sports Illustrated*, June 17, 1993: 68.

_____. "Nothing Stopped the Dodgers." *Sports Illustrated*, September 30, 1993: 26.

Durslag, Melvin. "Perfecto Larsen Viewed Sandy's Classic Curving." *The Sporting News*, May 25, 1963: 6.

Finch, Frank. "Roebuck Put on Retired List in Six-Player L.A. Shuffle." *The Sporting News*, August 6, 1958: 8.

_____. "DUMBO—The Dodgers' Newest Star." *Baseball Digest*, October 1958: 25.

_____. "Larker Big Blaster with Borrowed Bats." *The Sporting News*, October 12, 1960: 3.

Fleischmann, Bill. "Many Veterans Included in Majors' Cut-Down." *The Sporting News*, May 21, 1958: 7.

Gavin, Michael. "A Whole Family Goes to the Mound." *Baseball Digest*, June 1955: 30.

Harmon, Pat. "Queen City Flips Lid Over Prince Charmings" *The Sporting News*, October 4, 1961: 12.

Herskowitz, Mickey. "Colt Fans Will Be Ushered to Seats by Trigger-Ettes" *The Sporting News*, April 4, 1962: 12.

Holzman, Jerry. "Fiber of the Pirates." *Baseball Digest*, October 1960: 23–24.

Horgan, Tim. "How Bucs Beat Senators to Groat." *Baseball Digest*, April 1961: 38.

Hunter, Bob. "Buzzie Will Buzz Three A.L. Clubs." *The Sporting News*, November 18, 1959: 2.

_____. "Buzzie Chills Sievers Swap When Nats Get Hot on Lillis." *The Sporting News*, December 16, 1959: 2.

_____. "Shortstop Battle Spices Dodger Training Tilts." *The Sporting News*, March 23, 1960, 7.

_____. "Muscle Injury Casts Doubt on Future of Veteran Furillo." *The Sporting News*, April 13, 1960: 11.

_____. "1,200 Serenade Dodgers at L.A. Writers." *The Sporting News*, April 13, 1960: 11.

_____. "Bad News for N.L. Hurlers—Snider's Knee Improved." *The Sporting News*, April 20, 1960: 11.

_____. "Fast-dealing Bavasi Shuffles Dodgers to Flag-fighting Size." *The Sporting News*, April 20, 1960: 11.

_____. "Craig Out for Two Months After Collision with Pinson." *The Sporting News*, May 11, 1960: 19.

_____. "Howitzer Howard puts Hefty Charge in Dodger Attack." *The Sporting News*, May 25, 1960: 16.

_____. "Smokey Locks Doors, Takes Cut at Ragged Dodger Play." *The Sporting News*, June 29, 1960: 6.

_____. "Handcuffed Hitters Bust Loose, Dodgers Out of Doldrums." *The Sporting News*, July 13, 1960: 26.

_____. "Red-Hot Dodgers Stomp and Fidget at All-Star Break." *The Sporting News*, July 20, 1960: 12.

_____. "Base Burglar Wills Preparing to Swipe Mays' Theft Crown." *The Sporting News*, August 17, 1960: 17.

_____. "Dodgers Wheel Out Flashy Youngsters." *The Sporting News*, September 14, 1960: 8.

_____. "Dodgers Set Trap Early, Hoping to Land Big Belter." *The Sporting News*, September 28, 1960: 20.

_____. "Bavasi, Alston Start Desperate Search for Slugger at Series." *The Sporting News*, October 5, 1960: 42.

_____. "Dodgers Weed out Vets—Clear Decks for Kid Stars." *The Sporting News*, October 26, 1960: 20.

_____. "Roebuck's Dead Arm Rated No. 1 Rally-Killer." *The Sporting News*, January 11, 1961: 5.

_____. "Wary Skipper Walt Warns of Pitfalls for Dodger Bandwagon." *The Sporting News*, April 12, 1961: 14.

_____. "Slumps, Bumps Slow Dodgers' Swifties in Jump from Barrier." *The Sporting News*, April 26, 1961: 17.

_____. "Injuries, Power Fizzles Helped to Paint..." *The Sporting News*, September 27, 1961: 6.

_____. "Line-drive Hitters No Longer Penalized by

Lofty Screen." *The Sporting News*, October 11, 1961: 16.

_____. "Buzzie Kayoes Rumors, Hands Dodger Reins to Alston for '62." *The Sporting News*, October 18, 1961: 6.

_____. "Mom Made Big Decisions—Steered Tommy to Dodgers." *The Sporting News*, March 28, 1962: 9.

_____. "Fast-Stepping Davises—Dodger Jet Jobs." *The Sporting News*, March 28, 1962: 9.

_____. "Willie Nixed Track Career." *The Sporting News*, March 28, 1962: 9.

_____. "Fast-Stepping Davises—Dodger Jet Jobs." *The Sporting News*, March 28, 1962: 9.

_____. "Hats Off! Sandy Koufax." *The Sporting News*, May 2, 1962: 259.

_____. "Ron Idolized Yankees but Signed $21,000 Cub Pact." *The Sporting News*, June 29, 1963: 4.

_____. "Ex-Spartan Sparkers Sponge Up Relief Honors." *The Sporting News*, June 29, 1963: 3.

_____. "Index Finger Ailment Sideline Koufax for 30 Days." *The Sporting News*, July 28, 1962: 16.

_____. "Howard Edges out Drysdale for July Player of the Month." *The Sporting News*, July 28, 1962: 16.

_____. "Don Hit 20 Mark Faster Than Any N.L. Ace Since '18." *The Sporting News*, August 18, 1962: 8.

_____. "Podres Johnny on the Spot in Jacking Up Dodger Staff." *The Sporting News*, August 18, 1962: 5.

_____. "Shook Up Dodgers Count Welts, Scars After Frisco Quake." *The Sporting News*, August 25, 1962: 7.

_____. "Alston Buttons Up the Lip." *The Sporting News*, September 1, 1962: 11.

_____. "Quick Work by Dodgers, Doc Save Lippy from Final Out." *The Sporting News*, September 8, 1962: 25.

_____. "Frick Puts 154-Game Limit on Wills' Record Theft Bid." *The Sporting News*, September 29, 1962: 7.

_____. "Dodgers Eye Koufax Pitch for Comeback." *The Sporting News*, October 6, 1962: 6.

_____. "Giants Plunge L.A. Fans into Smog of Defeat." *The Sporting News*, October 13, 1962: 10.

_____. "Dodger Yelpers to Face Bavasi's Pruning Shears." *The Sporting News*, October 27, 1962: 8.

_____. "'Dodgers Tired, We Didn't Fold' Snider Declares." *The Sporting News*, November 10, 1962: 19.

_____. "'Dodgers Expect Moose's Muscle to Pep Up Attack' Snider Declares." *The Sporting News*, December 27, 1962: 11.

_____. "Sandy's Pinkie Give Dodgers Rosy Hue." *The Sporting News*, February 16, 1963: 3.

_____. "Dodger Spirits Soar in Wake of Koufax' Flying-Colors Start." *The Sporting News*, March 16, 1963: 17.

_____. "Oliver Wraps Up Dodger Keystone with Tidy Show." *The Sporting News*, March 23, 1963: 30.

_____. "'Wills Cost L.A. Flag'—Boggess." *The Sporting News*, March 23, 1963: 3.

_____. "Classy Kids Closing Dodger Infield Gap." *The Sporting News*, April 20, 1963: 18.

_____. "O'Malley Stymies Rumors, Says Alston's Job Is Safe." *The Sporting News*, May 18, 1963: 8.

_____. "Tommy D 3-D Dandy in Delayed Debut at Dodgers' Hot Corner." *The Sporting News*, May 18, 1963: 7.

_____. "Koufax' No-Hit Voodoo Kayoes Injury Hex." *The Sporting News*, May 25, 1963: 6.

_____. "Tommy D Dents Fences, Powers Dodger Take-off." *The Sporting News*, June 8, 1963: 8.

_____. "Dodgers, in Throes of Injury Plague, Still Find Time to Grin." *The Sporting News*, June 15, 1963: 25.

_____. "Willhite Stirs Up Dodger Wind After Buzzie Whiffs on Trade." *The Sporting News*, June 29, 1963: 8.

_____. "Dodgers Sniff Happy Hunting as Big Moose Starts to Stir." *The Sporting News*, July 6, 1963: 18.

_____. "Gilliam Grabs Hero's Role with Storybook Socking for Dodgers." *The Sporting News*, July 13, 1963: 16.

_____. "Dodgers' Bats Trip Critics Reaching for Panic Button." *The Sporting News*, August 10, 1963: 9.

_____. "Roebuck Sears Alston in Farewell." *The Sporting News*, August 10, 1963: 9.

_____. "Dodgers' Bats Trip Critics Reaching for Panic Button." *The Sporting News*, August 31, 1963: 9.

_____. "Tommy D Sounds Dodger 'Charge' with Sock Salvo." *The Sporting News*, September 7, 1963: 9.

_____. "L.A. Fans Have Circus Watching Dodger Feast." *The Sporting News*, September 14, 1963: 9.

_____. "Dodgers Pluck Fine-Feathered Birds." *The Sporting News*, September 28, 1963: 5.

_____. "Couldn't Be Done—But Dodgers Did it." *The Sporting News*, October 28, 1963: 25.

_____. "Dodger Flag Dream Wrapped Up in Stout Left Wing of Koufax." *The Sporting News*, December 13, 1963: 20.

Hurwitz, Hy. "Sandy First Hill Ace to Win N.L. MVP Since 1956." *The Sporting News*, November 9, 1963: 8.

Joyce, Bob. "Hurlers Hail New Strike Zone, Expanded by 10 to 12 Inches." *The Sporting News*, February 9, 1963: 4.

Kahan, Oscar. "Bargain Hunters Baffled." *The Sporting News*, December 16, 1959: 7.

_____. "Groat Third Buc Shortstop to Cop Bat Title." *The Sporting News*, December 21, 1960: 19.

_____. "Kids Shine on Every Club in Big Time." *The Sporting News*, April 13, 1962: 14.

Keck, Harry. "FAT-FREE BUCS GREASE PLANK FOR RIVALS." *The Sporting News*, May 11, 1960: 1–2.

King, Joe. "The Prodigals Return." *The Sporting News*, June 9, 1962: 8.

Kremenko, Barney. "Kids Shine on Every Club in Big Time." *The Sporting News*, April 20, 1962: 3.

Kuenster, John. "Milwaukee's Return to the National League Revives Fond Memories." *Baseball Digest*, March 1998: 21.

Leggett, William. "Koo-foo the Killer." *Sports Illustrated*, October 14, 1963: 21.

Lieb, Frederick. "Powerful N.L. Looks for Banner Year." *The Sporting News*, April 6, 1960: 1.

McDonald, Jack. "Jocko Shouts 'Foul' Over Giants' Sand Bar." *The Sporting News*, October 13, 1962: 7.

_____. "50,000 Hail Heroes at 'Frisco Airport." *The Sporting News*, October 13, 1962: 7.

Munzel, Edgar. "For Shame!" *The Sporting News*. June 1, 1960: 14.

_____. "Scrappy Zim Fires Up Cubs at Hot Corner." *The Sporting News*. April 20, 1961: 29.

Murphy, Tom. "Modest Howard Brash Belter as L.A. Farmhand." *The Sporting News*, June 18, 1958: 38.

Park, Charlie. "This Howard Has 50 Coat, Bat to Match." *Baseball Digest*, March 1961: 57.

_____. "The Versatile Maury Wills." *Baseball Digest*, February 1962: 35.

Povich, Shirley. "Scouts Tips Sold Nats on Nabbing Lees." *The Sporting News*, December 9, 1959: 19.

_____. "Nats Plug 2 Holes with Pair of Swaps." *The Sporting News*, April 13, 1960: 10.

_____. "Kennedy Sets Presidential Mark with Fireball Pitch." *The Sporting News*, April 19, 1961: 3.

_____. "Kennedy's Quick Pitch Launches New Season." *The Sporting News*, April 20, 1963: 7.

Reidenbaugh, Lowell. "Stan Whacks Pair of Hits in Grande Finale." *The Sporting News*, October 12, 1963: 22.

Russo, Neal. "Cautious Keane Eyes Cards' Comet." *The Sporting News*, May 11, 1963: 9.

_____. "Oh Wotta Spree Before Bubble Burst!" *The Sporting News*, September 28, 1963: 5.

Spink, C.C. Johnson. "Writers Back Frick's Homer Decision." *The Sporting News*, August 2, 1961: 1.

Stevens, Bob. "Traffic Boo-Boos Throw Brakes on Giants' Jitney." *The Sporting News*, June 22, 1963: 8.

Wolf, Bob. "Spahn Ends a 15-Year Hex in Road Win Over Dodgers." *The Sporting News*, July 13, 1963: 18.

Newspapers

Chicago Daily Tribune
Los Angeles Times
New York Times
Washington Post

Index

Numbers in **bold italics** refer to photographs.